صدام

Saddam

THE SECRET LIFE

CON COUGHLIN

MACMILLAN

Also by Con Coughlin

Hostage: The Complete Story
of the Lebanon Captives (1992)

A Golden Basin Full of Scorpions:
The Quest for Modern Jerusalem (1997)

First published 2002 by Macmillan
an imprint of Pan Macmillan Ltd
Pan Macmillan, 20 New Wharf Road, London N1 9RR
Basingstoke and Oxford
Associated companies throughout the world
www.panmacmillan.com

ISBN 0 333 78200 3 (HB)
ISBN 1 405 02081 4 (TPB)

Unless otherwise noted, the photographs in the photo insert are
from the collection of the Saddam Hussein Museum in Baghdad, Iraq

Designed by Kris Tobiassen
Iraq map on page xv drawn by Paul Pugliese;
all other maps drawn by Kris Tobiassen

9 8 7 6 5 4 3

A CIP catalogue record for this book is available from
the British Library.

Printed and Bound in Great Britain by
Mackays of Chatham plc, Chatham, Kent

In memory of Juan-Carlos Gumucio (1950–2002)

"Emerge tu recuerdo de la noche en que estoy."

—PABLO NERUDA

CONTENTS

LIST OF ILLUSTRATIONS

SADDAM'S FAMILY TREE

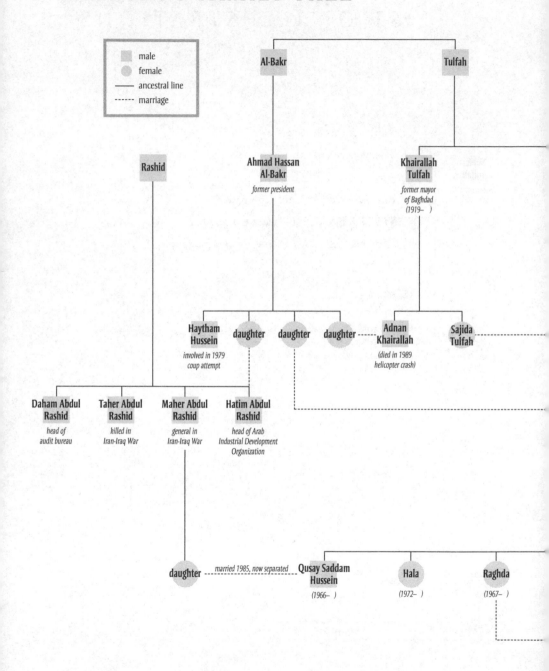

male
female
ancestral line
marriage

Al-Bakr

Tulfah

Rashid

Ahmad Hassan
Al-Bakr
former president

Khairallah
Tulfah
*former mayor
of Baghdad
(1919–)*

Haytham
Hussein
*involved in 1979
coup attempt*

daughter

daughter

daughter

Adnan
Khairallah
*(died in 1989
helicopter crash)*

Sajida
Tulfah

Daham Abdul
Rashid
*head of
audit bureau*

Taher Abdul
Rashid
*killed in
Iran-Iraq War*

Maher Abdul
Rashid
*general in
Iran-Iraq War*

Hatim Abdul
Rashid
*head of Arab
Industrial Development
Organization*

daughter

married 1985, now separated

Qusay Saddam
Hussein
(1966–)

Hala
(1972–)

Raghda
(1967–)

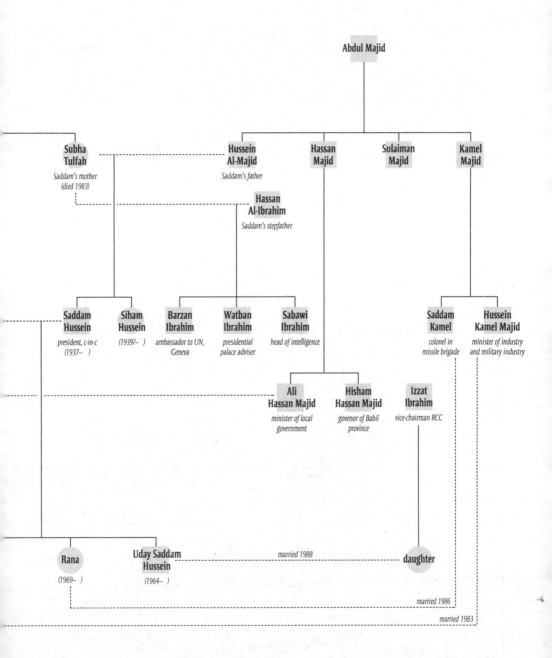

Abdul Majid

Subha
Tulfah
*Saddam's mother
(died 1983)*

Hussein
Al-Majid
Saddam's father

Hassan
Majid

Sulaiman
Majid

Kamel
Majid

Hassan
Al-Ibrahim
Saddam's stepfather

Saddam
Hussein
*president, c-in-c
(1937–)*

Siham
Hussein
(1939?–)

Barzan
Ibrahim
*ambassador to UN,
Geneva*

Watban
Ibrahim
*presidential
palace adviser*

Sabawi
Ibrahim
head of intelligence

Saddam
Kamel
*colonel in
missile brigade*

Hussein
Kamel Majid
*minister of industry
and military industry*

Ali
Hassan Majid
*minister of local
government*

Hisham
Hassan Majid
*govenor of Babil
province*

Izzat
Ibrahim
vice-chairman RCC

Rana
(1969–)

Uday Saddam
Hussein
(1964–)

married 1988

daughter

married 1986

married 1983

xi

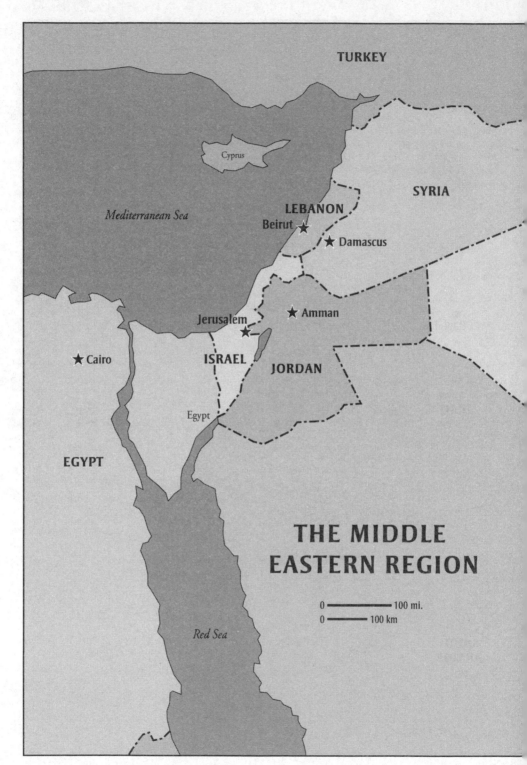

TURKEY

Cyprus

Mediterranean Sea

SYRIA

LEBANON

Beirut ★

★ Damascus

★ Amman

Jerusalem
★

ISRAEL

JORDAN

★ Cairo

Egypt

EGYPT

THE MIDDLE
EASTERN REGION

0 ———— 100 mi.
0 ———— 100 km

Red Sea

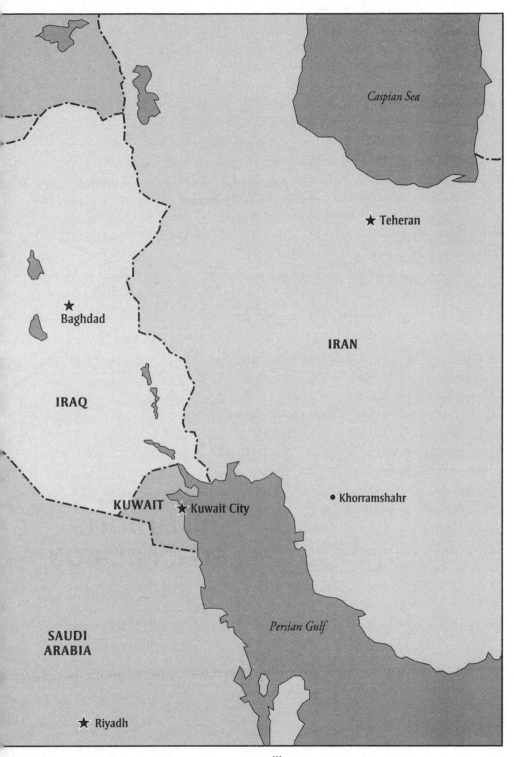

Caspian Sea

★ Teheran

IRAN

★ Baghdad

IRAQ

● Khorramshahr

KUWAIT ★ Kuwait City

Persian Gulf

SAUDI
ARABIA

★ Riyadh

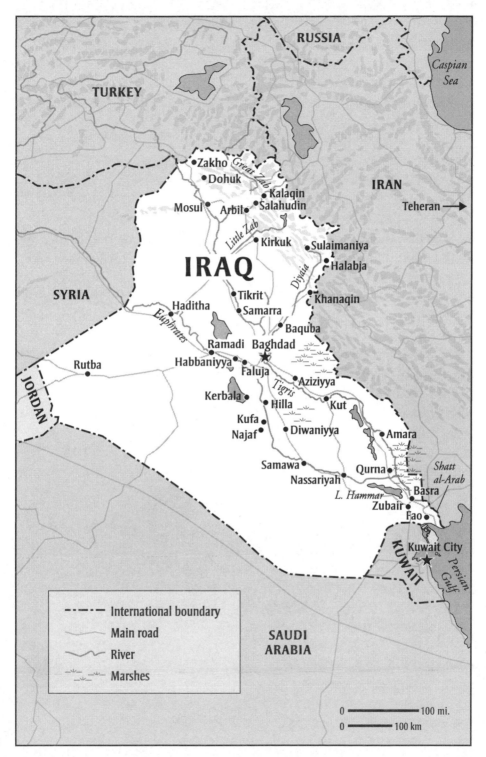

RUSSIA

Caspian
Sea

TURKEY

IRAN

Zakho
Dohuk
Great Zab
Kalaqin
Salahudin
Teheran →
Mosul
Arbil
Little Zab
Kirkuk
Sulaimaniya
Halabja

IRAQ

Diyala
Tikrit
Samarra
Khanaqin
SYRIA
Haditha
Euphrates
Baquba
Ramadi
Baghdad
Habbaniyya
Faluja
Aziziyya
Rutba
Tigris
Kerbala
Hilla
Kut
Kufa
Diwaniyya
Amara
Najaf
Shatt al-Arab
Samawa
Qurna
Nassariyah
Basra
L. Hammar
Zubair
Fao

JORDAN

KUWAIT
Kuwait City
Persian Gulf

SAUDI ARABIA

—··— International boundary
⌇⌇⌇ Main road
〰 River
☘︎☘︎ Marshes

0 ————— 100 mi.
0 ————— 100 km

xv

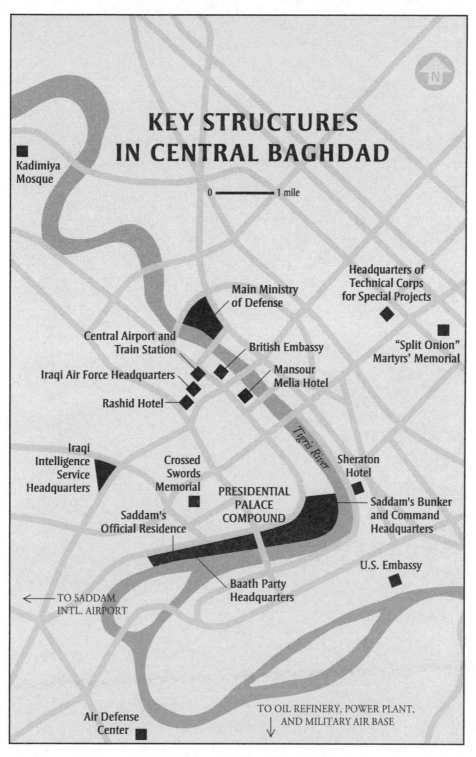

KEY STRUCTURES
IN CENTRAL BAGHDAD

0 ——— 1 mile

Kadimiya Mosque

Headquarters of Technical Corps for Special Projects

Main Ministry of Defense

Central Airport and Train Station

British Embassy

"Split Onion" Martyrs' Memorial

Iraqi Air Force Headquarters

Mansour Melia Hotel

Rashid Hotel

Tigris River

Iraqi Intelligence Service Headquarters

Crossed Swords Memorial

Sheraton Hotel

PRESIDENTIAL PALACE COMPOUND

Saddam's Bunker and Command Headquarters

Saddam's Official Residence

Baath Party Headquarters

U.S. Embassy

← TO SADDAM INTL. AIRPORT

TO OIL REFINERY, POWER PLANT, AND MILITARY AIR BASE
↓

Air Defense Center

SADDAM'S PRESIDENTIAL PALACE COMPOUND

Shari Yafa Road
South to the banks of the Tigris is a restricted area controlled by military and security services

Ministerial Buildings

Military Industrialization Organization
Headquarters for organizing arms and oil smuggling

Special Security Organization Staff

Special Security Organization Headquarters

Communications Mast

Tomb of the Unknown Soilder

Presidential Palace

Saddam's Private Office

Saddam's Private Secretaries' Office

Housing for Palace Staff

Interrogation Center

Special Protection Squad Guard the Inner Perimeter of Saddam's Office

Reception Building for Visiting Dignitaries

Bomb-Damaged Bridge Rebuilt

Tigris River

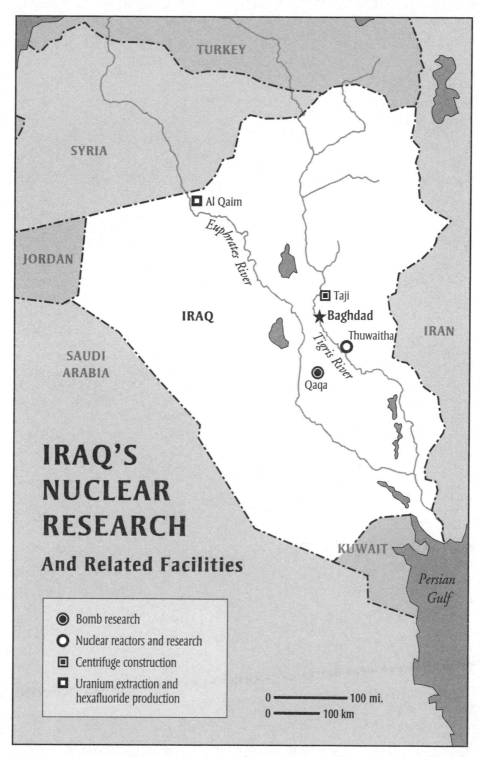

TURKEY

SYRIA

JORDAN

IRAQ

SAUDI
ARABIA

☐ Al Qaim

Euphrates River

☐ Taji
★ **Baghdad**
Thuwaitha ◯

IRAN

◉ Qaqa

Tigris River

IRAQ'S
NUCLEAR
RESEARCH
And Related Facilities

KUWAIT

Persian Gulf

◉	Bomb research
◯	Nuclear reactors and research
▣	Centrifuge construction
☐	Uranium extraction and hexafluoride production

0 ———————— 100 mi.
0 ———————— 100 km

PREFACE

Writing a biography of Saddam Hussein is like trying to assemble the prosecution case against a notorious criminal gangster. Most of the key witnesses have either been murdered, or are too afraid to talk. Even those former associates of Saddam who have not seen him for more than two decades live in the constant fear that, if they speak out of turn, they might receive a visit from one of his assassination squads or that their surviving relatives in Iraq might be punished for their indiscretions. However, in the course of the three years I spent researching this book, a number of Saddam's surviving former associates agreed to be interviewed. Only those who were prepared to be named have been identified; in the majority of cases, however, this was not possible. Similarly, many of the scores of government, diplomatic, and intelligence officials, both serving and retired, in the United States, Europe, and the Middle East who have assisted with this undertaking have asked that their names be withheld. To everyone who enabled this project to reach fruition I offer my sincerest thanks. Naturally I take full responsibility for the interpretations and conclusions I have reached in the course of writing this book.

I would like to express my gratitude to Linda Bedford and the librarians at the Royal Institute for International Affairs in London for their expert and efficient assistance in locating important source material, to the staff of the *Telegraph* library for their help in finding obscure press articles, and to Jules Amis for her unfailingly good-natured assistance. I am also indebted to my colleagues, friends, and family for their encouragement and support.

In the interest of readability, no attempt has been made to give a scholarly transliteration of Arabic names for people or places, and the style adopted is the one generally used in British and American newspapers.

PROLOGUE

The Outlaw

Shortly before a carefully orchestrated series of terrorist attacks devastated the eastern seaboard of the United States on the morning of September 11, 2001, Saddam Hussein, the president of Iraq, placed his troops on "Alert G," the highest state of military readiness Iraqi troops had seen since the 1991 Gulf War. Saddam himself retreated to one of his heavily fortified bunkers in the family fiefdom of Tikrit, in northern Iraq. His two wives, Sajida and Samira, women who in normal circumstances shunned each other's company, were moved to another of Saddam's secret bunkers. The reason, it appeared, that Saddam had retreated to Tikrit in early September 2001 was that he had prior warning of the September 11 attacks, in which groups of suicidal al-Qaeda terrorists flew fully laden civilian airliners into New York's World Trade Center and the Pentagon in Washington, D.C., killing thousands of innocent civilian office workers and military officials. A fourth team of Islamic terrorists had attempted to fly their hijacked aircraft into the White House, but were prevented from doing so by the heroism of some of the passengers who tackled the hijackers, thereby causing the aircraft to crash in a field south of Pittsburgh, killing everyone on board.

In the chaotic days that followed the world's worst terrorist atrocity, Saddam Hussein's Iraq soon emerged as one of the most likely targets for retaliation. The intense secrecy and security that surrounded Saddam's every move meant it was impossible to say for sure why the Iraqi leader had placed his country on high alert and retreated to a bombproof shelter, but the timing alone was sufficient to raise suspicions. Even though there was no specific proof that Saddam was directly involved in the September 11 attacks, Washington's deep-seated institutional antipathy toward the Iraqi dictator was such that President George W. Bush, in the days immediately following the atrocity, found himself having to urge restraint on his more hawkish colleagues. Bush wanted to keep the immediate focus of his response on al-Qaeda, the Islamic terrorist group led and funded by the fanatical Saudi dissident, Osama bin Laden. All the available evidence linked the hijackers directly to bin Laden. In the speech Bush made to Congress on September 20, he made no mention of Iraq. He spoke in general terms of fighting a "war on terror," and his main demand was that Afghanistan's Taliban regime hand over bin Laden and his al-Qaeda accomplices, or face the consequences.

Although the main emphasis of President Bush's speech was concentrated on al-Qaeda, scraps of intelligence, such as that concerning Saddam's whereabouts on the morning of September 11, began to percolate in the Western intelligence community. The most compelling report was that issued by the Interior Ministry of the Czech Republic, which was that Mohamed Atta, one of the ringleaders of the September 11 bombings, had met with an Iraqi intelligence officer five months before the attacks were carried out. Atta had tried to enter Prague in the summer of 2000 but had been turned away because he did not have a valid visa. Having acquired the proper travel documentation, Atta returned to Prague in April 2001, where he met with Ahmed al-Ani, an Iraqi intelligence official whom the Czech authorities were about to expel. Ani, who worked as a second consul at the Iraqi embassy in Prague, was suspected of "engaging in activities beyond his diplomatic duties," the euphemism used to denote espionage. Although there was nothing to link the Iraqi agent with September 11, the very fact that the formidable intelligence apparatus controlled by the world's most notorious dictator was in contact with the world's most ruthless terrorist organization meant that Saddam would quickly find himself in the crosshairs of the Pentagon's military planners.

That Saddam should be implicated in the September 11 atrocities came as no surprise to those counterterrorist specialists who had been investigating the Iraqi dictator's links with international terrorism since the early 1970s. In the past Saddam had been directly involved with such infamous terrorists as Abu Nidal, the leader of the radical Palestinian group that was held responsible for, among other atrocities, the attacks on the Rome and Vienna airports in 1985; and the legendary Venezuelan Ilich Ramírez Sánchez, or Carlos the Jackal as he was more commonly known.

The whiskey-drinking Saddam was not by disposition a devout Muslim or well disposed toward the forces of radical Islam; between 1980 and 1988 he had fought a murderous war against the hard-line Islamic regime that had been established in Teheran by Ayatollah Khomeini. Throughout the 1990s, however, when radical Islamic groups, such as Hizbollah in Lebanon and al-Qaeda in Afghanistan, had been successful in attacking Western targets in the Middle East and elsewhere, intelligence reports began to circulate that suggested Saddam's security forces were helping to train, fund, and equip Islamic terrorists. Two high-ranking defectors, who were debriefed by Western intelligence in late 2001, revealed that Saddam had established a terrorist training camp at the Salman Pak military base south of Baghdad, which had hosted groups of Islamic fighters from Saudi Arabia, Yemen, and Egypt. The camp contained a disused Boeing 707, which was used to teach the recruits how to hijack a plane using only their bare hands or knives, techniques similar to those used by the September 11 hijackers.[1] Although the defectors could not say for certain that the recruits trained at Salman Pak belonged to al-Qaeda, the fact that the majority came from Saudi Arabia and were from bin Laden's uncompromising Wahhabi sect was sufficient to arouse suspicions in Washington and London.

A more direct connection between Saddam and bin Laden related to terrorist activities based in Sudan in the mid-1990s, a country that at the time ran several Islamic terror training camps. Saddam channeled funds through Sudan to support Islamic insurgencies in Algeria and other parts of the Middle East. In the late 1990s details emerged of a plan devised by Saddam in which a specially selected detachment of his security network, Unit 999, would collaborate with al-Qaeda to undertake a number of attacks in Europe and the Middle East against designated targets. By forming an alliance with bin Laden's operatives, Saddam hoped to remove any suspicion of Iraqi involvement in terrorism. As a consequence of this collaboration several prominent Iraqi dissidents were murdered in Jordan, and plans were laid to destroy the Radio Free Europe headquarters based in Prague.[2] In April 1998 bin Laden even sent a delegation of his al-Qaeda fighters to attend the birthday celebrations of Saddam's eldest son, Uday, who responded to this gracious gesture by agreeing to train a number of al-Qaeda recruits in Iraq.

Another indication of Saddam's attempts to develop his links with al-Qaeda emerged in August 2002 when it was revealed that Sabri al-Banna, the Palestinian terrorist otherwise known as Abu Nidal who had been closely associated with Saddam during the 1970s and 1980s, had died in mysterious circumstances in Baghdad. At first the Iraqis claimed that Abu Nidal had committed suicide when Iraqi intelligence officers went to visit him to question him about his alleged involvement in a plot to overthrow Saddam. In fact Saddam had ordered his agents to kill Abu Nidal after the veteran terrorist, who had been invited to Baghdad to undergo medical treatment for skin cancer, had refused the Iraqi leader's request to train a number of al-Qaeda fighters who had taken refuge in eastern Iraq following the collapse of the Taliban regime in Afghanistan. Saddam also wanted to make use of Abu Nidal's terrorist network in the Middle East to undertake operations on behalf of al-Qaeda. Abu Nidal, who was said to be in the process of attempting a reconciliation with the mainstream Palestinian leadership, declined the offer, believing that forging an alliance with al-Qaeda would damage his political aspirations. Saddam responded by having him killed.[3]

Information linking Saddam personally to bin Laden and al-Qaeda, however, remained sketchy. In the three decades that he had effectively run Iraq, Saddam had constructed one of the most powerful, and all-pervasive, security structures in modern history, making the task of extracting genuine information about Saddam's own activities a significant challenge for Western intelligence agencies. Consequently many of the claims made about Saddam's activities turned out not to be true. In October 2001, for example, there were allegations that Saddam was behind the anthrax outbreaks that had occurred in Florida and New York soon after the September 11 atrocities. These and other reports concerning Saddam's activities caused President Bush to come under intense pressure from a number of high-ranking hawks in the administration to take action against Saddam. Prominent among them were Vice President Dick Cheney, who a generation before had been defense secretary to President Bush's father, President George Herbert Walker Bush, who led the international military coalition that defeated Saddam's forces following the 1990 invasion of Kuwait. Others in favor of undertaking military action against Saddam were Defense Secretary Donald Rumsfeld, a veteran of the former Reagan and Bush administrations; and Paul Wolfowitz, the deputy defense secretary. Although the main priority of these veterans of previous Republican administrations was to ensure that the United States and its allies were fully protected against Islamic terror groups, they had not forgotten that Saddam had attempted to assassinate George Bush senior during his visit to Kuwait in 1993. The only senior member of the administration involved in foreign policy who urged caution was

Secretary of State Colin Powell, who had been the elder Bush's chief of staff during the war to liberate Kuwait in 1991.

President George W. Bush's ambivalence about targeting Saddam in response to the September 11 attacks began to change only toward the end of October 2001 when American intelligence received warnings that Islamic militants were planning an even more spectacular attack on the United States than those of September, one that, in the words of Condoleezza Rice, Bush's national security adviser, would "make September 11 look like child's play by using some terrible weapon."[4] The intelligence suggested that bin Laden's associates were planning to use a "dirty bomb," which employs conventional explosives to spew radioactive material. One device could devastate an area the size of Manhattan, making it uninhabitable for years. Emergency security arrangements were implemented to ensure that Bush and Cheney were never together, and private notices were sent to Washington police and congressional intelligence committees warning of the new threat.

The attack did not materialize, but the scare made a deep impression on the American president. It was clear to him that al-Qaeda was aggressively searching for weapons of mass destruction, and it was obvious to all concerned that the one country that might be tempted to make such weapons of mass destruction available to terrorist groups was Saddam Hussein's Iraq. Since the 1970s, when Saddam first emerged as the "strongman of Baghdad," Iraq had concentrated enormous resources into acquiring chemical, biological, and nuclear weapons. Furthermore, whereas in the West such weapons were developed as a deterrent, Saddam had demonstrated he was willing to use them in an offensive capacity against his enemies, most notably when he used chemical weapons against innocent civilians in Kurdistan in 1988. Saddam's willingness to use his nonconventional weapons arsenal, coupled with al-Qaeda's desperation to acquire such weapons, convinced Bush that effective action had to be taken to remove the threat posed by Saddam. The other factor that helped to concentrate the minds of the Bush administration in the autumn of 2001 was the emergence of fresh evidence that suggested Iraqi involvement in the 1993 bombing of New York's World Trade Center by Islamic extremists.[5] Condoleezza Rice later explained the evolution in Bush's thinking thus: "It is not because you have some chain of evidence saying Iraq may have given a weapon to al-Qaeda. . . . It is because Iraq is one of those places that is hostile to us and, frankly, irresponsible and cruel enough to make this available."[6]

The threat to the West posed by the forces of fanatical Islamic terrorism forced the United States to undertake a fundamental reassessment of its national security doctrine. During the cold war the United States and its NATO allies had relied on the threat of massive retaliation to deter attacks from hostile countries. But when it came to dealing with an enemy for whom the normal rules of warfare did not apply, and for whom the notion of martyrdom was inextricably linked to the success of any mission, it was clear that the war against militant Islam would need to be fought by a very different set of rules. The Bush administration became convinced that in the "war on terror," as Bush dubbed it, the United States would need to strike first against its enemies. As Bush would later tell a group of graduating cadets at West Point Military Academy in the spring of 2002, "If we wait for threats to fully materialize, we will have waited too long." Veterans of the cold war such as Cheney and Rumsfeld also regarded the conflict with Saddam as leftover business from the superpower era. Saddam's attitude to the West had, in a sense, been conditioned by the support, both military and diplomatic, he had received from the Soviet Union. With the Soviet Union no longer in existence, Saddam's Iraq had become a dangerous anachronism.

For the first nine months of George W. Bush's presidency, Iraq had not featured very prominently as an issue. Indeed, since the collapse of the United Nations–sponsored program to dismantle Saddam's weapons of mass destruction arsenal at the end of 1998, which had resulted in President Bill Clinton launching a series of largely ineffectual air strikes against Iraq, Western policy toward Baghdad had entered a state of limbo. The guiding principle of what remained of the allies' policy toward Iraq was "containment," which was essentially defined by the wide-ranging UN sanctions that had been imposed in the immediate aftermath of Saddam's invasion of Kuwait in 1990. Halfhearted efforts were also made to coerce rival Iraqi opposition groups to settle their differences and present a unified front against Saddam, but these invariably ended in failure. American and British warplanes continued to patrol the no-fly zones in northern and southern Iraq that had been established in the early 1990s to protect Iraq's Kurdish and Shiite minorities, and there were occasional clashes when Iraqi antiaircraft missile systems locked onto allied aircraft. In the summer of 2001 Iraq was reported to have upgraded its air defense systems, and demonstrated its new capability by firing on a U.S. U-2 spy plane, nearly bringing it down. But despite these occasional acts of provocation, President Bush had seemed in no hurry to formulate his policy toward Iraq. At the time of the September 11 attacks, Bush's review of U.S. policy toward Iraq had been languishing in the doldrums because of the American president's apparent lack of interest in the issue.

Given the long history of tension between Washington and Baghdad, Saddam Hussein did not exactly help his cause during the crucial weeks of late 2001 when the Bush administration was formulating how best to prosecute the war on terrorism. In late October Saddam published a rambling "open letter" to the American people, which condemned U.S. military action in Afghanistan against the Taliban, claimed that U.S. foreign policy was being driven by "Zionism," and suggested that the U.S. mainland could be subjected to further terrorist attacks. In November, when the United Nations suggested that the sanctions against Iraq could be eased if Saddam agreed to allow UN weapons inspection teams to return to Baghdad, Saddam rejected the offer without a moment's hesitation. And adding insult to injury, an Iraqi government survey commissioned at the end of the year proclaimed Osama bin Laden as Iraq's "Man of the Year 2001," an accolade awarded for his dedication in defying the United States and championing Islam. The government-owned Iraqi television showed an Iraqi tribal chieftain reciting a poem he had written for Saddam in celebration of the events of September 11.

> *From inside America, how four planes flew.*
> *Such a mishap never happened in the past!*
> *And nothing similar will happen.*
> *Six thousand infidels died.*
> *Bin Laden did not do it; the luck of President Saddam did it.*[7]

Saddam continued to irritate Washington in the spring of 2002 when he ordered his security officials to provide aid to the families of Palestinian suicide bombers.

As the Bush administration formed the view that the "war on terror" should be extended to include Saddam Hussein, many of Washington's Western allies continued to express strong reservations about attacking Iraq, particularly as no conclusive proof had emerged linking Saddam to September 11. Tony Blair, the British prime minister, was alone among European leaders in supporting the U.S. position. He had delivered an emotional speech to the House of Commons on September 14 in which he pledged his full support to the United States in fighting terrorism. But by the late autumn many European leaders were publicly expressing their disquiet about renewed hostilities against Saddam. Blair, however, remained support- ive even though British intelligence, which had worked closely with the United States in the hunt for clues linking Saddam to the September 11 attacks, were only able to give Blair some "bits and pieces" showing that Iraq and al-Qaeda had worked together, but nothing that related directly to September 11.[8]

Despite the reservations expressed by his European allies, by the end of 2001 President Bush was determined to extend the war on terror to include Saddam. As the success of U.S. forces in defeating the Taliban seemed assured, Bush gave a strong indication that Saddam would be America's next target. "Saddam is evil," Bush bluntly declared. "I think he's got weapons of mass destruction, and I think he needs to open up his country to let us inspect."[9]

Bush's intentions toward Saddam were confirmed two months later when he delivered his State of the Union Address at the end January 2002. In his speech he outlined the two key objectives that would dominate America's "war on terror." The first was to shut down the terrorist camps that trained Islamic fighters, to disrupt the plans of terrorist organizations and bring them to justice. The second objective broadened significantly the terms of reference of the "war on terror" as they had been defined by his address to Congress on September 20. From now on, Bush declared, U.S. policy would be dedicated to preventing "terrorists and regimes who seek chemical, biological or nuclear weapons" from threatening America and the world. And the American presi- dent left his audience in no doubt as to the identity of the "regimes" he had in mind. Referring to North Korea, Iran, and Iraq as an "axis of evil," Bush reserved his severest criticism for Saddam Hussein's Iraq.

"Iraq continues to flaunt its hostility toward America and to support ter- ror," said Mr. Bush. "The Iraqi regime has plotted to develop anthrax, and nerve gas, and nuclear weapons over a decade. This is a regime that has already used poison gas to murder thousands of its own citizens—leaving the bodies of mothers huddled over their dead children. This is a regime that agreed to inspections, then kicked out the inspectors. This is a regime that has something to hide from the outside world. States like these, and their terrorist allies, con- stitute an axis of evil, arming to threaten the peace of the world. By seeking weapons of mass destruction, these regimes pose a grave and growing danger. They could provide these arms to terrorists, giving them the means to match their hatred. They could attack our allies or attempt to blackmail the United States. In any of these cases, the price of indifference would be catastrophic."

This, then, was President Bush's justification for extending the terms of reference of the war on terrorism from one fought against those directly responsible for September 11 to a wider conflict against any regime that either harbored terrorists, or might provide them with the means to carry out their missions. Saddam qualified for inclusion in Bush's definition on two counts: first, there was evidence that he had funded Islamic terrorists and provided them with training facilities; and second, Saddam had acquired a substantial quantity of chemical, biological, and nuclear weapons. Even though no evidence had been uncovered to suggest that Saddam had afforded terror groups access to his nonconventional weapons arsenal, there was always the possibility that he might do so at some point in the future. He had already demonstrated his willingness to use such weapons in the past, and had only been dissuaded from deploying them during the Gulf War after the United States threatened him with retaliatory nuclear strikes. According to the Bush administration, the United States had every legal right to resume hostilities against Saddam as he had reneged on his commitment, made at the end of the Gulf War as part of the cease-fire agreement, to destroy his weapons of mass destruction. The threat that Saddam posed to the civilized world was one, in Bush's view, that could be tolerated no longer.

But Bush's strategy toward Saddam did not attract universal support, and many of America's allies in Europe, which had been so quick to condemn the September 11 attacks, had grave misgivings over the president's decision to extend the war on terror. Hubert Vedrine, the French foreign minister, described Bush's "axis of evil" remark as "simplistic." The German foreign minister, Joschka Fischer, complained that the United States was treating its European allies as "satellites." And Chris Patten, the EU commissioner for foreign affairs, denounced Bush's approach as "absolutist" and "unilateralist overdrive." The response from America's traditional Arab allies was equally dismissive. Saudi Arabia, which has been struggling to come to terms with the fact that most of the September 11 hijackers were Saudi citizens, indicated it was unwilling to allow Saudi bases to be used for renewed attacks against Baghdad, as did most of the other Gulf states.

By adopting a negative approach to George W. Bush's State of the Union Address, these allies had misunderstood one of the other key principles upon which Washington's post–September 11 foreign policy was based. During his address to Congress back on September 20, the president had made it quite clear how the United States intended to prosecute its war on terror. "Every nation, in every region, has a decision to make," Bush declared. "Either you are with us or you are against us." The Bush administration had no desire to pursue a unilateralist agenda, but if its allies were not prepared to help, then Washington was quite prepared to go it alone.

The only ally of any note who fully backed Bush's decision to target Saddam Hussein was Britain's Tony Blair. Although the Labour leader in the autumn of 2001 had expressed reservations about tackling Saddam, by the spring of 2002 he appeared to have become a ready convert to the anti-Saddam cause. Addressing a press conference at a Commonwealth summit in Australia in March, Blair's arguments for confronting Saddam bore an uncanny resemblance to those articulated by Bush in his State of the Union Address the previous January. Referring to Saddam's weapons of mass destruction, Blair declared: "If these weapons fall into their [the terrorists'] hands, and we know they have both the capability and the intention to use them, then I think we have got to act on it because, if we don't act, we may find out too late the potential for destruction."[10] Even if Blair's arguments had been borrowed from Washington, it nevertheless made sense for Britain to back the United States. British warplanes were still regularly flying joint missions with their U.S. counterparts to enforce the no-fly zones over northern and southern Iraq. Blair's decision also received a ringing endorsement from Lady Thatcher, the former British prime minister who had played a central role in creating the coalition that confronted Saddam in 1990 following Iraq's invasion of Kuwait. "Saddam must go," she declared in her indomitable fashion. "His continued survival after comprehensively losing the Gulf War has done untold damage to the West's standing in a region where the only unforgiveable sin is weakness. His flouting of the terms on which hostilities ceased has made a laughing stock of the international community."[11]

So far as Washington and London were concerned, the die was cast. Saddam Hussein was an international outlaw. Either he agreed to dismantle Iraq's weapons of mass destruction and renounced his support for international terrorism or the United States, with British support, would undertake to effect a "regime change" in Baghdad, if necessary removing Saddam by force.

ONE

The Orphan

The young Saddam Hussein had a harsh and deprived childhood. The man who was to become one of the most powerful Arab leaders of modern times came from an impoverished village situated on the banks of the Tigris River on the outskirts of the provincial town of Tikrit. He was born into a poor family in one of the country's most inhospitable regions. At an early age Saddam was orphaned and sent to live with relatives, who oversaw his upbringing and education. No profound knowledge of psychology is required to estimate the effect these circumstances had upon the child's development. As with Hitler and Stalin, those two great tyrants of the twentieth century, both of whom overcame their less than auspicious starts in life to take absolute control of their respective nations, Saddam was to rise above the disadvantages of his childhood to become the undisputed master of Iraq. The shame of his humble origins was to become the driving force of his ambition, while the deep sense of insecurity that he developed as a consequence of his peripatetic childhood left him pathologically incapable in later life of trusting anyone—including his immediate family. Given the disadvantages of his birth, Saddam deserves credit for overcoming these seemingly insurmountable social obstacles to reach the pinnacle of Iraq's political pyramid.

Saddam was born in the village of Al-Ouja, which means "the turning," and is so named because of its location on a sharp bend in the Tigris River eight kilometers south of Tikrit, in north-central Iraq. The village was then a collection of mudhuts and houses and the inhabitants lived in conditions of abject poverty. Amenities such as running water, electricity, and paved roads were unheard of, and although there were a number of wealthy landowners in the region, the village itself was barren. Infant mortality was high, and survival for many was a full-time occupation. The big estates, situated in the Fertile Crescent, produced a variety of crops such as rice, grain, vegetables, dates, and grapes, and their owners, who resided either in nearby Tikrit or the ancient metropolis of Baghdad, were held in high esteem within Iraqi society. In what was essentially a feudal society, the function of the impoverished inhabitants of Al-Ouja was to provide a fund of cheap labor to work as farmhands on the estates or as domestic servants in Tikrit. There were no schools at Al-Ouja. The wealthier parents sent their children to school in Tikrit, but the majority could not afford it, and their barefoot children were left to their own devices.

While most of the inhabitants were gainfully employed in these mundane pursuits there were some who preferred to sustain themselves through illicit activities such as theft, piracy, and smuggling. Historically Al-Ouja was known as a haven for bandits who would earn their keep by looting the *doba,* the small, flat-bottomed barges that transported goods between Mosul and Baghdad along the Tigris, one of Iraq's most important trade arteries. The looters were particularly active in the summertime when they could more easily go about their business from their vantage point on the bend in the river where the passage of the boats was of necessity slow, and where the *doba* would sometimes become stuck on the shallow banks. Poaching was another popular activity, and some of the villagers felt no compunction about helping themselves to chickens and fresh produce from the neighboring estates.

Officially, Saddam was born on April 28, 1937, and, to lend the date authenticity, in 1980 Saddam made it a national holiday. Given the primitive nature of Iraqi society at the time of his birth, it is, perhaps, hardly surprising that this date has been challenged on several occasions, with some of his contemporaries arguing that he was born a good couple of years earlier, in 1935, while other commentators have claimed that he was born as late as 1939. This might be explained by the fact that the whole process for registering births, marriages, and deaths was exceedingly primitive. At this time it was the custom for the authorities to give all peasant children the nominal birth date of July 1; it was only the year that they attempted to get right. This would certainly explain why a certificate presented in one of Saddam's official biographies[1] gives July 1, 1939, as the date of his birth. In fact, Saddam acquired his official birth date from his friend and future co-conspirator, Abdul Karim al-

Shaikhly, who came from a well-established Baghdad family and so had the advantage of possessing an authentic birth date. "Saddam was always jealous of Karim for knowing his own birthday. So Saddam simply copied it for himself."[2] Not content with stealing someone else's birthday, it is now generally accepted that Saddam also changed his year of birth to portray himself as being older than he actually was during his meteoric ascent through the ranks of the Baath Party. This is explained by his marriage to his first wife, Sajida, who was born in 1937. It is frowned upon in Arab society for a man to marry a woman older than himself, and Saddam appears to have amended his year of birth to that of his wife. The fact that Saddam cannot even be clear about his precise date of birth says a great about his inner psychology.

Although the date of birth may be disputed, the location is not. Saddam was born in a mudhut owned by his maternal uncle Khairallah Tulfah, a Nazi sympathizer who was later jailed for five years for supporting an Iraqi anti-British revolt during World War II. He was born into the Sunni Muslim al-Bejat clan, part of the al-Bu Nasir tribe, which was dominant in the Tikrit region. Tribal loyalties were to play a significant role in Saddam's rise to power. By the 1980s there were at least a half-dozen members of the al-Bu Nasir tribe—including the president and Saddam—who held key government positions. In the 1930s, however, the clan was known primarily for its poverty and for its violent disposition. Its leaders took great pride in eliminating their enemies for the most innocuous offense. As a Sunni Muslim, the child was born into the majority orthodox doctrine of Islam, although the Sunnis are a minority sect in Iraq: only one in five Iraqis is Sunni. The child was named Saddam, which literally translates as "the one who confronts" and which, given his exploits in later life, could not have been more appropriate.

The enduring controversy, however, concerns not so much the date of Saddam's birth as the whereabouts of his father, Hussein al-Majid, a poor landless peasant, so typical of the inhabitants of Al-Ouja. Irrespective of the details contained in the official accounts of Saddam's life, most of the biographies and profiles previously published on his life have intimated that he was an illegitimate child. The Iraqi records state that Saddam was born out of the union between Subha Tulfah, a fiesty peasant woman and sister of the Nazi-supporting Khairallah, and Hussein al-Majid. The lack of known information about Hussein, however, has made even this simple fact the subject of considerable dispute. The gossipmongers have thrived on the fact that, whereas Saddam constructed a huge mausoleum in his mother's memory after her death in 1982, no such monument was ever constructed for his father, nor is there any record either of his death or of where he is buried.

As a consequence, most accounts of Saddam's life have suggested that his father had either departed the family home before the child was born, or that he departed soon after. Various notions have been advanced to explain this absence, such as the suggestion that he died of natural causes, not itself an uncommon event among such an indigent community. The most widely believed Iraqi account of Hussein al-Majid's fate is that he was killed by bandits, also not an unlikely eventuality. There were numerous variations on this theme, including the theory that he was killed while in the act of committing some form of banditry himself—few questions were asked of landowners or tradesmen who committed capital crimes while in the act of defending their property. Another version suggested that he abandoned the family home to escape the demanding and domineering Subha. One Arab expert on Saddam claimed that Hussein had worked as a servant for a former Iraqi prime minister during the monarchy,[3] while others refuted this, saying that he was either an unemployed laborer or else that he participated in the illicit piracy and poaching for which the inhabitants of Al-Ouja were then notorious. Yet another account suggested that he was murdered by vengeful relatives of Subha for impregnating her out of wedlock, a plausible theory given the proclivity of his clan for blood feuds and honor killings. The most irreverent of all these propositions is the suggestion that Hussein never even existed, and that Saddam was the product of his mother's activities as the village whore. The latter assertion was understandably popular in Western media circles at the time of the Gulf War and one that, if repeated in the wrong circles in Iraq, was punishable by death. After Saddam had become president of Iraq, a senior Iraqi army officer confided to his mistress that he had slept with Saddam's mother. Unfortunately for the officer, the conversation was taped by the Iraqi secret police, and a transcript was duly handed to Saddam. The officer, his son, and the mistress were all executed.[4] Despite these dire threats of retribution, Subha herself has been the subject of many colorful stories. One account suggests that she was so distraught at the prospect of being a single mother that at one point during her pregnancy she tried to throw herself under a bus, exclaiming: "I am giving birth to the devil."

While the fate of Saddam's father remains something of a mystery, the sensitive question of Saddam's legitimacy can be answered by the simple fact that he had a younger sister, Siham, whose name loosely translates as "spear."

Siham, who shunned the limelight in Iraq despite her brother's success, was born a year or two after Saddam to the same parents in the same village. In later life she married a district judge and had two children. The only time that her family came to prominence in Iraq was during the harshest period of the Iran-Iraq War in the mid-1980s when her husband refused Saddam's call to all Iraqi males to volunteer for military service. The family was briefly placed under house arrest, and Siham's husband was sacked. A few months later, however, Saddam made it up with his sister and her husband was reinstated to his position. The fact, however, that Saddam's sister, unlike all his other close relatives, never received any public recognition in Iraq, inevitably raised questions marks about whether or not Siham was directly related to Saddam.

As for the fate of Saddam's natural father, the most that can be said is either that he died sometime after Siham's birth, or simply abandoned the family home. Tikriti contemporaries of Saddam's have stated that Hussein al-Majid left Subha for another woman and lived for many years after Saddam's birth, although relations between the two sides of the family were, not surprisingly, poisonous.[5] Whatever the truth of the matter, the fact that Saddam had to endure the absence of his natural father throughout most of his childhood was a cause of great distress, even if the presence of a younger sister meant that he could defend himself against claims of illegitimacy.

Although it is difficult to establish a precise chronology of Saddam's early childhood, it is possible to piece together a rough outline of his whereabouts. After Hussein al-Majid had departed the family home, Saddam's mother, Subha (whose name translates as "dawn"), was too poor to bring up the infant on her own. Subha's only known employment was as a clairvoyant. Former residents of Tikrit have said they remember her always wearing black dresses, her pockets filled with seashells which she used to help her with her prophecies. Some accounts say she received financial support from Khairallah, who lived in nearby Tikrit, while others suggest the young child was soon handed over, as an interim measure, to Khairallah's care. Once an important textile town, Tikrit had become something of a provincial backwater by the 1930s. Historically its claim to fame was that it had been, in 1138, the birthplace of Saladin, the legendary Muslim commander who defeated the Crusaders in Palestine. In 1394 the Tartar hordes of Tamurlane, a descendant of Genghis Khan, had also paid it a visit during their Mesopotamian campaign, stopping to construct a pyramid made entirely from the skulls of their defeated victims.

Khairallah Tulfah, who at the time was serving as army officer in Tikrit, was a fervent Arab nationalist who was to become one of the most formative influences on the young Saddam. An indication of the deep bond that developed between uncle and nephew is that, after he had become president, Saddam rewarded Khairallah by appointing him mayor of Baghdad. By all accounts an argumentative and bad-tempered individual, Khairallah nevertheless managed to inspire in the young Saddam a depth of respect that bordered on hero worship. It is not difficult to imagine the impression made upon the boy during his formative years by this father figure who was an unapologetic supporter of Adolf Hitler and the Nazi ethos. Certainly when Khairallah's enthusiasm for the Nazis led, in 1941, to him being expelled from the army and jailed for five years, Saddam is said to have badly missed him. Years later, in a wide-ranging interview with Fuad Matar, one of his official biographers, Saddam made a telling reference to his uncle's imprisonment: "My maternal uncle was a nationalist, an officer in the Iraqi army. He spent five years in prison. . . . 'He's in prison,' was my mother's constant reply whenever I asked about my uncle. He always inspired us with a great nationalistic feeling."[6] Khairallah instilled in the boy a deep dislike of the Iraqi royal family, which then ruled the country, and their foreign backers, i.e., the British. Indeed, this sense of xenophobia was so deeply imbued that Saddam himself was to write, shortly after becoming president: "Our children should be taught to beware of everything foreign and not to disclose any state or party secrets to foreigners . . . for foreigners are the eyes of their countries."[7]

Khairallah's imprisonment meant that Saddam had to return to live with his mother. By the time Saddam returned to his mother's home in Al-Ouja, she had found herself a new husband. Having taken a second cousin for her first husband, Subha took as her second husband a first cousin. Intermarriage of this sort was commonplace in Iraq. The lack of social and physical mobility, together with the obligations of tribal loyalty, meant that such unions were actively encouraged, and intermarriage was regarded as necessary for strengthening and maintaining the bonds of kinship. Subha, who appears from the various portraits of her written by Saddam's official biographers to have been a strong-willed woman, was not someone who wanted to be on her own. There was even a suggestion that she had another husband between the official first and second, although there no convincing evidence has been produced. Her second husband was Hassan al-Ibrahim. Subha, so it was rumored, had persuaded Hassan to leave his wife for the delights of her own marriage bed. According to one of Saddam's Tikriti contemporaries, Subha's second marriage represented a significant downgrade in the family's social standing, even by the impoverished standards of Al-Ouja. "The Majids had a bad reputation, but the Ibrahims were even worse. The Majids were bad enough; they were thieves and criminals. But the Ibrahims were the lowest of the low. Everyone in the area hated them."[8] The Ibrahim clan were known as local brigands. Hassan himself was a poor, work-shy peasant, whose only known job was working as a caretaker at the local school in Tikrit. Unlike Khairallah, who, through his army rank, could lay claim to a degree of social status, Hassan was rooted firmly at the foot of the social ladder. The union with Subha, however, appears to have been a success, and the couple produced three half brothers for Saddam—Barzan, Watban, and Sabawi—and a number of girls.

Subha's new family was well established by the time Saddam returned to their mudhut at Al-Ouja after Khairallah's incarceration. Saddam was still a child—aged anything between two and seven—but even so he did not receive much of a reception. At home he seems to have been badly neglected, save for the occasional, brutal attention of his stepfather who, when he could rouse himself from his natural indolence, would delight in beating the young boy with an asphalt-covered stick, forcing him to dance in the dirt to avoid being hit.[9] Conditions in the village remained exceedingly harsh. The family home had no running water or electricity, and the dwelling housed the livestock as well as the children. At night the family would sleep on the mud floor, huddled together for warmth. According to another of Saddam's official biographers, Amir Iskander, he was under no illusions about the deprivations of his upbringing. Saddam confided to Iskander that he was never young, but a melancholy child who shunned the company of others. There is also a certain pathos in the comment that his birth "was not a joyful occasion and that no roses or aromatic plants bedecked his cradle."[10]

Apart from having to endure these harsh conditions, the young Saddam had to contend with the distinctly corrupting influence of his stepfather. Subha's new husband was known in the village as "Hassan the Liar" because he claimed that he had made a pilgrimmage to Mecca, one of the seven pillars of Islam prescribed in the Koran, when in fact he had never been anywhere near Saudi Arabia, let alone Mecca. What Hassan lacked in honesty, however, he made up for with a feckless attitude to life. He had no other job after his brief employment as a school caretaker, but he compensated for his own idleness by getting the most out of his stepson. While Hassan passed his days gossiping with his friends at the local coffeehouse, Saddam was denied the opportunity to attend the local school and was put to work on menial tasks around the house. Saddam was sent to steal chickens and eggs from neighboring farms, and Saddam may have spent a spell at a juvenile detention center as a consequence. One former Iraqi minister claimed that Subha was just as deeply involved in encouraging Saddam's acts of theft. "They'd steal and divide the spoils the same night. Saddam's mother used to preside over the division of the loot—wheat or rye, sheep, maybe a few pieces of gold and silver."[11] The young Saddam may even have been subjected to sexual abuse by Hassan, which certainly would not have been an uncommon experience for someone in Saddam's position. To say that there was no love lost between Saddam and his stepfather is something of an understatement. Villagers remembered Hassan screaming at Saddam on many occasions: "I don't want him, the son of a dog."

If life was difficult at home, it did not get any better once young Saddam was able to escape the unwanted attentions of his stepfather. It was generally believed throughout the village that the boy was fatherless, a reputation that Hassan would have done little to refute. As a consequence Saddam was teased mercilessly by the other children, and frequently attacked. Indeed, he was so badly bullied that he took to carrying an iron bar with which to defend himself whenever he ventured outside the family home.[12] One legend has it that Saddam often amused himself by putting the bar on a fire and, once the heat had turned it red, would stab a passing animal in the stomach, splitting it in half.[13] In view of Saddam's later fascination with the gruesome pursuits undertaken in his torture chambers, the story has a degree of credibility. Saddam was so lonely that the only creature he really cared for was his horse. Saddam was so attached to this horse that when it died, he claims, his hand was paralyzed for more than a week.

It is possible to gauge Saddam's own view of his childhood through his official biographers. Hardly any mention is made of Hassan, who like Subha's first husband, has quietly been erased from the script. The only references he is known to have made about Hassan are uncomplimentary, such as claiming that his stepfather would wake him at dawn shouting, "Get up, you son of a whore. Go tend the sheep." Saddam has also been fairly frank about the appalling poverty of his youth. To one of his biographers he baldly stated, "We lived in a simple house." In the 1970s, when Saddam was attempting to

build his power base in Iraq, it suited him to stress his humble origins, which
he hoped would broaden his appeal to ordinary Iraqis. In June 1990, on the
eve of the Gulf War, he was more expansive when interviewed by Diane
Sawyer of ABC TV. "Life was very difficult everywhere in Iraq. Very few
people wore shoes and in many cases they only wore them on special occasions. Some peasants would not put their shoes on until they had reached
their destination so that they would look smart."

If Saddam's recollections of his stepfather and home life are authentic, the
same cannot be said of his recollections of Subha. Like most sons, Saddam
idolized his mother, as is demonstrated by the massive tribute he built for her
in Tikrit—with, it must be said, state funds—after her death. The tomb pro-
claims her as "the Mother of the Militants" while, on a personal note, Saddam
stressed the closeness of his relationship with her when he confided to a biographer that he would visit his mother as often as possible. In view of the hard-
ships he suffered during the time he lived with Subha, Saddam's devotion to
his mother is intriguing. Pictures of her show a rather dumpy, scowling
woman wearing the long black dress typical of Arab peasant women. Her face
is tattooed with small black circles, and in none of the surviving photographs
is she smiling. Contemporaries of Saddam who met her in the 1960s recall a
bad-tempered woman who littered her conversation with expletives, even
when talking to complete strangers. But Saddam was blind to her faults and
remained devoted to her memory.

Saddam has similarly kept on good terms with his half brothers, even
though he clearly had a difficult relationship with them during childhood.
Barzan, Sabawi, and Watban were all rewarded with important official posts
once Saddam had achieved his ambition of becoming president of Iraq, and
for several years Barzan even came to regard himself as Saddam's heir apparent. Saddam's childhood was to have a considerable bearing on how he conducted himself in public life, particularly after he achieved positions of real
power. His upbringing taught him to trust no one, the importance of self-
reliance, and the value of using brutal force to intimidate anyone who got in
his way, iron bar or no iron bar. He learned that no matter how dysfunctional
his own family might be, these were the only people he could trust to help
keep him in power.

However much Saddam may have romanticized the memory of his
mother, there is little doubt that the most exciting moment of his childhood
came when his uncle Khairallah was finally released from jail, in either 1946

or 1947, and Saddam was able to escape the misery, poverty, and repression of life with Subha, Hassan, and his half brothers for the altogether more exciting possibilities of life with his Nazi-loving relative.

If Saddam's experience with his stepfather helped to form his character, the period spent living with his uncle in Tikrit and Baghdad undoubtedly contributed to his political outlook. While Khairallah himself was no more than a bit player in the wider struggle among the Iraqi people for the right to self-determination, his active participation in the great nationalistic currents of the day made an indelible mark on the young Saddam, not least because Khairallah's activities were to deprive him of his uncle's company for five crucial years during his childhood.

The cause to which Khairallah was so vehemently committed has its roots in the creation of modern Iraq in the chaotic aftermath of the First World War. For almost four hundred years of Ottoman rule, the area that is known as modern Iraq was one of the most backward and underdeveloped regions of the empire. Under the Ottoman Turks what is now Iraq was three separate provinces based around the main trading centers of Mosul, Baghdad, and Basra. Ottoman control of the region was finally broken by the British-backed Arab revolt that culminated in 1917 with the capture of Baghdad. The campaign to destroy Ottoman control over the Middle East, remembered primarily for the exploits of T. E. Lawrence of Arabia fame, was not without mishap. A British expeditionary force was sent to Basra, at the head of the Gulf, at the start of war in 1914 as a precautionary measure against the Turks, who had sided with the Germans. Having captured Basra easily in 1915, the overconfident British commanders decided to advance on Baghdad. Ill equipped for a campaign in the grueling conditions of southern Iraq, however, the British force got within twenty-five miles of Baghdad before it was completely overwhelmed by the reinforced Turks. The remnants of the British force retreated to Kut, an evil-smelling town on a bend in the Tigris, where they were besieged by the Turks for 146 days. Eventually a surrender was negotiated, but not before most of the troops had died of starvation or disease. Altogether 10,000 British troops lost their lives and another 23,000 were injured.

The British conquest of Mesopotamia, Palestine, and Syria during the First World War was, therefore, achieved at considerable cost and after the war, as one of the victorious powers, Britain was determined to fashion a settlement in the Middle East that either placed the key, strategic areas, such as Palestine, under direct British control, or else under British protection, as was to be the case in the newly created kingdoms of Transjordan (later modern Jordan), Iraq, and the Gulf states, including Kuwait. The process of deciding the postwar settlement of the Middle East, which began during the Versailles negotiations and was later concluded by Winston Churchill in Cairo in 1922, was further complicated by an underhand deal that Britain had struck with France in 1916. The Sykes-Picot agreement, as it came to be known, gave Lebanon and Syria to the French, who were becoming concerned at Britain's postwar imperial ambitions, while Britain obtained control over Iraq and Palestine. The fundamental flaw in this cosy carve-up of the former Ottoman territories was that it overlooked the well-documented promises the British had made to the indigenous Arab leaders to grant them independence if they agreed to back the British in the war against the Turks.

The main loser in the Sykes-Picot deal was Sharif Hussein of Mecca, the leader of the Arab province of the Hejaz (in what would become modern Saudi Arabia), whose tribesmen had fought with T. E. Lawrence. In the protracted negotiations that followed, the British tried to placate him by making his sons the respective heads of the newly created kingdoms of Transjordan, Syria, and Iraq. While the old king refused to sign Churchill's agreement setting out the structure of the new Middle East, his sons had no such qualms in assuming their new positions. In Baghdad this meant that Faisal, Hussein's third son, became the first king of Iraq.

Although the establishment of a monarchy in Baghdad suited the British, it was not popular with the newly liberated citizens of Iraq, most of whom were opposed even to the creation of the new state. When it had first been proposed, in 1919, that the provinces of Mosul, Baghdad, and Basra be joined together to form one nation, even the local British administrators argued that it was a ludicrous suggestion. Arnold Wilson, the civil administrator in Baghdad, said it was a recipe for disaster because it meant trying to force three distinct groups—the Shiites, Sunnis, and Kurds—to work together, even though it was well known that they detested each other.[14] Tensions among the various tribes at that time were so great that in July 1920 the country suffered the greatest revolt in its history. The revolt was caused by a combination of factors, but Britain's failure to fulfill its wartime promise of allowing the Arab leaders self-determination was a significant factor. As one Arab leader told Gertrude Bell, the British writer, on the eve of the revolt:

"Since you took Baghdad, you have been talking about an Arab government, but three years or more have elapsed and nothing has materialised."[15]

The rising, which lasted until 1921, was suppressed, but not before almost an entire battalion of the Manchester regiment was wiped out by Shiite guerrillas. At least ten thousand people died in the revolt and, if nothing else, it persuaded the British that it would be far better to establish a puppet regime to run the country for them rather than burden themselves with the huge cost in men and resources that would be required to subdue the warring tribes. While efforts were made by the rival warlords in Basra and Baghdad to patch up their differences and present the British with a viable, local leadership, the British, mainly through their sentimental attachment to Sharif Hussein, resolved that one of his sons should be made king. Sayyid Talib, the preeminent local leader of Basra, was the only politician who had any realistic claim to leadership of the country. He received widespread support from tribal leaders when he toured the country campaigning under the slogan: "Iraq for the Iraqis." As it was Britain's intention to legitimize Faisal's accession by means of a plebiscite, the emergence of a genuine, secular contender caused alarm in the British government. The crisis was resolved, however, by the resourceful Sir Percy Cox, the British Resident in Baghdad, who invited Talib to afternoon tea at the British Residence to discuss his plans. When Talib arrived at the residence, Sir Percy was nowhere to be seen, and so he was entertained by Lady Cox. As he left the residence after the tea party, Talib was arrested by one of the other guests, who was acting on the orders of Sir Percy. Talib was then deported to the island of Ceylon (modern Sri Lanka) in the Indian Ocean, leaving Faisal free to ascend the throne, his coronation taking place in Baghdad on August 23, 1922.[16]

The establishment of the monarchy in Iraq, consequently, did not enjoy the most promising of starts, and the British acquired a well-deserved reputation among the country's new citizens for double-dealing. Faisal was a weak king who was served by a number of weak governments that never properly established their nationalist credentials. The British, who showed more interest in the newly discovered oil fields around Mosul than the internal politics of their newly created state, established two Royal Air Force squadrons on the outskirts of Baghdad and Basra as a deterrent against any future tribal revolts. Faisal's cabinets were filled with a group of former Ottoman officers who had fought with the British in the war. Although membership of the cabinet was changed frequently in an attempt to placate the complaints of genuine Iraqi nationalists, the outlook of the government remained the same.

The opportunity for the nationalists to enforce the changes that had been denied to them in the settlement of 1922 did not arise until the outbreak of the Second World War. Faisal died in 1933, to be replaced by son Ghazi, a Sandhurst-educated homosexual who, despite making populist noises, was incapable of ousting the British from their positions of influence, to the immense irritation and frustration of Iraq's emerging governing classes. By 1941, after Hitler had conquered most of western Europe, a group of Iraqis led by the pro-Nazi prime minister Rashid Ali, who was backed by four colonels known as the Golden Square, decided to challenge British influence in the country by attacking one of the RAF bases on the outskirts of Baghdad. Having committed himself to driving the British out of Iraq, Ali appealed for German support. The Germans were, however, slow in responding, and the British were able to crush the revolt easily. Rashid Ali and some of his supporters managed to flee the country, but other participants, including Saddam's uncle, Khairallah Tulfah, were rounded up and punished. The four colonels who had supported Ali were hanged and their bodies publicly displayed outside the Ministry of Defense building in Baghdad, as were some of the other ringleaders. Others were jailed and thrown out of the armed forces. Khairallah, who had been a willing participant in the revolt, was stripped of his army rank and jailed for five years.

Both nephew and uncle had changed a great deal by the time that Saddam and Khairallah were once again reunited in Tikrit. Khairallah was bitter and vengeful after his treatment by the British. Apart from having to serve his jail sentence, Khairallah had also lost the social status that went with his rank as an officer in the Iraqi armed forces. After his release from jail, the cashiered Khairallah found himself a post teaching at a local private school where, no doubt, he was able to disseminate his uncompromising nationalistic, and anti-British, views among the impressionable young minds of his students. A former Iraqi pupil who attended the school at the time it was being run by Khairallah recalls that he was "a very tough man, a Nazi and a Fascist. All the pupils were in awe of him, both because of his record in fighting the British and because of his political views."[17]

The young Saddam was in awe of his uncle's heroic exploits in the 1941 revolt, and Khairallah's new position as a schoolmaster added to the attractiveness of him moving to Tikrit. During his uncle's enforced absence, Saddam had graduated with full honors in the art of being a street tough but, thanks to the capriciousness of his stepfather, the boy was completely illiterate. For most boys of Saddam's low social standing, learning how to read and write was not high on their list of priorities when they could better amuse themselves by stealing from their neighbors or beating up and intimidating those who caused them offense. And Saddam would have happily continued to live a life of random thuggery had it not been for his desire to emulate his heroic uncle and fight for the liberation of his homeland from its foreign oppressors.

A career in the armed forces was about the only avenue open to someone of Saddam's class to improve their social standing; not only were they poor peasants from the provinces, but they were also Sunni Muslims, who in the new Iraq were regarded as a minority sect by the more populous, and politically influential, Kurds and Shiites. The ambition of any young Iraqi with military pretensions was to enroll at the prestigious Baghdad Military Academy, established by the British to produce a well-trained, and loyal, cadre of officers. The tradition of young Tikriti men joining the armed forces can be traced back to Mawlud Mukhlis, who was born in Tikrit and made a name for himself during the Arab revolt against the Ottoman Turks in the First World War. After the creation of Iraq, Mukhlis became a close confidant of King Faisal I and vice president of the Senate under the monarchy, and he used his considerable influence to appoint young Tikritis to senior positions in the armed forces and the police, a practice that was continued by his protégés, thereby creating, by the late 1950s, a powerful Tikriti clique at the heart of Iraq's military and security establishment. Saddam, who had already acquired some of the more aggressive attributes necessary for a career devoted to the art of making war, aspired to join the elite at the Baghdad Military Academy. Unfortunately for him, he had no formal qualifications and no realistic prospect of acquiring them so long as he languished at Al-Ouja.

Exactly how the ambitious young nephew came to be reunited with his embittered and disgraced uncle in Tikrit is another episode in the life of the young Saddam that has become cluttered with an array of fanciful and highly imaginative folktales. A commonsense explanation would be that Khairallah who was, after all, the boy's foster father, had offered to help the boy obtain a proper education. His sister Subha, who had her work cut out simply keeping her growing family above the subsistence level, would have jumped at the prospect of having one less mouth to feed. And Hassan al-Ibrahim, while perhaps ruing the loss of the boy's cheap labor to run his unedifying errands, would be relieved at the prospect of this particular cuckoo being removed from the family nest.

Throughout his career Saddam has been well aware of the enormous importance of propaganda and the cult of personality. It is hardly surprising, therefore, that the official accounts of Saddam's life provide an altogether more lurid description of how he came to leave the family home to be reunited with Khairallah. The account provided by Fuad Matar (for example) in his officially sanctioned biography is filled with drama.

According to Matar (who was, after all, only repeating what he had been told by Saddam himself) Saddam's family wanted him to become a farmer and believed there was no point in him receiving a formal education. But Saddam became interested in the idea of going to school when he met up with his younger cousin Adnan, Khairallah's son, who told him how he was learning to read, write, and draw. Adnan was Khairallah's son by his first marriage, which also produced a daughter, Sajida, who was to become Saddam's first wife. During his imprisonment Khairallah had become estranged from his wife, who moved, with her two children, to her parents' home in Baghdad. After his release from prison Khairallah remarried, and Adnan and Sajida moved back to Tikrit. Adnan was to become Saddam's closest childhood friend, and in later life became Iraq's defense minister, a position he held until he died under mysterious circumstances in a helicopter crash. In 1947 Saddam was so impressed by what his young cousin had told him that he resolved to travel with him to Tikrit to attend the village school. This, according to the official biography, was Saddam's "first act of rebellion," as his family remained convinced that education would be a waste of time for their brutish boy.

"When everyone was asleep, he [Saddam] left the house and walked through the dark until he reached a place where some other relatives worked. They were very surprised by his sudden appearance, but understood once he had explained that he wanted to attend school in Tikrit against his family's wishes. The young Saddam was greatly encouraged by these relatives. They gave him a pistol and sent him off in a car to Tikrit. There he was welcomed by other members of his family, who applauded his decision. After completing his first year at the school, he moved to Baghdad with his maternal uncle, Khairallah Tulfah, who had looked after him because his father had died before he was born. He completed his primary education at schools in Baghdad and entered the secondary stage."[18]

Even in a lawless community like rural Iraq in the 1940s, the idea of giving a boy of ten or so a gun to ensure that he gets his own way seems more than a little farfetched. Modifications to this stirring account have, on occasion, graced the pages of the government-controlled Iraqi press, the main alteration to the narrative being that Saddam walked on his bare feet to Tikrit, rather than taking a taxi, an embellishment designed to portray his heroism in an even more romantic light. Certainly the move to Tikrit should not be underestimated in terms of Saddam's self-esteem. In rural Iraq men generally take their surname from their birthplace, so that technically his name should be Saddam Hussein Al-Ouja, whereas he persists to this day in being known as Saddam Hussein al-Tikriti, an altogether more cosmopolitan nomenclature.

Saddam's education was not an experience, at least to start with, that he relished. It could not have been very enjoyable for the rough, almost feral, street child from a poverty-stricken village, who did not even know how to spell his name, to be thrown in with a group of five-year-olds who were better educated. Saddam most likely acquired more psychological scars from the bullying and mockery he suffered at school, even though he was probably better equipped than most to deal with the bullying. Inevitably he got into fights with some of the other boys. Some of these childhood scars ran deep, for in adult life he was said to have returned to Tikrit to exact revenge on his tormentors. Some accounts portrayed him as a high-spirited boy who attempted to charm his better-educated classmates by playing practical jokes on the teachers, such as embracing his old Koran teacher in a deceptively friendly hug and then inserting a snake beneath his robe. A more easily recognizable anecdote about Saddam's conduct at school was provided by one of his direct contemporaries. "My headmaster told me that he wanted to expel Saddam from school. When Saddam heard about this decision, he came to his headmaster's room and threatened him with death. He said: 'I will kill you if you do not withdraw your threat against me to expel me from the school.' "[19] The expulsion threat was quietly dropped.

Saddam received much encouragement from Khairallah and from his younger cousin Adnan, who was three years his junior, to get him through his schooling. After a difficult start, Saddam seems to have settled into the rhythm of the education process. Photographs taken of Saddam at the time show a square-jawed, unsmiling boy with sharp, piercing eyes, a boy who looks well capable of looking after himself. Saddam had to overcome many handicaps simply to attend school, and he was not regarded as a star pupil, although he did have an excellent memory and an almost photographic ability to remember details. The Palestinian writer Said Aburish, another of his apologists, has claimed that "Saddam was an exeptionally intelligent child, a fast learner who was calculating and methodical from the start."[20] This assessment of the schoolboy Saddam, however, was rather undermined by the fact that Saddam was unable to pass the basic requirements of the entrance examination for the Baghdad Military Academy. Nor was there much doubt that Saddam was extremely keen to join the academy. But he was deeply offended by his rejection, and in 1976, after he had firmly established himself in the government, he had himself appointed an honorary general; after he became president, he appointed himself the country's first field marshal. For good measure he executed by firing squad the son of Mawlud Mukhlis, the legendary Tikriti officer responsible for establishing his kinsmen in influential positions in the Iraqi armed forces.

Saddam did, however, manage to complete his primary education so that, in 1955, he graduated in Tikrit and, together with his cousin Adnan, moved to Baghdad with Khairallah where the two boys enrolled at the Karkh High School. The move from Tikrit to Baghdad was to have just as important an effect upon Saddam's development as had the move from Al-Ouja in 1947. Baghdad in the 1950s was a hive of intense political activity and rivalry. This was a period when Arab nationalist sentiment, encouraged in particular by Britain's withdrawal from empire after the Second World War, believed the moment had finally come to throw off the quasi-colonial shackles that had been imposed after the First World War. The independence movement was best articulated in Egypt by the charismatic leader, Gamal Abdel Nasser. His determination to liberate Cairo from Britain's intrusive sphere of influence helped to create the Suez crisis of 1956, which proved to be the final nail in the coffin of Britain's imperial pretensions. Nasser's diplomatic success at Suez reverberated around the Middle East and greatly encouraged other nationalist groups, particularly in Iraq where the monarchy created by Britain in 1922 was still in place and still deeply unpopular. King Ghazi, the only Iraqi king who had had any genuine popular support and who had upset his British overlords as a consequence, had been killed in a mysterious car crash in 1939. The British, and their allies in the Iraqi government, were blamed, rightly or wrongly, for his death. His successor, Faisal II, was only four years old at his accession and the country was effectively run by his uncle, Abdul Ilah, and the veteran Iraqi politician Nuri Said, both of whom were staunchly pro-British. After Nasser's exploits at Suez, the pro-British sympathies of Said and Ilah were increasingly at odds with Iraqi nationalist sentiment, and in Baghdad numerous political parties sprung up, the mainstay of whose campaign platforms was the overthrow of the monarchy.

The other crucial geopolitical dynamic that had a bearing on the politics of Baghdad in the 1950s was the emergence of the Soviet Union as a superpower. Not only were the Soviets keen to export their ideology to the Middle East; they were eager to break what they regarded as the West's monopoly of control over the region's vast oil wealth. The communist menace was regarded as a very real threat both in Washington, which after American president Dwight Eisenhower's intervention over Suez, had increased its involvement in the Middle East, and in London, which was still trying to maintain some vestige of control. In 1955 the Iraqi government was instrumental in setting up the Baghdad Pact, a regional defense organization comprising the unlikely alliance of Britain, Turkey, Iran, and Pakistan. The pact's raison d'être was to confront the Soviet threat, although Nuri Said secretly hoped it would provide Arab opinion with an alternative rallying point to Nasserism. Nasser's response to the pact was to sign a massive arms deal with the Soviets and the following year to nationalize the Suez Canal. Apart from making Nasser the undisputed champion of Arab nationalism, the pact made the Iraqi government appear the stooge of Western interests.

As one of the veterans—and in Saddam's eyes, one of the heroes—of the 1941 uprising, Khairallah was heavily involved in the political currents of the day. Khairallah's family moved to the Karkh neighborhood of Baghdad, a rough, run-down residential area on the western outskirts of the city. Karkh was a mixed neighborhood of Sunnis and Shiites, and there were frequent outbreaks of violence between the two communities. While working as a schoolteacher, Khairallah was very much involved in political agitation and, not surprisingly, his main political contacts tended to be among those of his own class and background. One of Khairallah's associates at this time was Ahmad Hassan al-Bakr, a Tikriti army officer and the future Iraqi president who would play a central role in Saddam's rise to power. Bakr was a leading light in the newly formed Baath (meaning renaissance) Party, an Arab nationalist movement that had been formed in Syria in the late 1940s. A radical and secular party, its main goals were the creation of a united Arab state that dispensed with the arbitrary imperialist boundaries that were imposed on the

Middle East after the First World War, and a more equal distribution of the vast oil wealth that was starting to transform the economics of the region. Nationalist and patriotic in outlook, the Baathists were the declared enemies of the Soviet-backed communists, whom they suspected of wanting to replace one form of colonialism with another, the only difference being that one emanated from London while the other had its roots in Moscow.

Saddam's recollections of these formative years in his political development are hardly profound. He told one of his biographers that his uncle's main motivation was "resistance and struggle" against the ruling elite that surrounded the monarchy and their British backers,[21] while to another he said his uncle "spoke in nationalist but not in communist terms."[22] A more illuminating insight into his uncle's political development is provided in a pamphlet written by Khairallah himself, entitled "Three Whom God Should Not Have Created: Persians, Jews, and Flies." Although published in 1981 after Saddam became president, it indicates the rudimentary thought processes to be expected from a keen adherent of the Nazis. Persians were "animals God created in the shape of humans" while Jews were "a mixture of dirt and the leftovers of diverse people." Flies, by contrast, were poor, misunderstood creatures "whom we do not understand God's purpose in creating."[23] This weak Iraqi attempt at imitating *Mein Kampf* nevertheless had a bearing on Saddam's future policymaking. As president of Iraq, Saddam's foreign policy was determined by his hatred of the Persians, or Iranians as they are now better known, and the Israelis. In 1980 he provoked the disastrous eight-year war with Iran that cost an estimated one million Iraqi and Iranian lives, while the high point for Saddam during the Gulf War in 1991 came when he fired a succession of Scud missiles at Tel Aviv. Khairallah's indoctrination of Saddam was rewarded with his appointment as mayor of Baghdad, a post he exploited with such exuberant venality that in the 1980s Saddam was forced to remove him from office, close down seventeen of his companies, and arrest their executives.

There is little doubt that Khairallah's influence on Saddam was as pernicious as his stepfather's had been, and it was not long before Saddam was running his own street gang in Karkh, intimidating political opponents or, as a true son of Tikrit, anyone else who caused him offense. By his late teens Saddam had grown into an impressive physical specimen. At six foot two inches tall, he was unusually tall for an Arab, and had a muscular build to go with it. He spoke with a thick, peasant accent and his speech was littered with Tikrit colloquialisms, much to the amusement of the more sophisticated

Baghdadis with whom he was beginning to associate. Saddam never lost his peasant accent or dialect, not even after he had become president. His public speeches were ungrammatical, as were his private conversations, which would later cause the official translators no end of problems. His inability to converse on equal terms with other members of Iraq's ruling elite would do little to help his deep-seated sense of insecurity.

In Baghdad during the late 1950s, Saddam may have been involved with the Futuwa, a paramilitary youth organization modeled on the Hitler Youth, which had been set up during the reign of the flamboyant King Ghazi in the 1930s. The Futuwa wanted Iraq to unite the Arabs in the same manner that the Prussians had united the Germans, and their ideology neatly dovetailed with that of the Baathists. Encouraged by Khairallah, Saddam was usually to be found at the forefront of any antigovernment demonstration or riot. In such an environment of perpetual violence and unrest, it was simply a question of time before Saddam killed someone.

As with so much else from Saddam's early history, there is a degree of uncertainty about the precise identity of his first murder victim. Although mainly resident in Baghdad, Saddam traveled frequently to Tikrit where he was involved on the periphery of politics, mainly organizing street violence. The inhabitants of Tikrit would have expected nothing less from someone like Saddam; the townsfolk have a saying to the effect that when the villagers from Al-Ouja come knocking, it is time to close up shop. One suggestion was that Saddam's first capital offense occurred when he murdered a cousin who had unwittingly offended his stepfather, Hassan al-Ibrahim. Although there is no supporting evidence to back the claim, such killings were so commonplace that it is not inconceivable that Hassan would have called on his burly stepson to apply his newly acquired skills to resolve a local dispute.

Where there is incontrovertible evidence of Saddam's involvement in committing murder concerns the case of Saadoun al-Tikriti, a Communist Party member who worked as the local party official and who was killed in October 1958. The Baathists were bitter enemies of the communists and Khairallah, who was one of the main Baath representatives in Tikrit, would have taken great exception to a communist holding a position of authority in the city. The real motive for the murder, however, was that Tikriti was well aware of Khairallah's unsavory background. In the summer of 1958 Khairallah managed to persuade the government to appoint him to a new position as director of education in Baghdad. When the communist Tikriti heard of Khairallah's appointment he informed the authorities about Khairallah's past, with the effect that a few months later Khairallah was sacked from his new job.[24]

Khairallah was incensed and reacted in the only way he knew how. Claiming that Tikriti had denounced him for political, rather than personal, reasons, Khairallah ordered his nephew to exact revenge. Saddam carried out his uncle's orders without hesitation. The killing took place in Tikrit as Tikriti was walking home, having spent the evening with some of his friends at a local coffee shop. His house was located in a road with no street lighting, and as he approached the gate Saddam stepped out from behind a bush and shot him dead with a single shot to the head with a pistol given to him by Khairallah.

Immediately following the shooting Saddam and Khairallah were arrested and detained for six months, but eventually the two men were freed through lack of evidence. There were no witnesses to the shooting and no one in Tikrit seemed too concerned about the murder of a communist. The "blooded" Saddam now enjoyed a degree of notoriety among Iraq's young revolutionaries, and made his way back to Baghdad where he resumed his activities as a political agitator while earning a modest living by working as a bus conductor.

A brief snapshot of Saddam and Khairallah at the time of their imprisonment has been provided by Hani Fkaiki, a former Baath Party official, who shared a prison cell with the two men in Tikrit. "What has stuck in my mind most of all was how Saddam and his uncle kept to themselves in prison. They would choose a far-away corner, away from the rest of the inmates. Despite the small size of the cell in which we were all held, the two of them never gave us a chance to enter into conversation with them. In an attempt to break down this barrier between us, I sent another imprisoned Baath party member to try to get close to them and find out the details behind their imprisonment." The overture was rebuffed.[25]

Saddam's only official comment on these events implied that he had been framed for the murder. "An official in Tikrit was murdered: the authorities accused Saddam Hussein of killing him and throwing him in jail," wrote one of his biographers.[26] However, the transcripts of court documents relating to another case, and seen by this author, confirmed that Tikriti was murdered by Saddam because he had crossed Khairallah. During the trial in 1959 of Abdul Salam Arif—who was later to become another of Iraq's postrevolutionary presidents—by a special military tribunal, Tikriti's brother gave evidence in support of Arif and, in passing, provided a detailed account of the murder. He related how Khairallah had been appointed a director of education, but then demoted to inspector because of Tikriti's intervention. In his witness statement Tikriti's brother states bluntly: "Accordingly Khairallah sent his nephew from his sister [Saddam] on 24th October . . . to shoot my brother and kill him."[27] Another indication of Saddam's guilt can be drawn from the fact that twenty years later, when Saddam had risen to the position of vice chairman of the Baath's Revolutionary Command Council, he visited the school of a relative of Tikriti in Baghdad and, in keeping with the tribal custom, gave him blood money and a Browning pistol.[28]

As a consequence of his murderous activities in Tikrit, Saddam had made a name for himself, not, as he had once hoped, as a dashing young officer training at the Baghdad Military Academy, but as a political agitator who was not averse to committing murder to achieve his goal. The Baath Party might be small (it had just three hundred members in 1958), but it had ambitions, and its leaders were not slow in recognizing the particular talents of their young recruit. If the Baath Party was to achieve its goal of taking over the country, first it had to get rid of the government. And so for his next official assignment, Saddam was to be given the task of assassinating Iraq's newly appointed president.

TWO

The Assassin

The overthrow of the Iraqi monarchy in the revolution of 1958 was one of the most bloodthirsty episodes in the recent history of the Middle East. Early on the morning of July 14, a group of army units calling themselves the "Free Officers" stormed the royal palace at Qasr al-Rihab. Artillery fire destroyed the top of the building, forcing the young King Faisal II, the regent, and their families to flee the building into the palace courtyard. There they were confronted by a semicircle of army officers who, without any regard for the women and children, massacred them all. The only survivor of the bloodbath was the wife of the former regent, and she only survived because she was left for dead in the middle of a pile of royal corpses. The coup leaders, perhaps taking their cue from the Bolsheviks' elimination of the Romanov dynasty at Ekaterinburg, were determined that no trace of the Iraqi royal family should survive as a rallying point for future loyalists. The only act of respect displayed by the coup leaders was to take the body of the young king to a secret location for burial.

The nonroyal victims, on the other hand, were shown no respect whatsoever. The body of the king's uncle and former regent, Abdul Ilah, was removed from the pile of corpses and handed over to the mob. Ilah and the prime minister, Nuri Said, were generally held responsible for Iraq's pro-British policy, and were even suspected of responsibility for the death of King Ghazi, the only monarch who had aroused anything approaching feelings of loyalty among the Iraqi people during his brief reign in the 1930s. Ilah's body was dragged through the streets tied to a car before being dismembered in the most grotesque fashion. The remains were then put on show at the Ministry of Defense at the same spot where the bodies of the four colonels hanged by the British for their part in the 1941 revolt had been displayed. The revolution was as much an attempt to rid the country of British influence as it was to dispose of the monarchy. Nuri Said survived the coup for another couple of days until he was caught, dressed as a woman, trying to escape. Said tried to fight off his captors with his pistol, but was quickly overwhelmed and killed. To make certain, his killers reversed their cars over his body several times. The remains were then buried, but a few days later the mob had second thoughts, and Said's body was disinterred and horrifically mutilated. Parts of his body were then paraded as trophies through the streets by the mob.

Saddam's precise whereabouts during the heady days of the 1958 revolution are not known, although it can safely be assumed that the young Baathist and his vehemently anti-British uncle acquitted themselves during the mob violence that erupted in the immediate aftermath of the monarchy's overthrow. Hundreds, if not thousands, of Iraqis died in the ensuing bloodshed and the Baathists, who fully supported the military coup, were determined to make sure that the revolution succeeded. Scant mention is made in Saddam's official biographies of his activities at this time, which claim he was then twenty-one years old, so it must be assumed that he was engaged in nothing more eventful than his customary rabble-rousing.

The new political agenda of the coup leaders was set out at 6:30 A.M. on July 14 in a special radio broadcast made to a stunned, but jubilant, Iraqi populace. The declaration was made by Abdul Salam Arif, one of the coup leaders. In the first proclamation of the new regime, Arif stated that the army had liberated "the beloved homeland from the corrupt crew that imperialism installed." The coup was immensely popular, and even though martial law and a curfew were imposed with immediate effect, no one appeared to take much notice. The first acts of the new government were to abolish all the main institutions of the ancien regime, including the monarchy, and to issue warrants for the arrest of all those who had supported the status quo ante.

The pressures for constitutional reform in Iraq had been accumulating almost from the time the country was first established by Winston Churchill in 1922. The desire for change increased significantly in the summer of 1958 as a consequence both of Iraq's support for the Baghdad Pact (discussed in Chapter One) and Nasser's success in defying Britain and France over the Suez Canal in 1956. Indeed by 1958, buoyed by his diplomatic triumph, Nasser was effectively trying to take over the Baathist cause for himself by proposing a prototype for a united Arab state. In February 1958 a political union of Syria and Egypt was established. Yemen joined later in the year and the new confederation became the United Arab Republic (UAR), with Nasser as its president and Cairo as its capital. Most of the Free Officers who had carried out the July 14 coup in Iraq supported the principle of joining the federation, especially those who were members of the Baath Party, who believed that this was the most likely means of achieving their goal of creating a pan-Arab state.

The Baathists consequently lent their full support to the new government established in Baghdad in the summer of 1958 by General Abdul Karim Qassem, the leader of the Free Officers. A thin-voiced and rather humorless army officer, Qassem appointed Baathists to twelve of the sixteen cabinet positions in his new government. Baathist support for Qassem was, however, contingent upon him promptly signing up for Nasser's prototype Arab nation. Some of the Free Officers had promised Nasser they would join the UAR in return for his support in helping them to overthrow the monarchy. Once in power, however, Qassem adopted a more cautious approach. In this Qassem was merely acting in a manner that would be copied by numerous Iraqi leaders in the turbulent years ahead. When in opposition it was customary for Iraqi politicians to support the notion of forming alliances with their Arab neighbors; once in power they quickly took up the cause of "Iraq First," a policy whereby Iraq's national interests were placed above all else. Having established himself in office, Qassem soon adopted an Iraq First approach. As an Iraqi nationalist, he had reservations about subsuming Iraq's hard-won independence under Nasser's control. He was also suspicious of the motives of some of his fellow coup conspirators, especially Arif, whom he suspected of pressing for membership of the confederation with Egypt and Syria as a means of strengthening his own political position in Iraq. As so often happens with the revolutionary process, the revolutionaries quickly found themselves at odds with each other over which direction the revolution should take. By the early autumn Qassem had rejected the notion of joining Nasser's confederation. Furthermore, in an attempt to assert his authority, he ordered the arrest of Arif and several other members of the Free Officers, who were then put on trial for treason (it was at this trial that Saddam's involvement in the murder of Saadoun al-Tikriti was revealed). Arif and his co-defendants were convicted and sentenced to death, although their sentences were later commuted to life imprisonment.

In a further attempt to strengthen his power base, Qassem struck up an alliance with the Iraqi Communist Party, which for its own ideological reasons was fundamentally opposed to joining the Nasser-sponsored union of Arab states: the only union Iraqi communists supported was with Moscow. Qassem's pact with the devil, as many of the nationalists came to regard it, and the show trials of noncommunist Iraqis, caused a rapid deterioration in relations between Qassem and many of the Free Officers who had supported the overthrow of the monarchy: they were not prepared to tolerate the replacement of one dictator-ship by another. The decisive moment came in March 1959 when a group of nationalist officers, in protest against the communists' mounting influence over the nation's affairs, staged a coup against Qassem. The coup was an ignomin-ious failure and, to teach the perpetrators a lesson, Qassem encouraged the communists to conduct a witch-hunt of their nationalist adversaries. The result was yet another blood-soaked episode in Iraq's modern history. In addition to disposing of all the officers who had staged the rebellion in Mosul, the com-munists killed many Arab nationalists who had supported them. Some of the Free Officers who had helped to overthrow the monarchy were tried as traitors. In Mosul itself a communist-inspired mob indulged in a weeklong orgy of rape, looting, and summary trials, which culminated in the accused being machine-gunned to death in front of cheering mobs.

For the Baathists, Qassem's conduct amounted to nothing less than betrayal. They felt that they had given the coup leaders their full backing in the summer of 1958 to overthrow the monarchy on condition that Iraq join Nasser's union of Arab states. Less than a year later their hopes had been dealt a cruel blow. So long as Qassem remained in power, it was quite obvious that they stood no chance of attaining their goal of creating a pan-Arab state. Their only chance of realizing that ambition was to remove Qassem from power, and this they resolved to do by the time-honored method of assassination.

That Saddam's name should have been put forward for the assignment is hardly surprising. At this stage in its development, the Baath Party of Iraq was more of an ideological sounding board than a fighting machine. Most of its three hundred members were either students or professional people who wanted to create a fairer society in which the government served the interests of the people, rather than the interests of foreign powers. When it came to imple-menting these high ideals, however, the Baath leadership counted on like-minded individuals to do the dirty work for them. The Baath Party had sup-ported the overthrow of the monarchy, but none of them was actually present when the royal family was butchered to death. The Baathists had supported the revolt in Mosul, but were not actively involved. Now that they had decided

Qassem must be removed from power, they had the will, but not the means. It is possible that the idea of assassinating Qassem did not come from the Iraqi Baathists themselves, but from Nasser, that master manipulator who had assumed control of the Baath, even though he himself, of course, remained a committed Nasserite. Some of the participants in the assassination attempt may have traveled to Damascus for training by Nasser's police, although no evidence has ever been produced to implicate Nasser directly in the plot.

Saddam claims he joined the Baath Party in 1957, when he was still a pupil at Karkh High School, and there seems no reason to dispute this. What is surprising is that Saddam should have chosen to join a party that, by the standards of the day, was relatively obscure and did not, at that stage, look as if it had the makings of an organization that would become one of the dominant forces in modern Arab politics. According to one of his official biographers, Saddam joined the Baath because "he found its principles a reflection of his own nationalist ideals." The biographer also drops a strong hint as to how the young Saddam was steered toward the Baathists. "He had considered himself a nationalist from the time his mother told him stories of how his uncle [Khairallah] Tulfah had fought against the British."[1]

Although Khairallah himself had no time for the Baath Party, and never joined it, he had befriended Ahmad Hassan al-Bakr, a fellow Tikriti who was a general in the Iraqi army with Baathist sympathies and who would become one of the key figures in the party and the first Baathist president of Iraq. Bakr liked to portray himself as a moderate, decent person, but behind this facade there was a brutal, ruthless streak, which would come to full prominence after he assumed the office of president. While Bakr's public persona was of a law-abiding officer, he nevertheless appreciated how Saddam's brutish force could be of use to him and, encouraged by Khairallah, he took Saddam under his wing to forge a powerful partnership that would ultimately result in the two men running the country for ten years. It was through Bakr, therefore, that Saddam was first introduced to the Baath Party. At this stage in his career, however, Saddam was a mere supporter of the party rather than a full member. Membership of the Baath was strictly controlled and limited only to those who had proved their loyalty to the party, and their commitment to its ideology. The account provided by Saddam's biographer of how he came to be involved with the party encapsulates Saddam's nascent nationalism.

"His relatives had been killed by the British, and their houses burned down; his forefathers had fought bravely against the Turks. With this background,

Saddam Hussein was all too aware of British imperialism and how the government in Iraq remained a prisoner of the imperialist will. He decided to become involved in political activity."[2] The same sentiments could easily have been attributed to Khairallah Tulfah.

Saddam's involvement in the plot to assassinate Qassem has contributed greatly to his cult status in Iraq, and in terms of capturing the full dramatic impact of the incident, there is no better account of his participation than that provided by Saddam himself.[3] Saddam's narrative traces his involvement back to the prison in Tikrit where he was held for six months from late 1958 on suspicion of murdering Saadoun al-Tikriti. Saddam's murder of Tikriti took place shortly after Qassem seized power. As a consequence Saddam was locked up in jail with Khairallah during the orgy of violence that erupted throughout the country. Saddam claimed that he used his confinement to save his fellow Baathists from being murdered by communists in Tikrit. Some of those communists, of course, may have well been seeking to avenge Saddam's murder of Saadoun al-Tikriti. According to Saddam's version of events, however, he bribed some of the more sympathetic prison guards to arrest Baathist activists on trumped-up charges and have them thrown into jail for their own protection. "A number of Baathists were thus brought into the jail. For many days they remained in prison until nightfall, when they were released to carry out their activities, returning to the jail before sunrise."

This would have taken place during Qassem's purge against the Baathists during late 1958 and early 1959. Saddam claimed he was released, sometime in early 1959, as a result of what he describes as "national pressure," whereas in fact it was because of the prosecuting authorities' inability, or unwillingness, to find sufficient evidence to charge him with Tikriti's murder. Saddam said that he then returned to Baghdad at the request of the party, where he was asked by one of his "comrades" if he would be willing to assassinate Qassem. He accepted at once because he "considered the assignment an honor." He then began training in the use of automatic weapons, "having already mastered the use of the revolver"—as his successful dispatch of Tikriti amply demonstrated. The plan was conceived by Fouad al-Rikabi, the Baath secretary-general who had briefly held a cabinet post in Qassem's cabinet and who was later murdered in one of Saddam's prisons.

The assassins were to shoot Qassem as he took his routine afternoon drive through Al-Rashid Street, one of Baghdad's central thoroughfares, on his way home from his office at the Ministry of Defense. Party activists had noticed that Qassem was not adequately protected, and a plan of attack was devised whereby one group of gunmen would open fire on the backseat occupants of Qassem's car, while another group was to kill those sitting at the front. Saddam's role in the five-man assassination team was to provide covering fire while the assassins made good their escape.

In fact Saddam's involvement in the assassination attempt on Qassem was very much a last-minute affair. The original four-man hit squad was made up of full members of the Baath, and was led by Abdul Karim al-Shaikhly, a teenage medical student from Baghdad who was to become one of the Baath Party's key ideologues and one of Saddam's closest friends. Soon after the plot was hatched, one of the gunmen announced that he did not want to take part because he had a young family, and was worried what would happen to them if he was killed or injured in the attack. It was at this point that Saddam's name was advanced.[4] Even at this relatively tender age, Saddam had acquired a reputation for ruthlessness. At six foot two inches with an impressive physique to match, he had already shown his mettle by murdering Tikriti, taking just a single shot to dispatch his victim. He had also taken great care to make sure that there were no witnesses to incriminate him.

The date for the attack was set for October 7, 1959. To familiarize himself with the area, Saddam rented an apartment, which was then used as a base for the operation. For several days he familiarized himself with the area, making notes on the best locations to carry out the attack and mapping out the best escape routes. The operation was duly launched on the late afternoon of the seventh. Unfortunately, in the excitement of the moment, Saddam drew his machine gun from the folds of a long cloak he had borrowed from Khairallah for the mission and prematurely opened fire at Qassem's car. Saddam's action preempted the carefully laid plan, and before the other assassins could open fire, Qassem's bodyguards dived into action. In the ensuing shoot-out, Qassem's chauffeur was killed and Qassem himself was hit in the arm and shoulder. One of the assassins was killed and Saddam received an injury to his leg. Saddam's apologists sought to give the impression that Saddam was shot by Qassem's bodyguards, but the more mundane reality is that he was shot by one of his fellow assassins who, panic-stricken, had simply sprayed machine-gun fire at anything that moved, including Saddam.

The surviving members of the assassination squad, believing Qassem to be dead and their mission accomplished, managed to make good their escape to one of the party's hideouts in the capital. Unbeknownst to the conspirators, however, Qassem was rushed to a hospital where he was saved by emergency treatment. According to Saddam's version of events, at the safe house the bleeding in Saddam Hussein's left leg got much worse. "As it was obviously impossible to go to a hospital, he took a razor blade and asked one of his comrades to cut into the flesh around the bullet and dig it out, using a pair of scissors and some iodine. He felt faint for a few minutes, but then recovered." This rather gruesome account, which has become enshrined in Iraqi legend as a central feature of Saddam's heroism, might seem more appropriate to the American Wild West than Baghdad in the late 1950s. It was certainly at odds with the recollection of Dr. Tahsin Muallah, the doctor who was called to treat the young Saddam immediately after the failed assassination attempt. "It was nothing more than a flesh wound, really, a graze," recalled Dr. Muallah who, like so many of Saddam's surviving contemporaries, eventually fled into exile.

Muallah was one of the founding members of the Baath in Iraq, a party that, at the time the assassination attempt was undertaken, still had less than a thousand members. "The Baath Party at that time was full of professional people—lawyers and doctors—who were not very good with guns," he said. "They needed to bring someone like Saddam in off the streets to do their dirty work for them. This was, after all, the first armed action that the Baath party in Iraq had ever undertaken."

At the time of the attempted assassination, Muallah was working in the outpatient division of the Republican Hospital in Baghdad. The day after the failed shooting a member of the Baath leadership stopped him in the street and informed him that there were some casualties being cared for at a safe house, and asked whether he could assist. The doctor agreed to attend the injured, and was taken to a house in the El-Wiya neighborhood of Baghdad. The most seriously injured, said Muallah, was a gunman called Samir al-Najm who had been shot in the shoulder. Using a local anesthetic, the doctor removed the bullet and treated the wound. When he had finished, he was informed by one of the Baathists that there was another casualty waiting to be treated in an adjoining room. "When I went into the room I came across a pale, yellow young man." It was Saddam and he was dressed in a *dishdasheh,* the traditional long white robe worn by Arab men. "He told me he had a bullet wound, but when I treated him I found that he had nothing more than a grazed shin." Muallah treated the wound and left. A few days later the security forces raided the house and arrested the occupants and Muallah. They had been tipped off by the gunman who, until his expulsion from the party, was originally supposed to have taken part in the assassination attempt. But by that time Saddam had already made good his escape. Muallah was tried for aiding and abetting the assassins by a special military court set up by Qassem, and jailed.

Even though the injury Saddam sustained during the botched assassination attempt was negligible, the incident later became so embellished by Saddam's propaganda machine that most Iraqis were convinced that Saddam nearly died of his wounds. In an autobiographical film of Saddam's early life called *The Long Days,* which was made by Iraq's Ministry of Information in the 1980s, the wound was portrayed as being so serious that Saddam was unable to walk. In the film Saddam came across as a bold and heroic figure, who did not even flinch as a comrade used a pair of scissors to dig the bullet out of his leg. Saddam himself has continued to perpetuate this myth. When interviewed by an Egyptian journalist about the ordeal many years later, Saddam claimed he had been unhappy with the actor's depiction of him because it was unrealistic. "I wanted the director to reshoot the scene because I remember the day when it happened. I did not grimace or move an inch until the bullet was out."[5]

The epic tale of Saddam's heroics in 1959 continued with his escape from Baghdad. Because, according to his version of events, he had difficulty walking, he "came across a man on a horse and bought it from the owner for ten dinars," the equivalent of about £20 ($30). He then rode the horse along the banks of the Tigris until he reached Tikrit. There Saddam bought some hay for his horse and some bread and dates for himself. He spent the night with a bedouin tribesman, and the following morning set off on the long journey to Syria, via Tikrit. He traveled for three days, at one point joining in an engagement party at Samarra. "A sheep had been slaughtered for the occasion, so he ate a hearty meal which made up for the diet of bread and dates, and slept in comfort and security." This almost biblical account of his flight from Baghdad was rudely interrupted on the fourth day when Saddam was suddenly intercepted by two carloads of armed customs officials. Saddam attempted to outrun them on his horse, but was soon overtaken and surrounded by the customs officials, who pointed their machine guns at him. "Saddam reined in his horse, and dismounted, making sure that his cloak covered the bandage on his leg as this was evidence that he was a wanted man." Saddam managed to bluff his way out of this potentially difficult encounter, first by demanding to see the officers' commander, and then demanding that the officer explain why he was being treated in this shameful manner. The commander was apologetic, saying that they had mistaken Saddam for a smuggler. When the commander asked to see Saddam's travel documents, Saddam replied that he did not have any as he was a bedouin, and it was well known that bedouin do not subscribe to any bureaucratic norm.

Saddam was allowed to continue with his journey until he reached a crossing point in the Tigris that would enable him to reach Tikrit. He tried to persuade a barge owner to take him across the river, but the boatman refused because a curfew was in force. In his desperation to get across, Saddam decided to abandon his horse and swim. Placing his knife betwen his teeth, Saddam swam across the river in the middle of the night. The water was freezing, and by the time that Saddam reached the other side he was in a state of near collapse. "Whenever he felt exhaustion creeping over him, he redoubled his efforts to reach the opposite bank." Finally he reached the other side, his teeth chattering with exhaustion. "It was like you see in the movies, only worse," Saddam himself later recalled. "My clothes were wet, my leg was injured, and I hadn't eaten properly for days."[6] Once out of the river Saddam stumbled to a nearby house in search of food and shelter. But when he knocked on the door, the woman mistook him for a thief. "She had no way of knowing that he was a revolutionary, not a robber." Saddam eventually managed to reassure the family that his intentions were innocent, and they gave him refuge. In the morning he took his leave and walked the whole day until the following night he finally reached his home village of Al-Ouja, where he was greeted by a tearful brother. Having safely survived the most hazardous part of his journey, Saddam then made his way into exile in Syria with some fellow Baathists, and they reached Damascus, the Syrian capital, a few days later.

Given the extent to which other aspects of Saddam's involvement in the assassination plot have been exaggerated, it is unlikely that the reality of his journey into exile justifies the drama of the narrative provided by his biographers. Most of those responsible for plotting the assassination managed to escape to Damascus. Shaikhly, for example, the assassins' leader, took a train to the northern Iraqi city of Mosul, and then made his way to Syria. The accounts of Saddam's involvement in the attempted assassination of President Qassem, however, does reveal some interesting insights into Saddam's personality at the time. Even though the young Saddam had already made a name for himself in nationalist circles as a street tough and killer, when it came to shooting Qassem it was generally agreed that Saddam lost his nerve and opened fire too early, thereby ruining the operation's chances of success.

Some accounts even blamed Saddam directly for the death of one of the assassins, Abdel Wahab Ghoreiri, whose body, despite Saddam's claims that he provided covering fire for the wounded to be carried to safety, was recovered by the security forces, enabling them to identify quickly those responsible for the plot. Saddam himself allowed one of his biographers to concede that the operation was not exactly a stunning success, saying that the whole organization of the plot was "elementary."[7] As, in later life, Saddam was to master fully every aspect of the art of assassination, both personal and political, it can only be assumed that the whole experience provided him with a salutary lesson.

The importance of maintaining the myth of his heroic escape in 1959 was underlined many years later when, in 1998, Saddam made a surprise visit to two remote villages in northern Iraq. It was one of the first times that Saddam had been seen in public since his defeat in the Gulf War in 1991, and he made the unannounced visit in an attempt to rally support. Apart from firing a rifle in the air to signal his appreciation of the warm reception he received from the startled villagers, Saddam recounted his exploits to the residents of Albu Dor, a village on the Tigris through which he had traveled during his escape. "It was like you see in the films, but worse," he said. "My clothes were wet, my leg was injured and I hadn't eaten properly for four days. How can I describe it?" he asked rhetorically. "It is hard to describe how I got out of the water."[8]

For the next three and a half years, Saddam was an exile, first in Damascus, and later in Cairo, then the undisputed capital of Arab nationalism. Damascus, the spiritual home of Baathism, was the obvious hideout for the coup plotters after their flight from Baghdad. For a young man barely in his twenties, Saddam, who was not even supposed to have taken part in the shooting, suddenly found himself thrust into the milieu of the most original and dynamic political theorists of their day. The doyen of the Syrian Baath Party was Michel Afleq, one of the founding fathers of the Baath in 1944, who through his unstinting pursuit of the pan-Arab cause had achieved an almost deitylike status in the minds of many contemporary Arabs. Unlike the Iraqi Baathists, who were still very much on the political fringe in Baghdad, the Syrian Baathists were a significant force and, through their association with Nasser, had already formed the first pan-Arab federation.

Although many of Saddam's contemporaries viewed him as little more than a thug, Afleq is said to have taken a personal interest in the young Saddam and promoted him to the highest rank of party membership by making him a full member.[9] This act of generosity may have been sparked by Afleq's genuine admiration for Saddam; more likely it was a gesture of thanks for his role in trying to eradicate the procommunist Qassem. Certainly, the Iraqi Baathists' inexpert efforts to overthrow the government in Baghdad made them heroes among Iraqi nationalists. The military trials of those, like Dr. Muallah, who were charged for their roles in the assassination plot, were closely followed throughout the Arab world, and the defiance of some of the accused Baathists, even though they faced execution if convicted, attracted widespread admiration, both inside Iraq and beyond. In essence they argued that they had a patriotic duty to murder Qassem because he was handing the country over to the control of the communists. When the trials concluded, six of the accused actually received the death sentence, although the sentences were never carried out.

The newfound notoriety of the Iraqi Baathists pleased Afleq, who sought to exploit for his own ends the political instability the failed assassination attempt had caused in Baghdad. At this juncture Afleq was playing a double game. He organized the expulsion of Fouad al-Rikabi and other members of the Baath leadership in Baghdad on the grounds that they should not have involved the party in the assassination plot. Afleq then sought to place his own supporters in key positions in the Iraqi Baath Party, and to this end he arranged for Saddam to acquire his much-coveted full party membership. Although Afleq later said that he could not recollect meeting Saddam until after 1963,[10] the quietly spoken ideologue and the restless young murderer would soon form a symbiotic attachment. It was mainly due to the efforts of Afleq, who for a time controlled the Baath Party in both Syria and Iraq, that, in 1964, Saddam was elected to a key position in the leadership of the Iraqi Baath Party. Saddam repaid the compliment by ensuring, when he finally achieved power, that Baathism became Iraq's official political doctrine. In the same way that Josef Stalin would use Lenin's name as a means of legitimizing his own rule, so Saddam would invoke Afleq's name to justify his own position in Iraq. Saddam had "a living Lenin who could be wheeled out on suitable occasions to ratify his decisions and above all his status as guardian of party orthodoxy against successive groups."[11] And when Afleq, who was himself later forced into exile in Baghdad, died in 1989, Saddam paid (or rather, the state did) for a massive tomb to be built for the founder of Baathism.

After two to three months in Syria, Saddam and the other surviving members of the assassination squad moved to Cairo where they joined up with a group of about five hundred exiled young Baathists who had congregated in the

Egyptian capital. These young Baathists were sent to Egypt by the Syrian government, the junior partner in the political union between Cairo and Damascus. The purpose of sending them to Cairo was to continue their education; at the time of his involvement in the assassination plot against Qassem, Saddam had still not completed his secondary education. President Nasser, as head of the first pan-Arab union, now opposed Qassem for reneging on his commitment to bring Iraq into the confederation. Afleq and the other Baathist leaders believed that the young assassins would be safer under Nasser's watchful eye than in Damascus, where the regime was less stable. The campaign to remove Qassem, meanwhile, was to be left to more senior, and experienced, Baathists.

This was the only time in his life that Saddam lived abroad, and soon after arriving in 1960 he enrolled at the Qasr al-Nil High School. After all the exhilaration of committing his first murder in Tikrit, and attempting his first assassination in Baghdad, life in Cairo was by comparison a relatively staid affair. Nevertheless, with Gamal Nasser in his full pomp, and Cairo the undisputed capital of Arab nationalism, Saddam could not help but be moved by a city that was a hive of political activity. Apart from his studies, Saddam involved himself fully in politics, joining the Egyptian Baath Party. Within months Saddam had become a member of its Regional Command, i.e., the Egyptian branch, although the influence of the Baathists was limited by the overpowering presence of Nasser, a fact that was ultimately to lead to Syria unilaterally seceding from the pan-Arab union in 1961.

Saddam's own recollections of his years in exile are uncharacteristically modest and low-key. One of his biographers reported that he "emulated Nasser and played a good deal of chess and was not distracted by night life and read a good deal."[12] This account was supported by Abdel Majid Farid, who was Nasser's secretary-general, and who was responsible for looking after the young Baathists. According to Farid, the Egyptian authorities helped him with his education and assisted with finding a suitable apartment. "He was one of the leaders of the Iraqi Baath. He used to come to see me now and then to talk about developments in Baghdad. He was quiet, disciplined, and didn't ask for extra funds like the other exiles. He didn't have much interest in alcohol or girls."[13] Abdul Karim al-Shaikhly, who became close friends with Saddam in Cairo, wrote to his family in Baghdad that Saddam spent most of his time trying to catch up on his education and finish his high school education. Shaikhly, a future Iraqi foreign minister, became such close friends with Saddam in Cairo that the two young men regarded each other as twin brothers. Shaikhly, who would be one of Saddam's first victims after he became president, spent his time in Cairo finishing his medical degree. In one letter to his family he described his new friend as "a quiet man, not a social person, someone who is trying hard to educate himself."[14]

Other contemporaries, however, do not paint such a rosy portrait. A Cairene café owner who served Saddam and his friends regularly described him as a troublemaker who never paid his bills. "He would fight for any reason," recalled Hussein Meguid, the owner of the Andiana Café, which, together with the Triumph, were Saddam's favorite haunts. "He would fight for any reason. We wanted to bar him from coming here."[15] But the police came back and said he was protected by Nasser, and when Saddam finally left Cairo he owed several hundred dollars. Perversely, it was not a debt that Saddam forgot. In the 1970s, when he was vice president of Iraq and had returned to Cairo on official business, Saddam made a surprise return to the café and paid his bill in full, leaving the owner a three hundred dollar tip. Saddam would not be Saddam if darker tales were not in circulation about his alleged misdeeds in Cairo. He was accused of killing an Egyptian in 1960 by throwing him out of his apartment window,[16] and also of killing a fellow Iraqi in 1963.[17] But as there are no records of the alleged offenses, and as Saddam was free to leave when he chose, they must be discounted as mere wishful thinking.

However much Saddam tried to put a brave face on his stay in Egypt, it was generally accepted that he regarded life in Cairo as the equivalent of a prison sentence. He did, however, manage to complete his high school education and in 1961 enrolled at the University of Cairo to study law. Saddam was provided with a modest allowance paid by the Arab Interest Section of Egyptian intelligence. Saddam never completed his studies, but still managed to secure a degree several years later when he turned up at the annual law examinations at Baghdad University in full military uniform. Before sitting down to take the examination, Saddam placed his gun on his desk to make himself feel "more comfortable." As with the headmaster who wanted to expel him, the sight of the gun did the trick, and Saddam was duly awarded his degree.

Saddam's sojourn in Cairo was the occasion of two other important events in his life—his first marriage, and his mysterious dealings with the Central Intelligence Agency. It was during his time at Cairo University that Saddam became engaged to his cousin Sajida, the daughter of his uncle Khairallah. Marrying within the family was the expected norm for someone from Saddam's background, and by becoming engaged to his uncle's daughter he was observing family tradition. Sajida was probably born in 1937 (which explains why Saddam may have tampered with his birth records to make him the same age as his wife, and not her junior), and Saddam spent most of his childhood growing up with her and her brother Adnan at Khairallah's homes in Tikrit and Baghdad. In effect Saddam and Sajida were brought up as brother and sister. According to Saddam, the marriage had actually been arranged when they were children and his grandfather betrothed Sajida to him. Saddam, aware of his tribal duties, observed Arab custom and asked his stepfather Hassan al-Ibrahim to approach his uncle and formally ask permission for him to marry Sajida. Relations appear to have improved between Hassan and Saddam, perhaps because Hassan sensed that Saddam might make a success of his life, and might therefore prove of use to the indolent stepfather. Hassan did as Saddam requested, Khairallah consented, and Saddam became officially engaged. Although the couple was not married until Saddam returned to Iraq in 1963, Saddam celebrated the engagement in traditional Arab style in Cairo in early 1962 and, to reassure Sajida of his good intentions, he sent her a wedding ring. The engagement party was organized by his good friend Abdul Karim al-Shaikhly.

The other significant development for Saddam during his residence in Cairo was the relationship he developed with the CIA. Like most of Saddam's activities in Cairo, his dealings with the Americans are shrouded in mystery, particularly as most of his direct contemporaries have been killed.[18] But there is nonetheless sufficient circumstantial evidence to indicate that Saddam made contact with the CIA's Cairo station. The early 1960s were a period when cold war tensions between Washington and Moscow were approaching a critical stage, as demonstrated by the Cuban missile crisis in 1962. The CIA saw its primary purpose as countering any attempt by the two communist superpowers, the Soviet Union and China, to extend their activities beyond their existing spheres of influence. China's move into Southeast Asia was ultimately to provoke the United States' ill-fated involvement in Vietnam's civil war. Moscow's desire to extend its influence in the Islamic world, from the Central Asian Soviet republics to the oil-rich Arab states of the Middle East, was to result in the region becoming a tinderbox, primed to ignite by the heated rivalries engendered by the cold war.

Iraq, situated at the heart of the Middle East, was regarded by Washington as a key strategic asset. For this reason the United States had encouraged the formation of the anti-Soviet Baghdad Pact, the regional defense organization set up in the mid-1950s comprising Britain, Turkey, Iran, and Pakistan. Indeed, the Americans were so concerned about the level of political instability in Baghdad following the overthrow of the monarchy that Allen Dulles, the CIA director, in 1959 declared that "Iraq was the most dangerous spot on earth."[19] By 1961, political developments in the region prompted the Americans to be proactive in countering what they regarded as a serious Soviet attempt to take over the Middle East.

Concern had been expressed about President Nasser's now notorious arms deals with Moscow, and the Soviets were suspected of being involved in General Qassem's decision to draw on the support of the Iraqi Communist Party to keep him in power. Qassem's decision unilaterally to withdraw from the Baghdad Pact in 1959, which made the region more susceptible to Soviet infiltration, and to rely increasingly on Soviet foreign aid and military supplies, did little to allay Washington's suspicions. The West was even more alarmed when in 1961 Qassem attempted to occupy Kuwait, which the Iraqis had always regarded as part of their own territory, and to nationalize part of the foreign-owned Iraqi Petroleum Company, a move that, for the Americans, had unpleasant echoes of the nationalization program Nasser had implemented during his early years in power.

The Egyptians under President Nasser were just as determined as the Americans to influence the political development of the modern Middle East, particularly as the decision by Syria in 1961 to withdraw from the United Arab Republic had seriously dented Nasser's ambition of creating a united Arab state. Iraq, therefore, which had reneged on its promise to join the UAR when Qassem seized power, was of particular interest to the Egyptians, and Egyptian intelligence was as active as the CIA in attempting to establish a sympathetic government in Baghdad.

As someone who had already participated in one attempt to overthrow Qassem, it was hardly surprising that Saddam and his exiled Baathist colleagues should find their activities arousing the keen interest of both the Egyptian and American intelligence services. Saddam was paid a modest retainer by the Egyptian authorities and allowed to study. But relations between the exiled Iraqi Baathists and the Egyptians cooled considerably after their fellow Syrian Baathists withdrew from the UAR, a move, moreover, that was actively encouraged by Michel Afleq, the founder of the Baath and who was Saddam's personal mentor. Saddam's biographers claim that Saddam was kept under close observation in Cairo, that he was continually harassed, and that his apartments were searched on several occasions.[20] This could, of course, have been due to Saddam's alleged criminal activities, and the Egyptians would have been obliged to search him for weapons if, as was alleged, he was threatening his opponents in Cairo with physical violence, in the same way that he had done in Baghdad.

None of the official biographers, however, made any mention of Saddam's frequent visits during this time to the American embassy in Cairo. The Americans, for different reasons, were as keen as Saddam to have Qassem removed from power, and there was strong circumstantial evidence to suggest that Saddam was in close contact with the CIA toward the end of his stay in Cairo.[21] Said Aburish, another of Saddam's sympathetic biographers, suggested that Saddam's meetings with the CIA were condoned by Egyptian intelligence, even though Washington and Cairo were pursuing diametrically opposed policies toward Baghdad. Although the true extent of Washington's courtship of the young Saddam may never be known, it cannot be discounted that Saddam Hussein started his political career as an agent of the CIA. The nearest anyone has come to shedding light on this intriguing aspect of Saddam's career was a meeting the authors Marion Farouk-Sluglett and Peter Sluglett had with a high-ranking former official of the U.S. State Department who confirmed to them "that Saddam Hussein and other Baathists had made contact with the American authorities in the late 1950s and early 1960s."[22] Certainly the issue was of sufficient sensitivity for Saddam that, later in his political career, he liquidated those Iraqi contemporaries who may have been in a position to shed light on his spying exploits.

Qassem survived until February 1963 when he was finally overthrown in a coup masterminded by the CIA. The coup, which, even by Iraqi standards, was particularly gruesome, was led by General Ahmad Hassan al-Bakr, another of Saddam's mentors to whom he had been introduced by his uncle, Khairallah, when he first moved to Baghdad. Bakr, a fellow Tikriti, had become a prominent member of the Iraqi Baath during Saddam's exile in Cairo. A quiet and determined man, he shared Khairallah's virulent hatred of communists and was consequently held in high regard by the Americans. Bakr had joined the Baath while in jail for plotting against Qassem. The Iraqi leader, who lacked the ruthless streak required to survive in Iraqi politics, was forever releasing political opponents he had jailed for trying to remove him. Bakr was no exception, and soon after he was freed he teamed up with other Baathists to plan the coup to oust Qassem.

The 1963 coup followed the gory tradition that had been established with the overthrow of the monarchy in 1958. The action against Qassem had to be brought forward because some of the conspirators were arrested, and when it was launched many army units refused to mobilize in support of the Baathists. Bakr, drawing on the services of four Hunter Hawker fighter jets, managed to launch an assault on Qassem's well-defended redoubt at the Ministry of Defense. The fighting lasted for two days, leaving hundreds of dead and wounded in central Baghdad, before Qassem was finally forced to surrender. His captors denied his request that he be allowed to keep his firearm, nor would they allow his trial to be held in public. After a summary hearing, Qassem was executed by firing squad. The whole process between his unconditional surrender and his execution took just one hour. To reassure the doubting Iraqi public that the president was indeed dead, Qassem's bullet-riddled body was featured in a grotesque film that was shown repeatedly on Iraqi television. "Night after night. . . . The body was propped up on a chair in the studio. A soldier sauntered around, handling its parts. The camera would cut to scenes of devastation at the Ministry of Defense where Qassem had made his last stand. Back to the studio, and close-ups of the entry and exit points of each bullet hole. The whole macabre sequence closes with a scene that must forever remain etched on the memory of all those who saw it: the soldier grabbed the lolling head by the hair, came up close, and spat full face into it."[23]

Once the television station had finished with the body, the deceased president was still not allowed to rest at peace. Initially Qassem's corpse was buried in a shallow, unmarked grave, but the body was unearthed by dogs who began eating it. Horrified farmers then reburied the body in a coffin, only to have the secret police dig it up again and throw it in the Tigris. Despite this gruesome turn of events—not dissimilar to the treatment Qassem's supporters had meted out to monarchists in 1958—Washington professed itself satisfied with the change of regime. James Critchfield, the head of the CIA in the Middle East at the time and a specialist in communist infiltration, later expressed himself deeply satisfied with the outcome. "We regarded it as a great victory," he recalled many years later. "We really had the ts crossed on what was happening."[24]

Saddam, much to his frustration, was marooned in Cairo for the duration of these dramatic events but, once the new regime had been installed, he lost no time returning to Baghdad to participate in the bloody purges that followed. Saddam flew back to Baghdad with Abdul Karim al-Shaikhly—his fellow conspirator in the plot to assassinate Qassem in 1959—and some of the other Iraqi exiles. They were met at the Baghdad airport by a large crowd of cheering Baathists, family members, and friends. Soon after his arrival Saddam reacquainted himself with Bakr, who had been rewarded for his role in overthrowing Qassem with the post of prime minister by the new president, Abdul Salam Arif. Bakr appointed many fellow Tikritis to positions of prominence, although Saddam initially found himself sidelined from mainstream politics. The party had moved on during his three years in exile, and the new leadership at first would not accept the membership Saddam had acquired in exile. Saddam was offered a lowly position at the Central Farmer's Office, where his duties were to look at ways of improving the lot of the Iraqi peasantry. Despite the difficulties he faced on his return to Baghdad, his friends and acquaintances noticed a significant change in Saddam's development. "When he fled Baghdad, he had not even finished high school. He was a thuggish kid who was good with his fists. But the Saddam who returned from Cairo was better educated and more adult."[25]

If Saddam was frustrated in his political ambitions, the bloody clashes that continued between the Baathists and communists after Qassem's overthrow provided him with a more familiar outlet through which to channel his frustrations. The street fighting that took place in Baghdad during the coup itself had claimed anywhere between 1,500 and 5,000 lives. For several weeks after the coup, house-to-house searches were undertaken in pursuit of communists and leftists. The searches were carried out by the National Guard (Haras al-Qawmi), the paramilitary wing of the Baath, which had joined in the street battles that eventually led to Qassem's defeat. The national guardsmen wore green armbands and carried submachine guns and, armed with lists of communist sympathizers, some of which had been provided by the CIA, they spent the first few weeks of the Baath Party's new government indulging in what can only be described as an orgy of violence.

Despite the assurances that the Baathists had given to the CIA that all those detained would be given a fair trial, many of those held by the National Guard were tortured and then summarily executed. Sports clubs, movie theaters, an entire section of Kifah Street, and a number of private houses were requisitioned by the National Guard to be used as prisons and interrogation centers. The liquidation of the communists in Baghdad was in many respects a forerunner of the anti-Leftist purges that were to occur in Chile and

Argentina in the 1970s and 1980s. Saddam's elite Republican Guard units were to behave in a similar fashion following Iraq's invasion of Kuwait in August 1990 when they commandeered government buildings and palaces and turned them into makeshift interrogation and torture chambers. The official Iraqi records claimed that 149 communists were executed, although it was generally accepted that hundreds, if not thousands, of communists suffered excruciating deaths at the hands of their Baathist tormentors. As often happens in such circumstances, many of those killed were either innocent, or the victims of local vendettas that had nothing to do with political ideology.

Dr. Ali Karim Said, a former Iraqi diplomat who was a leading figure in the Baath during this period, said that many innocent Iraqis died in the government-orchestrated purges of the communists. "I still remember when my brother . . . , who was then a deputy commander of military intelligence and one of the main interrogators, came to my house and threw down his machine gun on the floor and said in a pained voice: 'I cannot go on, because they arrest and send simple men to the execution courtyard. It is unacceptable and unbearable. They all shout: Please Mohammed, for your sake, Ali, and then they shout: God is Great three times before they die.' My brother continued: 'If you oppress these simple and helpless people they will definitely turn to the communists.' After this episode I . . . opposed all execution orders."[26]

One of the most notorious torture chambers was located at the aptly named Palace of the End (Qasr al-Nihayah), so called because it was the site where the monarchy had been wiped out in 1958. One of the most notorious practitioners of the torturer's art was Nadhim Kazzar, who would later become Saddam's head of national security. Even by the brutalized standards of modern Iraq, Kazzar's reputation for sadism stood out. Kazzar had joined the Baath Party as a student in the 1950s and quickly rose through the ranks. A hard and ascetic man, Kazzar was one of the party's few Shiites to hold a position of power. He came into his own following Qassem's overthrow when he revealed himself to be a fearsome persecutor of the communists. Kazzar's reputation for indulging in gratuitous violence was such that he even succeeded in terrorizing members of his own party. He had a particular liking for conducting interrogations personally and for extinguishing his cigarette inside the eyeballs of his victims.[27] Most of Kazzar's atrocities were committed in the Palace of the End, which the Baathists managed to turn into a laboratory for developing the mechanics of interrogation and where they were able to refine a range of abominable practices that were later to become standard once Saddam was in power. Hanna Batutu, the distinguished historian on modern Iraq, has, for example, managed to piece together from official government files a horrifying account of what took place at the Palace of the End under Kazzar and the Baathists in 1963:

"The Nationalist Guard's Bureau of Investigation had alone killed 104 persons. In the cellars of the *al-Nihayah* palace, which the bureau used as its headquarters, were found all sorts of loathsome instruments of torture, including electric wires with pincers, pointed iron stakes on which prisoners were made to sit, and a machine which still bore traces of chopped-off fingers. Small heaps of blooded clothing were scattered about, and there were pools on the floor and stains on the wall."[28] This was the work of the party that was to act as the springboard for Saddam's dramatic rise to power.

So what was Saddam's role in these atrocities? There are few precise details of Saddam's whereabouts at this time. The only comment Saddam personally made concerning this period related to the internal battles that were taking place within the Iraqi Baath Party. "There was an atmosphere of terror, and blocs and groupings were formed in the party; obstacles were placed in the way of comrades who wanted to work along proper party lines."[29] As Saddam was later to make Kazzar his security chief, giving him a free hand to institutionalize the diabolical interrogation methods he had developed at the Palace of the End, it is more than likely that the two men became acquainted during their eradication of the communist opposition. Saddam, fresh from his meetings at the American embassy in Cairo, may even have been able to provide some names and addresses of communist sympathizers in Baghdad. Some of Saddam's surviving contemporaries from this period have suggested that, apart from his mundane duties at the Central Farmer's Office, he became closely involved in organizing the National Guard, the Brownshirts of the Baath Party. He visited detention camps in Baghdad and helped to supervise the "punishment" of communist detainees.[30] Some of the detainees were held at the Fellaheen, or peasant, camp, which provides an intriguing insight into the likely nature of Saddam's duties at the Central Farmer's Office. Saddam's task, it appeared, was to improve the lot of the peasants, so long as they were peasants who did not have communist sympathies.

As a reward for his diligence in tracking down communists, Saddam was appointed to the Baath Party's intelligence committee, which assumed overall responsibility for the interrogations. In the 1990s an Iraqi communist who was tortured at the Palace of the End claimed that Saddam had personally supervised his interrogation. "My arms and legs were bound by rope. I was hung on the rope to a hook on the ceiling and I was repeatedly beaten with rubber hoses filled with stones."[31] Saddam has been accused of disposing of the bodies of his torture victims by dissolving them in bathtubs of acid. He was said to have experimented with the various torture techniques developed by Kazzar, sometimes offering the victims a menu from which they could choose their preferred method of interrogation. In the Iraqi-made autobiographical film, *The Long Days,* Saddam comments on his participation in the events of 1963, saying, "We must kill those who conspire against us."

A more mundane sketch of Saddam at this time was provided by Baha Shibib, who was a member of the Baath Party leadership in Baghdad in 1963 and briefly served as foreign minister. "In the greater scheme of things Saddam was pretty insignificant," said Shibib. "He was involved with the interrogations, but he was not involved in policymaking. When he came back from Cairo, his main concern was to get a job that paid a monthly salary. He came to us begging for a job, so we gave him something with the farmer's bureau. But the main thing I remember about Saddam then was the way he was always hanging around Bakr. He was the prime minister and clearly had lots of influence and Saddam, as a fellow Tikriti, was always hanging around his office, trying to ingratiate himself. He hung out with Bakr's bodyguards, trying to play the tough guy. But no one took him too seriously. We were far too busy with other matters."[32]

Fortunately for the Iraqi people, this particular Baathist reign of terror was short-lived. Factional infighting between rival Baathist groups resulted in the party being ejected from power in November 1963, thereby drawing to a close, for the time being at least, the gratuitous bloodletting taking place at the Palace of the End. The Baath, which had been the dominant party in the government established by President Arif the previous February, soon fell prey to factional infighting. The main cause of the ideological split was the vexed question of whether Iraq should pursue the stated Baathist objective of pan-Arab unity, and form a federation with either Syria or Egypt, or both. The civilian wing of the Baath, led by Ali Salih al-Sadi, favored political union, especially after the Syrian Baath had staged a successful coup d' état in Damascus in March. Sadi was opposed within the Iraqi Baath, however, by the party's more conservative, military wing, which favored the traditional "Iraq first" policy. By the autumn of 1963 Iraq's military establishment had become increasingly irritated by the ill-disciplined behavior of the National Guard, the Baath Party militia, which was being used by Sadi and his gangs of Baathist thugs to intimidate his opponents and persecute the communists.

In early November the military wing of the Baath conducted a coup of the party's leadership against Sadi and his associates. Sadi was put on a plane and sent into exile in Spain. The National Guard came out onto the streets in protest and attacked the government's main Rashid military base on the out-skirts of Baghdad. At this point Bakr, who had been attempting to reconcile the ideological differences between the rival wings of the party, called a meet-ing of the Baath National Command, the party's governing body, an umbrella organization, which controlled the different national groups, such as the Syrian Baath and the Iraqi Baath. (The individual Baath Party Regional Commands represented the interests of Baathists in their respective countries; thus the Iraqi Regional Command and the Syrian Regional Command were both subordinate to the National Command, which was based in Damascus.) Throughout this period Saddam, more through family loyalty than ideologi-cal conviction, supported Bakr, his fellow Tikriti, and soon found himself act-ing as the prime minister's de facto personal bodyguard. Saddam was to be found constantly in public at Bakr's side, armed with a loaded revolver.

The arrival of Michel Afleq and several other prominent Syrian Baathists to attend the special conference convened in Baghdad by Bakr to resolve the ideological conflict within the Baath did not, however, improve the mood of the "Iraq first" contingent, especially when Afleq, who regarded himself as the figurehead of pan-Arab Baathism, suggested that he should take control of Iraq's political affairs. With the National Guard continuing to pose a threat to public order, President Arif finally lost patience with the Baath and decided to act. On November 18 he mobilized those army units on whose loyalty he could rely. Several disillusioned military members of the Baath, including General Tahir Yahya, the chief of staff, and Brigadier Hardan al-Tikriti, the commander of the air force, lent their support when Arif gave the order to attack the National Guard in Baghdad. Within hours Arif's forces were suc-cessful and the president was in full control of the city.

President Arif's decisive intervention ended the Iraqi Baath Party's first, brief, flirtation with power. The twelve Baath members of the government were expelled, and replaced by military officers upon whom Arif felt he could rely. Bakr, Saddam's mentor, was sacked as prime minister and Iraq submitted itself to government by military dictatorship. The National Guard was dissolved and replaced by the Republican Guard, an elite unit in the armed forces that was commanded by a member of Arif's own tribe. Well armed and stationed strategically near Baghdad, the main function of the Republican Guard was to protect the regime against future coup attempts.

The disastrous reversal in the fortunes of the Baath Party in late 1963 was not, however, a complete disaster for Saddam Hussein. The peremptory dismissal of not one, but two, sets of party leaders meant that the Bakr faction, which Saddam supported, became the dominant force. During the next couple of years Bakr made his way through the ranks of the Baath Party to become secretary-general of the Regional Command—i.e., the section of the party responsible for Iraq. As Bakr's position strengthened in the Baath, so did Saddam's. The full membership of the party that he had acquired in Cairo was finally recognized in Baghdad and he was promoted to the Iraqi Baath Party's Regional Command in the summer of 1964—according to some commentators, with the backing of Michel Afleq—and used this position to consolidate his control of the party's internal security. The crisis of late 1963, in which the military wing of the party had colluded with the government to form a military dictatorship, taught the civilian wing of the Baath Party an important lesson, namely that in future they would need to be better organized if they were not to succumb to the superior firepower of the armed forces.

Salim Shakir, a former general in the Iraqi army who was active in the Baath Party during this period, recalled that Saddam carefully exploited Bakr's diffident nature to increase his own power base. "Until 1963 Saddam Hussein was nothing more than a gangster. If you wanted someone killed, you called for Saddam. But after Bakr started to move up the party ranks, Saddam was very smart and attached himself to him. Bakr was a good politician, but he was useless in public. He was a backroom operator. He needed someone to carry out his orders, and so he asked Saddam. As a fellow Tikriti he believed Saddam was loyal to him, and so he gave Saddam a lot of responsibility. Saddam was therefore able to use Bakr to strengthen his position in the party."[33]

Saddam now concentrated his energies on improving his social position. He married Sajida, to whom he had been betrothed during his exile in Cairo. Although it was an arranged marriage, the bride and bridegroom appear to have enjoyed a genuine affection for each other. A photograph taken shortly after their nuptials in 1963 depicts an attractive young couple, with Saddam clean-shaven (the trademark mustache had still to make its appearance) and smartly dressed in a dark suit and tie, and a rather serious-looking, dark-haired

Sajida wearing a modest dress with a plain floral print. Later Sajida dyed her hair blond after her husband developed a penchant for blond women, but in these early days of innocence they appeared much like any other young couple preparing to tackle the challenges of married life. Even after a couple of murders, a failed assassination attempt and four years' exile in Cairo, Saddam himself looked far from menacing; he comes across as self-conscious and shy, a fresh-faced young man who seems ill-at-ease in front of the camera lens. Saddam's social ineptitude was confirmed by one of his Baathist contemporaries who remembered him as being "very shy and introverted." At social gatherings "he did not say much. When he did speak, though, all he did was express ferociously anticommunist views." Nor did Sajida herself make much of an impression on Baghdad society. "She looked like her father wearing a wig and, as no one liked her father, people gave her a wide berth."[34]

From the point of view of Saddam's future career, however, his choice of Sajida for his bride was a good one. Khairallah Tulfah, her father and his uncle, was a close associate of Bakr, even if Khairallah detested the Baath Party's socialist sympathies. During the party's first flirtation with power in 1963, Bakr rewarded Saddam's uncle for his support in helping the Baathists to seize power by making him director general at the Ministry of Education. Saddam's alliance with Bakr was further strengthened when one of Bakr's sons married a sister of Sajida, and one of Bakr's daughters married a brother of Sajida.[35] Even at this early stage in the Baath Party's development, the clannish Tikritis were using the traditional bonds of marriage and kinship to secure their power base in Baghdad.

Saddam devoted all his energies to building up the Baath Party's internal security structure, a body that would become one of the main platforms for his own ascent to power. Like many Baathists, particularly those in the civilian wing of the party, Saddam had been appalled at how lack of party discipline had resulted in its expulsion from office in late 1963. With Bakr's encouragement, Saddam resolved to establish an organizational structure that could deal both with external enemies and internal dissidents. During his Cairo years, Saddam was greatly influenced by Josef Stalin, and studied his life and work. While it is difficult to believe that a mediocre student like Saddam, who spent most of his time running gangs and intimidating opponents, was capable of undertaking a serious study of the Soviet despot, it does seem that some of the more ruthless aspects of Stalin's philosophy found favor with the Baathist's apprentice. After the humiliation of November 1963, Saddam was often to be heard uttering Stalinist maxims such as "If there is a person then there is a problem; if there is no person then there is no problem."

Saddam was one of a group of committed Baathists responsible for establishing, sometime during 1964, the party's secretive security apparatus, which was called Jihaz Haneen, or the "instrument of yearning." Following the coup of November 1963, which had resulted in most of the remaining Baathist leaders—including Bakr—eventually being jailed, Saddam took a calculated risk by remaining in Baghdad, a decision that was contrary to the wishes of the party's high command in Damascus, which wanted him to flee once more to Syria. Saddam correctly reasoned that he would be regarded as a coward if he left Baghdad, and as a traitor if he sought refuge with a group of foreign Baathists in Syria. Together with some of the few Baathists who had not been jailed by Arif, Saddam set up an underground security force that owed more to the Nazi Brownshirts than the Red Guards in its outlook. The principal aim of Jihaz Haneen was to act as a counterweight to the large number of military officers in the Baath who in 1963 had sided with Arif to expel the civilian wing of the party. With people like Nadhim Kazzar holding senior positions, however, the organization was soon to become one of the most feared security apparatuses in the entire Middle East.

Saddam's freedom in 1964 was to prove short-lived. With most of the Baath leadership either in exile or in jail, Saddam was left to his own devices, and it was not long before he was involved in yet more plots to overthrow the government. As with the 1959 plot to assassinate Qassem, Saddam was joined by his "twin brother," Abdul Karim al-Shaikhly. Several possible scenarios were explored for assassinating President Arif in September 1964. There was a plan to shoot down his plane when it took off from the Baghdad airport, and there was another, much favored by Saddam, in which he and a group of Baathists would storm the Presidential Palace, break into a conference room where Arif and the rest of the government were meeting, and machine-gun them all to death. This plot, which gave Saddam the honor of firing the machine gun, had to be abandoned after a palace official who was to have allowed the plotters access to the palace, was transferred to another post. Finally the plotters had to resort to a crude plan to attack the Presidential Palace with homemade bombs made with TNT that they had purchased on the open market. But this plot, like the others, was foiled by the security forces. In mid-October Saddam's hideout in the suburbs of Baghdad was surrounded by the security forces. After a brief exchange of fire, Saddam was forced to surrender after he ran out of ammunition. According to one of his official biographers, Saddam was cool and composed when Arif's security forces burst into the room. "My dear fellow, what's this about?" he inquired. "Machine guns? Is there no government?"[36]

Salim Shakir, who was involved in one of the plots to overthrow Arif and later became one of Iraq's most distinguished generals, met Saddam for the first time at a house in Baghdad that was being used to plan the coup attempt. "It was a rather convoluted plan, and Saddam was trying to get me to mobilize army units to support a coup attempt. Looking back it all seemed rather farcical, but I must confess that Saddam was very impressive. He came into the room to address the meeting and said quite simply: 'We are going to take over the regime.' I must confess I thought there was something about Saddam that made him stand out among most other Baathists of his generation. My first impression was that I was dealing with a natural leader, a man with a clear idea of what he wanted to do."[37]

As with many other episodes from Saddam's early life, a degree of mythology has been allowed to develop about his "heroic" attempts to rid Iraq of the Arif government, and the stoicism he displayed during his two years of imprisonment. His official biographers relate how he was kept in solitary confinement for long periods, and how he was singled out for special treatment by the authorities because of his refusal to cooperate with them, the clear implication being that he was tortured. On one occasion, he claims, he was made to sit on a chair for seven days, not in itself a great hardship, and he also claims the government made several overtures to him in the hope of persuading him to join the Arif government. Just as Stalin was said to have spent his time in prison reading, generally trying to improve himself, and becoming one of the chief debaters in the prison commune, so Saddam "spent his time in prison trying to raise the morale of those comrades whose spirit had been broken by torture. He read a number of books and encouraged the others to read too; he also initiated discussions about the Party and its future."[38]

This inspiring account of Saddam's imprisonment, however, does not square with the recollections of those surviving Baathists who were jailed with him. Ayad Allawi, a young medical student and Baath Party activist who was imprisoned at the same time as Saddam, recalls that, far from being given a hard time, Saddam received preferential treatment from the prison authorities. "Most of us were held in a special camp where the regime was very tough," says Allawi. "Many of us were tortured, some quite badly." Saddam's "twin" Abdul Karim al-Shaikhly, for example, was given particularly harsh treatment. At one point his interrogators drove a nail into his back to make him confess. At another he was dragged around the prison compound, tied to the back of a jeep, and suffered appalling injuries. Saddam, however, was detained separately from the other prisoners. He was held at an old police training college, according to Allawi, where the conditions, compared with those experienced by the other Baath detainees, were similar to "being in a holiday camp. Even though the security forces had about thirty incriminating statements from witnesses denouncing Saddam—including one that he had smuggled guns from Syria to Iraq—they turned a blind eye."[39]

The preferential treatment Saddam received during his detention between 1964 and 1966 aroused suspicions in the Baath Party that he had made a secret deal with the Arif government; some former Baath Party members have claimed that Saddam was actively working with the government to inform on his own party.[40] During the summer of 1963, when Saddam was involved in the persecution and torture of communists and leftists, he worked in conjunction with the state authorities. There is also the possibility that he was working in conjunction with the CIA contacts he made in Cairo. Certainly that was the suspicion shared by many of the other Baathists who were jailed by the Arif regime, but did not enjoy Saddam's preferential treatment. Even though Saddam was actively involved in trying to overthrow the Arif regime, it seemed that he still had friends in the government, and even abroad, who were able to ensure that he was not badly treated in prison. And however much Saddam liked to think of himself as a Stalin-like figure, who looked after and helped to indoctrinate his fellow prisoners, in reality he was not well liked by his fellow inmates. Many of the other prisoners were well educated and came from better families and from a higher social class; many of them were also army officers. They tended to treat with disdain the thuggish young man from Tikrit, who was of low social standing, conversed in a strong peasant dialect, and had very modest educational qualifications. The only qualification to which he could lay claim was the secondary school certificate he obtained in Cairo, but no evidence of this was ever actually produced. Saddam developed a grudge against many of his fellow inmates for the patronizing tone they adopted toward him, and took his revenge against them once he had assumed a position of power in the Baathist government.

Khairallah Tulfah was detained during this time, even though he was not a member of the Baath Party. For a period Allawi shared the same cell as

Saddam's uncle, and it was not an enjoyable experience. According to Allawi, Khairallah was a "tall, well-built man who was very aggressive, and whose language was littered with expletives." Khairallah, apparently, was incensed by his arrest, and complained bitterly to the guards. "Why have they imprisoned me?" he would shout at the guards. "I am not against the regime." Khairallah was visited by Sajida, his daughter, who had just given birth to Saddam's first child, Uday. Apart from bringing food and books to Khairallah, she would visit Saddam who was held at a different prison. According to Saddam's biographers, Sajida would bring him messages from Bakr, who had been released from prison, that were hidden in baby Uday's clothes, which enabled Saddam to keep abreast of Baath Party affairs.

Saddam's second period of incarceration (the first had been for murdering Saadoun al-Tikriti in 1958) ended on July 23, 1966, when, together with two Baathist colleagues, he managed to escape. The official account of his escape[41] claimed that Saddam had befriended the guards to the extent that he was able to persuade them to stop at a restaurant for lunch while transporting him between the prison and the court, where he was being tried for attempting to overthrow the regime. Once inside the restaurant, Saddam and his accomplices, who included Shaikhly, were able to escape through a back door to a waiting car driven by Saadoun Shakir, an army deserter from Baghdad who had befriended Saddam, in which they then sped off while the guards were waiting for them outside the front entrance. Another version of the event, which has since become firmly enshrined in the heroic myth of Saddam, was that the escape took place when Saddam and Shaikhly feigned illness in the prison, and persuaded the guards to take them to a nearby hospital for treatment, where they made good their escape with Saadoun Shakir's assistance. The ease with which Saddam and Shaikhly escaped raised the obvious question of whether it was a genuine escape, or whether the authorities were complicit. Whatever the truth, his escape meant that Saddam was now free to start working on his next plan to overthrow the government and seize power.

THREE

The Revolutionary

The coup of 1968, which finally brought the Baath Party to power in Iraq, was, by comparison with the violent bloodletting that had accompanied previous changes of government in Baghdad, a relatively civil affair. The secret password given to those who were to participate in the historic events of that night was *rashad,* or "guidance." In the early hours of the morning of July 17, a number of military units, accompanied by civilian Baath Party activists, seized several key military and government installations, including the television and radio stations, the electricity station, the Ministry of Defense in Baghdad, all the city's bridges, and a number of army bases around the capital. All telephone lines were cut and at 3 A.M. precisely the order was given to move on the Presidential Palace. A number of tanks then rumbled into the palace courtyard, and came to a halt beneath the windows where the president was fast asleep in bed. Sitting astride the lead tank dressed in the uniform of an Iraqi army lieutenant, his pistol in his hand, was none other than Saddam Hussein.

One of Saddam's fellow conspirators that night was Saleh Omar al-Ali. In 1968 Ali, like Saddam, was a member of the Baath leadership in Iraq, and had been involved in all the secret meetings leading up to the coup attempt. Having worked with Saddam since 1964 and shared a jail cell with him, Ali had formed a high opinion of Saddam's ability. "He had a self-confident air about him. He was brave and courageous," Ali recalled.[1] The plotters were broken up into different cells that were assigned different tasks. Ali was in the same cell as Saddam, which was given responsibility for capturing the

Presidential Palace. The Baath leadership had insisted that civilian activists assume this responsibility to avoid a repetition of the 1963 coup where the military, having taken a leading role in overthrowing the Qassem government, took control of the government and forced the civilian Baathists to assume a secondary role.

Having collected weapons that had been kept at secret locations, Saddam's group drove to the palace in private cars. Although the cell was predominantly civilian in makeup, the group was accompanied by General Hardan al-Tikriti, the former air force commander who in late 1963 had helped President Arif suppress the Baathists (see Chapter Two), who still commanded respect within the military establishment. On the way to the palace the group met up with army sympathizers, who provided them with armored cars. They then proceeded to the military headquarters at the side of the palace, where they were met by Saadoun Ghaydan, who was in charge of palace security and, although not a member of the Baath, was sympathetic to the coup. The military headquarters contained a number of tanks and the plotters, having dressed themselves in army uniforms, took control of the tanks and maneuvered them into position around the palace. "Saddam was in a very excited state," said Ali. "This was the moment we had been waiting for, and Saddam was keen to be involved in every stage of the operation."[2]

The first that President Abdul Rahman Arif knew of the coup was when he heard some of the more exhuberant members of the Republican Guard firing their weapons in the air in a premature gesture of triumph. Saddam's mentor, General Ahmed Hassan al-Bakr, who had mastermined the plot and who oversaw the operation from military headquarters, used the military communications network to make contact with the president, informed him that his government had been overthrown, and invited him to surrender. Arif asked for time to consider the request and contacted other military units to see if anyone was willing to come to his aid. He soon discovered that his position was hopeless and that he had no alternative other than to surrender. He telephoned Bakr and offered to stand down, in return for which Bakr said he would guarantee his safety. Bakr then deputed Hardan al-Tikriti and Ali to enter the palace and escort the president off the premises. "I am empowered to inform you that you are no longer President," Tikriti dryly informed him. "The Baath Party has taken control of the country. If you surrender peacefully, I can guarantee that your safety will be ensured." Arif, a weak man who had only become president after his brother, Abdul Salam Arif, was killed in a helicopter crash in 1966,

accepted the coup as a fait accompli. His only demand was that the coup plotters spared his life and that of his son, who was a serving army officer.
Throughout the whole episode Saddam's role was to keep guard over the palace
and make sure that none of the soldiers loyal to Arif attempted to intervene.

General Tikriti and Ali then escorted Arif to Tikriti's house in Baghdad.
By 3:40 A.M. the coup had been completed without the loss of a single life,
which, by Iraqi standards, was quite an achievement. As the Baathists had no
great argument with Arif, they were able to conclude the affair in an almost
gentlemanly fashion. Tikriti went out of his way to make Arif comfortable at
his home, making him coffee and urging him to lie down and rest before his
flight to London, where he was to join his wife who was receiving medical
treatment. After a few hours' rest, Arif is quoted as saying, "I bade farewell to
all the officers and wished them every success."[3] Later that morning the Iraqi
people awoke to discover they had a new government. A Baath-sanctioned
radio broadcast announced that the party "had taken over power and ended
the corrupt and weak regime, represented by the clique of the ignorant, the
illiterate, the profit-seekers, thieves, spies and Zionists."

Saddam's version of his role in the events of July 17, needless to say, is
rather more action-packed. He claimed that, in the heat of the battle for control of the Presidential Palace, he learned how to fire the gun on top of his
tank. He has deliberately embellished the role of Barzan al-Tikriti, his half
brother, who he claims was riding on the same tank as Saddam (a considerable number of those who participated in the July 17 coup were, like Saddam,
Tikritis). According to others who took part in the occupation of the
Presidential Palace, just two tank rounds were fired following a false report
that Arif intended to resist. For the rest of the proceedings the only gunfire
came from overexcited soldiers who, in keeping with the Arab custom, fired
their guns in the air to celebrate the coup's success.

The explanation for Saddam's appearance that day, dressed in military
fatigues and riding on a tank, lies in the Baath Party's concern that its civilian
leaders, and not the military, should be installed in power if the coup succeeded, the opposite of what had happened during the 1963 coup. Ideally
Saddam and his Baathist colleagues would have preferred to carry out the coup
on their own, but in the crucial weeks leading up to Arif's overthrow it became
clear that they would need the support of the military if they were to succeed.
Saddam's Jihaz Haneen, the secret security force set up to combat what it
described as "the enemies of the people," was proficient at employing bullyboy

tactics to intimidate Saddam's enemies, but it had neither the muscle nor the expertise to take over the country. The Baath leaders therefore made contact with military commanders thought to be sympathetic to their cause. Some, like Hardan al-Tikriti, were already members of the Baath, and so were prepared to oblige. Others took more persuading. Two of the key converts to the cause were Abdul Razzak Nayif, the deputy head of military intelligence, and Colonel Ibrahim Daud, the commander of the Republican Guard. Although their cooperation was crucial to the coup's success, neither of them was particularly committed to the Baathist cause, and their support was determined more by opportunism than ideology. With a president as weak as Arif in office it was clear that the regime would not survive for long. Nayif and Daud were also well aware that the coup stood little chance of success without them and, in return for lending their support, Nayif demanded that he be rewarded with the office of prime minister, and Daud that of defense minister.

The conspiratorial nature of Baghdad café society meant that even someone as disconnected from the political currents of the day as President Arif became aware that trouble was brewing. The Baathists' carefully laid plans for the coup were thrown into considerable disarray when, on the afternoon of July 16, Arif summoned Nayif and Daud to the Presidential Palace, where he asked them if there was any truth in the rumors of the impending coup. Both men tearfully denied knowing anything about a coup attempt and, to demonstrate their loyalty to Arif, they fell to their knees and kissed his hand.

When the Baathists heard what had happened, Bakr convened an emergency meeting of the Baath leadership at his house that evening. It was clear that the Baathists needed to act quickly if their plans were not to be exposed. It was equally clear that they would need the support of Nayif and Daud, as well as other key military commanders, if they were going to succeed. Thus while the Baathists were not exactly enthusiastic about the demands made by Nayif and Daud, they nevertheless agreed to them. Saddam, who claims to have been present at the meeting when the decision was made to form a tactical alliance with the officers, reached an equally cynical conclusion about the merits of the alliance. In a speech to his fellow Baathists at Bakr's house, he declared, "I am aware that the two officers have been imposed on us and that they want to stab the Party in the back in the service of some interest or other, but we have no choice now. We should collaborate with them but see that they are liquidated immediately during, or after, the revolution. And I volunteer to carry out this task."[4] Stalin himself could not have put it better.

The July Revolution was a classic military coup, a coup d'état rather than a popular revolution, and the Iraqi public remained wary. Iraqis had not forgotten the orgy of violence that had proceeded from the last Baathist takeover of the country in 1963, and few people were inclined to be too enthusiastic about the new regime until they had a good idea about who was in government, and how good were its prospects of survival. Over the next two weeks, however, it became clear that the military takeover was merely a prelude for a more far-reaching change of regime. Having ridden on a tank to the Presidential Palace to make sure that the Baathists' military collaborators did not depart from the agreed script, Saddam and his fellow conspirators lost no time consolidating their position in the new government. The services of Nayif and Daud were required to gain power, and once that had been achieved the Bakr/Saddam Hussein alliance was determined to get rid of them, a sentiment that was warmly reciprocated by Nayif and Daud. Immediately after the coup, General Ahmad Hassan al-Bakr was appointed president, while Nayif and Daud assumed the portfolios of prime minister and defense minister respectively. Bakr, who remained secretary-general of the Baath Party, also became chairman of the Revolutionary Command Council (RCC), the body set up the morning after the coup that assumed supreme executive and legislative authority. For a party that had made its name fighting communism, the Baath Party in power quickly acquired all the attributes needed to govern a one-party state. Saddam, a high-ranking member of the Baath, might have been disappointed not to have figured in the new cabinet, but he was given responsibility for national security, a position that would be crucial to the new government's survival. Saddam was ideally suited for the position, having served his apprenticeship setting up the Jihaz Haneen paramilitary organization, which was dissolved once the Baathists came to power to be replaced by more formal security structures. Even though he did not enjoy official recognition, Saddam had a far more important power base that would ultimately deliver him the presidency.

Within days of the coup a bitter power struggle developed between Bakr and Nayif for control of the country, with both men believing that they could now dispense with the services of the other. Technically Nayif and Daud, who were both career officers, should have had the upper hand, as they were well-known and respected figures within the Iraqi military establishment. Bakr had demonstrated considerable political cunning in persuading Nayif and Daud to help the Baathists overthrow Arif. He had gotten Hardan al-Tikriti and

Saadoun Ghaydan, two of the Baath's leading military figures, to employ their powers of persuasion. Tikriti and Ghaydan had persuaded them that the new government would be run by the military, with the Baath playing a secondary role, and it was on this basis that they had participated in the coup. But once Bakr was established in power, he was determined to bring the Baath into the government at the expense of Nayif and Daud, who had underestimated the Baathists' superior organizational skills. Bakr was prepared to allow military officers who were also Baath members, such as Hardan al-Tirkiti, to participate in the new government, and in the days following the coup he increased the Baathists' military influence by appointing more than 100 Baathist officers to positions in the Republican Guards and other key units. Saddam, meanwhile, was busy helping to organize the Baathists' security apparatus and paramilitary units, which he believed were essential for keeping the Baath in power. On July 29, Daud, completely misreading the situation in Baghdad, left for a tour of inspection of Iraqi troops that were stationed in Jordan, part of the garrison that had been sent to reinforce the Jordanian border following the Six Day War with Israel. While Daud was away from Baghdad, Bakr, with Saddam's assistance, was able to strike. As one of Saddam's official biographers commented: "He [Saddam] felt that Abdul Razzak Nayif's participation [in the government] was an obstacle."[5]

Given the dire threats Saddam had made at Bakr's house on the eve of the coup, Nayif's removal was a relatively civilized affair. On July 30, the day after Daud went to Jordan, Nayif was invited to lunch with Bakr at the Presidential Palace. As the lunch drew to a close, Saddam, acting in his new position as the country's head of internal security, burst into Bakr's room brandishing a gun and accompanied by three accomplices. When Nayif saw the revolver pointed at him, he put his hands over his eyes and cried out, "I have four children." Saddam, according to the official biographers, was conciliatory. "Do not be afraid," he replied. "Nothing will happen to your children if you behave sensibly." Saddam then proceeded to give Nayif a short lecture on why he was being deposed from office: "You know you forced your way into the revolution, and that you are a stumbling block in the way of the Party. We have paid for this revolution with our blood, and now it has come out. The decision of the Party is that you should be put out of the way. You should leave Iraq immediately."[6] Precisely whose decision it was to remove Nayif is debatable. Saddam's biographers give the impression that it was all Saddam's doing, but most of the surviving participants say the decision was made by Bakr, who then gave Saddam the order to intervene. Nayif was persuaded to accept an ambassadorial post, and Saddam personally escorted him to the airport to catch his flight. As they left the palace, Saddam kept a concealed gun in his pocket to make sure Nayif did not try to make contact with any of the guards, some of whom would have been loyal to him.

The official account of Saddam's involvement in the removal of Nayif reads thus: "He warned Nayif that his gun was in his jacket, and that if he saw the slightest sign that Nayif was about to disobey his orders he would end his life there and then. He asked some of his comrades to remain at the Palace to protect President Ahmad Hassan al-Bakr. Saddam sat next to Abdul Razzak Nayif all the way to Rashid Military Camp. The plane was waiting. After it took off, Saddam Hussein felt tears come to his eyes. One shot could have aborted the whole operation to get rid of Nayif, but fate decreed that the operation went without a hitch from beginning to end."[7]

Saddam's tears were shed more out of relief that the mission was a success, rather than sadness at Nayif's departure. The tension that accompanied Nayif's removal from office suggests that the July 30 coup, or "correctional coup" as it became known, was a close-run affair. Had any of the forces loyal to Nayif and Daud been aware of what was taking place they may well have tried to intervene, prompting an ugly bloodbath in Baghdad, similar to what had occurred when the Baathists launched their attack to remove Qassem in 1963. As Daud, in particular, had widespread support in the military, it is by no means certain that the Baathists, relying heavily on the ill-disciplined paramilitaries trained by Saddam, would have prevailed, and the history of Iraq might have been very different. With fate on their side, however, the Baathists won the day, and Nayif was forced into exile in Morocco (Nayif's personal preferences for Beirut or Algiers having been dismissed on the grounds that these capitals were too politicized, places where he might have found allies to help him launch a countercoup). Daud was arrested in Jordan by the commander of the Iraqi detachment, General Hassan Naquib, and was returned to Baghdad on a military plane and sent into exile to Saudi Arabia. Nayif was regarded as such a potential threat that, ten years later in 1978, he was shot dead on Saddam's orders in London, having survived a previous assassination attempt in 1973.

The removal of Nayif and Daud finally allowed the civilian Baathists, rather than the military, to declare themselves the real driving force behind the July revolution. Bakr further consolidated his position by assuming two new posts to go with the presidency and his chairmanship of the RCC; he became prime minister and commander in chief. It was at this point, following the completion of the "second stage," as Baathist historians refer to it, of the July revolution, that the Tikriti wing of the Baath emerged as a force in its own right. Apart from Bakr himself, many of the key appointments in the new government went to Tikritis. Hardan al-Tikriti, who had been instrumental in appointing Saddam a principal full-time organizer of the nonmilitary wing of the Baath in 1964, became minister of defense, while Abdul Karim al-Shaikhly, Saddam's "twin" who had participated with Saddam in the failed assassination attempt on Qassem in 1959 and had joined him in exile in Cairo, became foreign minister. Even Saddam's uncle Khairallah, who was not a Baathist, was made mayor of Baghdad. Not only were there a large number of Tikritis in key government positions, many of them were Tikritis with whom Saddam was intimately connected.

The most intriguing appointment of them all, however, was that of Saddam himself. Although, as his biographers clearly state, Saddam played a key role in both the removal of Arif and Nayif, he was the only member of the conspirators' hierarchy who was not officially rewarded with a government position. Saddam was appointed deputy chairman of the RCC, the all-important body that would control the government of Iraq, but, at Saddam's insistence, the appointment was not made public. He claimed that he declined to accept an official government position. This reticence may have been because of Saddam's relative youth—he would only have been between twenty-nine to thirty-one years old. A more likely explanation is that Saddam preferred to stay in the shadows, working quietly away from the spotlight to ensure that the revolution was a success, and that any elements hostile to the Bakr regime were liquidated. Saddam's biographers ascribe his refusal to accept an official position to the fact that "he had fulfilled his role in bringing the Baath party to power." A measure of Saddam's anonymity at this time can be drawn from the fact that he made no impression whatsoever on the legion of Western diplomats based in Baghdad during the July revolution and its aftermath, most of whom were filing lengthy dispatches on the turbulent events unfolding in Iraq.

The murder of a lawyer in Baghdad at dawn on July 17, just as the revolution was beginning, provided a more telling insight into the precise nature of Saddam's activities at this time. While in general terms the coup was a bloodless affair, the one exception was the killing of Harith Naji Shawkat, who was murdered inside his home in Baghdad. At first no one could understand why Shawkat had been shot. A respectable middle-class man with a family, he had briefly flirted with membership of the Baath, but had not been involved directly in the July coup, which he neither supported nor opposed. Inquiries carried out by local officials, however, led them to the conclusion that Saddam had ordered the killing, which had been carried out by members of his new security service. It transpired that when Saddam was released from prison in 1966 Shawkat had been looking after funds worth some 20,000 dinars, a sizable sum, on behalf of the party. Saddam approached Shawkat and asked him to hand over the money, which he claimed he needed to help rebuild the party. Shawkat, however, refused, claiming that the money belonged to a different, left-wing group. Saddam, never one to forget, or forgive, a grudge had him killed the moment the Baath was reestablished in power. According to a Baath Party activist who worked closely with Saddam at this time, the killing was typical of Saddam's behavior. "Saddam was never an ideologue. He was the tough guy who was brought in to do the dirty business. But no one took him very seriously in the party. That was our big mistake, and that is why he was able to work quietly behind the scenes and eventually take us all over."[8]

Another example of Saddam's readiness to commit violence is provided by Saadoun Shakir, the army deserter who drove his escape car in 1966 and was appointed to the RCC after its formation. He recalls that Saddam had decided to remove Nayif "on the first day of the revolution." During the initial planning Saddam asked Shakir "to have ten committed party members ready to assassinate Abdul Razzak Nayif if he asked them to." Apart from gate-crashing the Baathists' takeover of the country, Nayif's main offense was that he "had links with foreign forces and that he would have sabotaged the revolution."[9] After his own flirtation with the CIA in Cairo, Saddam was not taking any chances that a fellow collaborator might be in a position to reveal unwelcome details of his own involvement with "foreign forces."

Even if Saddam's methods lacked sophistication, they clearly had a place in Bakr's new regime, which is why Saddam, who was still young and inexperienced compared with other senior members of the Baath, such as General Hardan al-Tikriti, found himself deputy chairman of the RCC. This appointment must have seemed especially pleasing to Saddam given that he had so abjectly failed in his youthful ambition to enroll at Baghdad Military Academy and pursue a career in the armed forces, the established channel for young men from the provinces seeking social mobility. He had been forced to watch on numerous occasions as rivals such as Tikriti made use of their military standing to further their political objectives. Bakr, however, who was more than capable of controlling the military side of things, needed someone who could take care of civilian affairs, in particular making sure that the military's recent stranglehold on Iraqi politics was broken. With his secretive security force and paramilitary storm troops, Saddam was perfectly suited for the task. And if Bakr had any doubts about Saddam, they were quickly allayed by Khairallah Tulfah, his friend and companion from Tikrit, who rarely missed an opportunity to reemphasize his nephew's many qualities. "Saddam is your son," Khairallah, the newly appointed mayor of Baghdad, would constantly advise Bakr. "Depend on him. You need the family to protect you, not an army or a party. Armies and parties change direction in this country."[10]

Saddam's dramatic trnasformation from jailbird to revolutionary leader in the space of just two years is a remarkable achievement by any standard. With Bakr's patriarchal backing, and with his own security apparatus at his disposal, there was only one likely trajectory for the young Tikriti's future career, and that was up. It is a testament both to the depths of Saddam's ambition and his ruthless sense of purpose that he managed to overcome the considerable disadvantages of his birth and background to reach the heights of Iraq's revolutionary establishment at such a young age. None of the other key players who emerged during the coups of 1968 were fatherless, indigent peasants without any formal training. Ever since he moved to Baghdad with his uncle Khairallah in the mid-1950s, the only qualifications that Saddam had acquired were in the dubious arts of gangsterism and political survival. His personal ideology, such as it was, consisted of an innate patriotism that bordered on the xenophobic, a condition much encouraged by Khairallah, and a profound understanding that political success in Iraq was determined simply by the acquisition, and retention, of absolute power, by whatever means.

Before his imprisonment in 1964 Saddam had acquired a standing of sorts in the Baath Party, having secured his appointment to its Regional Command in 1964 as a result of the enthusiasm he had displayed for persecuting Iraqi communists. The collapse of the Baath Party through internal bickering had played into Saddam's hands in late 1963 and early 1964, and circumstances conspired to move in his favor both during his imprisonment and after. In

political terms the most important development was the deterioration in relations between the Syrian and Iraqi parties, which was precipitated in February
1966 when the Marxist wing of the Syrian Baath seized power in Damascus
in a military coup. Michel Afleq and other, more traditional, Syrian Baathists
were arrested and the party's National Command, which technically oversaw
control of Baathists throughout the Arab world—including Iraq—was dissolved. Not only did the success of the Marxists in Damascus raise fears of a
communist revival in Baghdad, but the new Syrian government made it
abundantly clear that it intended to assume control of all Baathist policy, a
move that meant all Iraqi Baathists would be placed under Syrian control.

The notion of taking orders from Syrian communists was deeply unappealing to Iraqi nationalists such as Bakr and Saddam, and soon after his jail
escape Saddam organized what was called an Extraordinary Regional
Congress, which was convened in Baghdad in September 1966. The congress
has come to be regarded as a watershed in Baath history, the moment when
the Iraqi Baathists irrevocably parted company with their Syrian counterparts, a rift that determined the strained relations that were to develop
between the rival ruling Baath factions in Baghdad and Damascus. The congress decided to abandon the system of a unified command, based in
Damascus, with regional commands established in various member countries. It was replaced by two rival National Commands in Iraq and Syria,
which both claimed to be the heirs of the original party, and which claimed
leadership over Baathists throughout the Arab world. Having effected this
initial schism, the Iraqi Baathists followed it up in February 1968 by insisting
on the supremacy of their own National Command, with Bakr appointed as
secretary-general and Saddam working as his deputy.

Apart from playing a key role in facilitating the establishment of an independent Baath Party in Iraq, Saddam, again with Bakr's support, spent the two
years leading up to the July 1968 coup assisting with the party's reconstruction
after the disasters of 1963, and purging the party of any surviving leftists. He
completed the formation and organization of Jihaz Haneen, the party's neo-
Nazi militia. The organization itself was the brainchild of Abdul Karim al-
Shaikhly, although Shaikhly himself was more of an ideologue, an intellectual
figure who, having argued for the creation of a paramilitary wing, was quite
content to leave the day-to-day administration to Saddam. The paramilitary
organization, under Saddam's guidance, came to be composed of individual
cells of committed and trusted party workers, with each cell working in isola-

tion from the others. Many of those recruited by Saddam to run the Jihaz Haneen cells had worked with him in the torture chambers at the Palace of the End in 1963. An indication of how the Baath was taking shape under Saddam can be drawn from the fact that all three of Saddam's half brothers—Barzan, Sabawi, and Watban—all passed through his training camps, learning skills such as firing machine guns and abducting opponents. Another head of a Jihaz Haneen cell was Saadoun Shakir, Saddam's friend who had driven the getaway car for his jailbreak. The Baath under Bakr and Saddam was very much a family concern, and Saddam's main goal was to make sure that the next time the Baathists made a bid for power, they not only succeeded but remained there.

During the period when Saddam was busily building the power base that would eventually lead to him becoming one of the most powerful figures in the new Baath government, he still remained a socially awkward individual who was often overcome by shyness when required to mix with his Baathist contemporaries. Although he was tall and well-built, he retained a strong peasant accent and his coarse, colloquial Arabic made him feel conspicuous among his more genteel contemporaries in Baghdad. Fellow Baathists who knew him at this time recall that on the few occasions that Saddam made a public appearance, he did not talk much and that when he did, most of his conversation was confined to a denunciation of the evils of communism. His wife Sajida, who soon became pregnant with Qusay, Saddam's second son, after his release from prison, usually accompanied him to these functions. But on the whole Sajida was a neglected wife who was left at home to look after her young son while her husband devoted his every waking moment to furthering his career. For much of the time Sajida and the infant Uday stayed at Khairallah's house. During the period immediately following his escape from prison Saddam hid in the houses of friends, such as Abdul Karim al-Shaikhly, or Baath Party activists. Even when it was safe for him to come out of hiding, he still stayed at different houses to protect himself from revenge attacks. It was a policy he continued long after he had become president. During the Gulf War in 1991, for example, it was said that he stayed at a different location every night of the conflict. As a full-time employee of the Baath, Saddam received a modest income of fifteen dinars per month (about thirty dollars), which was paid for out of the five dinars a month subscription that all Baath Party members were required to donate. He was given an old Volkswagen Beetle, which had been looted from the communists in 1963, in which to conduct his official Baath business. This was later upgraded to an old Mercedes, which had been acquired by similar means.

For the first few months after his escape Saddam remained in hiding. Even though there were suspicions that the government had somehow been complicit in his liberation from jail, he still needed to keep a low profile. By the autumn, however, the charges against Saddam were quietly dropped and he was able to assume a more public role. Other Baath Party activists came to regard Saddam as Bakr's "second son." Few of them had much respect for Saddam, who was still blamed by many for the horrific excesses carried out in the name of the Baath against the communists in 1963. But Bakr, who headed a powerful group of officers, was regarded as the party's best chance of obtaining power, particularly after the mysterious helicopter crash that killed President Abdul Salam Arif in April 1966. Arif commanded respect, while his brother, who replaced him, possessed no natural authority, so that a destabilizing power vacuum was soon created. "We believed that Bakr was our best chance of delivering Iraq on a golden plate," commented one of Saddam's direct Baathist contemporaries from this era. "Because we supported Bakr, we did not question his relationship with Saddam."[11]

Apart from enjoying a reputation for violence, Saddam was viewed with suspicion by his Baathist contemporaries because of the relatively easy time he had enjoyed during his imprisonment. Mindful of the brutal scenes that had accompanied the coups of 1958 and 1963, President Abdul Salam Arif was a firm believer in meeting violence with violence, and the Baathists rounded up in 1964 for plotting his overthrow were treated severely. The least any of them could expect was to have their arms bound tightly behind their backs, and to be beaten with a thick black rubber hose about their bodies and on the soles of their feet. Others were dragged around the prison compound tied to the back of army trucks and a variety of other excruciating tortures were inflicted on the prisoners, such as, in the case of Abdul Karim al-Shaikhly, having nails driven into their backs. But despite his deep and well-documented involvement in both Baath politics and the 1964 coup to overthrow Arif, Saddam suffered hardly any ill-treatment during his confinement.

Saddam's comparatively benign treatment by the authorities has naturally raised suspicions about where his true loyalties lay. As has already been explained, Saddam, using lists provided by the CIA, was heavily involved in hunting down and liquidating communists during the purge of 1963. During this time it is also likely that he made contacts with senior figures in the Arif government. Saddam was never an ideologue, and always tended to follow those who were best placed to improve his own position. Saddam may have been informing on his Baath Party colleagues for the Arif government.[12] Alternatively Saddam may have been working as an agent for either the British or American government (the CIA was the more likely suspect, given what is known of Saddam's dealings with the American embassy in Cairo). Certainly many of his contemporaries believed that there must have been a foreign power intervening on his behalf during his incarceration. Suspicions were further raised about Saddam's loyalty when, after his escape, he made contact with Robert Anderson, a CIA officer who made frequent trips to Baghdad to monitor efforts by the Soviets to take control of Iraq's oil reserves. Anderson maintained such a high profile during his visits that he actually provoked demonstrations in Baghdad, with the crowds chanting, "Go back home, Anderson." The CIA man, who was keen to see a government installed in Baghdad that would act as a counterweight to the new Marxist regime that had recently been established in Damascus helped to draw up pamphlets that were distributed by Saddam's paramilitaries. The precise nature of Saddam's dealings with Anderson was unknown, but suspicions about his real loyalties at this time were further complicated by the fact that Saddam was the author of a note sent to the British consulate in the southern Iraq port city of Basra asking for their help in overthrowing the Arif government.[13]

Apart from carrying out his Baath duties, Saddam decided to finish his education and enrolled at the law faculty at Baghdad University. At the time that Saddam enrolled for the law course, in September 1966, the university did not require high secondary school grades; merely to have completed secondary school was regarded as qualification enough. The only official qualification that Saddam had actually obtained was the secondary school certificate that all the exiled Baathists had received in Cairo, but Saddam never produced this in Baghdad. The course was so overenrolled that it was taught in two shifts. Saddam quickly distinguished himself as anything but the model student. Although socially shy, he was more forthcoming in the political hothouse of the university campus, and added to his physical presence was compensated was a commanding personality. "By comparison with all the other students he was very hawkish and hard-line," recalled one former student. "He was brimming with aggression." Apart from his extremist views, Saddam stood out from the other students because he was generally accompanied by four of five "bodyguards," members of the Jihaz Haneen, and he was always armed with a pistol. "Saddam gave the impression of great physical strength because he was always surrounded by this group of thugs. Saddam would

come into the canteen of the medical school, one of his favorite haunts, surrounded by his guards. These guys were real heavies, and were built like
wrestlers. None of the other students ever felt like arguing with Saddam, even
though we didn't agree with his policies. He was the only Baathist on the
campus who behaved like this."[14]

Saddam's group of guards were known by the other students as the
"Saddameen" and, apart from protecting their leader when he ventured onto
campus, they spent their time intimidating anyone who did not subscribe to
Bakr's right-wing Baathist agenda. In most respects the *Saddameen* were no
different from the Nazi Brownshirts, and they certainly shared the Nazis' hatred
of communists and leftists. The *Saddameen* were used by Saddam to intimidate and terrify anyone who did not agree with his philosophy. They would
break into the homes of leftists and loot them. On other occasions they would
spray their homes with machine-gun fire. A classic example of their modus
operandi was provided in the autumn of 1967 when Saddam himself appeared
at a coffee shop in Baghdad that was frequented by young Baathists. Without
pausing to greet his acquaintants, Saddam announced to anyone who cared
to listen that he had just killed a left-wing Baathist called Hussein Hazbar on
the al-Jadiria bridge in central Baghdad. "I beat him over the head with my
revolver until he could move no more," Saddam boasted. "You won't be seeing
him again."[15] Contrary to Saddam's expectations, the other Baathists gathered
at the Baladia coffee shop in central Baghdad were horrified by the revelation,
and protested vigorously that this was not the way in which to settle differences of opinion within the Baath Party. Saddam merely laughed and walked
out, accompanied by his bodyguards. The remainder of the Baathists in the
bar hurried to the local hospital, where they learned that the badly injured
Hazbar was being treated. Both his arms had been broken, and he had sustained a fractured skull, but in spite of the severity of his injuries he survived.
The young Baathists comforted him as much they could, telling him that they
abhorred Saddam's tactics. "We tried to impress upon him that we did not
believe this was what the party was about," said one of those present. "After
what he had been through, it was difficult to make him understand that not
everyone in the Baath party was a homicidal maniac."[16]

Saddam's bullyboy tactics were to play a crucial role in the buildup to the
1968 coup. The coup itself undoubtedly had its origins in the tumult that
engulfed the Arab world in the aftermath of Israel's resounding victory in

the Six Day War in June 1967. The Iraqi expeditionary force that had been stationed in Jordan to take part in the proposed pan-Arab invasion of Israel was completely routed without hardly firing a shot in anger. Israel's victory traumatized the Arab world, not least because it dealt a devastating blow to President Nasser's belligerent claim that a unified Arab assault would be sufficient to destroy the "Zionist entity," the euphemism by which he referred to Israel. Nasser himself never recovered from the shock of defeat, and died a broken man in 1970. Elsewhere in the Arab world the defeat provoked an outpouring of hostility toward the Arab governments held responsible for the disaster, which left the Israelis in control of the West Bank, Gaza, the Golan Heights, and the Sinai Peninsula. In Baghdad the outrage of the Iraqi people was directed at President Abdul Rahman Arif.

Defeat in the Six Day War was the opportunity the Baathists had been looking for to agitate for a change of government, and from the autumn of 1967 Bakr, with Saddam's help, began developing a concerted plan of action that would result in the coup of 1968. During the last months of 1967 and early 1968, the Baath was involved in a series of strikes and demonstrations that denounced the regime's corruption and ineptitude and called for its replacement. Saddam himself played a prominent role in the strikes, particularly those taking place on the campus at Baghdad University. Perversely, in one of the earlier strikes, which had been called by all opposition parties other than the Baathists, Saddam acted as a strikebreaker, rather than as an enforcer. For a party to succeed in Iraq it had to demonstrate that it had street credibility, and so when, in late 1967, the major opposition parties called a nationwide strike to protest against the government, the Baathists decided to oppose it. This gave them an opportunity to show their organizational strength, which they did by forcing the strikers back to work. Saddam, backed by his *Saddameen*, was ideally suited for the task and concentrated his energies on forcing the students striking at Baghdad University back to their classes. "Saddam would arrive at the campus, firing his gun in the air to frighten the students and intimidate them," recalled one of Saddam's university contemporaries. "He would run around with the *Saddameen* and force them back to class to resume their studies. The tactic worked brilliantly and the strike at the university was quickly broken."[17]

Through tactics such as this the Baath quickly established itself as the main party of opposition. Having displayed their organizational skills by breaking a strike, the Baathists determined to demonstrate their political power by organizing their own strikes and demonstrations. The early months of 1968 were a period of intense political instability in Baghdad with the Arif government desperately struggling to hold on to power. In April 1968 thirteen retired army officers, five of whom were Baathists, submitted a memorandum to Arif demanding the removal of the prime minister, Tahir Yahya; the establishment of a legislative assembly; and the formation of a new government. It is an indication of the Arif government's weakness at this time that, rather than becoming alarmed by the growing confidence of the Baathists, it did nothing to suppress their activities and bent over backward to try to accommodate their demands. Yahya even conducted a number of clandestine meetings with the Baathists to see if the government could reach a political accommodation with them. At Yayha's initiative Bakr and the Baath leadership, which was technically a banned organization, attended regular meetings at the Presidential Palace between 1966 and 1968 to discuss with the president the possibility of forming a government of national unity.[18] With the Iraqi government on the defensive, it was simply a question of time before Bakr and his associates took control. Indeed, the coup might actually have taken place in the summer of 1967 were it not for the untimely intervention of the Six Day War.

Amid all this political turmoil Saddam was working hard to consolidate his position within the Baath Party. Already well established in the hierarchy of the Iraqi Baath, Saddam attempted to have himself elected to the Baath's international leadership at a special summit held in Beirut in December 1967, the Ninth Pan-Arab Congress of the Baath Party, which was convened ostensibly to resolve the party's differences, particularly those between the left-leaning Syrians and the right-wing Iraqis. This time, however, Saddam's attempt to further his career was a humiliating failure. Saddam himself was not able to attend the meeting, but his good friend Abdul Karim al-Shaikhly was present and put forward Saddam's name for inclusion in the new governing body. But Saddam's reputation preceded him, no doubt because of the role he had played the previous year in helping Bakr to reconstitute the Iraqi Baath Party. Not only did the delegates refuse to vote for him; they would not even let his name be put down on the election list. One of those present at the Beirut meeting said that the main reason for Saddam's rejection was that he was widely disliked within the Baath, and had no credibility. "The man was regarded as a thug. He was widely suspected of having links with foreign powers. He had no proper constituency within the party apart from his friendship with Bakr. No one was going to give him their vote. Shaikhly thought he was doing Saddam a big favor by putting his name forward, but all he did was humiliate him."[19] The rejection was certainly a massive blow to Saddam's pride, and one that he never forgot. Added now to the list of those against whom Saddam was to hold a lifelong grudge, which till then had included all those who had patronized him in prison for being uneducated and having no social standing, were all those Baathists who had sought to curb his political ambition.

By the summer of 1968 the momentum was moving in favor of the Baathists, and their growing popularity was demonstrated at a rally held in the center of Baghdad in June on the first anniversary of the Six Day War. This, it should be remembered, was the same year that revolutionary demonstrations were taking place at campuses all over Europe and America, a time when youthful rebellion really believed it had a chance of changing the world. In Baghdad the revolutionaries were to succeed. For one of the demonstrations a makeshift platform was set up in Al Rashid Street, and Bakr, accompanied by Saddam, Shaikhly, and five retired Iraqi army officers, addressed the crowd. Bakr's speech focused on criticizing the Arab regimes for their weakness in failing to confront Israel, and accused many of them of actually being infiltrated by Jewish spies, an ominous allegation in view of the anti-Jewish persecution that would take place once Bakr was safely installed at the Presidential Palace. The speech was so well received that even the police commanders, who had come to maintain order, came onto the platform and publicly applauded Bakr. Nor was the impressive public display of support for the Baath lost on the country's military leaders who, since the overthrow of the monarchy in 1958, had ultimate control over who ran the country. The realization began to dawn on them that either they got behind the Baathists, or found themselves left behind in the revolution that was inevitably to come.

Ayad Allawi, who was a young medical student and head of one of the Baath Party cells in Baghdad, believed that the decision by key military commanders to support the coup was the crucial factor in the revolution passing off peacefully. "We had the commanders of the Republican Guard and military intelligence behind us, as well as the commanders of key military units in and around Baghdad. At least 25 percent of the officer corps were members of the Baath Party, and their support meant that the coup attempt, when it came, worked like clockwork." Allawi was in charge of one of three cells that carried out the coup on the morning of July 17. One cell, mainly comprising the Republican Guards but also including some Baathists, including Saddam, was responsible for taking the Presidential Palace while another, led by the 10th Armored Brigade, was to take control of central Baghdad. A third group was detailed to take control of the television and broadcasting centers and the main bridge crossings into Baghdad. "The reason there was so little opposition is that nearly everyone knew that the revolution was going to happen, it was simply a question of when."[20]

The morning after the coup Allawi ran into Saddam, who was on his way to make a broadcast and was brimming with excitement. "In hindsight we all underestimated Saddam," said Allawi, who headed the Baath Party's students committee. "We thought Saddam was the weakest link in the leadership and that he would soon be sidelined. Indeed none of us took the Tikriti crowd seriously. Our priority was to build a modern, democratic Iraq. It never entered my mind at that stage that Saddam would play a critical role in Iraq. There were far better candidates who were experienced in politics and government." Such was the general mood of idealistic euphoria among the young Baathists that they made no objection when Bakr proposed carrying out the "correctional coup" to remove Nayif. According to Allawi's recollection of events, the "correctional coup" was Bakr's idea, although the proposal enjoyed widespread acceptance within the party. "Bakr masterminded the whole affair," insisted Allawi. "He liked to present himself as a decent, moderate guy. But in reality he was two-faced. He was a first-class conspirator." For the Baathists the arrangement with Nayif and the other non-Baathist military officers had been a marriage of convenience, and now the time had come for the divorce. As the old Iraqi saying goes: It is better that you have your enemy for lunch so that they don't have you for dinner. Allawi said there was another reason that the Baathists were keen to distance themselves from Nayif. "It was generally believed that Nayif worked with the Western powers and that, if we were to win the respect of the Iraqi people, he had to go."

This obsession with the CIA and "foreigners," such as Jews, was to be one of the main distinguishing characteristics of the Baath regime after the "correctional coup" of July 30 had consolidated the power base of Bakr and his fellow Tikritis. It was a development that appalled the young, idealistic Baathists, such as Allawi, who had naively supported the July Revolution in the belief that they would turn Iraq into a modern country. "The Baath Party before the coup wanted nothing to do with violence," said Allawi, who later became the head of one of the main opposition groups, the Iraqi National Accord. "The only violence we contemplated was a war at some stage against the Israelis." But the new ruling elite, of whom Saddam was a key member, had other ideas, and it was not long before, with Saddam's help, the high ideals that had inspired the July coups were corrupted with violence and bloodshed.[21]

Saddam was suspected of involvement in the only killing that took place on July 17, the day of the original coup. Four months later he was implicated in yet another murder, this time the killing of Nasir al-Hani, who had briefly served as Nayif's foreign minister in the summer of 1968. Hani was a career diplomat of no particular political orientation. After his removal from office and replacement by Saddam's longtime fellow conspirator, Abdul Karim al-Shaikhly, Hani became vociferous in his criticism of the new government, which he felt was not observing the promises on which it had been brought to power. He, like Nayif, was suspected of having close contacts with the CIA, which, after all, was still keen to ensure that the new Iraqi government, irrespective of its politics and personalities, did not fall under the influence of the Soviets. Iraqis are deeply suspicious of any politician with foreign links, and if Hani had links to the CIA, then he may well have been in a position to shed some light on Saddam's own dealings with the Americans, both during his sojourn in Cairo and beyond. Whatever his motives, Saddam was determined to rid himself of Hani, and so on the night of November 10, Hani was abducted from his house by an armed gang and stabbed to death.

"The gang that committed the murder was the same gang that was run by Saddam Hussein," said Allawi, who himself has been subjected to several assassination attempts by Saddam's henchmen. "The Baath Party was outraged by the murder of this man. We wanted to build a new country, not return to the violence of the past. But with people like Saddam in charge, it was clear that this was not going to happen."[22] Although Saddam was never prosecuted for the murder, it was generally accepted in Baghdad that he was responsible, and that he had ordered Hani's murder "because he knew too much." Saddam's own denial of involvement in the killing is singularly unconvincing. When challenged about the murder his reply was merely rhetorical: "Who was Nasir al-Hani and what danger did he constitute for the regime and the party? He was neither a politician nor a competitor of ours. . . . Why should we kill him at all?"[23] Whatever the reason for the murder, Saddam Hussein's violent repression of anyone who stood in his way was gradually laying the foundations for the reign of terror that was to become the hallmark of the new Iraqi government.

FOUR

The Avenger

As a publicity stunt, the public execution of fourteen spies took some beating. On the morning of January 27, 1969, the day the hangings were due to take place, the police withdrew from the center of Baghdad, leaving the streets under the control of gangs of Baath Party activists. Directed by Baath-appointed commissars, groups of volunteers constructed the gibbets at intervals of seventy meters around Liberation Square. Nine of the condemned men were Iraqi Jews, and their trial, at which they were accused of spying for Israel, had been the most sensational in Iraqi history. The authorities were consequently expecting huge crowds to turn out for the hangings, and they wanted to make sure that everyone in the audience had a good view of the spectacle. A national holiday had been proclaimed, and the government had helpfully arranged transportation for an estimated one hundred thousand "workers and peasants" to be bussed in for the event. By the time the condemned men were led out to meet their fate, an almost carnival-like atmosphere had taken hold over the city. In Liberation Square itself, entire families had spread out on the flower beds for a picnic. For those who were unable to attend, the whole event was broadcast live on Iraqi television and radio. Just as the executions were about to commence, President Bakr and Saddam Hussein, his able deputy, drove around Liberation Square in an open-topped limousine to the acclaim of the Baathist students who lined the streets.

This gruesome affair continued for twenty-four hours. After the executions had been carried out, the bodies—including that of a sixteen-year-old boy—were left hanging for all to see. One eyewitness who was present in Liberation Square on the day of the hangings recounted how he was pushed up against the bodies by the crowd four hours after the executions had taken place. "You could see that their necks had been broken and they had been stretched to about a foot long." Film footage of the event, which was shown on Iraqi television, showed crowds of smiling militiamen and supporters dancing and cheering in front of the cameras. Later in the day Bakr climbed onto a platform and made a rabidly anti-Zionist and anti-imperialist speech before a cheering crowd, with the corpses of the recently executed "spies" dangling behind him. "We shall strike mercilessly with a fist of steel at those exploiters and fifth columnists, the handmaidens of imperialism and Zionism." Other leading luminaries of the Baath addressed the crowd, whipping the audience of bemused peasants into a chanting, spitting, stone-throwing frenzy. A good example of the rhetorical flourishes emanating from the podium was provided by Saleh Omar al-Ali, who had accompanied Saddam on a tank into the Presidential Palace during the July 17 coup the previous year (see Chapter Three). The revolution had been good to Ali who was now the Baathist "minister of guidance" and the Revolutionary Command Council (RCC) official to whom had been entrusted the successful prosecution of the "Israeli ring of spies." Ali had personally supervised the interrogations and helped arrange the show trials. "Great People of Iraq! The Iraq of today shall no more tolerate any traitor, spy, agent or fifth columnist! You foundling Israel, you imperialist Americans, and you Zionists, hear me! We will discover all your dirty tricks! We will punish your agents! We will hang all your spies, even if there are thousands of them! . . . Great Iraqi people! This is only the beginning! The great and immortal squares of Iraq shall be filled up with the corpses of traitors and spies! Just wait!"[1] Saddam's comment was brief and to the point. The spies had been hanged "to teach the people a lesson."

The infamous trial of the "Israeli" spies was a graphic illustration of what can only be described as the Stalinization of Iraq in the aftermath of the 1968 revolution. Saddam might have been imbued with a deep hatred of communism, but he undoubtedly owed a great debt to Stalin for providing him with the means to create and maintain a one-party state. The Baath Party that assumed power in 1968 was based on the traditional Marxist-Leninist model in terms of organization, structure, and its methods; hierarchy, discipline, and secrecy were its dominant characteristics. As in Soviet Russia, the party became the government. All promotion was channeled through the ranks of the party, which had a pyramidic structure. At the base was the individual cell, or neighborhood unit. These reported in turn, in order of seniority, to the division, the section, and finally the branch, of which by 1968 there were twenty-one (one for each of Iraq's eighteen provinces and three for Baghdad). At the top of the pyramid was the Regional Command Council, the highest executive and legislative body of the state. According to the new constitution that was enacted by the Baathists in 1970, the Revolutionary Command Council (in effect, the ruling clique of Baathists who headed the Regional Command Council), of which Saddam was vice president, became "the supreme body of the state." The RCC was empowered unilaterally to promulgate laws and decrees, to mobilize the army, to approve the budget, to ratify treaties, to declare war, and to make peace. The RCC also took charge of all aspects of national security. The constitution stipulated that the RCC was to be self-selecting and self-perpetuating; it alone could choose and discharge its members, and all new members were to be selected from the Regional Command Council. Saddam was unique among the members of the new Baath government in that he had not worked his way up through the party machinery; his rise to prominence was entirely due to the patronage of Bakr, who had appointed him to key positions in the party.

Immediately Bakr's position as head of the new Baath government was secure, Saddam's task was to make sure not only that the Baath Party survived in power in Iraq, but that it was the only party in Iraq. Even after its success during the coups of 1968, the Baath was by no means a populist movement; most estimates put the total party membership in late 1968 at no more than five thousand. And given the narrow tribal and geographical base of the leadership, which was drawn from a small number of Sunni Muslim families based around Tikrit, the likelihood of it becoming a party of genuine mass appeal was distinctly remote. Saddam was well aware of the party's limitations, and once he was established as Bakr's right-hand man, it became his personal mission both to eradicate any potential enemies of the party, and any potential rivals to his own position. Contemporaries from this period ascribe to Saddam numerous quasi-Stalinist maxims, such as "Give me the authority and I will give you a party capable of ruling this country," which is what he is supposed to have told Bakr after his appointment as vice president of the all-powerful RCC, or "Mr. Deputy" as the title-conscious Saddam now preferred to be known. A more telling exposition of Saddam's authoritarian vision of Iraq's political system was provided in one of the first public pronouncements he made after the Baathists came to power. "The ideal revolutionary command should effectively direct all planning and implementation. It must not allow the growth of any other rival centre of power. There must be one command pooling and directing the subsequent governmental departments, including the armed forces."[2]

Iraq might not have been a communist state, but the methods employed by the Baathists to impose their will on the country were almost identical to those used by the Soviets, and perfected by Stalin. The masses had to be "reeducated" and incorporated into the party's organizational machinery. Rivals were to be eliminated and a deep sense of fear and respect had to be struck into the hearts and minds of ordinary Iraqis. Saddam, as head of the Baath's security apparatus, was ideally suited for the task. It was also an opportunity for him to excel at the expense of the army officers who were competing against him for promotion within the party. Purges, propaganda, and indoctrination are not skills that come naturally to men of action; they tend to be more the preserve of backroom apparatchiks such as Saddam.

The sensational trial of the ringleaders of what the government claimed was a major Zionist spying ring, which finally got under way in January 1969, was an example of how the new Baathist regime intended to adopt the concept of the show trial as a means of persecuting its enemies and instilling fear among the population at large. In the years immediately following Israel's success in the Six Day War, anti-Zionist sentiment was rampant throughout the Arab world. The Iraqi armed forces based in Jordan were frequently involved in skirmishes with the Israelis, from which they mostly emerged second best, and the government rarely missed an opportunity to blame the country's woes on Zionist spies and fifth columnists. When, for example, sixteen Iraqi soldiers were killed in an Israeli air attack in December 1968, Bakr personally addressed an anti-Israeli demonstration held outside the Presidential Palace at which the bodies of the dead Iraqis were paraded through the streets. "We face treacherous movements of a rabble of fifth columnists and the new supporters of America and Israel," he declared. "They are hiding behind fronts and slogans which the people have seen through and exposed." Every so often Bakr would interrupt his speech to ask the crowd, "What do you want?" To which they would reply, "Death to the spies, execution of the spies, all the spies, without delay!"[3]

The atmosphere of mass hysteria being created by the Baathists played perfectly into Saddam's hands. As head of the Baath Party's security apparatus it was his job to track down and destroy what were described in Baathist literature—with no conscious acknowledgment of Stalin—as the "enemies of the state." In October 1968 the regime claimed it had compelling evidence of this international treachery when it revealed that it had broken a Zionist spy ring based in Basra. The "discovery" of the spy ring was actually part of a carefully prepared scheme Saddam had devised for eliminating some of his principal rivals. Saddam's plot, as opposed to the Zionist's alleged misdeeds, went back two years to the time when a genuine Israeli agent had been killed in the Hotel Shattura in Baghdad. An incriminating notebook, containing the names of several leading Iraqis, was found on the dead Israeli. Saddam did not do anything with it at the time, but after the Baath came to power the notebook was again produced, only this time many other names had been added, most of them people whom Saddam wanted removed, including Saadoun Ghaydan, the commander of the Presidential Guard's tank battalion, which had participated in the July coup.

Shortly after the discovery of the Zionist conspiracy, Saddam set up a special "Revolutionary Court" to try "spies, agents and enemies of the people." The court consisted of three military officers with no legal training; no one appearing before such a tribunal could expect a fair and impartial hearing. Indeed, the lawyer representing the seventeen Zionist plotters who went on trial in January 1969 actually opened the defense by apologizing to the prosecution for having to defend the "spies," stating for the record that "he would not like to see the traitors go unpunished."[4] As the hearing got under way the defendants were publicly humiliated when their "not guilty" pleas were subjected to derisive peals of laughter from the press benches. At the end of the two-week trial fourteen of the accused were convicted of espionage and sentenced to hang.

The carefully stage-managed executions in Liberation Square that were carried out within days of the verdicts being delivered were Saddam's way of whipping up public support for the Baathists. Baghdad Radio summoned people to "come and enjoy the feast," and called the hangings "a courageous first step towards the liberation of Palestine." In a retort directed at international criticism of the hangings, Baghdad Radio declared: "We hanged spies, but the Jews crucified Christ." The only criticism of the executions in the Arab world came from the Egyptian newspaper *al-Ahram*, which commented: "The hanging of fourteen people in the public square is certainly not a heartwarming sight, nor is it the occasion for organizing a festival."

The trial of the so-called Zionist spy ring set the tone for a nationwide purge of any opponents suspected of posing a challenge to Saddam and the Baath Party, which lasted for most of the next twelve months. Further public executions of the regime's opponents took place on February 20, April 14 and 30, May 15, August 21 and 25, September 8, and November 26. Executions became so commonplace in Liberation Square that it became known colloquially as "the Square of the Hanged." Victims were brought before the Revolutionary Court, where they were obliged to confess their crimes in front of a televised audience before being escorted off to face the firing squad or, in civilian cases, the hangman's noose. If Saddam thought it unlikely that a confession would be forthcoming, opponents were dealt with by his gangs of paramilitary thugs, as happened to Nasser al-Hani, the former foreign minister in the first cabinet of the July revolution. The only significant difference between Saddam's purges and Stalin's terror is that in Iraq there were no gulags; with few exceptions, Saddam's intended victims stood no chance of survival. The purges basically fell into two categories: first, those constituencies, such as the Kurds, communists, Shiites, and even left-leaning Baathists, who were considered hostile to the Bakr regime; second, any member of the Iraqi government or military establishment who posed a threat to Saddam.

Until the Baath Party came to power in 1968, the army had been the mainstay of the repressive regimes that had ruled Iraq since 1958, and had overseen the detention and interrogation of political opponents. Once established in the Presidential Palace Saddam used his experience of running the Baath Party's Jihaz Haneen security operation to undertake a substantial reorganization of the country's intelligence infrastructure, which placed him firmly in control of all aspects of national security. Jihaz Haneen was replaced by a security structure consisting of three main elements: the Amn al-Amm, or State Internal Security, which oversaw domestic security and dated back to the monarchy; the Mukhabarat, which started its existence by the unlikely name of the Public Relations Office but later became known as either Party Intelligence or the General Intelligence Department, and was the Baath Party's security arm, and by far the most powerful and feared agency; and the Istikhbarat, or military intelligence, which, apart from keeping the military in check, also undertook operations abroad, in particular the assassination of foreign dissidents.[5] Later in his career Saddam would set up yet another body, the Amn al-Khass, or Special Security, which superseded the Mukhabarat and reported directly to the president's office and was to become Saddam's personal secret police. To ensure he maintained total control over the Baath's new security apparatus, Saddam mainly appointed close family members or trusted friends to head either the Mukhabarat or Amn al-Khass. The first head of the Mukhabarat was Saadoun Shakir, the Baath colleague who had helped him to escape from prison in 1966 and who had helped him to run Jihaz Haneen. Saddam trusted no one, and so he made Barzan al-Tikriti, his half brother, Shakir's deputy. Barzan later took charge of the Mukhabarat between 1974 to 1983, and Saddam's other half brother, Sabawi, ran the organization from 1989 onward. After Saddam was made president, Amn al-Khass was headed by Hussein Kamel Hassan, Saddam's son-in-law.

Soon after the Baathists took power, Nadhim Kazzar assumed control of the internal security operation. Kazzar had already proved his credentials as a torturer during the bloody persecution of the communists in 1963 (see Chapter Two). The Baath leadership of Bakr and Saddam were well aware of the diabolical methods used by Kazzar to terrorize opponents of the regime, but nevertheless gave him free rein to eradicate any hint of opposition to the new regime, whether it came from within the party or outside. Hundreds if not thousands of people perished at the hands of Kazzar's security forces, many of them tortured to death at the Palace of the End. In 1971, for example, one faction of the Iraqi Communist Party issued a list of 410 members whom it claimed had died at the palace. One former Baathist activist who was present in Baghdad at the time recalled that Kazzar was afforded special treatment by the Bakr/Saddam government. "He was highly trusted. He was the only member of the Baath who was allowed to go armed with a firearm when he visited the Presidential Palace. This was because he had so many enemies in the Baath he felt he had to protect himself against an assassination attempt." A former engineer by training, Kazzar is remembered as a quiet man who never smiled. "In all the years I knew him I never saw him smile once."[6]

At the top of Saddam's list for retribution after the Baathists were established in power were his long-standing foes, the communists. From November 1968 onward there were a number of confrontations between communist sympathizers and Saddam's paramilitaries. The communists, like the Kurds, were becoming increasingly concerned at the decidedly autocratic nature of the new Bakr government, and staged several protests calling for a more democratic administration. Saddam reacted to their demands with his customary delicacy: in November 1968 two communists were killed when a group of striking factory workers in Baghdad came under fire, and another three were shot dead the following day at a rally to mark the fifty-first anniversary of the Bolshevik revolution. In each instance an accusing finger was pointed at Saddam's paramilitaries.[7] The outraged communists reacted by forming small, armed detachments with which they aimed to overthrow the regime. These guerrilla units staged a number of daring raids on businesses in Baghdad and other cities to raise money, blew up a number of official vehicles, and even sprayed Saddam's house with machine-gun fire. Saddam responded by launching a nationwide hunt for the communist cells, which his security forces eventually succeeded in catching in February. The captured men were predictably transported to the Palace of the End for interrogation: no fewer than twenty were said to have subsequently died under torture, including two members of the Politbureau that controlled the Iraqi Communist Party. The effectiveness of Kazzar's torture methods was illustrated by Aziz al-Haj, the head of the Politbureau, who broke down and recanted his sins against "the revolution" in a televised broadcast. Al-Haj, who had previously experienced the horrors of the Palace of the End in 1963, is said to have exclaimed upon his arrest, "I can no longer bear torture, I will cooperate."[8] Over the next two years a number of prominent communists were either murdered by Saddam's "security officials" or died at the hands of Saddam's torturers in the palace, and the movement's ability to mount an effective challenge to the Baathists was gradually eroded.

An altogether more serious threat to the Baathists was presented by the country's large Shiite community, which, apart from being hostile to the Sunni clique that was now running the country, had close ties with the shah of Iran, the leader of the world's most populous nation of Shiite Muslims. Ignoring protests from the United Nations over the show trials of the "Israeli ring of spies," Saddam persisted with his witch-hunts for spies and plotters, and the show trials were prosecuted with greater vigor: in February 1969 another seven people were publicly executed for plotting against the state, followed by another fourteen in April. Most of these executions were carried out in the southern city of Basra, the capital of the Shiite community, which adjoins the border with Iran. The shah, who had reached an entente with the Israelis to keep Iraq weak and destabilized, was keen to exploit the perceived weakness of the new regime and, without any provocation from the Iraqis, his government in April 1969 abruptly declared null and void the 1937 treaty that had granted Iraq control of the all-important Shatt al-Arab waterway at the head of the Gulf. For good measure he massed his troops on the border with Iraq and sandbagged buildings in Teheran.

The general sense of unease that the shah's belligerence created in Baghdad came to a head in January 1970 when a triumphant Saddam was able to expose a plot by a group of Iranian-backed Iraqi officers to overthrow the Bakr government. On January 20, the day fixed for the projected coup, Mahdi Saleh al-Samurrai, a retired colonel in the Iraqi army, set off with a group of fifty men, who had earlier assembled at the main Rashid military camp on the outskirts of Baghdad, for the Presidential Palace as part of a coordinated plan to overthrow the government. According to Saddam's account of the coup attempt, the plotters, who were led by Major General Abed al-Ghani al-Rawi, a retired officer and former protégé of the two Arif presidents, intended to form a number of "hit squads" that would assassinate key party and government officials in a number of coordinated attacks. The only action that actually took place, however, was Samurrai's march on the Presidential Palace where, to his surprise, on arrival he was warmly greeted by Saleh Omar al-Ali, the Baathist activist who had ridden on a tank with Saddam during the 1968 coup (see Chapter Three), and Colonel Fadhil al-Nahi. Believing that Ali and Nahi were party to the coup, Samurrai gratefully accepted their invitation to enter the Presidential Palace, and the gates were duly thrown open to allow his band of adventurers to enter. Unfortunately for Samurrai and his fellow conspirators, as soon as they were inside the palace compound the gates slammed shut, leaving them trapped inside. According to the official Iraqi account of the incident, Samurrai was then shown into a large hall. As the bemused plotters weighed their options, the door was thrown open, and Saddam entered the hall, accompanied by several officers. Realizing that they had been lured into a trap, the plotters opened fire, killing two of the palace guards. But they were quickly overpowered and forced to surrender.

Later that same day Saddam convened a Special Court to try the plotters. The court was headed by Captain Taha Yasin al-Jazrawi, a member of the RCC and a close associate of Saddam, and the other two members included Saddam's favorite henchman, Nadhim Kazzar. In all, forty-four plotters were convicted and executed,[9] including Samurrai. The executions started on January 21, and were completed by the twenty-fourth. The military officers were shot, and the civilians hanged. The officers were allegedly shot with the weapons they had received from the Iranian security services to carry out the coup.[10] Fifteen others were imprisoned. Nayif, the exiled prime minister who was implicated in the affair, was sentenced to death in absentia, as was General Rawi. The Iranian ambassador was given twenty-four hours to leave the country, and the Iranian consulates in Baghdad, Karbala, and Basra were closed and Iranians living in the country deported.

The exposure and swift dispatch of the plotters was a triumph for Saddam Hussein. It was his security forces that had uncovered the plot, and the exposure of a military coup attempt by Saddam's civilian officials constituted a victory for the civilian Baathists over their military rivals, a point that was not lost on President Bakr. Saddam, the ever-vigilant "Mr. Deputy" was able to make the point that it was he and his formidable security forces, rather than the military, that had guaranteed the party's safety. Saddam was able to turn exposure of the coup into a brilliant propaganda exercise, just as he had done with the "Israeli ring of spies." Every detail of the coup uncovered by the authorities was made public: the enormous sums of money, the sophisticated electronic transmitters, the 130 tons of arms, all of which was elaborately displayed in a central exhibition hall in Baghdad, each item carefully presented behind glass partitions. It was revealed that the whole affair had been arranged through the Iranian embassy in Baghdad, and details of the correspondence between the Iranian ambassador and General Rawi were published. Apart from the dispute with Iran over the Shatt al-Arab waterway, the other motive Saddam provided for the coup attempt was that it was part of a conspiracy to return Iraq to Anglo-American imperialist control and to weaken the country in its ongoing war with Israel.

Large demonstrations were organized to publicize "the invincibility" of the revolution and a state funeral was held for the two Baathist soldiers killed during the skirmish at the palace. Taped confessions and photographs of huge arsenals of weapons were widely circulated; handwritten letters giving code words were made available, and the wives of the plotters denounced their husbands. It was even alleged that the conspirators had planned to flood Baghdad and other cities in the event that they could not kill off the Baathist leaders immediately. The authorities claimed to have recovered from the conspirators' pockets lists of future ministers and other proposed government appointments, which provided Saddam and his acolytes with a wealth of ammunition to use against their enemies.[11] According to the official account of how the authorities apprehended the conspirators, which was provided in the government newspaper *Al-Thawra*, or "the revolution," the plot had actually been uncovered the previous year, at the same time that the government was prosecuting the Zionist plotters, and rather than round them up immediately, Saddam had placed thirty agents in their ranks. Saddam was keen to make as much political capital as possible from the affair which, apart from convincing the Iraqi people that they faced a genuine threat from foreign forces, would enable him to send a resounding signal to the shah of Iran that the Baathists were not to be intimidated by their neighbor's growing regional power.

The other powerful faction that needed to be neutralized by the new Baathist government was the Kurds, arguably the most problematic of all the Iraqi constituents. The Kurds are an ethnic minority distinct from the Arabs. They speak a different language and have different habits and customs. During the final years of Ottoman rule the vast majority of Kurds lived in what has today become Turkey. At the end of the First World War the victorious Allied powers denied the Kurds the statehood they believed they had been promised. The lands they had occupied for generations were divided among Syria, Iraq, Turkey, and Iran. From the outset of Iraq's creation successive Kurdish leaders campaigned for autonomy from Baghdad, a campaign that generated substantially more enthusiasm once the Kurds discovered that the Kurdish regions of northern Iraq around Mosul and Kirkuk contained some of the world's most lucrative oil reserves. The discovery of the region's oil wealth, however, only served to strengthen Baghdad's resolve to maintain control over the region, and the "Kurdish question" was a perennial issue that demanded tactful and skillful handling by Baghdad. The Baathists, forever mindful of their narrow power base, decided to placate the Kurds on the basis that they could only deal with so many rival factions at once.

From 1969 onward Saddam was given personal control by Bakr to bring the Kurds into line. From the outset Saddam's efforts to deal with the Kurds were hampered by the fact that the main Kurdish leader, Mustapha Barzani, was receiving the backing of the Soviet Union. The Soviets, who remained committed to their goal of extending their influence throughout the Gulf, had taken a dim view of the new Baathist government's persecution of the Iraqi Communist Party, and saw the Kurds as a means of putting pressure on Baghdad. Saddam's first instinct was to confront the Kurds on the battlefield and in April 1969 he called out garrison troops and the small Iraqi air force. On August 8 the army razed the Kurdish village of Dakan, near the northern city of Mosul. But the rugged terrain of Kurdistan was not well suited to the tanks and heavy armored vehicles of the Iraqi troops. The Kurdish guerrillas, called *peshmergas* ("those who walk before death") used the high mountain passes and steep valleys to their advantage. When the air force tried to bomb them, they simply dug in and hid in caves. The valleys were so narrow that the Iraqi pilots had difficulty in maneuvering. On occasion, unable to pull up in time, they crashed their jet fighters into the mountain peaks. To make matters worse for Saddam, the Iraqi communists threw in their lot with the Kurds. Potentially the Kurdish-communist threat was a deadly combination for the Baathists.

Facing a humiliating defeat on the battleground, Saddam decided to seek a diplomatic solution. In January 1970 he made his first visit to Moscow, which during the 1960s had become Iraq's main supplier of arms, hoping to negotiate a deal with Prime Minister Alexei Kosygin to withdraw Soviet support from the Kurds. The Russians were amenable, but stressed that if they withdrew their support, there was to be no massacre of the Iraqi Kurds. Saddam reluctantly agreed to the Soviet terms and, on his return from Moscow, triumphantly announced a new "autonomy plan" for Kurdistan. The March Manifesto, as it became known, promised the Kurds many of the political and cultural rights they had been demanding for years. The only catch for the Kurds was that Saddam was able to insist on the concession from Barzani that the autonomy agreement should not go into effect for another four years. Saddam had no intention of giving up control over the three oil-rich Kurdish provinces, but the agreement provided the Baathists with the breathing space they needed to deal with all the other threats they faced, such as the communists, the military, and Shiites, not to mention Israel and Iran.

The gloss was somewhat taken off the deal the following year, however, when a carefully planned attempt was made on Barzani's life, which bore all the hallmarks of Saddam's security forces. Relations between Saddam and Barzani quickly became strained because Saddam proved reluctant to stick to the terms of the March Manifesto, and probably never had any intention of doing so when the deal was originally struck. The Iraqi army was not withdrawn from the region, as had been agreed, on "security grounds," and Saddam created numerous obstacles to prevent Barzani from implementing his side of the agreement, such as appointing Kurdish politicians to government positions in Baghdad. The final straw for Barzani was the attempt on his life, which took place while he was entertaining eight religious leaders sent by Saddam to discuss implementation of the manifesto. As Barzani was talking two explosions rocked the room, killing two of the clerics. Barzani's bodyguards immediately opened fire, killing five of the remaining clerics. Barzani himself escaped, and it later transpired that the clerics had been duped into carrying out the assassination attempt by Saddam's associate, Nadhim Kazzar.

Kazzar provided the clerics with tape recorders and asked them to record their conversation with Barzani. The moment they activated the machines the bombs went off. Barzani was particularly incensed because not only had he agreed to see the clerics following a meeting with Saddam, but because Saddam had implicated Barzani's estranged son Ubaidallah in the plot, promising him that he would succeed his father if the attack were successful. Confronted with such incontrovertible evidence of Saddam's involvement, Barzani declared, "Iraq is a police state run by Saddam Hussein who is a power-obsessed maniac."[12]

Barzani's comment struck a chord with many Iraqis who came to know only too well how Saddam's security forces extended their pernicious influence into every area of Iraqi society. Immediately after the 1968 revolution all government offices were purged of any non-Baathist staff members who refused to accept the new order. The military was a harder nut to crack, but Saddam found a way around the resistance of the officer corps by reverting to the Soviet system, introduced by Lenin during the First World War, of appointing political commissars to report back on their activities. The commissars reported directly to Saddam, thereby bypassing the formal chain of command. Officers of questionable loyalty were replaced by Baathists or their sympathizers. Many of those dismissed from the armed forces, which included a number of division commanders, were arrested and tortured. Saddam similarly increased his control over the lives of ordinary Iraqis. Baathist militiamen patrolled the streets, and surprise raids on private homes in the middle of the night drove home the message that no one was beyond their control. Iraq was being transformed into a totalitarian regime, "a place where men vanished, and their friends were too frightened to inquire what had happened to them; people arrested on trivial charges "committed suicide" in prison; former officials were mysteriously assassinated; politicians disappeared."[13]

While Saddam was busy establishing this labyrinthine network of spies, commissars, torturers, and murderers, he nevertheless found time to keep himself acquainted with the gruesome practices being applied to his luckless victims at the Palace of the End. A Shiite dissident who managed to survive the torture chambers at the Palace of the End provided a chilling description of how Saddam personally killed another Shiite detainee by the name of Dukhail. "He came into the room, picked up Dukhail and dropped him into a bath of acid. And then he watched while the body dissolved."[14] While corroboration of such stories is hard to come by, they nevertheless bear an uncanny resemblance to some of the legends that have arisen relating to Saddam's activities at the Palace of the End in 1963. Whether true or false, from Saddam's point of view the most important consideration was that stories such as this were in the public domain in Iraq, and were widely believed. So long as the population was persuaded to live with the fear that any Iraqi might at any moment suffer a similar fate, the position of the Baath Party would remain secure.

Apart from terrorizing the various factions confronting the Baathists, Saddam concentrated his energies on eliminating anyone who might be considered a potential rival, together with anyone who knew him well enough to have information that might be considered harmful to his future career prospects. As discussed earlier, the motive for the murder of Nasser al-Hani, the former foreign minister, in November 1968, was widely attributed to the fact that he may have been able to shed unwelcome light on Saddam's dealings with the CIA. The official explanation for Hani's death was that he had been killed by criminals. A similar explanation was provided four months later following the murder of Colonel Abed al-Karim Mustafa Nasrat, a former special forces commander who had spearheaded the attack on the Ministry of Defense during the 1963 coup that overthrew General Qassem. His offense was that he had remained sympathetic to the Syrian Baath, another of Saddam's pet hates. To allay public suspicions, Saddam's security officers produced a public "confession" from a petty criminal who admitted to stabbing Nasrat to death in his home during a robbery. Saddam was also implicated in the death of Fouad al-Rikabi, the former secretary-general of the Iraqi Baath, who had been personally responsible for giving Saddam his first Baath assignment, the failed assassination attempt on General Qassem in 1958. Rikabi had been forced out of the party shortly afterward by the Baathist ideologue Michel Afleq and had become a Nasserite. After the 1968 revolution the Baathists jailed him for one and a half years on a trumped-up charge. A few days before he was due to be released, "the authorities brought in a hooligan with a knife. Rikabi was stabbed in the chest and then dragged to the hospital. They left him unattended until he died."[15]

There was a chilling degree of professionalism about the way in which Saddam systematically set about dispensing with his rivals. Samir al-Khalil, whose book *Republic of Fear* provides a fascinating examination of the repressive state security structures that were created by the early Baathists, sets out a detailed list of more than thirty high-ranking officers, senior Baathists, and politicians of ministerial rank or higher who were purged after the July Revolution of 1968, most of them on Saddam's orders.[16] The show trial remained Saddam's preferred method of humiliation, so long as he could be sure of securing a conviction, which was usually possible through the good offices of either the Palace of the End torturers or the willingness of the court officials to accommodate their Baathist masters. Thus Rashid Muslih, a former minister of the interior, publicly admitted at his televised trial that he had spied for the CIA, and was duly executed. Abed al-Rahman al-Bazzaz, who had served as prime minister under the second President Arif and had been generally well-disposed to the Baath, was put on trial in the summer of 1969, together with Abed al-Aziz al-Uqayli, a former minister of defense. Both these men denied the Baathists the pleasure of hearing public confessions, but received lengthy prison sentences nevertheless.

Saddam's sadistic streak was demonstrated by his treatment of Tahir Yahya, who had been Iraq's prime minister when the Baathists took power in 1968. Yahya had served Iraq as a military officer his entire adult life, and had at one time even been a prominent member of the Baath Party and one of Saddam's superiors. After seizing power Saddam had Yahya, a well-educated man whose sophistication he resented, confined to prison. On his orders Yahya was assigned to push a wheelbarrow from cell to cell, collecting the prisoners' slop buckets. He would call out, "Rubbish! Rubbish!" The former prime minister's humiliation was a source of great delight for Saddam until the day Yahya finally died in prison. He would tell the story to his friends, chuckling to himself over the words "Rubbish! Rubbish!"[17]

While the show trials proved to be a useful tool for persuading Iraqis that their country was riven with plots and conspiracies, Saddam needed all his cunning to dispense with more formidable rivals, such as General Hardan al-Tikriti, the gruff former air force commander who had persuaded President Arif to surrender during the bloodless coup of 1968, and Salih Mahdi Ammash, a veteran Baathist apparatchik and close ally of President Bakr. After the revolution Tikriti, a ruthless, arrogant man who posed a genuine threat to Saddam, gloried in the titles of chief of staff, deputy minister of defense, and deputy prime minister, while Ammash had become minister of the interior and deputy prime minister.

Tikriti, who ran the military as his personal fiefdom, believed that he was immune to Saddam's intrigues because, as the architect and hero of the 1968 revolution, he had become a close confidant of Bakr's, who trusted him implicitly. In this he underestimated Saddam's inherent suspicion of the military establishment, which he constantly feared would attempt to usurp the civilian Baathist government. Saddam reasoned that if he could remove Tikriti, he would negate the threat posed by the military.

Despite his high standing in the government and the army, the only chink in Tikriti's armor was that, while he supported the Baath, he was not regarded as a committed ideologue, as were Bakr and Saddam. Tikriti was nevertheless an astute operator and recognized the threat posed by Saddam, and lobbied hard behind the scenes to persuade Bakr to get rid of him. At one point in 1969 Saddam so enraged Tikriti during a row at the Republican Palace that the former general was actually able to persuade Bakr to send Saddam into exile. Saddam was put on a plane and sent to Beirut, where he remained for a week until Tikriti's temper cooled. It was a humiliation Saddam would not forget.

Ammash, on the other hand, was a dedicated Baathist, a short, stocky former army officer who, unlike Saddam, had dutifully risen through the ranks of the Baath. A cultivated man who liked poetry and had written three history books, he was put in charge after the revolution of the administrative side of the government, chairing meetings on various aspects of government policy, such as planning and reconstruction. Apart from being a close associate of Abdul Karim al-Shaikhly, the new foreign minister, Ammash was an accomplished plotter and it was for this reason that Saddam came to regard him as a threat that had to be eliminated.

Although Saddam had great influence over the highly secretive security apparatus, he was still regarded as a lowly functionary by senior figures in the Baath government such as Tikriti, Ammash, and Shaikhly, who, while generally supportive of the purges being carried out against the government's enemies, were unaware of the formidable power base Saddam was quietly acquiring for himself. At this point in his career Saddam did not enjoy any of the trappings of power. His office was still a small room located next to Bakr's in the Presidential Palace; he had no secretary or receptionist. To the other ministers he was regarded more as Bakr's errand boy than a figure of authority in his own right. He was often to be seen at the various government ministries, hanging around the reception area, waiting for the minister to find a spare moment in which to see him.

Saddam was neverthless successful in gradually undermining the reputations of his superiors. In this he was aided on two counts: he could draw on

the resources of the security forces; and he had the ear of Bakr. One indication of the all-pervasive nature of Saddam's security apparatus, even during
these early days of the Baath regime, has been provided by a former Baathist
official who was the recipient of a chilling demonstration of the Baath Party's
institutionalized paranoia. As a senior member of Bakr's government, the
official received an invitation to attend a cocktail party at the British embassy
that was being hosted by the commercial attaché. The invitation had been
vetted by the Iraqi Foreign Ministry, and the official duly attended the function at which he attempted to reassure Britain's diplomatic representatives
that the Baath was committed to modernizing the Iraqi economy. A few days
after the function the official received another invitation for drinks, this time
with Saadoun Shakir, who had been appointed head of the Amn al-Amm, or
State Internal Security, one of Saddam's key security agencies. The two men
met for dinner at one of the main hunting clubs in Baghdad. After thirty
minutes or so of general conversation Shakir, who was one of Saddam's most
trusted lieutenants, suddenly produced a pile of photographs, and asked the
official to examine them. The photographs, which had been taken by a pho-
tographer working for the Iraqi News Agency, showed the official conversing
with British diplomats at the embassy party he had attended several days previously. "Do you recognize these?" asked Shakir. The official replied in the
affirmative. "Then you should take more care," Shakir continued. "We
would prefer it if you did not go to any more functions of this nature. They
will only arouse our suspicions." The official got the message, and resolved
never to attend another reception at a foreign embassy.[18]

Under Saddam's guidance, the Baathists established an all-pervasive network to monitor the activities of all government officials. In the same way that
commissars had been appointed to oversee the activities of the armed forces, so
civilian commissars were appointed to government offices to report on the
activities of ministers and civil servants. The civilian commissars were generally university graduates who were trusted members of the Baath. They
reported back both on the performance of ministers and their professional and
social contacts. Apart from the commissars, whose positions were clearly identified, the activities of government officials were closely monitored by a secondary layer of informers who worked as secretaries or messengers. All telephone and postal communication was intercepted and analyzed, so that all
government officials had to become accustomed to working in a Kafkaesque
environment where there was no alternative other than to follow Baath Party

doctrine. "From the moment they came to power the Baathists were obsessed with buying bugging devices of every shape and form," recalled one former senior official. "They were buying all the latest, high-technology equipment from countries such as Germany. They were convinced that everyone was trying to plot against them if they got the chance. We quickly learned that we were being watched every time we went somewhere and that we were being bugged every time we picked up the telephone."[19]

With the formidable resources of the state's security apparatus at his disposal, Saddam was able to plot against his political rivals, and concentrated his energies on undermining their reputations. In particular he seems to have been successful in persuading President Bakr that the ambition of both Tikriti and Ammash could ultimately pose a threat to his own position. Bakr certainly seems to have taken this on board for, in November 1969, a reorganization of the Baath was announced, at which Saddam's position as deputy chairman of the RCC was officially confirmed, even though he had been carrying out the deputy's functions since the start of the year. Simultaneously the two positions of deputy prime minister were abolished, thereby depriving Tikriti and Ammash of the privilege of chairing cabinet meetings in Bakr's absence (among his many titles, President Bakr was also prime minister). In April 1970 they were made vice presidents, but relieved of their other positions; two of their main rivals in the military replaced them in their cabinet posts, Hammad Shihab as minister of defense and Saadoun Ghaydan as minister of the interior. It was simply a matter of time before Saddam applied the coup de grace.

For Tikriti this came in October 1970. He was stripped of all his positions on the spurious pretext that he had failed to help the Palestinians during the Black September uprising against King Hussein of Jordan, even though it was official Iraqi policy, personally endorsed by Bakr and Saddam, not to get involved. Tikriti heard the news while in Madrid on an Iraqi mission that Saddam had devised to get him out of the country. Saddam even drove Tikriti to the airport, kissing him on both cheeks before he boarded his flight. The next day the government-owned Baghdad press carried front-page pictures of Saddam and Tikriti embracing at the airport. But no sooner had Tikriti arrived than he was informed that he had been stripped of his government position and was to be made Iraq's ambassador to Morocco. Saddam had arranged to have the photograph published so that when news of the popular Tikriti's demotion was announced, his supporters would be unlikely to hold Saddam directly responsible. When Tikriti heard the news he was outraged, and ignoring an order to take up the post, flew back to Baghdad to face down Saddam. Upon arrival, however, he was seized by Saddam's security agents and bundled onto a waiting plane and flown to exile in Algeria. The irony of Tikriti's fate could be attributed to Saddam's perverse sense of humor. The man who had led the tanks into the Presidential Palace on July 17, 1968, to depose President Arif would now share the same fate as his fellow conspirator and the Baath Party's first prime minister, Abdul Razzak Nayif—escorted to the Baghdad airport by Saddam and forced into exile in Algeria. And like Nayif, who was murdered in London in 1978, Saddam's gunmen would eventually catch up with Tikriti; he was gunned down in Kuwait in March 1971, where he had moved to be closer to his children, who were still at school in Baghdad.

Tikriti's murder was a textbook Baathist assassination, inspired by fears that his presence in Kuwait might make him a rallying point for disgruntled Iraqi officers. On the morning of March 20, Tikriti, accompanied by the Iraqi ambassador to Kuwait, set off for an appointment at the government hospital. As the car arrived at the hospital four armed men ambushed the car. As one of the assassins forced open the car door, another, standing behind him, fired five shots at Tikriti at point-blank range, killing him instantly. They then made good their escape. The Baathists had clearly improved their assassination techniques from those early days when a nervous Saddam Hussein had ruined the plot to murder General Qassem by firing his weapon too early.

By contrast to the dramas that attended Tikriti's bloody exit from the Baathist stage, the removal of Ammash was a more civil affair. After Tikriti's fall, Ammash was fully aware that his own position was untenable. He made a series of scathing comments about his Baath Party colleagues, which only served to isolate him further. The end came in September 1971 when he was stripped of his government positions and sent into exile as Iraq's ambassador to the USSR. Unlike Tikriti, Ammash accepted his demotion with grace—no doubt he was fully briefed on the circumstances concerning Tikriti's murder—and made the most of his new posting in Moscow. Indeed, he made such a success of his diplomatic career that three years later he moved to be ambassador to Paris, and served one last posting in Finland where he died. Despite his continued service to the country, many Iraqis believed that Ammash was poisoned, while on a visit to Baghdad after Saddam had become president, with thallium, a heavy metal used in commercial rat poison and one of the Iraqi security forces favored methods of dispensing with its opponents.[20]

The removal of Tikriti and Ammash, who had both enjoyed distinguished careers in the Iraqi armed forces, represented the triumph of Saddam and the civilian wing of the Baath Party over the military echelon. Henceforward the Iraqi military establishment would be firmly under the control of the government, and the prospect of the military mounting a successful coup, as it had done on several occasions since the overthrow of the monarchy in 1958, became more and more remote. After the departures of Tikriti and Ammash, several leading military officers who were suspected of being supporters or friends of the deposed men were themselves removed, or arrested. With the rest of the officer corps constantly under surveillance by Saddam's commissars and security services, Saddam felt sufficiently confident of his control over the military that he was moved to declare that "with our party methods, there is no chance for anyone who disagrees with us to jump on a couple of tanks and overthrow the government."[21] As someone who had done just that in July 1968, Saddam knew precisely what he was talking about.

With the military safely in his pocket, it was time for Saddam to turn his attention to senior civilian officials in the Baath Party who might present an obstacle to his vaulting ambition. Even while he was engaged in suppressing the communists, laying traps for the Shiites, destabilizing the Kurds, and persecuting the armed forces, Saddam still found time for the odd purge of the party's nonmilitary hierarchy. In March 1970, Abdullah Sallum al-Samurrai, the minister of culture and information and one of Saddam's associates since the late 1950s, was removed from office and made ambassador to India. Several other members of the RCC, even those who were Tikritis and claimed kinship with President Bakr, were purged during the summer of 1970. But by far the most important, and most significant, scalp claimed by Saddam was that of Abdul Karim al-Shaikhly, his long-standing comrade-in-arms and the country's foreign minister.

Shaikhly, it will be recalled, participated with Saddam in the abortive assassination attempt on Qassem in 1959. Like Saddam, he fled to Damascus, and later moved to Cairo where he continued working for the Baathist cause. In Cairo he organized, and was guest of honor at, Saddam's party to celebrate his engagement to Sajida Tulfah. He returned to Iraq in 1963 and helped Saddam to establish the party's new security apparatus. After the Baath's expulsion from government in late 1963, he again linked up with Saddam and helped to draw up plans for the assassination of the first President Arif. On one occasion in 1964 he even saved Saddam from arrest when they were sitting in his apartment in Baghdad. "It was just one o'clock in the morning. Saddam rose to his feet and was about to leave. 'Where are you going?' Shaikhly asked. 'To sleep in the hideout where the arms are hidden,' replied Saddam. 'The police patrols are very active these days,' said Shaikhly. 'You had better spend the rest of the night here.' That night the arms cache was raided and, had it not been for Shaikhly's advice, Saddam would have been caught red-handed."[22] When the pair was finally detained during Arif's crackdown on the Baathists in 1964, he was the only party member jailed with Saddam himself. Shaikhly was at Saddam's side when the two men escaped from jail in 1966, and Shaikhly was heavily involved in preparing the party for government, and deposing the second President Arif. At times Saddam felt so close to Shaikhly that he referred to him in public as "my twin." In short, if anyone should expect a display of loyalty from Saddam, with, perhaps, the exception of his uncle, Khairallah Tulfah, it was Abdul Karim al-Shaikhly.

It has been said that attempting to untangle the various personal feuds that afflicted the early years of the Baath in ideological terms is rather like a historian of Chicago during the Prohibition era attempting to explain the interaction between Al Capone and his rivals. Inasmuch as any of the participants in the rise to power of the Baath Party were interested in ideology, then Shaikhly passed for an ideologue. Born about the same time as Saddam in 1935, Shaikhly came from a distinguished Baghdad family whose ancestors had been responsible for administering Baghdad during the Ottoman Empire. Saddam, who had no idea of his own birth date, had taken Shaikhly's birthday, April 28, for his own. One of the first members of the Baath, the university-educated Shaikhly was highly regarded by the founding fathers of the party and was regarded as someone who actually understood the principles of Baathism. By the summer of 1971, however, Shaikhly's own career was progressing too well for Saddam's comfort. As foreign minister and a senior figure in the RCC, Shaikhly was regarded in some circles as a future prime minister, or even president. Apart from Saddam, he was also the regime's highest-ranking civilian.

Unlike Saddam, however, Shaikhly was a dilettante Baathist. As a bachelor in his early thirties, Iraq's intelligent young foreign minister had the world at his feet, and took full advantage of the opportunity, so much so that he acquired a reputation as something of a womanizer. There were many aspects of the new Baath government that did not appeal to Shaikhly's sensitive nature, such as the public executions that were regularly taking place in Liberation Square. "We did not like this kind of thing. We considered it uncivilized, as we did all the torture and disappearances that were going on," recalled one of Shaikhly's contemporaries. "But he was too involved in his own affairs to do anything about it. And he became too full of his own importance to take care of his position in the party."[23]

On the same day that Saddam carried out his purge of Ammash, Shaikhly was relieved of his post as foreign minister and given the lesser title of ambassador to the United Nations. It has been generally assumed that the main reason for Shaikhly's removal was ideological, namely that Saddam suspected him of trying to promote a reconciliation between the Iraqi and Syrian Baath parties, a move that Saddam felt would undermine his position as he was the person held responsible for creating the rift in the first place. Shaikhly's appointment to New York was tantamount to being sent into exile, as it was impossible for him to influence events in Iraq from the United States. Shaikhly eventually returned to Baghdad when he retired, and, after Saddam became president, was murdered in 1980 as he visited a post office in Baghdad to pay his telephone bill.[24]

Another explanation for Shaikhly's removal, however, which affords a fascinating insight into the family intrigues that dominated the Baath Party's inner sanctum during this period, is provided by Shaikhly's cousin, Salah al-Shaikhly, who became Saddam's deputy director of planning before fleeing into exile in the late 1970s. According to his version of events, Saddam and Shaikhly were such close friends that Saddam had hoped that Shaikhly would one day marry his younger sister Siham, as is generally the custom among Arab men. Even though the Shaikhly family would previously have dismissed the idea out of hand of allowing their menfolk to marry into a peasant family from Al-Ouja, Shaikhly was actively encouraged by the family elders to give serious consideration to marrying Saddam's sister as they regarded that the balance of power had moved from the traditional ruling elite and was now with the peasants. Although Shaikhly and Saddam were close, their relationship was more professional than personal. The urbane, intelligent Shaikhly appreciated Saddam's bravery and physical prowess, and saw him as someone who would ensure the success of Baath Party. But away from politics Saddam was not someone whose company Shaikhly sought.

When it came to marriage Shaikhly might have been disposed to keep Saddam happy, but the situation was further complicated by the fact that

President Bakr, who had five daughters, was keen to marry off one of his own offspring to one of the government's rising stars. On several occasions Bakr dropped heavy hints to Shaikhly that he should marry one of his daughters. Caught between a rock and a hard place, Shaikhly opted to marry a woman of his own choice, who was unrelated either to Saddam or Bakr. Saddam is said to have been so upset by Shaikhly's decision that, although he attended the wedding ceremony, he stayed only a half hour at Shaikhly's reception. And within two to three weeks of his wedding, Shaikhly had been thrown out of the government and forced into exile in New York.[25] The fact that the political career of one of the Baath Party's most respected performers could be destroyed over a dispute such as this was indicative of the strength of the family and tribal ties that bound together the ruling Baath clique, ties that would lie at the very heart of many of the crises that would have serious implications for the regime's future stability.

Unlike the dismissal of Hardan al-Tikriti, Saddam appeared to have effected Shaikhly's removal without acrimony. On the night of Shaikhly's dismissal from the government the two men were photographed dining at Baghdad's Farouk restaurant. The following day the Baghdad newspapers carried front-page pictures of Saddam and Shaikhly happily dining together. Saddam was keen to absolve himself of any blame for the dismissal of Shaikhly, who had a strong following both within the party and the military. Even if Shaikhly's choice of bride had not soured their relationship, it is unlikely that Shaikhly would have survived in office for much longer. In the opinion of Salah al-Shaikhly, his cousin's dismissal had as much to do with the success he had achieved in Bakr's government as the perceived insult he had caused Saddam by not marrying his sister. "Karim posed too much of a threat to Saddam. He was popular and talented. But, like so many of us, he should have seen it coming. If he had done something about Saddam then, the history of modern Iraq might have been a lot happier."[26]

Shaikhly's demotion and expulsion from Baghdad, coming at the same time as the purge of Tikriti and Ammash from the armed forces, sent shock waves through the country's ruling elite and revealed Saddam's position as a significant power behind President Bakr's throne. If Saddam could act against Shaikhly, then no Baathist was safe. As a final act in eradicating Baathist opposition, in July 1973 Saddam moved against Abdul Khaliq al-Samurrai who, like Shaikhly, enjoyed a reputation as a leading "theoretician" and was touted as a future candidate for the party's leadership. In July he was imprisoned and held in appalling conditions in solitary confinement for six years. Then, a few days after Saddam had succeeded in his ambition of becoming president of Iraq, he was dragged out of his prison cell and shot.

Samurrai's imprisonment was related to one of the most serious attempts that were made to depose the Bakr/Saddam axis. Thanks to Saddam's efforts, by 1973 most of the known opponents of the regime had been dealt with. Saddam's enthusiasm for cutting down his personal rivals, however, understandably engendered much bitterness within the party among those who survived, particularly as, in view of what had happened to their colleagues, they could expect to share a similar fate. The deep sense of paranoia that Saddam had managed to create at the heart of the government resulted in one of the most bizarre, but nonetheless dangerous, episodes in the early history of the Baath government. What made the coup attempt of late June 1973 all the more remarkable was that it was mounted by Nadhim Kazzar, one of Saddam's closest associates and someone whose reputation had been built on the brutal techniques he had devised at the Palace of the End for eradicating dissent.

In many respects Kazzar, who shared with Saddam similar disadvantages of background, acquired the same ruthless ambition and determination as his Baathist colleague. The son of a policeman, he came from Al-Amara, one of the country's most wretched and poverty-stricken communities. One of the few Shiites to reach the higher echelons of the Baath, Kazzar had joined the party in 1959, when he moved to Baghdad to study at the Technological Institute. He distinguished himself as a party member during the persecution of the communists following the 1963 coup. Indeed his activities at the Palace of the End, during which he initiated the young Saddam in the barbaric art of extracting information and breaking the human spirit, was so impressive that he was made chief of the Security Police in 1969—at Saddam's personal insistence. Kazzar was in many respects the Beria of the Baath Party. Fearless and impulsive, he was responsible for the arrest, torture, and secret executions of several hundred opponents, including communists, Kurds, Nasserites, dissident Baathists, and any other group foolhardy enough to challenge Saddam's wing of the Baath.

As Kazzar's reputation was built on violence, it was hardly surprising that he was a consistent advocate of using violent methods to attain political goals. He believed that force was the only way to deal with the Kurds and the communists, and repeatedly demanded that the Kurdish military apparatus should be crushed. On this issue he came into conflict with those Baathists, including

Saddam, who argued in favor of a less confrontational approach, especially so far as the Kurds were concerned. Even if Saddam had no intention of honoring his deals with the Kurds, that was nevertheless his official position.

Underlying Kazzar's restlessness was a mounting frustration within the Baath that the country was dominated by a small clique of military officers and Tikritis, whereas the original intention of the Baathists when they undertook the 1968 revolution was to have a broad-based government. Kazzar and his supporters, who included long-standing party ideologues such as Samurrai, wanted to convene a special conference of the Baath to elect a new leadership. If Kazzar had good reason for wanting the Bakr/Saddam clique removed, the way in which he set about attaining his objective left much to be desired. Even by the standards of revolutionary Iraq, the scheme devised by Kazzar to seize control of the country was particularly harebrained. As head of the Security Police, he believed that by kidnapping the heads of the army and the civilian police force he would somehow assume control of the country's entire security apparatus. Furthermore, if he could assassinate Bakr and Saddam, Kazzar would then easily persuade his captives to back him (his ultimate powers of persuasion, of course, were located in the cellars at the Palace of the End), and he would be able to take control of the country.

The first act of this highly credulous scheme was put into effect on the morning of June 30, 1973, when Kazzar invited General Hammad Shihab, the defense minister, and Saadoun Ghaydan, the interior minister, to inspect new electronic surveillance equipment that he was having installed at an espionage and counterespionage center he was building on the outskirts of Baghdad. Ghaydan has recalled how he was surprised to receive the call from Kazzar, as he had already previously visited the center.[27] He was nevertheless persuaded by Kazzar to make the trip, and he left his office with his bodyguard. When he arrived at the center, he left his bodyguard outside, "trusting Kazzar as a party member." No sooner had he entered than four security policemen, armed with machine guns, surrounded him and told him he was under arrest. He was taken to an underground prison cell where he was held, handcuffed, until later that evening. After a while Ghaydan realized that Shihab, the defense minister, was imprisoned in an adjoining cell. When he inquired about their detention, Shihab informed him that an uprising was taking place and that they were being detained "for their own protection."[28]

With Shihab and Ghaydan safely out of the way, Kazzar moved on to the second stage of his scheme, namely the assassination of Bakr and Saddam.

His plan was to kill them when President Bakr's plane touched down at the Baghdad airport at 4 P.M. on his return from an official visit to Poland. Saddam would be waiting at the airport to greet Bakr, and Kazzar arranged for a detachment of his Security Police to be at the airport to kill them the moment that Bakr stepped off the plane. The plan went awry, however, when Bakr's plane was late in leaving Warsaw, and then delayed further when it touched down in Bulgaria to refuel, only for Bakr's party to discover that the Bulgarian government had laid on an impromptu welcome for Bakr during his brief stopover. Consequently it was nearly 8 P.M. before the presidential plane finally arrived at Baghdad, by which time the head of the security squad, believing the plot had been discovered, dispersed his men and made good his escape.

Kazzar, meanwhile, had settled down in front of his television set to watch the assassination, as the state-controlled television network had been ordered to interrupt its programming to report on the president's activities—even something as mundane as his return from a routine visit to somewhere like Poland. When Kazzar saw Bakr safely disembark and disappear in an armed convoy with Saddam, he concluded, wrongly, that the plot had been discovered, and decided to flee the country. To guarantee his safety, Kazzar took Shihab and Ghaydan along with him as hostages. The party left Baghdad in a fleet of armored cars and headed straight for the Iranian border where Kazzar believed the Iranians, because of their dispute with Baghdad over the future of the Shatt al-Arab waterway, would provide them with refuge. On his way he contacted Bakr and offered to meet him to discuss his differences with the regime, and to resolve them peacefully. Among his demands he called for a purge of "opportunist elements" in the Baath Party, a clear reference to Saddam. Kazzar threatened to kill Shihab and Ghaydan unless his demands were met. Bakr refused to negotiate and ordered Kazzar's capture, dead or alive. Saddam was given the task of apprehending Kazzar, and responded with relish to the challenge. Having secured Baghdad, the army and air force were scrambled to stop Kazzar before he reached the border. His group was intercepted by helicopters and warplanes, and brought to a halt. Before surrendering, Kazzar ordered his soldiers to shoot Shibab and Ghaydan: Shihab was killed, but Ghaydan, although severely wounded, survived because Shihab's body fell in front of him and took the brunt of the machine-gun fire.

From the moment of his surrender Kazzar must have known his fate; his only consolation was that he was spared the horrors normally meted out to traitors at the Palace of the End. A Special Court of four RCC members was convened, and on July 7, eight security officials and thirteen officers, including Kazzar, were sentenced to death and executed later that same day. The following day another thirty-six people were tried, including two members of the Regional Command, Abdul Khaliq al-Samurrai and Muhammad Fadil. It was their misfortune that Kazzar had telephoned them during his coup attempt to inform them that it was taking place. The Special Court took the view that they should have passed on this information to the relevant authorities. Their failure to do so was tantamount to treason, and they were sentenced to death, together with twelve others. Samurrai, because of his importance as one of the party's main ideologues and because his previous record was unblemished, had his sentence commuted to life imprisonment, but the others were executed as soon as judgment was passed.

The crushing of the Kazzar plot confirmed Saddam's position as the second most powerful man in Iraq after President Bakr, a formidable achievement in view of the fact that immediately after the 1968 revolution he had been regarded by many Baathists as the "weakest link" in the party. In the space of just five years he had eradicated all his main rivals, be they friend or foe, and had neutralized the factions hostile to the Baath government, such as the Kurds and Shiites. One prominent Baathist, who had not seen Saddam for several years but ran into him in Baghdad at about this time, inquired why Saddam had not been seen much in public. "I have been dealing with all the jackals," was Saddam's enigmatic reply.

Following the exposure of the Kazzar plot, the Baath lost no time restructuring the government to ensure that the position of the ruling elite became even more unassailable. Even while the trial of Kazzar and his fellow conspirators was taking place, an emergency meeting of the Baath leadership was called at which it was agreed to hold new elections, which would allow candidates loyal to Saddam to be elected to the Baath's governing council. The Security Police was to be purged and brought under Saddam's control for its failure to prevent the Kazzar coup, and it was agreed to demolish the Palace of the End, as the party now felt sufficiently confident that it no longer had any need for Kazzar's torture chambers. The government resolved to undertake a new mission whereby it would consolidate its position by easing the restrictions on civil liberties, and embark on a program of social and economic development, which would create an atmosphere of well-being in the country, and further inspire confidence in the government.

FIVE

The Nation Builder

With power came affluence. For the first two years after the July Revolution, Saddam occupied a small side office in the Presidential Palace, which befitted his status. As his standing in the party improved, so too did his accommodation, and by the early 1970s he had moved into a larger office in the National Assembly building, which also housed the Ministry of Foreign Affairs. The National Assembly complex, which was located in the same compound as the Presidential Palace, had been commissioned in the late 1950s when the idea of creating democratic institutions in Iraq had been in vogue. From 1970 onward, after Salih Mahdi Ammash had been purged from the government, Saddam moved into Ammash's office, which had previously been used by Iraqi prime ministers, and came complete with an infrastructure of secretaries, advisers, researchers, and assistants. Saddam continued to work long hours, arriving at his office at dawn and staying until late at night, but his industry, combined with his extensive, and all-pervasive, intelligence network, gave him the crucial advantage of always being one step ahead of his colleagues.

For the first time in his career, Saddam was lucratively rewarded, and he soon developed expensive tastes to match his status as the country's strongman. In common with many wealthy men of peasant origins, his primary interest lay in expensive clothes and cars. He started to frequent one of Baghdad's most expensive tailors, Haroot, which was located in the city's Chaakia district and which was well beyond the price range of most Iraqis. Later, once he had become president, Saddam indulged himself by visiting his tailor often, as much as once a week, ordering several suits at a time. His interest in cars was confined to purchasing three or four top-of-the-line Mercedes limousines, which he bought each year in Kuwait—complete with all-important air-conditioning, an essential prerequisite for surviving the heat of a Baghdad summer.

Saddam also had to accommodate his growing family. By 1972 three daughters had been added to his two sons, Uday (1964) and Qusay (1966); Raghda was born in 1967, Rana in 1969, and Hala in 1972. For the first few years after the 1968 revolution, Saddam and his family lived in a large house on the grounds of the Presidential Palace, which, apart from housing the main presidential residence and the National Assembly, was a large, heavily fortified complex that provided accommodation for most leading members of the regime. Saddam's family lived in some comfort, and most of the houses were equipped with swimming pools and teams of servants. Access to the compound was gained by crossing one of two heavily guarded bridges: the Muallak, or hanging, bridge (because of its proximity to Liberation Square) or the al-Jamhuriyya bridge situated on the Tigris, which were located at either end of the compound.

This was also the period when Saddam began acquiring land to build houses for himself and his family outside Baghdad. Construction began on the first of Saddam's many houses in 1970, and Saddam exploited his close professional relationship with Bakr to seize key plots of land. In time the houses would become so lavish that they were more like palaces than ordinary family homes, and in later years they would be used for a very different purpose than that for which they were originally intended—storing his illicit arsenal of weapons of mass destruction. There was, of course, a strong whiff of corruption about the personal fortunes being amassed by the new Baathist elite. Saleh Omar al-Ali, who became minister of information after the revolution, claimed he had to deal with a deluge of complaints from party members in the Tikrit region about the amount of land being sequestered by Bakr, Saddam, and Khairallah Tulfah. "It started off on a small scale, but after a time they were just taking what they wanted," Ali recalled. "People were being thrown off their land and being deprived of their livelihoods. Khairallah Tulfah was the worst offender, but Bakr and Saddam were soon just as bad. They caused a lot of ill feeling among ordinary Baath members."[1]

Never one to miss a propaganda opportunity, Saddam was keen to exploit the stability of his family life, which was deliberately portrayed in the government-owned Iraqi media as the model to which the socially mobile

Iraqi middle classes should aspire. Saddam placed particular emphasis on the fact that Sajida, his wife, was working as a part-time schoolteacher while raising five children. Pictures began to appear of Saddam and his family in the state-owned Iraqi press, including pictures of him playing in the sea with his children while on vacation. The development of a personality cult around Saddam was to be a key part of his strategy for seizing power and, at this early stage in his career, the propaganda campaign was mainly concentrated on the Hussein family's contented family life. In the portraits published in the Iraqi press Saddam's family appears genuinely happy, and it did Saddam no harm at all to be presented as the head of the perfect Iraqi family.

Even Saddam's eating habits changed. The poor peasant boy from Al-Ouja, who had been raised on a subsistence diet of rice and beans, now developed a taste for American-style food, which was becoming highly popular among the newly emerging Iraqi bourgeoisie. He was particularly fond of barbecues, and his favorite dish was spare ribs. This he washed down with his favorite drink, Portuguese Mateus rosé wine, a rather saccharin affair and not exactly the most sophisticated choice for a future head of state. As a young man Saddam smoked a pipe, an affectation that appears to date from his sojourn in Cairo. Gradually, however, he switched to cigars, which he continued to smoke throughout his career. When not working hard at his office, Saddam started to frequent some of Baghdad's smarter restaurants, establishments that would have been well beyond his range before the Baathist takeover. His favorite haunts were Dananir and Matam al-Mataam. For relaxation he liked to go hunting, which in the Arab world consists of shooting game. In the early 1970s his hunting companions were his political associates, such as the head of his Security Police, Saadoun Shakir, and his half brother, Barzan. Their favorite locations were Kut, Swaika, Sammara, al-Dour, and Tikrit, and the hunting expeditions were a weekly fixture in Saddam's routine. He was usually accompanied by one of his bodyguards and some Baath Party officials. The hunting party would mostly shoot pheasants, which would later be barbecued. Saddam, who enjoyed a reputation as a good shot, would invite his family and friends for an al fresco picnic. An invitation to one of Saddam's hunting parties, however, did not necessarily mean that the future career of a young Baathist was secure; the event could also be used by Saddam to identify any possible future rivals, or, by taking advantage of the relaxed atmosphere, to bring any ideological differences to the surface. At least two of Saddam's hunting companions were to regret the experience;

Tahir Ahmed Amin was executed for treason in 1969, and Saad al-Sammurai
was assassinated in 1982.

When not out hunting, Saddam's favorite haunt in Baghdad was the Nadi
al-Said club, which literally translates as "the hunting club" and is located in
the city's Mansour district. Since the establishment of the monarchy,
Baghdad had boasted a number of hunting clubs. The British had socialized
at the al-Alwiya club during the heyday of the monarchy, and there were a
number of other clubs, most of them located close to the Tigris, that were frequented by different social groups: the Hindya club, for example, was patronized by Christian families, while membership of the newer al-Mansour club
was mainly drawn from Baghdad's newly emerging middle class. From the
early 1970s the Nadi al-Said club tended to be associated with the country's
new governing elite. Apart from a comfortable clubhouse, the club's extensive, and immaculately maintained, grounds contained a swimming pool,
tennis courts, and horse-riding facilities. The club would also arrange a variety of activities, such as shooting parties and social functions, for the entertainment of its members. It was a place where the country's ruling elite could
visit during their spare time for much-needed relaxation.

Once he had firmly established himself in power, Saddam used the club
almost as his personal fiefdom, so much so that in the early 1970s he authorized a development program to extend the club's facilities. Saddam took an
intense, almost proprietorial, interest in the building project and was often to
be found at the construction site inspecting progress on a Friday afternoon,
the middle of the Islamic weekend. This was a time when middle-class Iraqis
would join senior Baath Party officials for a relaxing lunch at the club with
their families. Former club members recall that the most striking aspect of
Saddam's inspection visits was the number of bodyguards he would bring
with him. "There would be at least eight armed men with him all the time.
Generally there would be two bodyguards on either side and four behind
him. No one else in the Baath needed protection like this, and the presence
of the bodyguards gave Saddam a rather sinister air."[2]

Despite his intimidating air, Saddam nevertheless went out of his way to
charm the other members of the club. The shy awkwardness that had afflicted
his early attempts at social intercourse in Baghdad appears to have been
replaced by an altogether more urbane approach. The hunting club was
Saddam's refuge, the place where he could seek sanctuary at the end of a long
working day, or on the weekends. He would usually arrive at the club with

some of his close colleagues, such as Abdul Karim al-Shaikhly or Saadoun Shakir, and the ever vigilant bodyguards. He would take a corner table and sit quietly talking with his circle of friends while drinking Johnnie Walker Black Label whiskey. Most of the time Saddam would prefer to keep his own company, and did not socialize much with the other club members. Unlike most of the other male members, however, who were often accompanied by their wives for lunch or dinner, Saddam was never accompanied by Sajida, even when the club had laid on evening social functions, such as a dinner dance or a cabaret. The only members of Saddam's family who came to the club were his children, particularly his sons, Uday and Qusay, who, when they were older, were brought to the club on weekends, and would play with the other children. But Sajida, who would have had her hands full with five children, was hardly ever seen in public, apart from her occasional appearances in the Baghdad press. Despite his reticence, Saddam knew most of the club members, and would engage them in polite conversation if the necessity arose. As most of them by the early 1970s were well aware of the activities of Saddam's security forces, even Saddam's attempts at making a joke could easily be misconstrued. One former club member, who was married to a British woman, recalled how one day he was at the club with his two young daughters, and was talking to them in English. Saddam overheard them, and came up to the member and remarked: "I think it is high time you spoke to them in Arabic." Saddam was smiling at the little girl as he made the remark, but the member, who held a senior position in the Baath government, was not convinced Saddam had made the comment in jest, and resolved in future to converse with his daughters in Arabic when in public.[3]

The early 1970s was a period when Saddam sought to cultivate a favorable public image, and many Iraqis were the recipients of impromptu acts of "generosity" on the part of "Mr. Deputy." Located close to the Presidential Palace in the middle of the Tigris is a small island known locally as "Pig's Island," which in the summer is a popular picnic spot for Baghdad families. Because of its proximity to the palace, however, the island was kept under constant surveillance in case opponents of the regime might try to use it as a staging post for an attack on the regime's nerve center. There were several occasions when Iraqi families who were picnicking on the island on public holidays had their festivities interrupted by Saddam, who would make his way to the island with his bodyguards from the Presidential Palace in a motorboat. Saddam would go from one family to another, making their acquaintance and inquiring as to their general well-being. Although the main purpose of his visit was to check that the island was not being used for any subversive activity, he would nevertheless attempt to make a favorable impression. When, for example, he saw that the men at one picnic party were drinking whiskey, he sent one of his bodyguards back to the boat to fetch a case of liquor, which was promptly delivered to the picnickers. Farther along the island he came across another party that was drinking wine, and so he sent his bodyguards to bring a case from the boat. These might have been token gestures on Saddam's part, but they nevertheless had the effect of winning him a reputation among the residents of Baghdad as someone who cared for ordinary Iraqis.

Somehow this opulent lifestyle had to be paid for, and Saddam proved himself to be adept at exploiting unconventional revenue streams to pay both for his own expanding needs and those of his security forces. One of the first such ventures initiated by Saddam was the reintroduction of horse racing. During the monarchy, horse racing had been a national sport and, even though betting is regarded as un-Islamic, gambling had generated a healthy income for the government. The puritanical President Qassem had banned horse racing, but once the Baathists were established in power Saddam lifted the ban. Gambling on horse races was tolerated, and the canny Saddam set up a system whereby some of the profits from the new gambling syndicates were channeled into his own accounts, thereby affording him the means to finance his own requirements and those of his security services.

The most significant development, however, in the attempts by Saddam and the Baathists to finance their grandiose plans for modernizing Iraq was the nationalization of the Iraqi oil industry. Iraq contains the world's second largest oil reserves after Saudi Arabia—in the 1970s Iraq was estimated to have known reserves of 130 billion barrels, compared with 150 billion barrels in Saudi Arabia. With the right market conditions, it was estimated that Iraq could be capable of producing 11 million barrels a day. Iraqi oil, moreover, is very cheap to extract—roughly six cents per barrel compared with eight cents per barrel in Saudi Arabia. Since the creation of modern Iraq, control of the country's oil industry had resided in the Iraqi Petroleum Company (IPC), which by the 1970s was in effect a consortium comprising five of the world's largest oil companies—BP, Shell, Esso, Mobil, and Compagnie Française des Pétroles (CFP). Foreign ownership of Iraq's key resource had long been an affront to generations of Iraqi nationalists, and many of the coups had been motivated by the desire that the government should have ultimate control over the country's fabulous oil wealth. Certain efforts had been made by various Iraqi administrations to rein in IPC's dominance over the industry, most notably when in 1961 President Qassem wrested control of 99.5 percent of the land from IPC, which was refusing to develop it. In 1964 President Arif set up the Iraqi National Oil Company (INOC) to develop the country's oil reserves and sell it on the open market, but this was thwarted by the international oil companies, which, among other retaliatory measures, refused to sell oil to countries that dealt directly with the Iraqi government. This was essentially the situation inherited by the Baathists after they seized power in 1968, and Saddam, with Bakr's backing, resolved to settle an issue that was widely regarded as a national disgrace.

From 1971 Saddam assumed responsibility for dealing with the oil consortium, together with Murtada al-Hadithi, the oil minister. Saddam's opportunity to engage in the confrontation the Baathists had been waiting for came soon afterward when the IPC decided to slow down oil production in Iraq in favor of that in other countries. The IPC decision meant that, in effect, foreign companies were dictating the earning power of the Iraqi government, an intolerable position for any self-respecting government and one that smacked of neoimperialism. It was a provocation that the nationalist wing of the Baath, as represented by Bakr and Saddam, could not let pass without a challenge. The manner in which Saddam engineered the course of events that would result in the nationalization of the Iraqi industry is an instructive case study in Saddam's ability, even at this relatively early stage in his political career, to manipulate circumstances to suit his own ends.

The Baath Party had, for some time, given consideration to forming an alliance with a "nonimperialist" power, the most likely candidate being the Soviet Union, which, perversely, was not deemed by the Baathists to nurture imperial ambitions. Although Saddam and Bakr were anticommunist, they realized that an alliance with Moscow would enable them to withstand any pressure that Washington might bring to bear on Baghdad. Although Bakr and Saddam had little sympathy with communism and had spent most of the past decade viciously persecuting members of the Iraqi Communist Party, an alliance with Moscow made good diplomatic sense for the Baathists. The centuries-old ambition of generations of Russians of reaching the warm southern seas was a constant source of consternation for the shah of Iran, with whom Iraq shared a one-thousand-mile border. An alliance with Moscow would help to curb any aggressive instincts the shah might nurture toward Iraq, particularly over sensitive issues like the Shatt al-Arab waterway, Iraq's only access to the Gulf which was crucial for its oil exports. Developing good relations with the Soviets would also give Iraq the opportunity to make massive arms purchases and build up the strength of its armed forces. This was a top priority for the Baathists, who were aware that they needed to strengthen their military position to defend themselves against the belligerence of the Iranians, to participate fully in any future war against Israel and to deal with any internal conflicts, such as the constant threat of the Kurds to declare autonomy. The foundations of an alliance with the Soviets had been laid during Saddam's 1970 visit to Moscow to sort out the Kurdish problem, and in February 1972 Saddam returned to Moscow as Bakr's personal emissary for a series of meetings with Soviet prime minister Alexei Kosygin. Saddam's mission must have been a success for, despite Soviet reservations about the Baathists' treatment of Iraqi communists, it was reciprocated the following April when Kosygin flew to Baghdad and signed a bilateral Treaty of Friendship and Cooperation. After the formalities had been concluded, Kosygin was given a conducted tour of the marble halls of the Presidential Palace, accompanied by a handsome blonde who had been provided by Saddam.

Saddam was forced to make many unpalatable concessions to the Soviets. The treaty guaranteed Soviet access to Iraqi air bases. By way of compensation the Soviets agreed to provide training of thousands of Iraqi officers at Soviet military academies. It also referred to the "harmonization" of Soviet and Iraqi foreign policy, a polite way of saying that the Baathists would take orders from Moscow on issues such as Iraq's votes at the United Nations. In return the Soviets agreed to help keep the Baathists in power, and to help them with their nationalization plans. Commenting on the deal years later, Saddam was quite pragmatic about the concessions he had made to Moscow. "We never expected that the Soviets would support us without guarantees that our friendship would serve their strategic interests."[4] Saddam did not enjoy being beholden to a superpower, and the terms imposed on him by the Soviets were to have an important bearing on his future dealings with Moscow.

Even so the Moscow pact put Saddam in an immeasurably stronger position to take on the foreign oil consortium, as the alliance gave him the confidence to tackle the oil barons. He was well aware that any attempt to break the IPC's stranglehold over the Iraqi oil industry would provoke a hostile reaction, with the big oil companies attempting to bully the Iraqis into submission, as they had done on many occasions in the past. The alliance with Moscow, however, together with the pledge the Soviets had given that they would purchase any Iraqi oil surpluses, bolstered Saddam's chances of success. He was also greatly assisted by indications that Iraqi oil officials had received from Valéry Giscard d'Estaing, the French trade minister, that France would decline to join an anti-Iraq boycott, so long as French interests were not harmed.

On June 1, 1972, two months after signing the pact with Moscow, the Baath nationalized the Iraq Petroleum Company. The importance of this event cannot be stressed enough, both in terms of its impact on Iraq and its future development, and in confirming the legitimacy of the Baath Party. Without oil, Iraq would be impoverished; with oil, Iraq had the potential to be one of the world's richest nations. The nationalization of the oil industry had been the long-standing cri de coeur of generations of Iraqi nationalists, and its implementation was arguably the single most revolutionary event to take place in Iraq since its establishment. Because of the alliance with the Soviets and the duplicity of the French, the ability of the expelled members of the consortium to protest was limited, particularly after Saddam traveled to France at the end of June and struck a deal with President Georges Pompidou. Pompidou agreed to accept nationalization in return for French companies being allowed to participate in the future development and exploitation of Iraqi oil fields, and to purchase Iraqi oil at a specially agreed low price.

Freed from the constraints imposed by the IPC, Iraq was able to exploit a range of oil fields that the IPC had declined to develop. The surge in Iraqi oil production resulted in a massive boost in government revenues. These enabled the Baath to embark upon its ambitious building project to turn the country into a modern state, and to raise the general living standards of ordinary Iraqis. They also financed the massive buildup in the country's armed forces, which saw the army's strength almost double in size between 1970 and 1975.

No one was more aware of the revolutionary implications of Iraq's oil nationalization than Saddam, who wasted no time making sure he received the lion's share of the credit for the takeover, while also ensuring that, in so doing, he did not detract from the standing of President Bakr. Saddam had, after all, conducted the crucial negotiations both with the Soviets and the IPC. Having fully discussed the available options with Bakr, Saddam had personally conceived the ultimatum that was made to the IPC in the full knowledge that they would refuse, thereby giving the government no alternative other than to proceed with nationalization. Radio Baghdad broadcast endless revolutionary slogans such as "Arab Oil for the Arabs," and Saddam named June 1, 1972, as "Victory Day." Saddam himself stated, "Our wealth has returned to us." A few years later, talking to one of his official biographers, Saddam reemphasized the role he had played personally in effecting the takeover of the IPC. "All the experts and advisers warned me against nationalisation; not one was in favour. Yet the decision was taken. . . . Had I listened to the Oil Minister, the decision would never have been made."[5]

Saddam's personal involvement in the nationalization of the IPC provides a telling insight into how, even as early as 1972, he had acquired a range of highly sophisticated political skills. As has been shown, oil nationalization did not happen overnight. Indeed, according to those Iraqis who were closely involved in the nationalization process, the plan to take IPC under Iraqi control was originally conceived as early as 1970, and most of the groundwork was carried out by Murtada al-Hadithi, the oil minister, rather than Saddam himself, a fact that may explain why Murtada would later perish in one of Saddam's purges. The Baathists were aware they needed to proceed with caution, knowing that any precipitate move on their part might cause the West, the main consumer of Iraqi oil, to close ranks and boycott the country's main export, which would quickly bring the country to its knees. The Baathists were hindered by the expert assessment of the Iraqi Oil Ministry that Iraq was not capable of running the oil industry on its own. Numerous economic studies were undertaken to assess how Iraq might be able to survive on a given percentage of its oil revenues. And in fairness to Saddam, the advice from the technical advisers, right up to the moment of nationalization, was that Iraq was not yet ready for such a dramatic move. The key to the success of the gamble on nationalization was the support provided by the Soviets, for which Saddam could take the credit, and the support of the French, for which he could not.

The moment Saddam believed nationalization was possible he sacked Murtada and took control of the whole project himself. "Saddam wanted to get his hands on the nation's oil wealth because he could see that this was his gateway to fame," recalled a former Iraqi official who was closely involved in the nationalization program. "After receiving all the technical advice, it was Saddam who took the political decision."[6] The manner in which Saddam made the historic decision to go ahead with nationalization reveals how Saddam, at this relatively early stage in his career, was able to exploit the Iraqi body politic for his own ends. Although the political decision was essentially

Saddam's, he nevertheless took care to ensure that he had President Bakr's full support before making his move. That such a momentous decision should have been taken by Saddam, and not Bakr, says a great deal about how the balance of power in Baghdad was shifting away from the president and into the hands of his deputy. Having secured Bakr's support, Saddam was careful to ensure that his decision had the full backing of the Baath Party's main decision-making body, the Revolutionary Command Council, of which he was vice president. A meeting of the RCC was duly called at which Saddam received its full backing to proceed with nationalization. Saddam wanted to make sure that, if his bid for glory backfired, it would be the Baath Party collectively, and not Saddam alone, that would bear responsibility for the consequences. But if the gamble succeeded, the glory would all belong to Saddam. This tactic of sharing the burden of political accountability in the face of adversity was to become a recurrent theme of Saddam's political career.

Saddam's role in negotiating the cooperation pact with Moscow and the oil nationalization program meant that, for the first time since the Baathists came to power in 1968, his reputation extended beyond Iraq. With the cold war at its height, the activities of "Revolutionary Command Council Vice President Takriti," as he was referred to in the *New York Times* in 1972, in seeking a "solid strategic alliance" with the USSR was regarded as a matter of grave concern in U.S. diplomatic circles.[7] Questions over the precise nature of the new Baghdad-Moscow alliance intensified in the spring of 1973 when Iraqi forces occupied a Kuwaiti border post, once more reigniting Baghdad's irredentist claims to the sheikhdom. Washington regarded the Iraqi action as being part of a plot by Moscow to challenge American oil interests in the Gulf, which had been a major concern of U.S. policymakers since the 1950s. This suspicion persisted even after the dispute was resolved by the mediation of the Soviets, which occurred during a visit by Saddam to Moscow in March 1973, at which he had further talks with Kosygin on improving Soviet-Iraqi cooperation. The key role played by Saddam in the oil nationalization program did not pass unnoticed. When Washington and London, outraged by the typically Gallic deal President Pompidou had negotiated with Baghdad to protect French interests, threatened Paris with punitive action, Saddam responded by declaring in an interview with *Le Monde,* "We will not tolerate any wrong inflicted on France. . . . Any attempt to harm French interests would be considered as an act of hostility against Iraq."[8] Saddam's emergence as a key player in Baghdad's power politics was recognized by both the State

Department in Washington and the Foreign Office in London and before long articles were appearing in the Western press in which Saddam was flatteringly described as Iraq's "Nasser."[9]

If the outside world was starting to take notice of Saddam, foreign observers were merely catching up on the political reality that had pertained in Baghdad since late 1970, when Saddam had successfully dispensed with his main political rivals, Tikriti, Ammash, and Shaikhly. For the two years that Ammash had held the office of deputy prime minister, senior advisers in the Iraqi government had enjoyed personal contact with Bakr, and meetings would be held at the Presidential Palace on an almost weekly basis. Officially, Bakr was head of all the government departments and committees, dealing with every aspect of the administration, such as education, health, and transport. In practice he left the day-to-day running to Ammash, and he chaired the meetings so that he could remain in touch with developments. But after Saddam moved into Ammash's office, the meetings at the Presidential Palace became more and more infrequent until they stopped altogether. Saddam took charge of all the main government departments, and chaired the key planning meetings, and Bakr became more and more removed from the machinery of government.

At this stage in his career Saddam's obsession with security was starting to manifest itself. Officials attending meetings at his office in the National Assembly Building were subjected to various checks. Saddam himself entered his office by a special, secluded entrance. Although he was gradually usurping Bakr's position at the heart of the administration, Saddam was careful not to give the impression that his status was in any respect superior to Bakr's. He made sure that his office was smaller than Bakr's, and when he traveled around the country he was insistent that he should have fewer bodyguards than Bakr. In everything he did Saddam took great care not to upset his mentor. When a government department had reached the point where a decision needed to be made, Saddam would visit Bakr and, in an amicable way, suggest that the president should authorize a particular course of action. Having heard Saddam's analysis of the issue, Bakr would invariably accept Saddam's judgment, as he did with the nationalization of the IPC. If for any reason Bakr did not agree, Saddam would be disinclined to challenge him directly, but would manipulate him over a period of time—weeks, if necessary—until he got his way.

Saddam's emergence as the driving force behind Bakr's regime still owed much to the support and encouragement he received from his president and fellow Tikriti, and Saddam was aware that he should not underestimate either Bakr's popularity or power. By the 1970s Bakr was well into his fifties, and appeared to be content with fulfilling a patriarchal role. As one of the last surviving members of the Free Officers responsible for overthrowing the monarchy in 1958, he enjoyed considerable support throughout the country. Not by nature an assertive individual, Bakr carried out the ceremonial functions of his office while allowing Saddam a free hand in consolidating the regime's position and eliminating its enemies. It has also been suggested that, from an early stage in the Baathist government, Bakr did not enjoy the best of health. As early as 1971 he was hospitalized for what was reported in the Iraqi media as a "slight indisposition." This might be one explanation why Saddam, who enjoyed robust health, acquired far greater powers than are normally invested in a deputy, so that he was soon able to put himself in a position where his services were indispensable to Bakr. This, of course, was precisely the role Khairallah Tulfah, Saddam's uncle, had envisaged when he encouraged Bakr to take on his nephew in the 1960s. By appointing a deputy twenty years younger than himself, Bakr had calculated that he would have many years in power before the issue of the succession arose. But with the benefit of hindsight it appears that from the early 1970s Saddam's sole game plan was to seize the presidency at the earliest available opportunity. If Bakr allowed Saddam more independence of action than most deputies receive, that is not to suggest that he was unaware of Saddam's intrigues, or of the reasoning that lay behind them. Bakr was fully apprised of the infrastructure of institutionalized terror that had been constructed under his auspices by Saddam, and personally condoned the use of violence—including the barbarity of the Palace of the End—against the regime's enemies. And as Saddam cut a swathe through the ranks of his political rivals, it gradually became apparent to the Iraqi public that the country was being governed by a dual leadership consisting of Bakr and Saddam; these were the men who made the important decisions, more often than not at Saddam's instigation. Even if he had his eye on the presidency, at this point in his career Saddam remained careful not to overstep the mark in his relations with Bakr. In a speech broadcast on Iraqi radio in late 1971, for example, he went out of his way to deny suggestions that he had usurped Bakr's position. "I know there are some who claim that Saddam Hussein is the number one man in Iraq," he said, "but we have a President who exercises his constitutional powers. In our view he is the number one man and, even more, we consider him the father and the leader."[10]

* * *

The period that followed oil nationalization was crucial to Iraq's future development, and Saddam resolved to be fully involved in every aspect of the Baath Party's master plan to modernize the country. The Baath now enjoyed popular, and widespread, support throughout the country. The Iraqi people at large believed that for the first time in their history they had a government that was neither a monarchy nor a military junta, but one that was genuinely concerned with improving their lot. Saddam and the Baath were more confident. Saddam had quashed most of his rivals, and the Baath had neutralized most of its political enemies. Saddam's position as head of the security infrastructure was also greatly assisted by a secret deal he had struck with Yuri Andropov, head of the Soviet KGB intelligence operation, to improve the quality of Iraq's surveillance techniques.

From the moment it had seized power in 1968 the Baath had attempted to fulfill its promise for a more equal redistribution of the country's wealth, but its efforts had been constrained by the limited oil revenues. Even after nationalization all departmental budgets were severely curtailed to enable them to cope with the anticipated backlash from the West. The quadrupling of OPEC oil prices that occurred in the wake of the 1973 Yom Kippur War, however, finally provided the Iraqi authorities with the opportunity they had been waiting for, allowing them to reap the rewards of the newly liberated oil wealth.

Saddam the nation builder was chairman of all the key committees and was personally responsible for the Baathists' ambitious plan to modernize the country. He more than anyone was aware that the key to improving his own popularity and that of the Baath Party would be how the new oil wealth was apportioned. By 1980, Iraq's oil revenues would be worth $26 billion compared with a figure of $476 million shortly after the Baath seized power,[11] and this phenomenal rise in the government's revenues was entirely due to Saddam's nationalization of the oil industry. In 1968 oil provided about 22 percent of national income; by 1980 this had risen to 50 percent. This enabled the government to fund the massive redevelopment program that had been promised by numerous regimes, but had never been accomplished. The Baath's restructuring of the economy, however, was to be conducted in a totalitarian fashion. The party set itself three main goals: (1) the elimination of an upper, and even middle, class of wealth and privilege and a more equal distribution of income and services; (2) the establishment of a socialist economy, with government ownership of national resources and the means of production; and (3) diversification of the economy, allowing Iraq as much economic independence as possible.

Every project, whether building a new school or hospital, was subjected to Saddam's personal scrutiny, and all proposed expenditures had to be authorized by the Planning Board, of which Saddam was the chairman. Saddam signed contracts with the USSR to expand Iraq's oil industry. He signed contracts with the French to build huge turnkey factory complexes, equipped with everything from machinery and production equipment to pencils on the director's desk. He negotiated with the Brazilians to build railroads, with the Belgians to build a phosphate complex, and with the Yugoslavs, Bulgarians, Germans, and Japanese for high technology, labor and expertise. He built schools and a powerful radio and television network capable of broadcasting Baathist propaganda throughout the Arab world. He extended Iraq's electricity grid into the most remote areas of the countryside. All this activity led foreign observers to point to Iraq as one of the success stories of the Third World. Unlike Africa, where money was all too often spent on useless prestige projects, Saddam's vast nation-building master plan was actually improving the living standards of ordinary Iraqis.

Even with the new oil wealth coming onstream, Saddam demanded value for money. His favorite tactic was to have Western and Soviet companies bid against each other on contracts so that Iraq would get the best deal. Saddam called this policy "nonalignment," and its main goal was to preserve independence of action. His experience with the Soviets had taught him the perils of being too dependent on one outlet. Saddam made sure that the influx of foreigners brought in to work on the various construction projects did not pollute the Baathist revolution. His security forces were instructed to ensure that "contaminating influences" did not come in contact with ordinary Iraqis. Foreign workers were followed, on occasion interrogated, and encouraged not to develop social contacts with Iraqi civilians. Foreign newspapers and magazines were confiscated and all foreign workers were required to apply for exit visas before they left the country, and the permits were sometimes withheld as a means of intimidation. Saddam explained his philosophy for dealing with foreign companies to a group of visiting Arab journalists in 1974. "We have no reservations about dealing with companies anywhere in the world, on a basis that guarantees the respect of our sovereignty and ensures both parties a legitimate profit. Our country has large-scale projects,

prodigious projects, and we have great ambitions. The idea that we might isolate ourselves from the world to live according to our own devices is foreign
to us, and we refuse it categorically."[12]

Most Iraqi technicians and officials involved in the various projects knew
that Saddam relied heavily on his security apparatus to keep himself in power.
Even so, they were still impressed by his ability to master even the most complicated brief. Salah al-Shaikhly, a first cousin of deposed foreign minister
Abdul Karim al-Shaikhly, was a British-educated economist who worked as
deputy director of planning for the Baath until he was obliged to flee the
country in 1977. For seven years he attended weekly meetings chaired by
Saddam and, despite the suffering Saddam has inflicted on his family, he has
not wavered from his view that Saddam was a gifted administrator. "He could
grasp an argument faster than many technicians," he said. "He could ask
questions that even those who had Ph.D.s could not answer. We could only
assume that he spent a lot of time reading up on the briefs. But even so it was
an impressive performance." On those occasions that Saddam did not understand a point, he would ask for it to be repeated "for the benefit of the rest of
the group who, like me, I am sure, would appreciate a little clarification." The
meetings were conducted in a businesslike manner and there was no hint of
the menace that afflicted so many other areas of Iraqi life. "There was no
sense of intimidation," said Shaikhly. "It was only when people were clearly
underperforming that it became a problem."

The drive to modernize Iraq was undertaken strictly on terms laid down
by Saddam. "Mr. Deputy" was under no illusions about the signficance of the
potential riches that were about to change the country forever, nor did he
underestimate the significance of Iraq's oil wealth to the outside world. "So
long as we have oil we have power," he was fond of telling his officials. "I want
Iraq to have the last barrel of oil in the world. The longer we can make our oil
last, the longer we will be recognized as a world power." It was for this reason
that he disdainfully dismissed the suggestion put forward by one of his senior
advisers to develop the country's solar energy resources, a reasonable enough
suggestion given the strength of the sun in Iraq's desert regions. "If we do this,
oil will be redundant," was Saddam's take on the proposal.

In other areas Saddam was fascinated with science, and was determined to
import the latest technologies to Iraq. Rather than follow the other oil-rich
Gulf states, and simply import technology, Saddam wanted Iraq to become
technologically self-sufficient. Saddam's enthusiasm was undoubtedly infec-

tious, and the officials and scientists who were invited to participate in this
new dawn in Iraq's development were inspired by Saddam's leadership. "We
all thought it was marvelous," recalled Shaikhly. "The good things outweighed the bad. We knew there was censorship and we knew unpleasant
things happened if you fell foul of the security forces. But for those of us who
were given the opportunity to rebuild the country, it was all tremendously
exciting." Saddam was always on the lookout for bright new talent. When he
chaired meetings, he would sit attentively when a newcomer was invited to
make a presentation. In these circumstances first impressions were crucial.
Anyone who made a good first impression could look forward to quick promotion. "Saddam was essentially looking for young people with good qualifications who were intelligent and courageous," said Shaikhly. "These were
the people he wanted to help him modernize the country. As for loyalty, he
took that for granted. After all, he had this extensive security apparatus
watching everyone all the time. If anyone displayed the slightest hint of dis-
loyalty, Saddam knew precisely how to deal with them."[13]

On those occasions when someone annoyed Saddam he had a unique way
of demonstrating his displeasure. The back of his left hand is marked by three
small dotlike tattoos, the tribal markings of a Tikriti that he had carried since
childhood. Saddam would simply wave his hand, displaying the tattoos in the
direction of the offending official, signaling that he should leave at once.
Later in Saddam's career, this gesture was taken as a sign for the security forces
to arrest the unfortunate official, who would be taken away for interrogation,
often never to be seen again.

Agrarian reform was one of the Baath's first priorities and the party initiated a widespread land redistribution scheme, breaking up the large land-
holdings and creating a network of small, self-sufficient farms that were
required to participate in local cooperatives. No compensation was paid to
the landowners. By 1976 more than 71 percent of state-owned land had been
given to 222,000 new farmers who were provided with modern agricultural
equipment while the number of farm cooperatives rose from 473 in 1968 to
1,852 in 1976. The egalitarian nature of the regime was reflected in education, an issue close to Saddam's heart, and student enrollment at educational
establishments doubled at every level during the 1970s. Saddam's personal
concern was to eradicate adult illiteracy.

In 1977, for example, when he was becoming frustrated by the inability of
his various education proposals to bring down the level of adult illiteracy, he

declared a Day of Knowledge to persuade Iraqis to participate in nationwide courses in reading and writing. To make sure that there was full enrollment in the courses, Saddam threatened those who did not take up his offer with prison. The scheme was such a success that UNESCO gave Saddam the Kropeska Award for promoting its campaign to wipe out illiteracy worldwide.[14]

The country still depended heavily on oil revenues, and Saddam was also involved in the Baath Party's attempts to diversify the economy and make the country more self-sufficient. From 1975 onward, the government drew up investment budgets that aimed at developing the nucleus of heavy industries, such as coal oil and petrochemical facilities. Saddam's office was closely involved with the development of the $45 billion fertilizer, steel, and chemical plant at al-Zubair and a massive petrochemical complex at Basra. Saddam claimed credit for construction of a nationwide network of oil pipelines that provided the government with oil terminal outlets in Syria, Turkey, and Basra. As part of the government's development program, remote villages were connected to the electricity grid. The Baathists gave away free televisions and refrigerators to poor families, especially among the Shiite communities in the south of the country. As part of their policy of social liberalization, the Baathists were committed to the emancipation of women, and passed legislation ensuring equal pay and outlawing job discrimination on the basis of sex. A family law code, known as the Code of Personal Status, was revised, making polygamy more difficult to practice and allowing women to choose their own husbands, rather than having them chosen by their families, and to divorce. At a time when in neighboring Saudi Arabia women were not even allowed out on their own in public, Iraqi women were allowed to enroll in the military and the Popular Army.

This massive development program, which constituted a genuine social and economic revolution in Iraq, naturally focused attention on those responsible for implementing it, and Saddam, who had already appreciated the importance of the personality cult, was the main beneficiary. Pictures of him and his family became an even more familiar fixture in the Iraqi press, and the story of his rise to power from his humble origins in Tikrit became the stuff of legend. Newborn babies were named after him, and it was reported that young party members were emulating his walk, his dress, and even his manner of speech. Saddam appeared constantly on Iraqi television, giving long, rambling monologues, which could last for up to four hours, on a wide range of topics, from education to family planning. The content might not make compelling viewing, but his constant appearance on television strengthened the impression among the populace of who was really running the country. Moreover, Saddam deserved a great deal of the credit for the genuinely progressive changes that were taking place in Iraqi society. To make sure that all the targets he set were being reached he would arrange "productivity meetings" all over the country, and he would make personal visits to make sure that the goals he set in Baghdad were coming to fruition in the country.

The nationalization of the oil industry and the treaty with Moscow provided the Baathists with an enormous confidence boost, and enabled them to tackle the other outstanding political issues of the day, foremost among which was the Kurds and the troubling relationship that they were developing with Iran, the Baathists' perennial bugbear. As part of their cozying up to the Soviets in the early 1970s, Bakr and Saddam had rather cynically brought the remnants of the persecuted Communist Party into the government by forming the Patriotic National Front. Although Bakr and Saddam had no intention of letting Iraqi communist leaders have a say in the running of the country, this gesture at reconciliation nevertheless found favor among the Soviets, who responded by trying to pressure the Kurds into ceasing their agitation against the Baath. Relations between the Kurds and the Baath were already strained following Saddam's failed assassination attempt on Barzani in 1971, and deteriorated further in the wake of the IPC nationalization, with the Kurds claiming that the Baathists had seized control of the Kirkuk oil fields, which they claimed was a clear breach of the March Manifesto of 1970. To put pressure on the Baathists, Barzani made encouraging noises to the Americans, who were none too pleased about Baghdad's new strategic alliance with Moscow and were still seething over the loss of the IPC. Barzani made it clear that U.S. firms would be allowed to develop the Kirkuk oil fields if the United States supported the Kurds in their quest for autonomy. The threat posed by the Kurds to the Baathist hegemony was enhanced by the fact that the shah, wary of the new alliance between Baghdad and Moscow and who himself was being armed by the United States, was providing Kurdish leaders with military and logistical support.

For Saddam, the threat posed by the Kurds was seen as nothing more than an attempt by "the agents of imperialism" to destroy all the achievements of the Baathist revolution.[15] Saddam was concerned that, far from seeking an autonomy solution, Barzani would stop at nothing less than full independence, and that an independent Kurdistan would then ally itself with countries that were hostile to Iraq, such as Iran, Israel, and the United States. With the positions of both sides so entrenched, it was inevitable that the conflict would escalate, and hostilities finally commenced in the spring of 1974 when the Kurds rebelled against an attempt by Baghdad to impose Saddam's autonomy plan, which had been rejected by Barzani. Initially the Iraqi armed forces acquitted themselves well, but by late 1974 they were forced on the defensive as they struggled to contend with the guerrilla tactics of the well-armed and ruthless Kurdish fighters. The Iraqi effort was further hindered by the refusal of the Soviets, their main arms suppliers, to provide fresh arms and ammunition. Moscow saw an opportunity to punish the Baathists for their purges against Iraqi Communists. With the Americans backing Barzani, and the Soviets deciding to aid Iraq, an unlikely U.S.-Soviet cold war alliance threatened the Baath government. The Iraqi position further deteriorated in January 1975, when the Iranian army entered the fray on the side of the Kurds, even deploying two regiments inside Iraq.

After the diplomatic triumphs of 1972, the war in Kurdistan was rapidly turning into the deadliest challenge the Baathists had faced since seizing power in 1968. Saddam, as the architect of the deal that was supposed to resolve the perennial Kurdish problem, was vulnerable, particularly as the Iraqi losses continued to mount without any sign of a breakthrough being achieved. Saddam tried to put a brave face on the party's fortunes in February 1975 when he declared that "the political and military situation in the northern area has never been so good."[16] But with casualties in excess of sixty thousand and the cost of the conflict threatening to bankrupt the Iraqi economy, drastic measures were needed if the Baathists were not to be driven from power.

Saddam's solution was to open a dialogue with the shah; if he could somehow persuade the Iranians to disengage from the conflict, he was confident that his forces would be able to suppress the Kurdish resistance. Opening a dialogue with the shah, however, was not a foregone conclusion. The authorities in Teheran were well aware of the brutal tactics the Baathists employed to keep themselves in power, and the shah had gone on the record as denouncing the Baghdad regime as "a group of crazy, bloodthirsty savages." The shah, moreover, was fully appreciative of the powerful position in which he found himself, and was determined to strike a hard bargain. He had long coveted an agreement whereby Iraq formally acknowledged Iran's claim to control the Shatt al-Arab, the strategically important waterway at the head of the Gulf. Iraq had vigorously resisted the Iranian claim on the grounds that such a concession would jeopardize Iraq's ability to export oil. It is an indication of the perilous position in which Saddam found himself in early 1975 that he agreed to enter into negotiations with the shah over the Shatt al-Arab and other disputed territories during a meeting of oil ministers in Algiers in early 1975. The negotiations were a success, certainly from the shah's point of view, and on March 6, 1975, Saddam and the shah concluded the Algiers Agreement. In return for Iraq conceding Iran control over the Shatt al-Arab, the Iranians agreed to withdraw their support from the Kurds.

In the immediate context of the Kurdish conflict, Saddam's gamble paid off. Within forty-eight hours of the signing of the Algiers Agreement, Iran had withdrawn its forces and its support for the Kurds, and within two weeks the Kurdish rebellion had effectively been suppressed. Saddam even found himself being singled out for praise by the shah, who, after the negotiations had been concluded, remarked, "Saddam Hussein has favourably impressed me. He is young and has courageous ideas."[17] In every other respect, however, the Algiers Agreement constituted a national humiliation for Saddam and the Baathists, as it effectively gave Iran control over Iraq's miniscule coastline at the head of the Gulf, the nation's only sea access. It was clearly an untenable position for Iraq, and one that would ultimately result in the bloodiest conflict the Middle East has seen. Iraq's foreign minister, Saadoun Hammadi, accurately summed up Baghdad's real feelings about the sellout over the Shatt al-Arab. "It was either that or lose the north of the country." But so far as Saddam was concerned, the agreement was essential because, apart from ending the Kurdish rebellion, it salvaged his political career. It was well known in Baghdad that Saddam had assumed personal responsibility for resolving the Kurdish question, and failure to do so, particularly after the 1974 rebellion, would have destroyed him. So faced with the choice of sacrificing the national interest or sacrificing his own career, Saddam took the option that guaranteed his survival.

For all its faults, Saddam managed to turn the deal with the shah into a personal triumph, another garland to be added to those acquired through the nationalization of the IPC and the groundbreaking cooperation pact with Moscow. In many respects, 1975 is the moment that Saddam's inexorable march on the Presidential Palace can really be said to have begun in earnest.

Apart from being able to boast these diplomatic triumphs, his known enemies in the military and the civilian wing of the Baath had been culled and
his security apparatus was all-pervasive. As Bakr's official deputy, he was con-
sulted on all policy matters, both domestic and foreign. Even so Saddam calculated that it was still too early for him to make his move on the
Presidential Palace.

That is not to say that the idea had not entered his thoughts. As he later
explained to one his official biographers: "It is certain that matters would have
been accomplished faster had I become the Republic's President five years earlier," he confided. "That was also President Bakr's conviction. But I used to
contradict him because I did not want him to leave his post as President."[18]
Saddam's argument for not ousting Bakr in 1975 was that such a move might
be regarded as cynical opportunism, even though he himself believed it would
have been the correct course of action. "If I had not behaved in this moral way,
what would I have told the people? My situation would have been exactly like
any other revolutionary situation in the world or in the Arab nation, with no
clear-cut moral difference. If the one who is better takes over his friend's place
and seeks only the reward, then we would be like so many other revolutionary
movements, whereas this is far from the truth."[19] These comments, made soon
after his inauguration as president, can hardly be taken at face value in view of
his subsequent treatment of Bakr. The simple truth of the matter was that at
this juncture in his meteoric career Saddam did not feel sufficiently confident
in his position to conduct a putsch against Bakr. An inherent cautiousness is
one of Saddam's more surprising character traits.

The gradual rise in Saddam's fortunes during the mid-1970s was accompanied by a parallel increase in the fortunes of the Baath Party. The Popular
Army, the Baath Party militia that was controlled by Izzat Douri, Saddam's
deputy at the RCC and one of his most devoted followers, increased its membership to an estimated 150,000 followers. The Baath Party, which had numbered just 5,000 members when it seized power in 1968, was attracting
record numbers of new recruits, ordinary citizens who saw membership of
the Baath as a means of improving their lot. By the late 1970s it is estimated
that membership of the Iraqi Baath passed the 1 million mark, an impressive
landmark in a country with a population of just 12 million.[20]

Having strengthened his position in the party and the military, Saddam
was well aware that if he were to fulfill his ultimate ambition of becoming
president he needed to cultivate genuine support among the Iraqi public at

large. An intriguing insight into how Saddam was thinking at this juncture in his career is provided by a British journalist who visited Baghdad in 1975 and was told by his government interpreter that "Saddam's half brother and Head of Intelligence, Barzan al-Tikriti, had asked him to procure books on Nazi Germany. He believed that Saddam himself was interested in this subject, not for any reason to do with racism and anti-Semitism . . . but as an example of the successful organization of an entire society by the state for the achievement of national goals."[21] Having drawn on Stalin's example to create a totalitarian regime, Saddam was now looking to Hitler for clues on how to improve his popularity.

To prepare the way for his eventual accession Saddam felt he still needed several more building blocks in place so that, when the time came for him to make his move, any opposition he encountered would prove futile. The first significant attempt by Saddam to weaken Bakr's position came in January 1977 when he arranged for ten new members to be appointed to the Baath Party's Regional Command, giving Saddam a comfortable majority of fourteen out of the twenty-one members. Seven months later all these newcomers were appointed to the RCC, providing Saddam with a decisive majority in the country's most influential decision-making body. Among those making their debuts within the party's ruling elite was one of the Baath's few Christian activists, Tariq Aziz. After studying at the University of Baghdad, where he obtained an M.A. in English literature, Aziz had started his professional life as a schoolteacher. In the 1960s he had joined and left the Baath Party, before rejoining in 1968. An educated and cultured man, who had managed to steer clear of the violence and bloodshed that was coming to characterize the Baath Party, he had a keen interest in international politics and enjoyed a reputation for being, like Saddam, a staunch anticommunist and committed Arab nationalist. In 1969 Aziz was appointed editor of the Baath Party's newspaper *al-Thawra* and in November 1974 he became minister of information. During his editorship of *al-Thawra*, Aziz had proved himself to be an ally of Saddam, penning helpful editorials in support of Saddam's policies. In 1976, for example, during one of Saddam's perennial spats with the communists, Aziz wrote simply: "There is no place for a communist party in our country."[22] When Tariq Aziz's son was born a few years later, he paid his mentor the ultimate tribute by naming the child Saddam.

Having sorted out the regime's civilian wing, Saddam turned his attention toward ensuring that he faced no threat from the military. This he achieved in

October 1977 by engineering the elevation of his favorite cousin, Adnan Khairallah, to be the new minister of defense. Adnan had already, like Tariq Aziz, been elected to the Regional Command the previous January, and of all the schemes Saddam devised to increase his own power base, Adnan's appointment was arguably the most significant. Saddam had looked up to Adnan ever since he had followed his example and forced his way into the Iraqi school system. Following Saddam's move to his uncle Khairallah's house in Tikrit, he and Adnan had been brought up together almost as brothers. They had moved to Baghdad together, although Adnan, who had better educational qualifications, had fulfilled every aspiring Iraqi schoolboy's dream of enrolling at the Baghdad Military Academy, while Saddam had been required to content himself with a career in the far less glamorous Baath Party. Saddam had married Adnan's sister Sajida, while Adnan, at the instigation of his father and Saddam, had married one of Bakr's daughters. It is difficult to imagine a more incestuous arrangement dominating the ruling elite of a modern republic. In 1978 the bonds of family and kinship triumphed, and Adnan joined Saddam in the government. The appointment could not have been easy for Adnan, who was effectively undermining his father-in-law. Until Adnan's appointment Bakr had held the defense portfolio himself, along with his many other government positions. Adnan's promotion stripped his father-in-law of a crucial executive function. It also meant that henceforth the armed forces would be under Saddam's control.

Adnan's elevation to defense minister was just one of many appointments made by Saddam where members of his own family and his Tikriti clan were gradually taking control of the country's security and defense infrastructure. Barzan, his half brother, had already become head of the directorate general of intelligence in the wake of the Kazzar affair, and had taken over the functions of some of the other security departments. The National Security Office was headed by Saddam's friend Saadoun Shakir—who helped Saddam escape from jail in 1966 and had been a member of his *Saddameen* gang of thugs— and reported directly to Saddam. Saddam's other two half brothers, Watban and Sabawi, had been made governor of the newly expanded province of Tikrit and deputy chief of police respectively. And Khairallah Tulfah, the father of the new defense minister, was mayor of Baghdad. The more Saddam's power increased, the more the government came to be controlled by a tightly knit Tikriti clique.

With Adnan firmly established in command of the armed forces, another round of purges was instigated to eradicate the last vestiges of anti-Baathist sentiment from the officer corps. In the summer of 1978 Adnan conducted his own "cleansing operation"; dozens of officers were purged, including the commander of the air force and several divisional commanders, and some sixty military personnel were executed.[23] In July 1978 the RCC enacted a decree rendering non-Baathist political activity an illegal act, punishable by death, for members of the armed forces. At the same time as the armed forces were being purged, Saddam was funding a substantial military buildup, mainly to counter the threat posed by the belligerence of the shah. Saddam had probably considered doing something to improve the strength of Iraq's armed forces in the past, but had hesitated because he did not feel that he could entirely trust the military establishment, and by arming them the cautious Saddam would have felt that he was merely strengthening the position of his political rivals. Despite his own personal failure to secure a place at the Baghdad Military Academy, Saddam had managed to persuade Bakr in 1976 to appoint him to the rank of lieutenant general (which he insisted on having backdated to 1973), the equivalent of chief of staff. Soon after his inauguration as president, Saddam would appoint himself field marshal.

Adnan's appointment to the Defense Ministry meant Saddam enjoyed more control over the military. Consequently the period between 1977 and 1979 saw Iraq embark upon a frenzy of military spending that resulted in the Iraqi armed forces purchasing some of the Soviets' most advanced weapons systems, including 450 T-52 tanks, and dozens of 122- and 152-millimeter self-propelled guns, Tu-22 bombers, Mi-24 helicopters, and Il-76 transport aircraft. But Saddam had learned his lesson during the Kurdish conflict about relying too heavily on the Soviets for his military hardware, and resolved to find new markets. The most logical alternative to the Soviets was the French, who had also provided much-needed moral support during the oil crisis. Thus the Iraqi air force received 40 top-of-the-line Mirage-F1 fighters, and Iraq's antitank potential received significant reinforcement with the purchase of 60 Gazelle helicopters.[24] Most of these purchases were negotiated by a special three-man committee Saddam had set up at the end of 1974, whose long-term aim was to guarantee Iraq's long-term independence of military supplies. Chaired by Saddam, the other committee members were his cousin Adnan Khairallah and Adnan Hamdani, the Iraqi deputy prime minister who was to play a key role in helping to build up Iraq's arsenal of weapons of mass destruction. The takeover of the military by Saddam and Adnan seriously reduced both the power and influence of President Bakr, who was increasingly becoming little more than a figurehead, so much so that by the late 1970s Iraqis were openly referring to the Presidential Palace as "the tomb of the well-known soldier."

By 1977, Saddam's position had become almost impregnable. Officially the country was run by the triumvirate of Bakr, Saddam, and Adnan, with their intricate network of family and tribal ties. Indeed, the preponderance of Tikritis in prominent positions had prompted the government in 1976 to make it an offense for public figures to use a name that indicated their tribe. From 1974 onward, a combination of bad health and family tragedies made Bakr, as has been shown, a peripheral figure, and Saddam's office became the central focus of power and decision making in Iraq. The extensive Baath Party organization, which extended to every village and town; the intelligence structure; and the key ministers, who under the constitution owed their allegiance to Bakr, all reported to Saddam's office.[25] Saddam was well aware of the importance of his position in the country, and apart from his insistence that he be called "Mr. Deputy" at all times, demanded strict observance of official protocol when engaged in public duties. When, for example, he was waiting outside Bakr's office, Saddam would insist that one of Bakr's officials formally invite "Mr. Deputy" to enter the president's office. It was now simply a question of time before he made that office his own.

SIX

The Terrorist

After Iraq, the world. If Saddam could dominate the Iraqi stage, then he saw no reason why he could not become a dominant figure in international affairs. Even while he was biding his time as Bakr's second-in-command, Saddam had acquired a taste for diplomacy and, armed with the new oil wealth, he firmly believed that it was Iraq's destiny to be the preeminent force in Middle East politics. The more power he acquired in Iraq, the more he felt he should be taken seriously as an international player. He had demonstrated his negotiating skills in the deals he struck with the Soviets, the Iranians, and the Kurds, even though in all three cases he would eventually renege on the agreements. Saddam saw himself as the natural heir to Nasser, a powerful figurehead providing leadership over the entire Arab world. But if he were to achieve the lasting glory he so patently desired, then he would need more than the skills of the negotiating table. To compete with the big superpowers like the United States and the Soviet Union it was essential that Iraq develop its military strength. And in Saddam's view that meant acquiring an arsenal of nuclear, chemical, and biological weapons.

The ease with which Saddam was able to strengthen Iraq's nonconventional military capability in the 1970s was greatly assisted by the indulgent attitude taken by the West toward the Baathist regime, particularly after Saddam's oil nationalization resulted in Baghdad's various government ministries being awash with petrodollars. Iraq was a wealthy country, and Western companies, including defense contractors, were lining up to do business with Baghdad. The impact of Iraq's new oil wealth can be seen in the dramatic rise in the country's military expenditure from $500 million in 1970 to $4.5 billion in 1975. Western companies leaped at the opportunity to exploit the new Iraqi arms market, particularly after Saddam came to the conclusion that his strategic alliance with Moscow, which had been so crucial to his ruse of nationalizing the IPC, had outlived its usefulness. Saddam was determined to avoid what he regarded as Iraq's crippling dependence on the Soviet Union for arms, and from the mid-1970s onward he controlled the three-man committee whose responsibility it was to diversify Iraq's arms procurement needs. When Andrei Gromyko, the Soviet Union's foreign minister, complained about Iraq's new arms purchasing arrangements, Saddam replied candidly, "I do not care where my weapons come from. What counts is that these weapons will serve my purpose."[1] The comment accurately summed up Saddam's philosophy, and not just with regard to arms deals.

No one seemed too concerned about the regime's brutal disregard for human rights, and by the late 1970s Iraq was buying arms from France, Italy, West Germany, Belgium, Spain, Portugal, Yugoslavia, and Brazil. While the Soviet Union remained Iraq's main arms supplier, its share of Baghdad's overall arms acquisitions dropped from more than 95 percent in 1972, when Saddam negotiated the cooperation pact, to 63 percent on the eve of the Iran-Iraq War in 1980. France, which had been the first Western country to make conciliatory gestures to Baghdad after the nationalization of IPC, was the main beneficiary and quickly became Iraq's second largest supplier after the Soviet Union. In the summer of 1977 Iraq concluded its first arms deal with France for the supply of Mirage-F1 fighters, to be followed a year later by further agreements on the sale of Alouette attack helicopters, Crotale-I surface-to-air missiles, and electronic equipment.

From an early stage in Iraq's military development, Saddam made it abundantly clear that he was not just interested in conventional weapons and from the mid-1970s onward he concentrated a significant amount of energy on building up Iraq's nonconventional capability. Iraq's attempts to acquire chemical and biological weapons can be traced back to 1974 and the creation of the three-man committee, known as the Strategic Planning Committee, which was dedicated to fulfilling this goal and was personally headed by Saddam. The committee members were the same as those on the arms procurement committee, Adnan Khairallah and Adnan al-Hamdani, a lawyer by training who became Saddam's bagman and chief negotiator. Hamdani had been a protégé of Abdul Karim al-Shaikhly, the former foreign minister whom Saddam had sent into exile at the UN in New York in 1971 for declining to marry his sister Siham (see Chapter Four). Saddam had come into contact with Hamdani when he was working on one of the planning committees and, impressed by his sharp mind and technical ability, promoted him to work as his aide-de-camp.

Hamdani's first initiative was to establish contact with a Beirut company run by two Palestinian entrepreneurs called Arab Projects and Developments (APD), which specialized in finding work for highly qualified Arabs. Estimates of the number of Arab scientists recruited by the Iraqis range from between several hundred and four thousand. Egyptians, Moroccans, Palestinians, Algerians, Syrians, and other Arabs were persuaded to leave good jobs in the United States, Britain, Canada, Brazil, and dozens of other countries, bringing to Iraq a wealth of expertise. Most of them were employed in petrochemical and infrastructure projects, but some of them inevitably found themselves employed on more sensitive scientific projects. The other key contribution APD made to Iraq's development was to help with the creation of Iraq's higher education system, which would provide Saddam with his own homegrown scientists to work on his various weapons projects.

Saddam's initial interest in biological weapons centered on the bacteriological variety, which were cheap, relatively simple to manufacture, and potentially deadly. A single vial of the anthrax virus, for example, dropped into an urban water system is sufficient, in the right conditions, to launch a full-scale epidemic. It was a terrorist's weapon if there ever was one. At Saddam's request, Izzat al-Douri, a high-ranking Baath official who served on the Revolutionary Command Council as minister of agriculture, traveled to Paris in November 1974 where he signed a contract with France's Institut Merieux to set up Iraq's first bacteriological laboratory. The spurious justification provided by the Iraqis for wanting such a facility was the need to manufacture large quantities of vaccines to help develop agricultural and animal production. The official Iraqi purchasing agency was called the General Directorate of Veterinary Services.[2] No one in France seemed in the least concerned. Douri was rewarded with a promotion on his return home to Baghdad, and was soon appointed minister of the interior, while still retaining special responsibility for "agricultural" development.

Having laid the foundations for the biological weapons program, in 1975 Saddam's committee decided on its next move—the acquisition of poison gas. At the meeting Adnan Khairallah argued that chemical weapons were a "force multiplier." Unlike the sophisticated electronics systems then being developed by the superpowers, the technology for chemical weapons was well within the grasp of a developing nation like Iraq. The committee decided to make an all-out effort to acquire the technology for producing various types of poison gas, including suffocating agents, like mustard gas, and nerve agents, like the more sophisticated Tabun and Sarin. Tabun had been discovered in 1937 by scientists working for the German company I. G. Farben, which gained international notoriety during the Second World War for providing the gas used at the Nazi extermination camps. The scientists discovered that certain organic phosphorous compounds, which were easy to obtain, could be transformed into a deadly gas that attacked the central nervous system. Hitler's Third Reich began manufacturing large quantities of the new nerve agent, but the Führer never used it in combat. After the war I. G Farben patented the new compound and called it Tabun.

Tabun, and its first cousin, Sarin, are almost identical in composition to the organic phosphate compound Parathion, a well-known and highly dangerous insecticide. Tabun and Sarin are so deadly that a single drop is sufficient to kill a man. Nerve gas also has the advantage of being odorless and colorless. It is easy to make and easy to spread, and it makes killing easy and efficient. Both agents can be obtained from organic phosphate compounds, which in turn are derived from different types of phosphate minerals. It was Saddam's good fortune that Iraq had large phosphate deposits in its western desert, close to the Syrian border.

In order to put the chemical weapons plan into effect in late 1975, Saddam moved Adnan al-Hamdani to the all-powerful Ministry of Planning where he could oversee Iraq's entire industrial development. Hamdani's job was to slip strategic weapons projects into large contracts ostensibly aimed at developing Iraq's civilian manufacturing or agricultural potential. For this task he was aided by two senior members of the Revolutionary Command Council, Izzat al-Douri, the new minister of the interior (who still retained his special responsibility for "agricultural development"), and Taha al-Jazrawi, the minister of industry and minerals. Hamdani cleverly concealed the strategic weapons projects in Iraq's Second Five-Year Plan. Under the heading "agricultural development" he inscribed a little-noticed entry that called for "the creation of six laboratories for chemical, physiological, and biological analysis." To operate the laboratories, the plan recommended training 5,000 technicians from foreign companies. Under the heading

"Chemical Industries" the plan proposed the construction of a pesticides plant at Samarra capable of producing 1,000 tons a year of organic phosphate compounds.[3] Most Western countries had stopped using these highly lethal compounds for pest control years before because of their high toxicity. The same organic phosphorous materials form the basis of nerve gas compounds such as Sarin and Tabun.

Although APD had been helpful in the general recruitment of technical expertise, the Iraqis realized that they would need outside assistance to achieve their goal of becoming self-sufficient in the manufacture of chemical and biological weapons. To this end Saddam established the Al-Haythem Institute in Baghdad's Masbah district. Although the Institute reported directly to Saddam, the day-to-day running was managed by Saadoun Shakir and the Mukhabarat. The institute developed close links with various dissident Palestinian groups such as the Popular Front for the Liberation of Palestine (PFLP), which helped the Iraqis to acquire sensitive material from countries such as East Germany.[4]

Procurement teams were dispatched to Europe and the United States disguised as commercial representatives for various front companies. The closest they came to duping a foreign country into building a poison gas plant was with an approach, made through French intermediaries, to the Pfaulder Company, of Rochester, New York, which specialized in the manufacture of equipment for mixing toxic chemicals. Believing that they were being asked to build a plant for the manufacture of pesticides, Pfaulder dispatched two engineers to Baghdad to meet with a team of officials from the Ministry of Agriculture. An amiable Iraqi official gave the Americans a detailed explanation of how Iraq's attempts to develop its agricultural productivity were being hampered by the inability of Iraqi farmers to protect their crops from the ravages of desert locusts and other pests. "A modern pesticide plant could change all that," said the official. The Americans were impressed, but aware of the difficulties of producing highly toxic pesticides in the Third World, they proposed constructing a pilot plant to train the local workforce and identify potential problem areas.

To this end in January 1976 Pfaulder presented a detailed proposal for a pilot plant. Apart from containing detailed design specifications, it stipulated the type of special equipment necessary for blending toxic chemicals. The Iraqis were unhappy about building a pilot plant; they wanted to go into production right away. The Iraqis' impatience disturbed the two engineers, as did the Iraqis' insistence that when production finally got under way they would want to manufacture four highly toxic organic compounds—Amiton, Demeton, Paraoxon, and Parathion. All four of these chemicals are first cousins to nerve gas agents, and could be readily transformed into deadly weapons. The final straw for the Americans came when the Iraqis indicated that they wanted to build production lines big enough to turn out 1,200 tons of these chemicals per year. At a stormy meeting in mid-1976 at New York's Waldorf-Astoria Hotel, the Iraqis said they wanted a full-scale plant immediately, and when the Americans stuck to their insistence on building a pilot plant first, the Iraqis withdrew from the negotiations.[5] The Iraqi team did not go away completely empty-handed. The blueprints and specifications for the pilot project provided by Pfaulder were sufficient to enable the Iraqis to build their own plant.

Next the Iraqis turned their attention to Europe. Saddam remained convinced that if Iraq could build up its chemical weapons capability then it could achieve total independence from its weapons suppliers. In late 1976 Saddam's procurement teams approached two British companies, Imperial Chemical Industries (ICI) and Babcock and Wilcox. Once again the Iraqis' cover story was that they wanted to build a pesticides plant capable of producing Amiton, Demeton, Paraoxon, and Parathion. The Iraqis even produced the plans that had been drawn up by Pfaudler the year before, showing the corrosion-resistant reactor vessels, pipes, and pumps that were needed for nerve gas production. ICI officials were immediately suspicious and declined the offer "because of the sensitive nature of the materials and the potential for misuse." At the same time ICI tipped off intelligence officers at the Secret Intelligence Service in London. Having failed in Britain the Iraqis visited two Italian companies, the giant chemical firm Montedison and the engineering concern, Technipetrole. Both companies have denied helping the Iraqis acquire chemical weapons, although both of them have since been named on the U.S. Senate Foreign Relations Committee's list of Iraq's chemical weapons suppliers. Still desperate for expertise and equipment, the Iraqis finally turned their attention to Germany, the spiritual home of poison gas.

During a meeting with Karl Heinz Lohs, the director of the Leipzig Institute for Poisonous Chemicals, in what was then East Germany, the Iraqis were unapologetic about their intentions. "You Germans have great expertise in the killing of Jews with gas," said the official. "This interests us in the same way. . . . How [can] this knowledge . . . be used to destroy Israel?" Lohs made many visits to Iraq to give lectures on the terrible effects of chemical weapons use, although he later claimed that his visits were used by the East German authorities as a cover to get their chemical weapons experts into Baghdad to assist with the development of Iraq's chemical weapons program.[6]

The final piece in the chemical weapons jigsaw concerned the development of the phosphate deposits in western Iraq, which the Iraqis wanted to exploit for nerve gas production. The Belgian engineering company Syberta was already contracted to build a huge phosphate mine at Akashat. Phosphate mining in itself is a perfectly acceptable enterprise for a developing country such as Iraq, and there were many countries, such as Morocco, that had become a major exporter of fertilizer, in Morocco's case manufactured from phosphate deposits in the Sahara. After work had begun on the mine, the Iraqis signed a second contract to build a fertilizer complex 150 kilometers (100 miles) away at Al Qaim. To move the raw material from Akashat to Al Qaim a Brazilian company was contracted to build a rail link. No expense was to be spared for Saddam's pet project. None of the companies involved in the project seemed concerned about the unusual specifications demanded by the Iraqis, such as reinforced concrete fortifications around certain buildings. British, French, American, Austrian, German, Swiss, Danish, and Swedish companies all contributed expertise to the Akashat/Al Qaim project, all believing that they were helping with the construction of a fertilizer production plant. But the project turned out to be a classic example of dual-use technology. American and British intelligence officials have since confirmed that Iraq's first nerve gas plant was constructed at Akashat at an estimated cost of $40 million, and a separate facility was constructed at Al Qaim.

The plant was completed at about the time Saddam became president and during the next ten years Saddam was able to draw on the expertise of a number of foreign companies that enabled Iraq to produce significant amounts of chemical weapons, including a refined form of Distilled Mustard (HD), as well as the Tabun nerve agent and the more potent VX nerve agent. The manufacture of biological weapons also underwent significant expansion to the extent that Iraq was able to produce agents such as anthrax, typhoid, and cholera. It was an irony not lost on the teams of United Nations weapons inspectors who were given the task of dismantling Saddam's weapons of mass destruction in the aftermath of the Gulf War in 1991 that many of the agents they were trying to track down originated in either Europe or the United States.

Of all the schemes to develop nonconventional weapons the one that was closest to Saddam's heart, however, concerned the Iraqi effort to acquire a nuclear arsenal. From the mid-1970s Saddam and other leading Baathists had preached about the necessity of Iraq making the most of the latest scientific developments if it were to turn itself into a modern nation. "For the Arab nation, the need for scientific advancement is tantamount to the need to live since it is impossible for any nation to lead a dignified existence . . . without respect for science and a defined role in its exploration and exploitation," Saddam had declared. Science had a key role to play in a wide variety of economic activities in Saddam's Iraq, from developing the petrochemical industry to the massive reconstruction program of roads, homes, and public utilities. But the area of science that most fascinated Saddam was that of nuclear technology. Indeed his fascination was so great that it rubbed off on his children. In 1980 one of Saddam's official biographers was given the opportunity to meet his family. During his visit to the family home he met Uday, Saddam's eldest son and a precocious sixteen-year-old. Uday informed his interviewer that he was good at physics and chemistry and that he wanted to go to the university to study nuclear physics. The reason he was set on this particular career path was that "Iraq would need scientists in this field once it had entered the nuclear club."[7]

At a special meeting in 1975 of his three-man committee on weapons procurement, Saddam had set a target for acquiring nuclear weapons of within ten years—i.e., by 1985. Apart from the status that accrued from having a nuclear weapons capability, there were many reasons why Saddam was so determined to acquire this particular arsenal. To start with there was a determination within the Arab world to match the nuclear capability that it was widely believed Israel had developed after purchasing the Dimona nuclear reactor from France in the 1950s. It would also be a useful deterrent against any future threat from Iran, a country that was three times larger than Iraq. Saddam was well aware that by joining the likes of the United States, Britain, France, China, and the Soviet Union in the elite "nuclear club," Iraq's position as the undisputed champion of the Arab world would be secure.

The Iraqi authorities had initiated their quest for nuclear technology as early as the late 1960s when the Arif government had purchased an experimental research reactor from the Soviet Union. The Iraqis built their first nuclear research center in the desert at Thuwaitha, about fifteen miles south of Baghdad, to house the modest-sized IRT 2000 light-water reactor. Later the Soviets upgraded the reactor and trained at least one hundred Iraqi nuclear physicists. But when in April 1975 the Iraqis asked to purchase more advanced technology, Brezhnev and Kosygin politely but firmly declined the request. According to the Palestinian writer Said Aburish, who makes no apology for assisting Saddam with his arms buildup in the 1970s, Saddam personally authorized his officials to conduct a worldwide search for suitable equipment: Aburish himself was instructed to approach Atomic Energy of Canada, which proved unsuccessful.[8] Saddam could easily have been assisted in his search for weapons of mass destruction by opportunists like Aburish who, apart from earning a handsome fee in commissions, felt "a special sense of elation" at being part of the effort to create "a balance of terror" between Israel and the Arabs.[9] The activities of Aburish and his associates, however, achieved little.

Thwarted by the Russians and everyone else he approached, Saddam finally got what he was looking for when he turned his attentions toward his most favored international ally, France. Saddam had already struck up a strong personal understanding with Jacques Chirac, the French prime minister. Although he had drawn heavily on Josef Stalin in his attempts to create a totalitarian regime in Iraq, Saddam remained at heart very much the nationalist his uncle Khairallah had brought him up to be. It was no surprise therefore that he should be attracted to a committed Gaullist like Chirac. General de Gaulle, who had withdrawn France from NATO's integrated military command structure rather than put France's nuclear weapons under NATO control, was a man after Saddam's heart. The Gaullists preached that national sovereignty was sacred, as did Saddam's wing of the Baath Party, and nuclear technology, as Chirac and his advisers constantly argued, was very much a sovereignty issue.

Saddam and Chirac had developed a close understanding during the lengthy negotiations that had taken place in 1975 for Iraq to purchase the new Mirage-F1 fighter plane, an upgraded version of the aircraft that had been used by the Israeli air force to defeat the Arabs in the 1973 war. During a visit to Paris in September 1975 to conclude the Mirage deal, Saddam was taken by Chirac on a tour of Provence. On their way to the bullfights at Les Baux, Chirac's party made a brief detour to enable Saddam to visit the Cadarache nuclear research center, a few miles north of Marseilles. The Commissariat à l'Énergie Atomique (CEA) had just set up its first experimental fast-breeder reactor, called Rapsodie. The basic principle of a fast-breeder reactor is to "breed" more nuclear fuel than it consumes. In the process it transforms significant quantities of uranium into plutonium, which can then be processed for use in the manufacture of nuclear weapons. Iraq's interest in fast-breeder reactors was simple: to obtain plutonium to build bombs.

As with their attempts to acquire chemical and biological weapons, the Iraqis claimed that they wanted the nuclear technology for peaceful purposes. Despite having the world's second largest oil reserves, the Iraqis claimed they were interested in developing an indigenous nuclear power industry. The French officials basically accepted Saddam's explanation, and offered to sell him an Osiris research reactor and a scale model called Isis, both of which could breed small quantities of bomb-grade plutonium. Saddam agreed to buy them on one condition—that France agreed to deliver an extra one-year supply of reactor fuel at start-up. If the fuel was processed correctly it would produce enough material for several bombs the size of the one dropped on Hiroshima.

The reactor was similar to the one the French had sold to the Israelis in 1956. As the French Socialists had been responsible for providing Israel with its Dimona nuclear research reactor, Chirac calculated that his Guallist Party was quite within its rights to provide the Arabs with similar technology. While the rest of the world was desperately trying to keep the Middle East a nuclear-free zone, the French, in their own inimitable fashion, were blithely negotiating deals to provide mutually hostile countries with the capacity to bomb themselves into oblivion. With characteristic Gallic cynicism Chirac's sole interest in selling a sophisticated reactor to Saddam "for peaceful applications" was commercial; the reactor was a quid pro quo for the French receiving favorable trading terms in Baghdad, including oil concessions, imports of French cars, and the understanding that Iraq would conclude the deal for the new generation of Mirage fighter planes. No one in the French government seemed at all bothered by the inherent contradiction of an oil-rich country like Iraq seeking to turn itself into a nuclear power. And Saddam left no one in any doubt as to his real intentions. Interviewed in the Lebanese weekly magazine *Al Usbu al-Arabi* in September 1975 shortly after the reactor deal had been concluded, Saddam proudly declared, "The agreement with France is the first concrete step toward production of the Arab atomic bomb."

At first the Iraqis called the reactor Osirak but later changed the name to Tammuz I and Tammuz II, the month that Saddam's Baath Party seized power. It is said that the Iraqis changed the name from Osirak at the request of the French government after the satirical French press had made it rhyme with the prime minister's name ("O'Chirac"). Once the party had returned to Paris, Saddam insisted on celebrating the deal by laying on a special feast for his special French ally. When Chirac had visited Baghdad the previous year he had shown a liking for the local Iraqi river fish called *masgouf.* Saddam ordered his cook to fly back to Baghdad on the presidential plane and return with one and a half tons of fish. When the cook returned, Saddam persuaded the maître d'hôtel at the Marigny Palace, where the Iraqi party was staying, to prepare a special barbecue for Chirac, and while Saddam's security guards patrolled the kitchens with their loaded machine guns, the cooks set to work roasting the huge, greasy carp over open fires. Chirac, who had to suffer the indignity of French television cameras filming him gamely swallowing the fish as it was served Baghdad-style on aluminium foil, later confided to an aide that the Iraqi delegation had caused quite a stir at the Marigny Palace. "The whole place smelled of charred flesh. It was amusing, but a mess."[10]

Saddam's visit resulted in a bonanza for French business that was potentially worth billions of dollars. The deal for the nuclear reactor, which was signed in Baghdad in November 1975, was alone worth about $3 billion. In addition there were to be contracts for petrochemical plants, desalinization plants, a new airport, and even a subway system for Baghdad. This was in addition to the massive arms deals that had already been negotiated. The French business community was so overwhelmed by the largesse delivered by Chirac's dealings with Saddam that they named him "Mr. Iraq." As Saddam prepared to leave, Chirac made an eloquent speech. French policy, he declared, "is dictated not merely by interest, but also by the heart. France deems it necessary to establish relationships between producers and consumers on terms that best conform to the interests of both parties."[11] The full text of the Franco-Iraqi Nuclear Cooperation Treaty was not made public until eight months later. One of the conditions set out in the treaty was the stipulation that "all persons of Jewish race or the Mosaic religion" be excluded from participating in the program, either in Iraq or France. The treaty also committed the French to training six hundred Iraqi nuclear technicians, more than enough for a bomb program.

Khidhir Hamza, one of the Iraqi scientists who worked on Iraq's nuclear project from its inception and who managed to defect to the West in 1994, has revealed how there was never any doubt about the Iraqis' intentions.

According to Hamza, Saddam took personal charge of Iraq's Atomic Energy Commission (AEC) from the mid-1970s, having first brought a team of scientists together to build the Iraqi bomb.[12] Most of the Iraqi scientists assigned to the project had been educated in Britain, the United States, and Canada and were greatly assisted in their efforts by the generosity of the United States Atomic Energy Commission which, under the Atoms for Peace program it was running at the time, had in 1956 donated to the AEC a complete set of the reports of the Manhattan Project, which had produced the world's first atom bomb in 1945. Hamza says the Iraqis decided to copy the Israelis, who had bought a small research reactor and then clandestinely changed its use.

Saddam was undoubtedly the driving force behind Iraq's nuclear project. He chaired the meetings of the AEC with the same professionalism that he chaired all the other government committees dealing with Iraq's modernization. He demanded detailed reports from the scientists on how they intended to go about developing the Iraqi bomb. He read the reports carefully and fully mastered the brief so that when he met the scientists he was able to ask pertinent and penetrating questions. It was through Saddam's personal initiative that Iraq secured a position on the board of governors at the International Atomic Energy Agency (IAEA), the international body responsible for policing the nuclear industry. Saddam calculated that the IAEA would be less suspicious of Iraq's nuclear "research" activities if it played a constructive role within the organization. Saddam rejected a proposal put forward by his scientists to build an "Atomic City" on the grounds that concentrating all the nation's nuclear research resources in one place would make it a soft target for anyone seeking to destroy it. As with the chemical weapons project, Saddam wanted to spread the resources around a number of secret locations throughout the country to protect them from attack.

Having reached an agreement in principle to buy a French reactor during his meeting with Chirac, Saddam dispatched Hamza and a small group of Iraqi specialists to Saclay, the headquarters of the French atomic energy agency on the outskirts of Paris, to sort out the technical specifications. When the Iraqi scientists were unable to provide a convincing explanation to their French counterparts as to why they needed a nuclear research reactor, the French simply responded by doubling the price. But even though the French could see nothing wrong with the nuclear deal, as soon as it became general knowledge it provoked a storm of international protest, particularly from Israel, Britain, Saudi Arabia, and Syria. As a sop to his critics, President

Giscard d'Estaing ordered the French atomic commission to develop a "clean" fuel for the Tammuz reactor that would be sufficient to power it up but that was totally useless for weapons production. Saddam was incensed, and threatened to cancel all the other trade contracts unless the French fulfilled the terms of the original deal. Eventually a compromise was reached whereby the French agreed to supply the original material, but in smaller consignments. To safeguard any further problems with the French, in 1979 Saddam secretly negotiated a ten-year nuclear cooperation agreement with Brazil, which committed the Brazilians to supply Iraq with large quantities of natural and low-enriched uranium, reactor technologies, equipment, and training. In addition American intelligence officials have claimed that Saddam signed secret nuclear deals with China and India, although no details have been published. The only piece of equipment Saddam lacked for completion of his nuclear adventure was the reprocessing laboratory necessary for extracting plutonium from the spent reactor fuel. This was rectified in April 1979 when the Italian company Snia Techint, a subsidiary of the Fiat group, agreed to sell four nuclear laboratories to the Iraqi Atomic Energy Commission. The Italian deal would give the Iraqis enough plutonium in a year to make one bomb, and the project would be ready to go operational by late 1981.[13]

Work continued on the quest for the Iraqi bomb throughout the 1970s, and the scientists involved in the project were carefully scrutinized and monitored by Saddam's security agents. On one occasion Saddam arrived at the research headquarters to lecture the scientists on the need to conduct their business in secret. "A scientist must be security conscious otherwise he is useless," Saddam declared, "and we don't want him. Security must be uppermost in your minds and it can take many forms. One way is to pretend that you don't know much."[14] Saddam's insistence that the scientists work in complete secrecy hindered the pace of the project, as the scientists were effectively cut off from their colleagues abroad and isolated from the latest scientific discourse and developments. The project's chances of success were not helped, either, when the cores of the two Iraqi reactors were severely damaged by sabotage in April 1979 at the plant at La Seyne-sur-Mer, near Toulon, where they were being assembled. The sabotage was the work of Mossad, the Israeli intelligence service, which had smuggled seven specialists into France to carry out the task. The attack was code-named Operation Big Lift, and the Israelis had carefully placed their bombs to cause maximum damage to the reactor cores, without damaging the rest of the complex.

The other difficulty hindering the project was the fact that not all the scientists were aware that they were involved in a bomb-making project. This
became painfully evident toward the end of 1979 when Saddam, shortly after
he had become president, paid a surprise visit to the AEC headquarters,
which were located at a military complex south of Baghdad. The scientists
were made aware of Saddam's impending arrival when armed guards suddenly appeared and locked the doors and filled the halls. Bomb-sniffing
German shepherds then scoured the building looking for booby traps. Finally
a motorcade of black Mercedes, filled with plainclothes agents carrying submachine guns, pulled into the compound. Saddam marched into the building and made his way to the office of the AEC chairman, Abdul Razzaq al-
Hashimi, and ordered him to assemble all his top nuclear officials. When they
were finally assembled, Saddam dispensed with the preliminaries and went
straight to the point. "When will you deliver the plutonium for the bomb?"
he demanded. Plutonium was crucial to the success of the bomb-making
project, and the French reactors had been purchased to help the Iraqis extract
their own supplies of the internationally restricted material. Responsibility
for producing it—a highly complex scientific task—had been entrusted to
Hussein al-Shahristani, a brilliant Iraqi scientist who was an expert in neu-
tron activation. But while Shahristani was in charge of plutonium extrac-
tion, no one had told him he was working on a project to build an atom
bomb. "Bomb, we can't make a bomb," replied the flustered scientist. He
then started to lecture Saddam that it would be impossible to use the French
reactors to produce weapons-grade plutonium because "they are covered by
the nuclear nonproliferation treaty, and we will be held in violation of our
treaty obligations." Saddam looked at the hapless scientist with contempt.
"Treaties," he replied, "are a matter for us to deal with. You, as a scientist,
should not be troubled by these things. You should be doing your job and not
have these kind of excuses." At that point Saddam cocked his head, a signal
for his security guards to remove Shahristani. As the trembling scientist
was led from the room, Saddam turned his back.[15] Shahristani was taken to
the headquarters of the Mukhabarat, the domestic intelligence service, in the
wealthy Mansour district of Baghdad where he was so severely tortured that
his children did not recognize his bloated face when they were allowed to visit
him. Eventually he was subjected to a show trial by a special security court
and jailed for life.

*   *   *

The primary motivation for Saddam's acquisition of weapons of mass destruction was his desire for Iraq to be self-sufficient in weapons production and to become a dominant force in both regional and world politics. Chemical and biological weapons would diminish Iraq's heavy dependency on foreign arms suppliers and enable it to defend itself from attack; nuclear weapons would make Iraq the first Arab superpower, capable of dominating its neighbors and in time fulfilling the long-held Baathist doctrine of creating a united Arab republic, headed, of course, by Saddam Hussein. Although in the mid-1970s Saddam's main concern was still the consolidation of the Baathist revolution in Iraq, he was nevertheless keen to implement the Baathist doctrine beyond Iraq's borders under his aegis. "The glory of the Arabs stems from the glory of Iraq," he declared on one occasion. "Throughout history, whenever Iraq became mighty and flourished so did the Arab nation. This is why we are striving to make Iraq mighty, formidable, able and developed, and why we shall spare nothing to improve its welfare and to brighten the glory of the Iraqis." Saddam remained committed to the notion of inheriting Nasser's mantle as a radical Arab leader, but was aware of Iraq's limitations, especially when it came to confronting Israel. For the time being, Saddam was content to opt for a pragmatic approach; as he openly admitted, the liberation of Palestine through military means was not feasible before building up a "scientifically, economically and militarily strong Iraq."[16]

In his desire to dominate the Arab agenda it was inevitable, therefore, that Saddam would eventually become embroiled in the intrigues of the Arab-Israeli conflict. Iraq up to that point had enjoyed an undistinguished history in its involvement in the various wars with Israel. The force sent to help the Palestinian Arabs fighting the establishment of the State of Israel in 1948 had performed so badly that the government had ended up being accused of colluding with the British to give Palestine to the Jews. An Iraqi expeditionary force was unable to prevent the Israelis inflicting their emphatic blitzkrieg against the Arabs in 1967, and the Iraqis fared little better during the 1973 Yom Kippur War. The Iraqis sent 30,000 troops and an armored division to help the Syrians who were battling to drive the Israelis from the Golan Heights, but a lack of tank transporters meant the tanks were late in arriving. The Syrians, who had begun hostilities without even informing the Iraqis of their plans, had given the Iraqi reinforcements a cool reception. The Iraqis were not even provided with maps, but simply given vague directions indicating the location of the front line. They were a sitting target when the

Israelis attacked, and lost more than 100 tanks and suffered heavy casualties. Saddam complained that throughout the battle he had to rely on the radio news to discover the fate of the Iraqi forces, and when the fighting was over he withdrew his forces from Syria in a huff.

The issue of liberating Palestine from Zionist control remained, how-ever, the most pressing issue of the day, and in the absence of a military option, by the 1970s the Arab states had turned to another cheap, but highly effective, means of waging war—terrorism. As with chemical weapons, terror cells are relatively cheap to run and are highly disruptive of the enemy. Although extremist Palestinian movements had been involved in interna-tional terrorism since the late 1960s, Iraq's involvement had been at best peripheral; Iraq's failure, for example, to back Yasser Arafat's Fatah movement during the 1970 Black September civil war in Jordan had not been forgotten by the PLO chairman. The other factor that weighed heavily against Iraq's attempts to become directly involved in the liberation struggle was that, unlike Jordan, Syria, Lebanon, and Egypt, it did not enjoy a common border with Israel, and it was therefore cumbersome for Palestinian groups to direct operations from Baghdad, from where they needed to pass through an inter-mediary before they could strike at an Israeli target.

The turning point for Saddam came in the diplomatic aftermath of the 1973 Yom Kippur War when the infamous shuttle diplomacy of Dr. Henry Kissinger, the U.S. secretary of state, resulted in persuading Anwar Sadat, the new Egyptian president, to pursue a peace dialogue with Israel, a process that would later result in the Camp David peace treaty. Arafat also appeared to be backing the Egyptian initiative. Anxious to isolate the Egyptians and portray itself as a truly radical regime, the Iraqi government attempted to forge its own alliance with the Palestinians. To this end the Iraqis went so far as to invite Yasser Arafat to join their cabinet as minister of Palestine affairs. The Iraqis also promised the Palestinians substantial financial aid. Arafat, who was still angry with the Baathists for failing to back him during Black September, and was keen not have the Iraqis assuming leadership of the Palestinian cause, declined the offer. Saddam was furious. He ordered the closure of Arafat's offices in Baghdad and started supporting a number of radical Palestinian groups, who were bitterly opposed to any deal with the Israelis and who were also opposed to Arafat's Fatah organization.

This was to be Saddam's first involvement in the world of international terrorism. Up to this point Saddam's terror tactics had generally been con-

fined to his own people and country, and on those occasions when his operatives ventured outside Iraq, it was generally to target dissident Iraqis, such as
with the murders of deposed General Hardan al-Tikriti in Kuwait in 1971,
and General Mahdi Saleh Samurrai in Beirut the same year. But with his
patronage of the infamous Palestinian terrorist Sabri al-Banna, otherwise
known as Abu Nidal or "father of the struggle," Saddam was sponsoring a
sophisticated network of fanatical terrorists. Even by the standards of Middle
East terrorism, Abu Nidal, had acquired almost legendary status through his
exploits, such as the bomb attacks against the Israeli airline El Al ticket desks
at Rome and Vienna airports in December 1985, which killed 18 people and
wounded 110, many of them American tourists. He was also held responsible in late 1984 for the murder of British diplomats Ken Whitty and Percy
Norris in Athens and Bombay respectively, and the brutal murder in 1986 of
British journalist Alec Collett, a videotape of whose execution, in retaliation
for the American bombing raid on Libya, was sent to his relatives.[17]

Abu Nidal had first moved to Baghdad in 1970 as chief representative of
Yasser Arafat's Fatah organization, which was the dominant force in the PLO.
To start with he was more involved with Bakr than Saddam, but as Saddam
increased his power, so the two men were required to work together.
Relations between the two were always strained, mainly because they recognized that they both shared the same sense of ruthless ambition. Abu Nidal
was also close to Tariq Aziz and Saadoun Shakir, Saddam's cousin and the
head of Iraqi intelligence. Shakir, who took his orders directly from Saddam,
is known to have worked closely with Abu Nidal from the mid-1970s when
Abu Nidal was mainly concentrating his energies on murdering his opponents in the Palestinian movement. Backed by Saddam, Abu Nidal spent the
late 1970s waging war against the PLO both in Europe and the Middle East.
The PLO's representative in London, Said Hammadi, a leading advocate of
opening a dialogue with Israel, was assassinated in 1978, and other PLO delegates were murdered in Paris and Kuwait. For good measure, Abu Nidal,
who described his relationship with Baghdad as a "close alliance," also conducted a series of terrorist attacks aimed at the neighboring Baathist regime
in Syria, which was then Saddam's sworn enemy. There were two attempts on
the life of the Syrian foreign minister, Abdul Halim Khaddam, and in 1976 a
team of Abu Nidal terrorists blew up the Semiramis Hotel in Damascus.

Another infamous Palestinian terrorist who was harbored by Saddam during this period was Dr. Wadi Haddad, one of the founding members of the

Popular Front for the Liberation of Palestine (PFLP), the PLO group responsible for turning the Palestinian cause into a vehicle for international terrorism in the early 1970s. Together with Dr. George Habash, the group's other founding member, the PLFP was responsible for the multiple hijacking of three aircraft at Dawson's Field in Jordan and the massacre of twenty-six people at Lod airport in Israel. The group's activities were so outrageous that they even merited condemnation by both the Soviet Union and China, and they were held responsible for King Hussein of Jordan's decision to expel the PLO from his country during Black September. The PLFP moved to Damascus, but when Habash turned against the policy of carrying out international terrorist attacks, Haddad moved to Baghdad in 1972, where he formed the splinter Special Operations Group. It was from there that he organized the infamous kidnapping of OPEC oil ministers during their meeting in Vienna in December 1975 and the hijacking of an Israeli airliner to Entebbe, Uganda. One of Haddad's closest associates during this period was the legendary Venezuelan terrorist known as "Carlos the Jackal." In addition to staging their own terrorist operations, Haddad's organization linked up with a wide variety of European terrorist groups, including Germany's Baader-Meinhof gang and the Japanese "Red Army." By 1977, when Saddam was effectively running Iraq, Haddad was described as "the spider in the net of the intertwined terrorist groups throughout the world." When Haddad died, of natural causes, in 1978, he was buried in Baghdad with full military honors. According to an Iraqi defector, a former member of the Iraqi security service with special responsibility for training foreign terror groups who escaped from Baghdad in late 2000, at least fifty members of the PFLP continued to reside in Iraq until the 1990s, and made frequent use of the Mukhabarat's terrorist training facilities.[18]

Iraq's dealings with terrorist groups such as those run by Abu Nidal and Wadi Haddad were handled by Saddam's personal office, and it was as a direct result of Saddam's support for these internationally condemned terrorist groups in the 1970s that the U.S. State Department added Iraq's name to the list of countries accused of sponsoring terrorism. David Mack, who was political officer at the U.S. embassy's interests section in Baghdad in the late 1970s, says the Iraqis made no attempt to conceal their involvement with the different terrorist groups. "We all knew precisely where Abu Nidal's house was located, although, of course, we weren't allowed to go there," he said. "Saddam liked to keep these groups there for show."[19]

The closest Saddam ever came to admitting in public his support for the Palestinian terrorist groups was during an interview with *Newsweek* in July 1978. Asked why Baghdad had become a haven for both Palestinian and European terror groups, Saddam responded: "Regarding the Palestinians, it's no secret: Iraq is open to them and they are free to train and plan [terrorist attacks] here."[20] By the summer of 1978 hardly a week passed when one of the terror groups linked to Baghdad was not committing some atrocity or another, whether in Paris, London, or Islamabad. A former CIA officer who specialized in Iraq during the 1970s said there was never any doubt in the minds of American officials that Saddam was personally involved in ordering the terrorist attacks. "From the mid-1970s Saddam controlled everything in Baghdad. And if Saddam was providing these groups with a safe haven, he would expect something in return. For Saddam, there is no such thing as free room and board." Indeed, by the late 1970s Saddam's reputation for being a generous backer had drawn a wide array of dissident groups to base themselves in Iraq: the hard-line Kurdish PKK movement, members of Syria's Muslim Brotherhood, and even Ayatollah Khomeini, who posed the biggest threat to the shah of Iran, all enjoyed Saddam's support. "Saddam liked to use these groups because it gave him great flexibility," according to the former CIA desk officer. "He could turn them on and off at will. So long as they did his bidding he was happy to support them."[21] Abu Nidal's group was one that frequently fell out with Saddam, particularly over Saddam's insistence that the Palestinian terrorist continue his attacks against Syria. Abu Nidal, who regarded himself as a significant player on the Palestinian political scene, sometimes refused to obey Saddam's instructions. As a result he would temporarily close his offices in Baghdad and relocate to places like Tripoli, Libya, where he found the interference of Colonel Gadhafi in his activities less intrusive. Eventually Saddam and Abu Nidal would reach a reconciliation and the Palestinian would move back to Baghdad.

Not all Saddam's terrorist activities during this period were confined to freelancers on the payroll of the Iraqi intelligence services. Dr. Ayad Allawi, a former senior member of the Baath who had fled to London in protest of Saddam's brutalization of the country, awoke one night at his Epsom home with his wife to find one of Saddam's assassins armed with an ax standing over their bed. "We were both subjected to an horrendous attack by this masked man," recalled Dr. Allawi, who became a leading Iraqi campaigner for Saddam's overthrow. "He hit us several times and left us for dead. Fortunately after he left I managed to drag myself to the phone and call for help."[22] Abdul Razzak Nayif, the former Iraqi prime minister who had helped the Baathists seize power in 1968, was not so fortunate. In July 1978 he was murdered as he left the InterContinental Hotel in London. The assassins fired two bullets into his head at point-blank range. The police later arrested two Iraqis who were charged with his murder. It later transpired that they were members of the Estikhbarat, the Iraqi equivalent of Britain's Special Air Service (SAS), military intelligence agents responsible for conducting overseas operations. The assassination sparked a diplomatic row between London and Baghdad, particularly as the British government was in the process of hosting the latest round of peace talks between Israel and Egypt. Britain expelled eight Iraqi intelligence officers and barred three others from entering the country, citing its "increasing concern at the threat posed by terrorist activities in London, particularly against Arab targets. The presence in London of a number of known Iraqi intelligence officers has led us to the conclusion that it would be best that they should leave."[23] The Iraqis did not take the expulsions lying down. A similar number of British diplomats were expelled from Baghdad. The Iraqis arrested British businessmen who were working in Iraq on contracts. The businessmen were charged and convicted on trumped-up spying charges, and given lengthy prison sentences. Saddam also issued a directive instructing ministries and state organizations not to do any business with Britain, and a total trade embargo on British goods was immediately enforced.

When diplomatic channels were eventually reestablished between London and Baghdad, and British diplomats made representations asking for the release of the jailed businessmen, the Iraqis made it clear that there would be no deal unless Britain first agreed to release the two Iraqi intelligence officers jailed for Nayif's murder. "We received several Iraqi delegations in London and they could not understand why we would not free the killers," recalled a British diplomat who handled the negotiations at the time. "They thought it was simply a matter of a trade-off. But there was no way the British government could interfere with the due process of law."[24] More than twenty years later the two assassins were still serving their life sentences in British jails.

Saddam's first flirtation with the world of international terrorism gradually came to an end in late 1978. The signing of the Camp David Accords in September 1978 between President Anwar Sadat of Egypt and the Israeli prime minister, Menachem Begin, was a watershed moment in the history of

Middle East diplomacy. While much of the world applauded the peace treaty between Egypt and Israel, Saddam saw it as an opportunity to reposition Iraq as the figurehead of Arab opposition against Israel, a position that had once been held by Nasser. The previous year Saddam had gone on the record in a rare interview with an American newsmagazine in stating his opposition to the peace deal being mooted by the Carter administration. By far the most significant message to emerge from the interview was Saddam's personal antipathy toward the existence of the state of Israel. While stressing that he personally had nothing against the Jewish people, he nevertheless declared himself to be a committed anti-Zionist. "We will never recognize the right of Israel to live as a separate Zionist state," he declared.[25] A year later Saddam saw in Sadat's "betrayal" an opportunity to assert his own position in Arab politics, and to that end he organized a summit in Baghdad in late 1978 to discuss how best to respond to Egypt. This required Saddam to improve relations with Saudi Arabia and the Gulf states, and to make overtures to President Asad of Syria to set aside the Baathist schism that had poisoned relations between the two countries for much of the 1970s. It was also in Saddam's interests to repair his relations with Yasser Arafat, who was still regarded as the undisputed leader of the Palestinian cause. Arafat, of course, felt badly betrayed by the outcome at Camp David, having been led to believe that the Palestinian issue would be resolved during the peace talks, only to discover that Sadat had in effect opted for a unilateral peace deal with the Israelis. While the Baghdad summit was in progress, Saddam called Arafat into his office to outline his new policy. According to Palestinian officials who were present at the meeting, Saddam promised to drop his support for Abu Nidal, who was still busily assassinating Arafat's key officials, if Arafat promised to support Iraq's anti-Sadat initiative. "I can tell you at once that we will sanction no further operations against you mounted from Baghdad," Saddam assured Arafat. "We will no longer take responsibility for his [Abu Nidal] actions—and we have told him so."[26]

Saddam's decision to scale down his involvement with terror groups provided him with an opportunity to reassess Iraq's international standing. The diplomatic spat with Britain in the summer of 1978 had meant that Baghdad now found itself facing diplomatic isolation from two of the West's key powers as it had already severed relations with the United States following the 1967 Six Day War. From the mid-1970s onward, however, there had been signs of a sea change taking place in Baghdad's diplomatic orientation. Saddam, who had been responsible for negotiating the Soviet pact in 1972, had been increasingly skeptical about the necessity of maintaining good relations with Moscow, particularly after the Soviets let him down so badly during his offensive against the Kurds in 1974–1975. An early indication of Baghdad's softening position toward the United States had been provided in April 1975 when Saddam granted an interview to the distinguished *New York Times* correspondent C. L. Sulzberger. Although the official Iraqi position remained staunchly anti-American because of Washington's support for Israel, Saddam was keen to send out a softer message because he wanted to incorporate the best Western technology, particularly that from the United States, in his master plan for modernizing Iraq. Even without formal diplomatic ties, trade with the United States had grown almost tenfold between 1971 and 1975. So far as Saddam was concerned, he saw no contradiction between Iraq maintaining its position as a fierce critic of American policy and being one of the largest consumers of American goods in the Middle East. "American policy as it is now conducted is our enemy," he informed Sulzberger. "But the Arabs, of whom we are a part, are not against the American state or the American people; only against American policy. We feel uncomfortable about U.S. meddling in our internal affairs, in the regional policy of the Middle East. If there is a change in this, we shall respond immediately."[27] Saddam returned to this theme again during his *Newsweek* interview in 1978. When asked about the prospect of a restoration of diplomatic ties between Baghdad and Washington, Saddam repeated his insistence that the United States must scale down its commitment to Israel. "There are other major issues, such as your complete support for the Zionist entity [Israel] and your deliberate strategy of dividing the Arab world, that stand in the way of normal relations."[28] As the American diplomat on the ground whose task it was to make sense of Baghdad's flirtation with Washington, David Mack found it hard to know just how seriously to take Saddam. "On one level they were supporting all these terrorist groups who were running around bombing Europe, and they never missed an opportunity to berate us for our policy on Israel. But on another level they were very keen to do business with the U.S. Our basic problem, though, with the regime at that time was Baghdad's support for all those terror groups. Until they sorted that out we were not going to play ball, and we made that perfectly clear."[29] Indeed, relations between Washington and Baghdad would not be properly restored until the summer of 1984, when the ruinous toll of the Iran-Iraq War would force Saddam to drop his opposition to Washington's pro-Israeli stance.

By the late 1970s Saddam's position as "the strongman of Baghdad" had gained general acceptance in the outside world and any Western diplomat or journalist seeking a meeting with the Baath leadership was steered toward Saddam, and not Bakr. Certainly by this time Saddam had taken complete control of foreign policy, as he was to make abundantly clear in his increasingly fraught dealings with Moscow. Saddam was determined to wean Iraq off its dependency on Soviet support, and in the May 1978 he fired another shot across Moscow's bows by executing twenty-one communist military officers who had been languishing in jail in Baghdad since 1975. The Baath had already declared that no political activity was allowed within the military other than Baath political activity. Even though the communists had been arrested before the Baath ruling was announced, in their cases Saddam decided to enact the ruling retroactively, and the officers were executed. To start with, a half dozen of the officers were shot. The Soviet ambassador was outraged and personally visited Saddam to protest. As a consequence of his visit ten more of the officers were shot. The Soviets then ordered the heads of the East bloc missions to plead for mercy. They too were ignored and the remaining five prisoners were marched before a firing squad. Not content with this humiliation for the Soviets, Saddam banned Soviet transport planes from using Iraq airspace to ferry military supplies to Ethiopia, which Moscow was backing in its war against Eritrean rebels. For good measure, Saddam supported the Eritrean campaign, and let rebel groups train in Baghdad. Finally Saddam demanded that the Russians relocate their embassy, which was situated next door to the Presidential Palace. Saddam suspected the KGB, no doubt correctly, of monitoring his conversations inside the palace and at the adjoining Baath Party headquarters. When the Soviets refused to move, Saddam reacted by cutting off the water and electricity supplies to the Soviet compound. A few days later the Russians announced that they would, after all, be moving into new premises.

Iraq's worsening relations with Moscow was one of the main subjects of discussion when Saddam agreed to be interviewed on the anniversary of the July 17 revolution, exactly a year before he was to seize power from Bakr. When asked whether the Iraqi officers had been executed as a warning to Moscow to keep out of Iraq's internal affairs, Saddam replied unhesitatingly: "Yes, it was." Then, giving vent to the visceral hatred of communism that had been the most compelling feature of Saddam's career in the Baath, he remarked: "They [the Soviets] won't be satisfied until the whole world becomes Communist." And asked whether, in view of Baghdad's uncompromising hostility to Israel, he believed that war was the only solution, Saddam replied simply: "Correct." He also predicted that in ten years time—i.e., by 1988—the Arab states would be strong enough to defeat Israel. "The Arabs won't always be weak. Their strength is growing daily. In ten years you will see a completely different equation."[30] This was a clear reference to Saddam's secret project for Iraq to develop its own nuclear arsenal, a project about which the outside world still knew very little.

While Camp David prompted the Iraqis to undertake a reassessment of their foreign policy goals, it was the waning fortunes of the shah in neighboring Iran that was to be the decisive factor in Saddam's calculation that the time had arrived for him to make his move against President Bakr. Saddam came to the conclusion that the aging Bakr would be unable to deal with the menace posed by the new radical Islamic government in Teheran. All the reforms carried out by the Baathists during the 1970s were designed to turn Iraq into a modern, secular state, albeit one governed by an autocracy. The prospect of an Islamic revolution enveloping neighboring Iran filled the Iraqi Baathists with deep conern. As the world's largest Shiite Muslim nation, an Islamic regime in Teheran would inevitably destabilize Iraq's large Shiite community in the south, which felt alienated from the Sunni Muslim, and secular, Baathist regime in Baghdad. Despite the Baathists' cynical attempts to buy them off with free television sets and refrigerators, the Shiites, like the Kurds and the communists, remained a perpetual thorn in the side of the regime. In 1977 bloody confrontations had broken out in the Shiite holy city of Najaf, which was then the home of the exiled Iranian Islamic leader Ayatollah Ruhollah Khomeini. Clashes between the Shiites and the government resulted in eight Iraqi clerics being arrested, tried by a revolutionary court, and executed. More than two thousand Shiites were arrested, and an estimated two hundred thousand were expelled to Iran by Saddam on the grounds that they were non-Iraqis. In October 1978 the Iraqis, at the request of the shah, expelled Ayatollah Khomeini, who had been living in exile in southern Iraq since the 1960s. In an attempt to shore up the shah, Saddam received Empress Farah in Baghdad, amid much pomp. Although the shah had not always been well disposed toward Iraq's Baathist regime, he was nevertheless the signatory, with Saddam, of the Algiers Agreement on the Shatt al-Arab dispute, and Saddam believed that maintaining the agreement, and therefore keeping the shah in power, was crucial to his own survival.

By now all these gestures of support were of no avail as it soon became clear that the Pahlavi dynasty was doomed. In February 1979 Khomeini returned in triumph to Teheran, signaling the start of the revolution that was to turn Iran into one of the world's most uncompromising Islamic regimes. The challenge posed by both the Camp David agreement and the emergence of a radical Islamic government in Iran persuaded Saddam that he could no longer afford to run the country from his position as "Mr. Deputy." The challenges ahead would require firm government, and Bakr was no longer capable of providing the leadership needed. Due to the gradual erosion of his authority by Saddam, Bakr was now reduced to a rather pathetic figure signing the pieces of paper Saddam placed on his desk. Bakr had become so ineffectual that Saddam was overheard complaining that Bakr did not even merit the salary he was receiving. A measure of the contempt Saddam felt for Bakr at the end of their professional relationship is provided by one of his biographers: "The military man spends his spare time on things that have no bearing on affairs of state. He wakes up early in the morning and goes into his garden; he waters the plants and trims the bushes. When he tires, he rests awhile in the company of his grandchildren. He lives with his memories."[31]

SEVEN

Mr. President

All the patience, all the hard work, all the plotting and scheming, all the betrayals, murders, executions, and assassinations finally paid off in July 1979 when Saddam became president of Iraq. The announcement was made, with exquisite timing, by the outgoing president, Ahmad Hassan al-Bakr, on the eve of the annual celebrations to mark the July 17 revolution. The date had been carefully chosen by Saddam to symbolize the continuity of the revolution, and was the culmination of months of carefully considered plotting. Saddam kept the precise details of his accession a closely guarded secret; the highly suspicious "Mr. Deputy" knew that a last-minute hiccup could ruin everything. Saddam's masterstroke, however, was to persuade Bakr himself not only to consent to the handover, but to appear on Iraqi television and portray his own purging as a natural transition of power. "For a long time," the sixty-five-year-old president told his listeners, "I have been talking to my Comrades in the Command, particularly cherished Comrade Saddam Hussein, about my health, which no longer allows me to shoulder the responsibilities with which the Command has honored me. My health has recently reached the stage where I could no longer assume responsibility in a manner that satisfies my conscience." In a voice shaking with emotion, Bakr went on to nominate Saddam as "the man best qualified to assume the leadership." Before bowing out of public life, Bakr paid a final tribute to Saddam, his erstwhile protégé.

"During the bitter years of struggle prior to the revolution, Comrade Saddam Hussein was a brave and faithful struggler who enjoyed the respect and trust of the party's strugglers. On the eve of the revolution, he was at the head of the brave men who stormed the bastions of dictatorship and reaction. During the revolution's march he was the brilliant leader who was able to confront all the difficulties and shoulder all the responsibilities."[1]

At the age of forty-two (or thereabouts) Saddam had taken control of one of the wealthiest countries in the Middle East. Buoyed by the oil wealth, Iraq was rapidly emerging as one of the region's dominant political, military, and economic powers. The government could boast some $35 billion in foreign exchange reserves, and the oil riches were beginning to permeate every aspect of Iraqi life. The armed forces were expanding rapidly and starting to benefit from the new, sophisticated equipment purchased from countries such as Spain and France. The Baathists had created the Arab world's first welfare state, with free education for all children from kindergarten to university, and a free national system of health care. The standard of living for ordinary Iraqis was gradually rising; basic foodstuffs were plentiful and cheap. For Iraqis who did not challenge the Baathist system, there had never been a better time to be an inhabitant of Iraq. The Baathists' success in diverting the new oil wealth toward building a modern, industrialized nation, a nation that was strong militarily and politically united, had prompted some commentators to describe Iraq as the Prussia of the eastern Arab world. Saddam could not have chosen a better moment to assume control of the country. Unlike his predecessor, however, Saddam had no intention of sharing power. His was to be an absolutist dictatorship. Apart from his position as president of the republic, Saddam held all the country's top positions: he was chairman of the Revolutionary Command Council, secretary-general of the Baath Party Regional Command, prime minister, and commander of the armed forces. Modeling himself on Stalin, Saddam had become the supreme leader of Iraq.

Precisely how Saddam managed to get Bakr to step down has always been regarded as something of a mystery. The issue of Bakr's declining health, the official reason given for his "retirement," cannot be entirely dismissed. Rumors were constantly in circulation among Baghdad's gossip-driven diplomatic community about Bakr's physical well-being. As early as 1971 Bakr had been hospitalized for what was reported in the Iraqi media as a "slight indisposition." In 1974 he was said to have suffered a cerebral hemorrhage, which prevented him from attending his wife's funeral.[2] His indisposition had also meant his being unable to receive French prime minister Jacques Chirac when he visited Baghdad; Saddam, that great Francophile, had effortlessly filled the breach. In May 1977 a distinguished medical team from George Washington University had flown in secret to Baghdad to treat "a top Iraqi official," whom everyone took to be Bakr.[3] Apart from his poor health Bakr had also had to contend with a number of deeply upsetting personal bereavements through the deaths of his wife, son, and son-in-law.

Even so it is unlikely that Bakr would have resigned his position without a fight and, according to former Baath Party members interviewed for the first time by this author, the meeting at which Bakr was persuaded to stand down quickly became acrimonious. Having decided to assume power on the anniversary of the revolution, Saddam, together with his cousin Adnan, the defense minister, and his uncle, Khairallah Tulfah, went to see Bakr in his office at the Presidential Palace on the evening of July 16, 1979. "They essentially presented him with a fait accompli," recalled one former Baathist. "They told him: 'You step down voluntarily and nothing will happen to you. But if we are forced to take action it could be very unplesant.' " At this point Bakr's son Haytham, who was in the room with his father, drew his gun and fired a shot in the air as a warning to Saddam's group, whom he denounced as traitors. But he was quickly overpowered and disarmed, and Saddam and his backers were able to get their way.[4] The next day Saddam assumed the presidency and Bakr made a dignified resignation speech.

Bakr should have anticipated Saddam's move. He had received plenty of warnings about Saddam's ambition to replace him and, earlier in the year, had revived the idea of unifying the Iraqi and Syrian Baath Parties, a plan devised in part to undermine Saddam, who was strongly anti-Syrian. Apart from putting Saddam in his place, the other, more pressing, motivation for the proposed union was the desire of the regimes in Damascus and Baghdad to present a united Arab front that could challenge Egypt's historic peace agreement with Israel, which had been negotiated at Camp David the previous year. Iraq and Syria, which were ideologically and vehemently opposed to the existence of Israel, regarded the Camp David agreement as a sellout, not least because it left the Palestinian issue unresolved. With Egypt no longer an ally in the struggle to destroy Israel, the Syrian and Iraqi Baath Parties in October 1978 agreed to set aside their own long-standing ideological differences in order to establish a "joint charter for national action"—i.e., against Israel.

Saddam was given personal responsibility for negotiating the deal to unite the two countries with Syria's president Asad, and in January Saddam became the first senior Iraqi politician to visit Damascus in ten years, during which he signed a deal to merge the two countries' respective ministries of foreign affairs, defense, and information. This was regarded as a first step toward a total union, which was scheduled to take place the following April. Apart from the challenge presented by Camp David, Iraq was also keen to cement its relationship with Syria as a means of protecting itself from the new threat posed by Iran's Islamic revolution after Ayatollah Khomeini seized power in February 1979. Speaking shortly after Khomeini had seized power, Saddam spoke enthusiastically about the proposed Iraq-Syria merger, declaring that "this unity was not a system, but rather the principal part of the entire Arab revolution." He also made a conciliatory gesture toward the new regime in Teheran, saying that "Iraq would support whatever the Iranian people decided."[5] The Iranian revolution had undoubtedly unsettled the Baathists, and even Saddam was prepared to set aside his natural anti-Syrian sympathies to build a united front against the Islamic extremists who had taken control in Teheran.

Even though Saddam was responsible for negotiating the union between Iraq and Syria, he was unable to overcome his strong reservations about the enterprise, which became more pronounced the longer the negotiations continued. His biggest concern appears to have been that a linkup with Syria would limit his power. Saddam therefore set about undermining the proposal, while at the same time giving the appearance that he was deeply committed to the union project. When President Asad, for example, came to Baghdad on June 16, 1979, to discuss the latest proposals, Saddam snubbed him by refusing to go to the airport to meet him. Bakr went in his place, and after three days of talks, Bakr and Asad announced a declaration of unity under which the governments of the two countries would be merged as a means of confronting "the Zionist-imperialist-Sadat onslaught."[6] Under the terms of the proposal, Syria and Iraq would become a loose federation, with Bakr at its head, Asad as deputy, and Saddam as number three. This arrangement was unacceptable to Saddam. As things currently stood in Baghdad, Saddam was already the de facto number one, and the prospect of being relegated to the position of number three in the newly merged nation did not appeal to him, particularly as he knew that, given Bakr's indifferent health, Asad would become the main power in the new union, in the same way that Saddam had become the undisputed power in an independent Iraq. If the union went ahead, moreover, Asad would purge Saddam in the same way that Saddam had dispensed with his own rivals. The only way for Saddam to prevent the federation from taking place, and remove the threat to his own career, was to seize power himself. No matter how much Bakr might desire the Iraq-Syria union, the initiative had come too late; from the mid-1970s onward, Saddam had effectively been running the country, and his vaulting ambition was not about to be inconvenienced by the new constitutional arrangements being advanced by his Baathist colleagues. The Syrian writer Patrick Seale wrote that, shortly before Saddam assumed control, Bakr sent a message to Asad, asking him to speed up the proposed union between Iraq and Syria because "there is a current here which is anxious to kill the union in the bud before it bears fruit."[7] No prizes for guessing the identity of the "current."

The brutal truth of the matter was that, by the summer of 1979, Bakr was powerless to reclaim the authority that he had gradually allowed to devolve to Saddam during the past decade. Former Baathist officials insist that the support Saddam received in his quest for supreme power from Khairallah Tulfah and his cousin Adnan was a decisive factor in persuading Bakr to step down. They were able to put pressure on Bakr to resign "for the good of the clan."[8] At any rate a special closed session of the Revolutionary Command Council was convened on July 11, 1979, at which it was decided to replace Bakr the following week, and for all his powers—and most of his titles—to be transferred to Saddam Hussein. Bakr's humiliation did not end with his removal from office. Three months after Saddam's takeover, Bakr was stripped of his last remaining title, that of deputy secretary-general of the Baath Party, which he had been given as an honorary title after being deposed as president; it was the same position that he himself had given the young Saddam in the late 1960s. Bakr died three years later in 1982 in complete obscurity during one of Iraq's darkest moments in the Iran-Iraq War, and amid rumors that he should be restored to power. According to previously unpublished information obtained by this author, Bakr was killed by a team of doctors who worked for Saddam's security apparatus and were sent to treat him when rumors began to circulate that Bakr was preparing a comeback. Apart from a heart condition Bakr was known to suffer from a variety of ailments, such as diabetes, hypertension, and kidney problems. His usual doctors were banned from attending to him for a month. During this period the team sent by Saddam injected Bakr with a large dose of insulin, which caused him to go into a coma. He never regained consciousness, and Saddam's doctors stayed by his side until they were sure he was dead.[9] In this way Saddam repaid the generosity, encouragement, and support of the mentor and kinsman who had been the most important influence on his life and career.

If Saddam's accession to the presidency was seamless, that is not to say it was unopposed. During the special meeting of the RCC at which it was decided to remove Bakr, Muhie Abdul Hussein Mashhadi, the RCC's secretary-general, summoned the courage to protest against Saddam's promotion. During the discussions Mashhadi had "suddenly stood up and demanded that they vote on the question of President Bakr relinquishing his responsibilities in the Party and the State to Saddam Hussein. He insisted that the decision be carried unanimously. 'It is inconceivable that you should retire,' he told Bakr. 'If you are ill why don't you take a rest?' "[10] Opposition such as this had to be eliminated, and Saddam acted quickly. On July 15, the day before Bakr was to resign, it was announced that Mashhadi had been relieved of all his duties at the RCC.

Even by the standards of Stalin's great purges in the 1930s, the process by which Saddam clinically set about removing any surviving Baathist rivals in the wake of his accession added a whole new dimension to the concept of state-inspired terror. Mashhadi had not been alone in opposing Saddam's accession, and many senior Baathists had supported Bakr's attempts to revive the union with Syria as a means of thwarting Saddam, irrespective of their feelings about the Camp David Accords. They had begged Bakr to provide them with the breathing space to put in place a strategy to counter Saddam's seemingly unstoppable march on the presidency, but Bakr was too old, weak, and exhausted to countenance a confrontation with his deputy. This last attempt by the Baath Party to bring the Saddam juggernaut to a halt therefore succeeded only in making the president-in-waiting aware that his popularity did not extend to all areas of the Baath.

True to character, Saddam resolved that his enemies would be shown no mercy, and the manner in which he set to work purging the party demonstrated not only his mastery of the psychology of terror, but his own formidable organizational skills. His first move, then, was to relieve Mashhadi of his duties as secretary-general of the RCC. The removal of Mashhadi was astute, for he was the only Baathist opposed to Saddam who had the authority to convene the RCC to discuss Bakr's successor. With Mashhadi out of the way, the party's ability to challenge Saddam was severely limited. Mashhadi, furthermore, was subjected to the customary interrogation by torture which, by 1979, had become even more sophisticated. Mashhadi's family was brought into the room where the sedated form of the former RCC secretary-general was sitting. Mashhadi was given two choices: he either cooperated with Saddam, and provided him with the list of names he required, or his interrogators would rape his wife and daughters in front of him before killing them. Mashhadi himself would be executed as an Israeli spy. Mashhadi went for the former option. Not only was Mashhadi persuaded to confess to any number of plots and conspiracies, he was willing to name his accomplices, who, conveniently for the new president, just happened to be the same people who were opposed to Saddam's accession.[11]

The stage, then, was set for Saddam to present his master class in state-sponsored persecution. Saddam was clearly delighted with the arrangements he had made for his Great Purge, so much so that he ordered that the entire proceedings be filmed for posterity, both as a warning to future opponents and to demonstrate his complete mastery over the regime's political and security structures. The venue chosen for the most brutal and far-reaching purge of his entire career was the Al-Khuld conference center in Baghdad, which resembled a large movie theater and was located opposite the Presidential Palace. On July 22, five days after his inauguration, Saddam convened an extraordinary conference of senior Baath Party members. Most of the one thousand or so delegates who had traveled from all parts of the country to attend this historic gathering would have been at least vaguely aware that the party's senior hierarchy had been indulging in yet another bout of infighting, but none of them could have guessed at the dramatic events that were about to unfold.

The film of the conference that was made especially for Saddam opens with Saddam nonchalantly sitting in a chair to one side of the platform, the personification of relaxation. As the proceedings get under way, he puffs, almost distractedly, on a large Cuban cigar. The conference opens with an address by Taha Yassin Ramadan, a close associate of Saddam who was the newly appointed vice president and head of the party's militia, the Popular Army. Other key loyalists are also visible on the stage including Izzat al-Douri, Saddam's second-in-command in the Baath and deputy secretary-general of the RCC; Tariq Aziz, the new foreign minister, and General Adnan Khairallah, the chief of staff and the cousin with whom Saddam had been raised by his uncle in Tikrit.

As Saddam looks on, his face almost concealed behind a plume of cigar smoke, Ramadan announces the exposure of "a painful and atrocious plot." Ramadan speaks in a sad and melancholic voice, trying hard to give the impression that the betrayal of the party by some of its most prominent members has caused him personal grief. The rapt audience is then moved to genuine astonishment when Ramadan announces that all the plotters are actually present in the conference room, and that they have been invited to the meeting without realizing that they are about to be exposed as traitors. Pausing for dramatic effect, Ramadan then invites Saddam to address the audience. Putting his cigar to one side, Saddam steps up to the podium. Dressed in a smart, tailor-made single-breasted suit with a neatly knotted tie, Saddam stands with his hands held loosely behind his back as he addresses the audience. His voice is measured and his demeanor oozes self-confidence. He speaks slowly, without notes, leaving lengthy pauses between each sentence for added impact. In the past, Saddam begins, he has always been able to rely on his sixth sense to warn him when there is trouble brewing. In this instance, however, although aware that the party was in danger—because of the planned merger with Syria—he has waited for the right moment before moving against his enemies. "We used to be able to sense a conspiracy with our hearts before we even gathered the evidence," he says. "Nevertheless we were patient and some of our comrades blamed us for knowing this but doing nothing about it."[12] But now he believes he has sufficient evidence to denounce the traitors. At that moment Saddam invites Mashhadi, who has been brought from prison to attend the meeting, onto the platform to narrate the details of the "horrible crime." Mashhadi, a middle-aged man with graying hair and a neat mustache, is also smartly dressed, and speaks in a measured tone as he explains the details of the plot, occasionally waving his finger in the air for emphasis.

Saddam had, in all probability, promised to spare Mashhadi's life in return for his agreement to address the conference and denounce his former colleagues. Certainly if he had known the true fate that awaited him it is unlikely that he would have been able to put on such a convincing show. As Mashhadi delivers his denunciation, the camera shows Saddam sitting back in his seat, puffing on his cigar and looking rather bored by the proceedings, as though he has heard it all before.

Mashhadi's speech has been well rehearsed. He provides the audience with full details of the conspiracy: dates, places of meetings, and, most shocking of all, the names of the participants. Mashhadi, a Shiite who has been a member of the Baath for twenty years, reveals how he has, since 1975, been part of a Syrian plot to overthrow both Saddam and Bakr in order to pave the way for a Syrian-Iraqi union. When the conspirators had realized that Bakr was about to step down in favor of his deputy, Mashhadi relates, they tried to persuade the president to change his mind, knowing that if Saddam took over, the prospects of a union with Syria would be dashed. President Asad himself is alleged to have had several meetings with the plotters to advise them how to deal with Saddam.

When Mashhadi has finished his testimony, Saddam returns to the podium. He tells the audience how stunned he has been to discover that he has been betrayed by his closest colleagues. "After the arrest of the criminals," he says, "I visited them in an attempt to understand the motive for their behaviour. 'What political differences are there between you and me?' I asked, 'did you lack any power or money? If you had a different opinion why did you not submit it to the Party since you are its leaders?' They had nothing to say to defend themselves, they just admitted their guilt." Finally Saddam ends his speech by declaring, "The people whose names I am going to read out should repeat the party slogan and leave the hall."[13] Saddam produces a list, which is read out by one of the security officials. A sense of terror grips the room as the first of the alleged conspirators is led from the room, escorted by specially selected, armed members of the Baath Party's security apparatus. The security operation is overseen by Barzan al-Tikriti, Saddam's half brother, who has worked closely with Saddam in making the arrangements for the purge. One by one the denounced delegates are escorted from the conference hall by Barzan's guards while Saddam watches from his chair at the podium, occasionally puffing on his cigar.

A total of sixty-six people, including some of Saddam's closest Baath Party colleagues, are denounced. Before leaving the conference hall, the condemned men are required to recite the party oath: "One Arab nation with a holy message! Unity, freedom and socialism!" The only time that Saddam takes an interest in the procession is when one of the accused attempts to speak out against the injustice of the event. Without raising his voice, Saddam interrupts him and, referring to Mashhadi's speech, says, "The witness has just given us information about the leaders of the organization. Similar confessions were made by the ring leaders." Then, with a distinct hint of menace entering his voice, Saddam simply states, "Itla, itla." "Get out, get out!"

As this grotesque ritual proceeds, the surviving members of the audience begin to grasp the significance of what they are witnessing, the brutal exposition of their new leader's unconstrained power. Iraq is inexorably moving from a military dictatorship to a totalitarian regime where the will of the

Saddam's mother, Subha Tulfah.

A 1930s view of Tikrit, the town where Saddam spent much of his early life.

Saddam's I.D. photo at age twelve.

Saddam at age sixteen.

General Qassem's car, riddled with bullets from the assassination attempt. (AUTHOR'S COLLECTION)

After his assassination attempt against Abdul Karim al-Qassem in 1959, Saddam had burned all his photos before fleeing to Syria. Authorities found this picture of him from the al-Karkh Secondary School and sent it to security centers all over the country, offering a reward for his arrest.

Saddam by the Nile in 1960, during his exile.

Saddam in Egypt, 1960.

Saddam (top row, second from right) and his comrades pose for a souvenir photo before leaving prison. Abdul Karim al-Shaikhly, his fellow conspirator, is pictured bottom right. Nearly all the other prisoners, including Shaikhly, were subsequently killed on Saddam's orders.

Saddam in prison (far left in both photos) in 1965.

The first photo showing Saddam with his wife Sajida whom he married soon after his return from Cairo following the February 1963 revolution.

Saddam in the drawing room of his house with his wife Sajida, his two sons Uday and Qusay, and his three daughters, Hala (the youngest), Rana, and Raghda (the oldest).

Saddam Hussein, now vice president, brings his family to visit a family of peasants living in the suburbs of Baghdad. Several other families dropped in when news of their presence spread.

Executions of Jews in Baghdad soon after Baath came to power in February 1969.

(AUTHOR'S COLLECTION)

Saddam (wearing the white visor) swims in the Tigris River in Salahuddin near Tikrit. The official Iraqi news agency said Saddam swam across "the immortal Tigris" three times to encourage participants in a national swimming tournament. The man behind him is his bodyguard.

Saddam smoking a cigar during the infamous 1979 meeting of Baath's Revolutionary Command Council, at which key party members were denounced and subsequently executed. (AUTHOR'S COLLECTION)

Saddam praying in Kuwait after the 1990 invasion, shown on the front page of *Babel,* a newspaper run by Saddam's son Uday.

Saddam during the Gulf War in 1990 with Stuart Lockwood, a seven-year-old British hostage. (AUTHOR'S COLLECTION)

Saddam (sitting) and his family, including his sons-in-law, General Hussein Kamel Hassan (far left) and Hassan's brother Colonel Saddam Kamel (second from left). General Hassan and his brother were shot and killed February 23, 1996, in Baghdad by relatives who wanted to restore the family honor.

Saddam in a village near Baghdad, where he celebrated the last day of the Eid al-Fitr festival, which marks the end of the fasting month of Ramadan.

Saddam flanked by his two sons, Uday Hussein (left) and Qusay Hussein, in a photo released by the Iraqi government on December 13, 1996. Uday was shot and wounded during an attack while driving in the smart district of al-Mansour in Baghdad December 12. This was the first reported attack on Uday's life.

A painting depicting Saddam liberating Jerusalem, on display in Baghdad.

supreme leader will be paramount. As their denounced Baathist colleagues are forcibly removed from the chamber, the surviving rump rise to their feet to acclaim the country's undisputed leader. "Long live Saddam!" they chant. "God save Saddam from conspirators," they cry, along with "Let me die! Long live the father of Uday." Some of the delegates are so overcome with emotion that they start sobbing. Saddam himself also seems moved by these sudden outpourings of loyalty, and can be seen reaching with one hand for a tissue to wipe away a tear while with the other he holds his cigar.

Once the alleged conspirators have been removed from the hall, Saddam invites the audience to discuss the day's events, which is the cue for the more sycophantic members to ingratiate themselves with Saddam. One delegate declares, "Saddam Hussein is too lenient. There has been a problem in the party for a long time. . . . There is a line between doubt and terror, and unbalanced democracy. The problem of too much leniency needs to be addressed by the party." At this Saddam allows himself a wry smile. Another of the speakers is one of Saddam's cousins, Ali Hassan al-Majid, who will later earn himself the epithet "Chemical" Ali for deploying chemical weapons against the Kurds in 1988. "Everything that you did in the past was good and everything that you will do in the future is good. I say this from my faith in the party and your leadership."[14] After several more speeches, in which the delegates demand that other "traitors" are exposed, Saddam brings the meeting to a close by declaring, "We don't need Stalinist methods to deal with traitors here. We need Baathist methods." At that point Saddam, as a gesture of solidarity, comes down off the podium and takes a seat in the main auditorium among the surviving members of the RCC. As a final touch he invites them to help form the firing squads that will carry out the executions of the denounced conspirators.

Among those who were led away on this unforgettable day in the history of modern Iraq were a number of senior Baathists, some of whom were longstanding associates of Saddam's who had actually assisted him in his rise to power. Five of the RCC's twenty-one members, for example, were implicated in the plot, including Mashhadi.[15] Murtada al-Hadithi, the former oil minister who had laid the groundwork for the nationalization of the IPC in 1972, was among the victims. The most surprising name on the list was that of Adnan Hussein al-Hamdani, whom Saddam had only five days previously appointed his deputy prime minister and head of the president's office. Hamdani, an industrious and dedicated member of the Baath, owed his rise to the top of the party to Saddam's patronage. After the purge of the Baath that had taken place in 1973 following the Kazzar affair, Hamdani had taken charge of Saddam's personal office and worked on a range of key issues, including helping to establish Iraq's nonconventional weapons program. According to one of Hamdani's former colleagues, Saddam regarded him as his principal troubleshooter. "Hamdani was Saddam's main fixer. If Saddam needed someone to solve a problem he would turn to Hamdani. He knew more about the running of the country than Saddam himself."[16] Hamdani had been an exemplary servant of Saddam's and was trusted to the extent that he and his wife Sanaa were regular dining companions of Saddam and Sajida.

Like so many capable Baath officials, the more success Hamdani achieved, the more he aroused Saddam's suspicious nature. Various theories have been advanced for the demise of a man who had played such a role in the regime throughout the late 1970s, particularly in drawing up the master plan for Saddam's weapons of mass destruction program. One theory is that Hamdani became too venal in his dealing with numerous shady arms dealers; another is that, as one of the few Shiites in Saddam's inner circle, he was suspected of nurturing secret sympathies with his rebellious coreligionists.[17] Why Saddam should have promoted Hamdani just days before denouncing him is yet another mystery concerning this unsavory affair. Saddam's officials claimed that they knew about the so-called Syrian "plot" long before they acted, and so Saddam must have known he was about to destroy Hamdani when he appointed him to his new positions. The most likely explanation is that Saddam did not want to arouse suspicions about the macabre spectacle he was planning to affirm his complete mastery of the Baath. One of Hamdani's former colleagues claimed that two of Saddam's closest relatives were behind Hamdani's downfall. "I believe that the main reason he was purged is that he fell out with Barzan al-Tikriti and Adnan Khairallah"—Saddam's half brother and cousin respectively. "They simply did not like him, and they did not like the power he exercised. And so they had him denounced."[18] Hamdani, who believed he could speak his mind with Saddam, may also have expressed his reservations about Saddam's plan to replace Bakr. Hamdani was in favor of the union with Syria, and feared that Saddam's promotion would ruin the project. Certainly neither Hamdani nor his family had any inkling that he had caused Saddam mortal offense. On the day of Hamdani's execution his wife was on a shopping trip to Paris with Sajida Hussein.

The same day that Saddam exposed the "plot," a special court, comprising seven of the surviving members of the RCC, was set up under Naim

Haddad, the deputy prime minister. A total of fifty-five Baathists were convicted of involvement in the plot, of whom twenty-two were sentenced to death through "democratic executions." This form of capital punishment had been devised specially by Saddam, and required loyal Baathists to participate in the dispatch of their treacherous former colleagues. The executions were scheduled for August 8, and regional Baathist associations were each invited to send a delegate to participate in carrying out the death sentences. The executions were held in the courtyard of the same building in which the accused were alleged to have conceived their treachery. All those participating in the executions were personally provided with a handgun by Saddam, who led the way as the orgy of killing commenced.

The video Saddam later released on the denunciation of his colleagues contains footage of the executions being carried out. The camera shows the condemned men kneeling with blindfolds over their eyes, their wrists tied behind their backs. The camera then closes in showing a hand holding a gun, which fires a shot into the temple. The victims jerk and then crumple over, blood oozing from their heads in the dust. In some cases the shootings prove inaccurate, leaving the victims still alive. Because some of the executioners were not professional gunmen, they had either missed the intended target, or had lost their nerve at the last minute. In these instances the camera shows a professional executioner applying the coup de grâce with a pistol shot to the head. It was later reported that the execution of Hamdani was one of those that was botched, and he was left writhing on the ground after the first bullet failed to do its job. Barzan al-Tikriti, Saddam's half brother who had been responsible for Hamdani's denunciation in the first place, finished him off by firing two bullets into his head.[19]

The idea of inviting the Baath leadership to participate in the "democratic executions" was a clever ploy by Saddam, turning the killings into a glorified tribal bonding session. In a country where blood feuds run deep, even over so-called judicial killings, Saddam had implicated the surviving Baath hierarchy in "cleansing" the party and thereby forced them to give him their undivided loyalty. For example, by making Naim Haddad, one of the leading Shiites in the new government, pass judgment over two other prominent Shiites in the Baath, Mohammed Ayesh and Hamdani, Saddam had guaranteed Haddad's ostracism from his own community and increased his dependence on the new president. This was to be a tactic that would become a distinctive feature of Saddam's rule; by forcing officers and officials to participate in barbaric acts, he was irredeemably tarnishing their reputations and linking their fate to that of the regime.

Having dispensed with the last of his rivals, Saddam set about turning the proceedings into a propaganda coup for himself. Copies of the video recording of the special conference were circulated to Baath members throughout the country. Details of the "plot" itself were not made public until the morning of the executions when an official announcement was broadcast on state radio. The executions, it was reported, in which hundreds of delegates, the president, and the entire RCC had participated, had been an "unprecedented event in the history of the party." The executions had been carried out "amid cheers for the long life of the Party and the Revolution, and the Leader, President, Struggler, Saddam Hussein."[20] Having spent the morning participating in the executions, a relaxed Saddam appeared later the same day to address the nation about the discovery of the conspiracy. All the old Baathist paranoia was in evidence when Saddam spoke. Not only was exposure of the "plot" a great achievement for the Baath revolution; it was also a humiliating defeat for the "foreign forces" that had backed it. "We pity the traitors and conspirators outside Iraq," he told the huge crowd that had gathered in the gardens of the Presidential Palace, "who laboured for more than five years and all they could win over were these 55 individuals."[21] Just like the Soviets after the 1917 revolution, Saddam was deliberately seeking to rally the nation behind his leadership by stoking the fires of xenophobia.

In Damascus President Asad, a formidable Baathist figure in his own right, was deeply disturbed to see the new entente between Syria and Iraq sacrificed on the altar of Saddam's irresistible ambition. After Saddam made his speech accusing Asad of masterminding the plot against the Iraqi Baath, Asad protested furiously, and demanded to see the evidence. He sent his foreign minister, Abdul Halim Khaddam, and his chief of staff to Baghdad to assure Saddam that if Iraq had any proof of Syrian wrongdoing, those responsible would be punished. All they brought back was a rambling tape recording of Mashhadi's confession. Saddam turned down Asad's suggestion that Iraq's allegations be examined by an Arab League committee. It is unlikely that Syria was entirely innocent of Saddam's allegations, and certainly Asad would have preferred to have an amenable figure such as Bakr in charge of the neighboring Baathist regime rather than Saddam. But once Saddam had emerged triumphant from his Baghdad power play, the more statesmanlike option would have been for the new Iraqi leader to put the past behind him and exploit Syria's willingness to improve relations. Saddam's insistence on snubbing Damascus, however, destroyed the entente and was mainly responsible for Asad forming an alliance with Iran's Ayatollah Khomeini, an alliance that would cause Saddam much heartache in the years to come.

The purge of the Revolutionary Command Council that accompanied Saddam's accession to the presidency in July 1979 was merely the start of a nationwide purge of party members and the military. From the outset of his rule Saddam was determined to ensure that the party and the armed forces posed him no threat. Although there are no precise figures, it is estimated that hundreds of party workers and military officers were purged from their positions; some of them were tortured and executed, and many received long prison sentences. Given that Saddam's security forces had already carried out an extensive purge of the Baath Party and the military during the early 1970s, it was quite an achievement that he was able to find any victims worth purging. The fundamental difference between the purges of 1969 and those of 1979 is that the earlier round of purges were directed at enemies of the Baath, while the 1979 purges were solely directed at anyone suspected of opposing Saddam Hussein.

Saddam's rise to supreme power provided him with the opportunity to settle several old scores. This was the moment that he chose to send his gunmen to murder his old friend and associate Abdul Karim al-Shaikhly, who had been out of active politics since 1971 when he was sent to the United Nations. Even in New York, Shaikhly did not take heed of the lessons he should have learned while indulging in his playboy lifestyle in Baghdad in the early 1970s. He should have known that everything he said, either in public or private, was being recorded and fed back to Saddam by his security agents, even in distant New York. But Shaikhly remained a model of indiscretion and never hesitated to speak his mind about what he thought the Baath had become under Saddam. Perhaps he felt that the close personal friendship he had once enjoyed with Saddam would protect him. Eventually, in late 1978, Saddam's patience snapped, and Shaikhly was ordered to return to Baghdad. Even this ominous summons did not unduly ruffle Shaikhly's composure, and he complied with the request. On arrival he was arrested and thrown into jail. Because he still enjoyed a strong following in the party and the country, the government decided that, rather than subject him to a show trial by a special military court, they would give him as normal a trial as possible. The judge complied with the request and when the trial eventually got under way the Iraqi public were treated to the unique spectacle of a defendant actually providing the court with a credible defense. After ten days, with Shaikhly calling a succession of witnesses to give evidence on his behalf, the trial was going nowhere, and Shaikhly faced the distinct possibility of being acquitted. At this point the government authorities intervened and, in a secret note to the judge, they ordered the court to resolve the case forthwith. Shaikhly was duly convicted of illegally criticizing the government and jailed for six years. But a year later, after Saddam became president, he was released. Thinking that his problems with Saddam were in the past, he attempted to adjust to normal civilian life. A few weeks after his release he set off with his pregnant wife to pay his telephone bill. As he got out of his car, he was shot dead by two of Saddam's assassins.

Similar treatment was meted out to other high-profile former Baathists. Another retired Baathist, Murtada Saad Abdul Baqi al-Hadithi, who had recently been Iraq's ambassador to the USSR despite losing his membership in the RCC in 1974, was executed in Baghdad in June 1980. Like Shaikhly, Hadithi had been recalled from Moscow in July 1979, arrested, and thrown in prison. Saddam had determined that his presidency would be run on the basis of absolute terror, a policy he rigorously pursued throughout his presidency. No dissent was too trivial or slight in Saddam's eyes. Any suggestion of opposition to Saddam's will was to be crushed ruthlessly and with the utmost brutality.

Salim Shakir, the former Iraqi army officer who had become a national hero in Iraq for his role in the 1973 Yom Kippur War, was one of the few survivors of Saddam's political purges of 1979. Shakir had been an active member of the Baath since the late 1950s, and had worked with Saddam to bring the Baath to power. A career army officer, he had commanded one of the tank units sent to fight Israel in the Yom Kippur War. After the war he served abroad as a military attaché, and by 1979 he was Iraq's ambassador to Senegal. Immediately after Saddam's accession he suddenly found himself accused of treachery, as were, according to his estimate, thousands of officers and officials from all walks of life. In common with many other Iraqi ambassadors at that time, Shakir received a call ordering him to return to Baghdad for "consultations" with Saddam. Shakir believed he was simply returning to Iraq to be briefed on the new government's diplomatic objectives, but as soon as he landed at Baghdad International Airport he was arrested and taken away for interrogation. When interviewed by this author many years later, Shakir, a short, smartly dressed, amiable man with a penchant for English tweeds, was suffering from partial deafness and tinnitus as a result of the beating he had received at one of Saddam's interrogation centers. "It is hard to describe the horror of that place. Everyone who went there was tortured to some extent. For Saddam torture was almost a way of life. I was lucky in that I was only beaten, but some of the others were not so fortunate. I believe I was only beaten because I was well-known as a war hero, and even these people had some respect for me."

Shakir was accused of plotting against Saddam and brought before the special revolutionary court chaired by Naim Haddad. The trial was a summary affair, so much so that Shakir was not even allowed to see his own affidavit, which, of course, he had no memory of making. "I had no chance whatsoever to defend myself," said Shakir. "The tribunal had already decided what to do with my case. I had been denounced as a traitor, and that was sufficient evidence for them." He received a seven-year jail sentence with hard labor. Shakir was never given specific details of his wrongdoing, and still does not know what he did to cause Saddam offense. "Saddam had always told me how proud he was of my military service and my role in the 1973 war," Shakir recalled. "Perhaps he was also jealous of me. He was very sensitive about the fact he had not served in the army himself, and it may well be that my record was an embarrassment for him." The only other explanation Shakir could provide for the treatment he suffered was a meeting he had with Saddam back in 1969, when he was asked to provide a list of officers' names for promotion. Saddam took exception to one of the names Shakir had put forward, claiming that the officer concerned nurtured pro-Syrian sympathies. Shakir attempted to defend the officer's reputation, but Saddam interjected by saying, "The problem between Syria and us is not political, economic, or philosophical. It is a matter of life and death." Shakir concluded that Saddam may have harbored a grudge against him since that exchange, and decided to act once he was in power. "You have to remember that Saddam had no real friends. He just had all those people around him who were terrified of him. Anyone who was close to Saddam was required to prove his or her loyalty to him all the time." According to Shakir, one of Saddam's favorite claims was "I can tell simply by looking in someone's eyes whether they are loyal or a traitor." Saddam was also prone to emotional displays, such as bursting into tears if one of his children hurt themselves in any way. "Saddam suffered from a split personality. He could be crying over his children while at the same time signing a death warrant for the execution of fifty people." On one occasion Shakir asked Saddam how he would feel if he executed the wrong man by mistake. "It is far better to kill an innocent man rather than to allow a guilty man to survive" was Saddam's unequivocal response.[22]

The purges removed any hint of opposition to Saddam's rule, and he quickly set about reorganizing the government in a way that further strengthened his power base. His first move was to increase the power of the cabinet while reducing its size to a handful of loyalist ministers. Many ministries were merged, and the day that he took office Saddam created the post of first deputy prime minister and five positions of deputy premier. Taha Yassin Ramadan was appointed to the first new position, and the five others were occupied by Adnan Khairallah, who still held the defense portfolio; Tariq Aziz, who had the foreign brief; Naim Haddad; Saadoun Ghaydan; and the ill-fated Hamdani. The restructuring of the cabinet, which was to hold regular meetings chaired by Saddam, was aimed at reducing the authority of the RCC, which Saddam continued to regard with suspicion, despite the purging of his enemies.

In March 1980 Saddam implemented another significant constitutional change by resurrecting the National Assembly, Iraq's state legislature that had fallen into abeyance after the overthrow of the monarchy in 1958. The new law provided for an assembly of 250 members who were to be elected by secret ballot every four years. If the assembly gave the impression, certainly to the outside world, that the new Iraqi regime had democratic pretensions, the reality was very different. The selection process for potential candidates was dictated by strict conditions. Each district was allowed only a single electoral list, thereby eliminating any competition among parties or groups. All candidates, who had to meet various criteria before they were accepted, had to adhere to the principles of the July revolution of 1968 and to submit themselves for examination by an election commission to receive permission to run. To ensure that the electorate was not left in any doubt as to how to cast its vote, Saddam declared: "We must ensure that the thirteen and a half million [the size of the Iraqi electorate] take the same road. He who chooses the twisted path will meet the sword."[23] The elections were held on June 20, 1980. Few voters opted for "the twisted path," and the assembly was filled with Baath appointees. Saddam's sardonic comment on the process was to the effect that his party's triumph in the elections was an indication that the Iraqi people had endorsed emphatically both the Baath candidates and Baathist principles.

Saddam's rise to power was accompanied by a significant increase in the activities of the Iraqi security services. A subtle restructuring of Saddam's security operations was undertaken, with the creation of Amn al-Khass, or Special Security, which became the state's all-powerful security arm. Amn al-Khass replaced the Mukhabarat, which had its size and authority substantially reduced. In effect Amn al-Khass became Saddam's personal security force, reporting directly to the president's office, which itself expanded to absorb the all-encompassing responsibilities of the new president. At the end of the 1970s it was estimated that the Presidential Affairs Department, which included Amn al-Khass, had nearly fifty-eight thousand employees on its payroll.[24]

New prisons were built and torture techniques devised to ensure the regime of terror functioned effectively. Technically torture was banned in Iraq under Article 22(a) of the Iraqi Constitution and Article 127 of the Code of Criminal Procedures. By the time Saddam came to power, however, it was estimated that the regime had perfected 107 different methods of torturing its enemies. Manual torture took the form of beatings, hair pulling, bastinado (beating with a stick on the soles of the feet), and the twisting of limbs until they broke. Electric shocks were commonly applied to extract confessions, and a wide range of psychological torture was also implemented. The standard form of torture was to place the victims in solitary confinement for long periods. Some prisoners were left in cold cells until their limbs froze, while on other occasions parts of the prisoners' bodies were set on fire. Another particular Iraqi specialty was to rape relatives of those detained—male and female—while the accused were forced to watch. Saddam's torturers could also make use of a variety of machines that were available for removing human limbs, from fingers to legs.

In a report issued in 1981, Amnesty International summarized the testimony of fifteen Iraqi exiles—twelve men and three women—who had been tortured by Saddam's security officials. All of them had been subsequently examined by physicians in London who found that in each case "the tortures described were consistent with the subsequent symptoms and the signs found during the physical examination." The Amnesty report provided a grueling account of the suffering inflicted on one of the Iraqi victims. "During the first two days he was taken to different rooms and beaten with fists, rods and a whip. . . . In one room he was caressed and sexually fondled, before being taken out and beaten and kicked. The torture then became more systematic, taking place every one or two hours. His head was whipped and beaten so hard that he lost consciousness. . . . After regaining consciousness on one occasion he was aware that his trousers had been removed and realized that he had been raped. He was then made to sit on a cold bottle-like object which was forced up his rectum. He was also burned with a hard object about the size of a pencil."[25]

As the apparatus of institutionalized torture became more widespread, so Saddam's security officials became less discriminating about their choice of victim. Another Amnesty investigation detailed the case of an Iraqi mother who went to the Baghdad morgue in September 1982 to collect her son's body. The boy had been arrested in December 1981 and held without charge or trial, and without his family knowing his whereabouts. When the woman entered the morgue, she could not believe her eyes. "I looked around and saw nine bodies stretched out on the floor with him . . . but my son was in a chair form . . . that is a sitting form, not sleeping or stretched. He had blood all over him and his body was very eaten away and bleeding. I looked at the others stretched out on the floor alongside him . . . all burnt . . . I don't know with what . . . another's body carried the marks of a hot domestic iron all over his head to his feet."[26] The detention of women and children was a common tactic used by Saddam's security forces, particularly when they were unable to capture the menfolk. There were well-documented cases of women being tortured in front of their families, or of husbands or children being tortured in front of their wives and mothers. When a female Iraqi journalist was detained, her inquisitors deprived her baby of food in an attempt to put pressure on her. Another female survivor of Saddam's torture chambers has recounted how sexual torture was commonly used against both women and children, and of children being placed in sacks with starving cats.[27]

By the mid-1980s the Iraqi authorities officially acknowledged that there were a total of twenty-four offenses that carried the death penalty: ten under the heading of offenses prejudicial to the external security of the state, ten for internal-security offenses, and the remainder for "offenses constituting a danger to the public." The definition of these capital offenses was deliberately vague so that any unauthorized disclosure of information could be interpreted as treason. Article 177 of the Iraqi penal code, for example, authorized the death penalty for "the disclosure of a state secret" by a public servant "in time of war or in furtherance of the interests of a foreign state." Almost all information in Iraq on government, the economy, and society was considered a state secret, and the disclosure of virtually any information to a foreign diplomat or journalist could be deemed a treasonable offense. The militant anti-Zionism of Saddam's regime was also reflected in Article 201 of the penal code, which specified the death penalty for "any person who propagates Zionist or Masonic principles or who joins or advocates membership of Zionist or Masonic institutions." In addition the death penalty was also applied to a range of civil crimes, such as murder, rape, arson, armed robbery, and sodomy. In the 1990s any Iraqi found to be suffering from the AIDS virus was subjected to summary execution.

There was precious little chance that those who found themselves accused of capital offenses might receive a fair trial. While the structure of religious, civil, criminal, and military courts remained intact, they were only allowed to deal with the more mundane cases. Any case that had a political dimension was likely to be referred to the Revolutionary Court in Baghdad, which had been established in 1969 and was made up of either three military or three civilian judges. Sentences passed by this court were final and not subject to appeal. Then there were the temporary special courts, which were run directly by the president's office. These courts did not require the services of professional lawyers but were drawn from members of the Revolutionary Command Council. It was courts such as these that were set up to try those involved in various coup attempts, and Saddam never had any difficulty securing the required verdict.[28] Amnesty International had the names of 520 people executed for political offenses between 1978 and 1981, and there were more than 300 executions in 1982.

In those cases where, for one reason or another, the security forces were unable to bring political opponents to trial, poison was used. Thallium was the most favored method, because it is odorless, colorless, and tasteless. From 1980 onward there were a number of reports of Iraqi activists being poisoned with thallium. In May 1980 two dissidents who had been in detention in Iraq made their way to London. They were examined by doctors and found to be suffering from thallium poisoning. One of them, Majidi Jehad, testified shortly before he died that he believed the poison had been given to him in an orange drink he was offered at the Baghdad police station where he went to pick up his passport.[29]

With the media firmly under government control, freedom of expression was not tolerated. From 1968 onward the Baath Party had set itself the goal of bringing the media under its control and making it an instrument for propagating Baath ideology. But in a report published in 1974, the party conceded that it had not yet reached these objectives, and lamented the fact that there were still too many "reactionary elements" lurking in the media and too few "competent and revolutionary executives." During the late 1970s these shortcomings were rectified, with membership of the Baath Party youth organization made a condition for entry to journalism school. Finally in 1980 Saddam established the General Federation of Academicians and Writers, and all journalists, writers, and artists were required to join, and any independent cultural and literary organizations that were still in existence were abolished. Saddam brought all artistic production, including music, under strict control and subjected it to government censorship. "For those who conform," a human rights activist wrote of Iraq in 1981, "there are excellent rewards. . . . For the first time in the country's history, poets can be found among the wealthy few." The price of conformity, however, was "to write verse for official occasions and festivities, praising the ruling Baath Party and its leaders . . . singing the praises of Saddam Hussein." Failure to do Saddam's bidding often resulted in imprisonment and torture, frequently ending in death, for hundreds of Iraqi writers and intellectuals.[30] A petition signed by Arab intellectuals and published in the Lebanese newspaper *As Safir* in December 1986 stated that in Iraq "more than 500 creative writers and thinkers have been subject to questioning and torture in order to extort avowals or to oblige them to modify their opinions."[31]

With the judiciary and media controlled directly by the government, the only redress open to Iraqi civilians was through the ranks of the Baath Party. But with Saddam's security forces monitoring all activity, the only criticism that was tolerated was that which glorified the achievements of the Iraqi leadership. The Baath was organized on classic Marxist-Leninist principles of hierarchy and discipline, and by the time Saddam assumed power the Baath had become a state within a state. It had its own training facilities, or "preparatory schools," where young members went to study ideology, economy, and politics. The party maintained "bureaus," which were run in parallel with government departments to ensure conformity and loyalty to Baathist principles. Other bureaus were charged with organizing and indoctrinating key groups of workers, such as the military, laborers, farmers, and professionals. Along with the military, the teaching profession was a prime target for Baath Party recruitment as the Baathists were determined to ensure the continuing indoctrination of young Iraqis. In 1979 all teachers were required to join the party, and those who refused, or were deemed ineligible, were fired. The party ran its own private militia, the Popular Army, as a coun-terbalance to the military establishment, which, despite all the purges that had been conducted over the years, was still viewed with deep suspicion by the Baathists. Saddam was particularly attracted to the concept of the Popular Army and in the first year of his presidency it more than doubled in size from 100,000 men to 250,000.

The situation in Iraq under Saddam's presidency was summed up by a group of moderate opposition writers living in exile, who wrote in a memo-randum submitted to the United Nations:

"The dictatorship of Saddam Hussein is one of the harshest, most ruthless and most unscrupulous regimes in the world. It is a totalitarian, one-party system based on the personality cult of Saddam Hussein. This man and his family and relatives have control over the regular army, People's Army, police and security services. All news media are under the strict control of the regime and there is no opportunity for freedom of expression. Political organization is limited to the Baath Party and a number of insignificant, obsequious organizations. Trade unions do not exist. Membership in any opposition party is punishable by death. Any criticism of the President is also punishable by death. Torture is the norm. The security system is all-powerful, omnipresent, and enjoys unlimited powers."

By 1980 every Iraqi institution, every government department, every aspect of public, private, and individual endeavor existed simply to glorify the achievements of Saddam Hussein. The deliberate attempt by Saddam to develop a cultlike status throughout Iraq had been under way since the mid-1970s. But after he was installed in the Presidential Palace, the cult of Saddam took on a life of its own. The cult of the leader under Saddam sur-passed anything seen elsewhere in the Arab world or, with the possible excep-tion of North Korea, beyond it. The glorification of the Iraqi president became one of the main enterprises of the country's press, radio, and televi-sion, and a thriving industry developed for the manufacture of posters, pic-tures, and other representations of the "father" of the revolution. Foreign journalists who were invited to cover the 1980 "election" for the National Assembly were struck at the number of posters of Saddam that adorned the offices of even the most mundane Iraqi officials. Every day the newspapers carried a front-page picture of President Hussein, regardless of whether there was a story to go with it. By the early 1980s some two hundred songs had been written in adulation of Saddam. Every night the evening television news would commence with what Iraqis called "the Saddam song," which was presented against a background of victorious soldiers and bursting fireworks by a smiling figure who chants:

> *Oh Saddam, our victorious*
> *Oh Saddam, our beloved;*
> *You carry the nation's dawn*
> *Between your eyes . . .*
> *Oh Saddam, everything is good*
> *With you . . .*
> *Allah, Allah, we are happy;*
> *Saddam lights our days . . .*

For those who dared to oppose Saddam there was the institutionalized horror of the torture chambers; for those who saluted him there was the promise of a share in the glory and success of Saddam Hussein's Iraq. Every action undertaken by the government was publicized as one of Saddam's personal initiatives. Saddam cleverly devised various material inducements to increase his popularity, such as awarding pay raises to selected groups of workers, including the armed forces. Frequently Saddam would make surprise visits to factories, schools, hospitals, and farms, and the entire proceedings would be filmed and shown on Iraqi television. Numerous public places were named after him, and it was at this time that authorized biographies of his life were written, in which particular attention was paid to glorifying the deeds of his youth, such as his involvement in the botched assassination of General Qassem in 1959. Even at this early point in his presidency Saddam had a highly developed sense of his own destiny. He told one of his biographers that he was not concerned so much with what people thought at the time but with "what people will say about us 500 years hence."[32] A special edition of the Baghdad newspaper *al-Jamhuriyya* was devoted to his life story, and a permanent exhibition dedicated to his life was established in Baghdad. Much was made in the Iraqi press of Saddam's devotion to his family, and his everyday involvement with his children. Iraqis learned about his hobbies, such as fishing and gardening. In everything he said and did Saddam presented himself as the role model for all Iraqi families. The hysteria surrounding Saddam even made its way to the United States when his propagandists, to celebrate his first year as president, took out an advertisement in the *New York Times* of

July 17, 1980. The advertisement claimed that, under Saddam's leadership, Iraq was on the verge of repeating "her former glories" and compared Saddam to the great warlords of the early Islamic period, the Abbasid caliphs al-Mansour and Harun al-Rashid.

The indoctrination worked. Western diplomats who were stationed in Iraq during this period reported back that, even though most Iraqis were well aware of the security forces' uncompromising tactics, Saddam was a genuinely popular leader. "At grassroots level he had a great deal of popular support," recalled a former ambassador to Baghdad. "He would make impromptu visits to the new towns that were being built all over Iraq. The quality of life had improved immeasurably for many people. There were schools, clinics, roads, water, and electricity, and this was very popular with ordinary Iraqi peasants. Superficially everything looked very good, and they were very appreciative of what Saddam had done for them."[33] Iraqis who wanted to show appreciation for their leader during these surprise visits needed to be on their guard, for soon after he became president Saddam's security guards began using sticks and electric rods on people who got too close to the man the Iraqi media dubbed Iraq's "knight," "leader," "struggler," and "son of the people."[34]

The sustained development of Saddam's personality cult, and the limited amount of time a man with so many responsibilities could reasonably devote to visiting his people, resulted in one of the more bizarre features of his presidency—the hiring of look-alikes. An Iraqi exile who called himself Mikhael Ramadan claimed that he acted as Saddam's double for more than ten years before defecting to the West. He provided an intriguing account of being brought to Baghdad from his village in southern Iraq shortly after Saddam became president after security officials noticed his strong facial similarities to the Iraqi leader. Ramadan said he was taken to meet Saddam at his house in Baghdad and that, when Saddam first met him, he was so struck by the similarities in their appearance that he jokingly asked whether his own father had enjoyed an illicit liaison with Ramadan's mother. Saddam then asked Ramadan whether he would be willing to stand in for him at some of president's more mundane official engagements. "I know the people of Iraq idolise their President, but my responsibilities are such that I do not have the time I would like to spend with my people. . . . Would you do me and, of course, the great people of Iraq an enormous service and perhaps stand in for me on occasion?"[35] Ramadan agreed and was sent for months of training, where he studied videos of Saddam's public appearances before himself undertaking low-scale engagements on his leader's behalf.

The quality of life had improved immeasurably for Saddam and his family. The Husseins occupied the Presidential Palace and were becoming accustomed to the trappings of high office. Saddam still worked sixteen to seventeen hours a day in a small office he had set aside for himself in the palace grounds. Saddam dressed well in tailor-made suits bought from his favorite tailors in Baghdad and Geneva, and there was something of the dandy about his appearance. One of his former Baath colleagues claimed that he owned more than four hundred belts. Despite his liking for the high life, Saddam remained something of a puritan when it came to his working practices. Dr. Mahmoud Othman, a Kurdish politician who negotiated with Saddam over several years, recalled how he visited the new Iraqi leader shortly after he had moved into the Presidential Palace. The meeting had been arranged for 7 A.M. and when he arrived he found Saddam still in his pajamas. Saddam had spent the night working in his small office, and Othman was surprised to see a small military cot in a corner of the room where the Iraqi president had slept. Next to the bed there were twelve pairs of expensive shoes, and the rest of the cramped office contained a small library of books about Stalin. Seeing the books Othman remarked, "You seem fond of Stalin," to which Saddam replied amiably, "Yes, I like the way he governed his country." Othman, perhaps pushing his luck a little, then asked Saddam if he was a communist, to which Saddam replied in a questioning voice, "Stalin, a communist?" from which Othman deduced that Saddam regarded Stalin more as a nationalist than a communist.

In 1980 Saddam's two sons, Uday and Qusay, were sixteen and fourteen respectively and were attending Kharkh High School, Saddam's alma mater, which had been run by Saddam's wife Sajida before he became president. Former classmates recall that Uday was loud and vulgar while Qusay was quiet and calculating. Both boys received special treatment at the school and were not obliged, like the other pupils, to obey the rules. Uday, in particular, seems to have been totally out of control. Both boys, of course, were accompanied by security guards at all times, and Uday often took advantage of their presence to behave outrageously. Former pupils claim that it was not uncommon for him to turn up for school wearing a bandolier filled with live ammunition. He was obsessed with cars and would order his guards to seize a car from the family of fellow pupils if he took a shine to it. On one occasion he broke his leg, and his class was required to move to a classroom on a lower floor. He started to imitiate his father's habit of smoking cigars. His legendary interest in the opposite sex is also said to have derived from his schooldays, and it has been suggested that the girls he dated had little choice in the matter.

Sajida Hussein, who had kept herself very much in the background during her husband's ten-year ascent to the presidency, had acquired a taste for the high life. By 1981 the shy, former schoolteacher was making personal use of the presidential jet to undertake shopping trips abroad. She made a secret trip to London with an entourage of twenty friends, where she spent most of her time at Hermès on Bond Street (Iraqi exiles claimed that she ran up a bill into the millions of pounds). A few months later Sajida flew to New York in a private Boeing 747 owned by the Iraqi government in the company of her cousin and future son-in-law, Hussein Kamel al-Majid, and an entourage of thirty. On this occasion she fell in love with Bloomingdale's department store, where she spent a small fortune replenishing her wardrobe. Every day that she was in New York Saddam, the devoted husband, phoned her to check on her progress and welfare.

EIGHT

The Warlord

Just as dawn was breaking on September 22, 1980, several squadrons of Iraqi fighter aircraft attacked ten Iranian air bases, including the military enclave at Teheran International Airport. Their objective was to destroy the Iranian air force on the ground and prepare the way for a land invasion by the Iraqi army. The tactic had worked brilliantly for the Israelis during the 1967 Six Day War, and Saddam Hussein, Iraq's newly promoted, and self-appointed field marshal, was confident that it would result in a glorious triumph for his own armed forces. Throughout the day the Iraqi pilots flew sortie after sortie, using their newly acquired French Mirage jets to devastating effect against the Iranian airfields and early warning radar stations. Initially taken by surprise by the attack, the Iranians soon managed to launch a counteroffensive, and ordered their American-built F-4 fighters to carry out retaliatory raids against the Iraqis, bombing two Iraqi airfields and destroying four missile boats stationed in the Gulf. The Iranians also attacked an Iraqi gas-processing plant and a number of oil installations near the Iran-Iraq border. Undeterred by the Iranians' spirited fight back, the next day Saddam ordered his tank commanders to lead the ground invasion of Iran. Six mechanized divisions of the Iraqi army crossed into Iran, thereby provoking one of the bloodiest, longest, and most costly conflicts since the Second World War. By the time the Iran-Iraq War finished eight years later, more than one million people would have perished and the economies of two of the world's wealthiest oil nations would lie in ruins.

Ultimate responsibility for the decision to invade Iran, which was to destroy all the progress the Baathists had made in modernizing Iraq, lay entirely with Saddam. Relations between the two Gulf states had been on a collision course, particularly after Ayatollah Khomeini's rise to power. From April 1980 onward a number of skirmishes had been reported along their shared one-thousand-mile border after Khomeini publicly called on Iraq's Shiite Muslims to rise in revolt and overthrow the Baathist regime. The official reason for the escalating tensions was the continuing dispute over the Shatt al-Arab waterway. Even though the Algiers Agreement negotiated between Saddam and the shah in 1975 had attempted to resolve the issue, Saddam had always felt that Iraq, which was at the time in no position to challenge its more powerful neighbor, had come out second best in the deal. With the change of regime in Teheran, Saddam saw an opportunity to revise the agreement in Iraq's favor, a move that was firmly resisted by Iran. Relations between the two countries continued to deteriorate to the point where, on September 17, 1980, Saddam addressed an emergency session of the newly reinstated National Assembly at which he unilaterally declared the Algiers Agreement null and void, blaming the "frequent and blatant Iranian violations of Iraqi sovereignty." Speaking slowly, and occasionally waving his finger for added emphasis, Saddam left his audience in little doubt about his intentions. "This river," he proclaimed, "must have its Iraqi-Arab identity restored as it was throughout history."[1] Five days later Iraq was at war with Iran.

Despite the many successes he had achieved in his ruthless rise to power through the ranks of the Baath Party, Saddam was singularly unsuited to be a war leader. For all the uniforms, titles, and honorific ranks he had awarded himself—including that of field marshal—Saddam had never had any military experience, had probably never read a military textbook, or ever considered the finer points of strategy and tactics. Nor had he ever participated in an armed conflict. Moreover the student who had been unable to muster the required grades to enter Baghdad Military College harbored a deep distrust, fueled by jealousy, of successful military officers that would taint his dealings with the Iraqi commanders for the duration of the war. To compensate for his obvious shortcomings as a war leader, Saddam's propaganda machine now went into overdrive to portray him to the Iraqi people as their dashing commander in chief.

Saddam's strategy in essence was to strike deep into Iran and capture sufficient territory to use as a bargaining chip with Teheran to negotiate a better deal over the Shatt al-Arab. Saddam, who was being advised by a collection of

the shah's generals exiled in Baghdad, had been told that the new Iranian
regime was in such a state of chaos that he could expect a quick victory—
probably within two to three weeks. The invasion plan was based on a staff
exercise that had been conducted by British military instructors at the
Baghdad War College as far back as 1941.[2] In addition to securing the eastern
bank of the Shatt al-Arab, Saddam had his eye on capturing the Arab-
inhabited region of Khuzistan from Iran, in the hope that this might trigger
a revolt among other non-Persian ethnic groups. If he could achieve these
goals he stood a good chance of precipitating the collapse of the Khomeini
regime.

In the first few weeks of the campaign the Iraqis looked like they were
achieving their war aims. The chaos engendered by the Iranian revolution
had, as Saddam correctly calculated, left the country's military institutions
unprepared for war, and certainly in no position to repulse a full-scale invasion. The Iraqis made rapid advances, capturing several key Iranian towns
along the central border and subjecting to severe bombardment the city of
Dezful, located in Iran's northern oil fields and the key transportation link
between Teheran and the south. In the south the Iraqi forces crossed the
Karun River, advanced on Abadan, and after a bitter battle involving house-
to-house combat and enormous casualties on both sides, took Khorramshahr
by late October. The Iranian defenders, armed only with light weapons and
Molotov cocktails, fought with great fervor and tenacity, and each side suffered about 7,000 dead and seriously wounded, while the Iraqis lost more
than 100 tanks and armored vehicles. By the time Khorramshahr was in Iraqi
hands on October 24, it had come to be referred to by both sets of combat-
tants as "Khunistan," meaning "city of blood." Iraq now occupied a strip of
Iranian territory 600 kilometers (373 miles) long and varying in width from
10 kilometers (6.2 miles) in the north to 40 kilometers (25 miles) in the
south. Saddam's lack of military experience did not prevent him from taking
direct control of the war effort himself. As had Hitler, he gave his generals
their objectives and told them when to strike. From the outset of hostilities
he went to the front and conducted military operations from forward headquarters. Whenever he ventured near the front line, his every move was
filmed and shown on Iraqi television later that same evening.

Even though Saddam could claim that the initial phase of the war was a
success, there were already worrying signs that the offensive would not
achieve the desired goals. The raids carried out by the Iraqi air force had

achieved little, and most of the Iranian air force remained operational and retaliated with strikes against Iraq. The Iraqis quickly discovered that their air defense systems were ineffective. Although the Iranian army was in no position to fight, the Iraqi invaders were taken aback by the ferocity of the resistance put up by the local population. The heavy casualties suffered in the assault on Khorramshahr meant that the Iraqis were not able to take Abadan, ten miles to the south. This was a serious setback, as failure to take Abadan meant that the Iraqis had failed in one of their main objectives, namely occupying the eastern shore of the Shatt al-Arab and thereby securing control of the all-important strategic waterway.

At this point Saddam called a halt to the Iraqi offensive and ordered the army to assume a defensive posture. This was the first of many miscalculations that would severely rebound against Saddam. By digging in around their new positions, the Iraqis were sending a signal to the Iranians that they were not interested in pursuing hostilities any further. Saddam assumed that he had made sufficient territorial gains to force the Iranians to the negotiating table. Buoyed by the gains achieved, Saddam may even have believed that the collapse of the Khomeini regime was imminent. But Saddam had completely misread the situation. The Iraqis' failure to capture either Dezful or Abadan meant that the Iranians' lines of communication remained intact, enabling them to regroup. Despite suffering massive casualties, morale in the Iranian regular army and in the irregular forces of the Revolutionary Guards remained high. And rather than weakening the Khomeini regime, the Iraqi offensive simply provided the opportunity for the more militant elements in Teheran to gain control of the political system.

Saddam soon had to face up to the shortcomings of his strategy. Surprisingly for someone who rarely showed much respect for human life, the heavy number of Iraqi casualties suffered in the first offensive—forty-five thousand Iraqis are thought to have been killed during the first two months of the war—persuaded Saddam against sustaining further casualties by attacking Abadan. The morale of the Iraqi army was an unknown factor and, as many of the troops were Shiites, there was no guarantee of their loyalty when ordered to attack their fellow Shiites in Iran. There were many Iraqis who opposed the war and believed that Saddam's objectives could be obtained by other means. And as the war dragged on, Saddam slowly began to realize just how badly he had underestimated the size of the challenge he faced from a country that was three times larger than Iraq. Iraq's capacity to sustain the long lines of communication that in-depth penetration of Iran would have demanded and to absorb the inevitable losses was questionable. Western military analysts have suggested that Saddam's insistence on exercising centralized control from Baghdad may have paralyzed the local commanders' ability to operate, and contributed to their failure to advance and hold ground. Iraq's strategic limitations were particularly a factor in the air war. Except for installations in Khuzistan, Iraq's air force had to penetrate hundreds of miles into Iran to hit major targets. The Iranian air force had to travel less than a hundred miles across the border to reach all major targets in Iraq. Six months into the war, Saddam finally came to terms with its strategic implications when he declared, "Geography is our enemy."

A more realistic assessment of Saddam's failure to achieve his war aims is that the offensive was halfhearted and lacked clear objectives. Only half of the Iraqi army—six out of twelve divisions—was involved in the actual invasion, and from the outset Saddam sought to confine the war by restricting his army's goals, means, and targets. He was particularly anxious to avoid Iranian civilian casualties, mainly because he hoped that the Iraqi invasion would somehow persuade the Iranian populace to rise up and overthrow the Khomeini regime. Indeed, Saddam's real motivation appears to have been to overthrow the Khomeini regime before the Khomeini regime overthrew him. Saddam had gone to war with Iran while at the same time attempting to send a signal to the Iranian people that he did not want an all-out war with Iran. The Iraqi position was succinctly summed up by Tariq Aziz, who was now Saddam's deputy prime minister. "Our military strategy reflects our political objectives. We want neither to destroy Iran nor to occupy it permanently because that country is a neighbour with which we will remain linked by geographical and historical bonds and common interests. Therefore we are determined to avoid any irrevocable steps."[3] Small wonder the Iranian people were utterly confused by the Iraqi objectives, and remained loyal to their own government.

Another factor that may have contributed to the failure of the Iraqi blitzkrieg is the claim that the Iranians had been in possession of the Iraqi war plan for fully two months before the offensive was launched. According to Abolhassan Bani-Sadr, the former Iranian president, who was appointed chairman of the Supreme Defense Council soon after the Iraqi invasion, the Iraqi plan was contained in a document that had been purchased by the Iranian foreign minister in Latin America for $200,000. The details of the battle plan had been given to Latin American intermediaries by the Soviets, who believed that Iraq had been given a green light by the United States to invade Iran. "Everything happened as set out in this document. There had been a meeting in Paris. At this meeting were Americans, Israelis, Iranian royalists: it was there that the attack plan was prepared."[4]

The economic consequences of the war were considerable for both sides, but more so for Iraq than Iran. The Iranian refinery at Abadan had been largely destroyed along with many facilities at Bandar Abbas. Iraq's pumping stations at Kirkuk and Mosul had been severely damaged, as had the massive petrochemical complex that Saddam had built at Basra. Consequently oil exports from both countries were suspended and when they did resume it was at a far lower level than prewar. When it came to wartime oil exports, however, Iran had a massive strategic advantage over Iraq in the form of the thousands of miles of coastline it enjoys both in the Persian Gulf and in the Indian Ocean. Iraq, on the other hand, was effectively landlocked as its failure to capture Abadan meant it had lost its only access to the sea.

Worse was to follow for Saddam the following year when the Iranians finally launched their counteroffensive in May 1981 on the central and northern fronts, forcing the Iraqi forces to pull back to Khorramshahr. By October the Iranians had pushed the Iraqis back across the Karun River and in November the Iranians launched a new offensive in which they employed a devastating new strategy that had a terrifying effect on the Iraqi soldiers. Hundreds of thousands of ill trained and lightly armed Revolutionary Guard volunteers, filled with intense religious fervor, joined the fighting. Led into battle by their clerics, the volunteers showed little fear of dying, for the regime had taught them that heaven was the reward for martyrs—the same tactics were later used by Islamic militants in the Palestinian territories during the second *Intifada* to persuade Arab teenagers to become suicide bombers. The Iraqi soldiers were an unequal match for this army of suicidal volunteers. One Iraqi officer later related to a British military observer how "they came at us like a crowd coming out of a mosque on Friday. Soon we were firing into dead men, some draped over the barbed wire fences, and others in piles on the ground, having stepped on the mines."[5] Another Iraqi commander recounted the demoralizing effect the Iranian tactics had on his own soldiers. "My men are eighteen, nineteen, just a few years older than these kids. I've seen them crying, and at times the officers have had to kick them back to their guns. Once we had Iranian kids on bikes cycling toward us, and my men all started laughing, and then these kids started lobbing their hand grenades and we stopped laughing and started shooting."[6] The tactics worked and for the duration of the Iranian offensive the Iraqis were gradually pushed back. In December the Iranians captured a key crossroads, the only road linking the entire southern sector. A monthlong Iraqi effort in February to recapture the junction failed, even though Saddam went to the front himself to lead the counterattack. At the end of March 1982 the Iranians achieved another dramatic victory, pushing the Iraqi army back thirty miles and taking 15,000 Iraqis prisoner. But Iran's greatest military success came in May 1982 when, in a monthlong campaign, they drove the Iraqis from their remaining positions and recaptured the city of Khorramshahr, together with 22,000 Iraqi troops.

The rumor was widely circulated in Baghdad during the March offensive that Saddam had himself come close to being captured by the Iranians. While driving around the rear of the fighting, near the Iraqi border, Saddam's convoy was besieged by Iranian troops unaware of Saddam's presence. The only Iraqi force close enough to relieve Saddam was commanded by General Maher Abdul Rashid, a fellow Tikriti, and one of Iraq's most competent soldiers. Rashid, however, was not on speaking terms with Saddam because some years previously he had arranged for his clan to murder the general's uncle during one of his purges. Before rescuing Saddam, Rashid made him beg for help, swearing by the name of the murdered relative. Under heavy bombardment and with his bodyguards piled on top of him to protect him, Saddam capitulated to the general's demand. Rashid promptly relieved the besieged president, and even though his daughter later married Saddam's son Qusay, the two men never overcame their mutual antipathy. Before the war ended, Saddam had placed Rashid under house arrest at his farm near Tikrit, where he remained for many years.[7]

Saddam's war plan was quickly collapsing around him, and unless he found a means of countering these setbacks, he faced the prospect of the Iranians mounting an offensive to remove him. The summer of 1982 was to be one of the most critical periods of Saddam's career. From the outset of the conflict the incessant drumbeat of his propaganda machine had made it clear that this was Saddam's war: if he was victorious, the victory would be his; if the war was lost, defeat would be Saddam's personal responsibility. But the failure of the Iranians to respond to Iraq's aggression in the way Saddam expected was a source of great frustration for the Iraqi leader. Saddam now lamented that the

Iranian leadership had perversely refused to abide by the anticipated rules of war. "Despite its military defeat in 1980, the Teheran regime insisted on its aggressive stands and expansionist trends," he declared.[8] In June 1982 Saddam responded to these reversals by declaring a unilateral cease-fire on the rather dubious grounds that Iraq had achieved its objective of destroying Iran's military status. Nobody inside or outside Iraq was deceived, particularly the Iranians, who threatened to reverse the tables and carry the war into Iraq, with the professed aim of toppling Saddam Hussein and the Baathist regime and replacing it with an uncompromising Islamic republic, along lines similar to the ones that had been established in Teheran by Ayatollah Khomeini. By this time Saddam must have wished that he had never invaded Iran, particularly as from this point on the conflict would degenerate into a bloody war of attrition, much like the trench warfare of the First World War, with both sides suffering heavy losses for little tangible gain.

In many respects the Iran-Iraq War can be seen as yet another episode in the long-running feud between the Persians and the Arabs for domination of the Gulf. The origins of the conflict can be traced back to the Arab Islamic conquest of Persia in the seventh century, which had continued, at various levels of intensity, up until the twentieth century when the discovery of the region's vast oil reserves only served to intensify the animosity. Apart from the cultural differences that distinguish the two peoples—Persians and Arabs have their own languages and literary traditions—they must also contend with the fierce rivalry of their competing Islamic traditions. The Iranians are Shiite and have a strong sense of religious hierarchy, which is why the ayatollahs, the leaders of Shiite Islam, are omnipotent. The Arabs, on the other hand, are predominantly Sunni, with its emphasis on the Koran and religious law, and enjoy a more democratic religious structure. One of the enduring fault lines in the composition of modern Iraq is that the majority of the population are Shiite, while the governing regime, from the monarchy onward, has been composed of Sunni cliques, such as Saddam's Tikritis.

From the outset of the conflict Saddam's propaganda machine was quick to mine the rich historical vein that had been created by centuries of conflict. Saddam drew parallels between the modern-day struggle with Iran and the battle of Qadisiya in A.D. 635, when a numerically inferior Arab army had inflicted a humiliating defeat on the Persians, and forced them to embrace Islam. Saddam, who claimed to share the same birthplace as Saladin, the great

Kurdish warrior who evicted the Crusaders from the Holy Land, now saw himself following in the tradition of Saad ibn-Abi Waqqad, the Arab commander who defeated the Persians. The war with Iran was hailed as a second Qadisiya. The Iraqi media, with monotonous frequency, referred to the conflict as "Saddam Hussein's new Qadisiya." Saddam encouraged comparisons to be drawn between himself and other legendary figures from history, even those who predated the Islamic era. The great ancient empire of Mesopotamia had been located in the area that is now Iraq, and Saddam had a particular affection for Nebuchadnezzar, the Babylonian king who had conquered Jerusalem in 587 B.C., destroyed the Jewish Temple, and forced the Jews into exile by the rivers of Babylon.

The blame for starting the war must, of course, lie with Saddam. He mistakenly calculated that with Iran crippled by Islamic fervor, he could take advantage of Teheran's weakness and strengthen Iraq's claim to be a significant military force in both the Middle East and the Gulf. But if Saddam was guilty of succumbing to hubris, it could equally be argued that some degree of conflict was inevitable once Ayatollah Khomeini had taken control of Iran. From Iraq's inception the majority Shiite Muslim community had believed that they merited a greater say in the running of the country, and were forever agitating to improve their lot. The emergence of an exclusive Shiite Muslim regime in Iran intensified the agitation by Iraqi clerics, most of whom had been close associates of Khomeini during his fifteen years of exile in Iraq, and who now openly called for the establishment of an Islamic republic in Baghdad. Not surprisingly Saddam came to see Khomeini as a threat to the Baathist regime and as a mortal threat to himself. In essence the dispute between Saddam and Khomeini was as much a clash of ideologies as a clash of personalities, with the Iraqis championing secular Arab nationalism and Iran preaching the Islamic revolution, and Saddam and Khomeini demanding each other's overthrow.

Officially, the principal casus belli of the Iran-Iraq War was the dispute over the Shatt al-Arab, although it was Iran's neglect of other protocols in the 1975 Algiers Agreement that provoked Saddam into action. Under the terms of the agreement both countries were to observe a policy of noninterference in each other's internal affairs and a rigorous enforcement of border controls. In the wake of the Khomeini revolution the Iranians no longer respected either condition. The absence of proper policing of the border enabled Kurdish rebels in northern Iraq to rearm, and in July 1979 the main Kurdish leaders, who had been living in exile, were allowed to cross back to Kurdistan by the Iranians. Iraq's Kurdish leaders in the north now joined with Shiite clerics in the south in calling for the overthrow of the Baathist regime. In retaliation the Iraqi government revived its support for dissident Arab groups in Iran's eastern Khuzistan province.

To give Saddam his due, he had gone out of his way to be hospitable toward the new Iranian government after it came to power. Soon after assuming the presidency he had reiterated his interest in establishing close relations with Iran "based on mutual respect and non-interference in internal affairs." Even though his statement received a dismissive response from Teheran, Saddam maintained his upbeat rhetoric. He declared that the Islamic Revolution, or any other revolution that purported to be Islamic, "must be a friend of the Arab revolution"—i.e., the revolution the Baathists had undertaken in Baghdad. Secular by nature, Saddam began praying with greater frequency, a development that was duly broadcast on Iraqi television. Saddam undertook a range of pro-Islamic initiatives aimed at placating Iraqi Shiites and the ayatollahs: Radio Baghdad was asked to broadcast excerpts from the Koran; Saddam visited both Sunni and Shiite holy shrines; the birthday of Imam Ali, the founder of the Shiite tradition, was made a public holiday; Islamic symbols were used more frequently. Saddam even pledged himself to "fight injustice with the swords of the Imams" while calling at the same time for "a revival of heavenly values."[9] Saddam the secularist became Saddam the Muslim.

The mullahs, however, remained intractable. Even before Saddam had become president, senior Islamic clerics were identifying him as their main target. As far back as 1978, after Khomeini had been exiled to Paris, Iran's spiritual leader, when asked in an interview to list his enemies, declared: "First, the Shah; then the American Satan; then Saddam Hussein and his infidel Baath Party."[10] After the ayatollahs seized power a militant member of the new leadership, Hujjat al-Islam Sadeq Khalkhali, claimed that Saddam was standing in the way of the their attempts to export the revolution. "We have taken the path of true Islam and our aim in defeating Saddam Hussein lies in the fact that we consider him the main obstacle to the advance of Islam in the region." From June 1979 Teheran was urging the Iraqi people—in particular the Shiites, who constituted about 60 percent of the population—to rise up and overthrow "the Saddamite regime."

The Iranians' anti-Saddam campaign continued in the autumn. Khomeini's main ally in Iraq was Mohammed Bakr al-Sadr, the head of Iraq's Shiite Muslim Dawa (the call) Party, whom he had befriended during his exile in Najaf. Sadr had been a constant thorn in the side of the Baath government and had been imprisoned on several occasions, the latest being during the bloody Shiite disturbances in 1977 (see Chapter Six). In the past the problem for the Baathists had always been that whenever they arrested Sadr—as they had done in 1972, 1974, and 1977—they only succeeded in increasing his popularity. But now Sadr overstepped the mark. He announced that he accepted Khomeini as the undisputed leader of the Shiites, and that he was acting as the Iranian ayatollah's official deputy. Sadr's treasonable actions, combined with the increasingly frequent anti-Baath demonstrations in Najaf, were a challenge Saddam could not ignore. The confrontation between Saddam and Sadr came to a head in April 1980 when members of Sadr's Dawa Party, which had already murdered a score of government officials in 1979, tried to assassinate Tariq Aziz, Saddam's deputy prime minister and a leading member of the RCC. Aziz himself was only lightly wounded but there were an unknown number of dead and wounded. A few days later the Dawa terrorists demonstrated their fanaticism by attacking the funeral procession of those killed in the failed attack on Aziz, causing yet more deaths.

Saddam's response, as one might expect, was brutal and uncompromising. The time for making Islamic overtures to the ayatollahs was over. "Our people are ready to fight to protect their honour and sovereignty, as well as maintain peace among the Arab nations," he declared. Having made membership of the Dawa a crime punishable by death, Saddam rounded up and executed hundreds of suspected Iraqi Islamic militants. He dispatched his special forces to Najaf, where they arrested Sadr and his sister. Obeying their orders to shoot to kill, they overwhelmed Sadr's guards and brought the prisoners back to Baghdad. There is little doubt that the cleric and his sister were tortured by Saddam's half brother, Barzan al-Tikriti, the head of General Intelligence, before being hanged in secret after a summary trial. No record of the trial has ever been produced. As news of the hangings reached the Shiite heartlands of southern Iraq, widespread riots broke out, and were brutally suppressed by Saddam's security forces. Hundreds more were killed and thousands arrested, never to be seen again. Saddam reinstituted the mass expulsion program carried out in 1977, forcing an estimated thirty-five thousand Iraqi Shiites out of their homes and deporting them to Iran. Khomeini reacted furiously when he learned of the execution of his friend and colleague. "The war that the Iraqi Baath wants to ignite is a war against Islam. . . . The people and army of Iraq must turn their backs on the Baath regime and overthrow it . . . because the regime is attacking Iran, attacking Islam and the Koran."[11] From this moment onward the border skirmishes escalated, and it became clear that the two countries were on a collision course that would inevitably result in war.

Nor was the dispute confined solely to Baghdad and Teheran. The Iranian revolution had a dramatic impact internationally, particularly when Iranian revolutionaries were held responsible for incidents such as the storming of the American embassy in Teheran on December 17, 1979, when the Revolutionary Guards took sixty-six American diplomats hostage. The following year the mounting tensions between Iran and Iraq spilled onto the streets of London when a group of six pro-Iraqi rebels from Khorramshahr in Iran's Arab province of Khuzistan seized control of the Iranian embassy in May, and held the staff hostage. The siege was ended when an elite unit from Britain's SAS stormed the embassy after the terrorists had shot dead one of the hostages. Five of the terrorists were killed during the ensuing operation, and one survived. But by the time the survivor went on trial at the Old Bailey courthouse in London in 1981, Khorramshahr was under Iraqi control. He later received a life sentence after being convicted of terrorism charges. It later transpired that the entire operation had been conceived by Iraqi intelligence, and that the Iranian gunmen had been trained in Iraq; they had also received false passports from their Iraqi trainers.

Desperate situations sometimes require desperate remedies, and with no end in sight to the increasingly destructive war with Iran, Saddam embarked on a wild gamble that he hoped would finally persuade the superpowers to intervene and bring hostilities to a halt. In the summer of 1982 the Begin government in Israel was straining at the leash to launch an offensive in Lebanon aimed at destroying the Palestine Liberation Organization. Aware of this, the PLO had been on its best behavior and had gone out of its way not to give the Israelis a pretext for launching an attack. Then on the evening of June 3, 1982, an assassination attempt was made on Shlomo Argov, the Israeli ambassador to London, as he left the Dorchester Hotel, where he had been giving a talk on the current situation in the Middle East. Argov was shot and seriously wounded, but the British authorities were able to round up the assassins. The British investigation revealed that the three gunmen who took part in the shooting were all members of Abu Nidal's terrorist organization, which was still based in Baghdad. One of the gunmen was one of Abu Nidal's relatives while the man who organized the attack was a colonel in Iraqi intelligence. It was also discovered that most of the weapons used in the operation had come from the military attaché's office at the Iraqi embassy in London.[12]

It was, of course, inconceivable that the attack could have taken place without Saddam's knowledge—Abu Nidal was still in regular contact with Saddam's private office and relied heavily on Saddam's patronage. And both Saddam and Abu Nidal were well aware of what the likely consequences would be of trying to murder the Israeli ambassador. Neither Menachem Begin, the Israeli prime minister, nor Ariel Sharon, his defense minister, was the type of person to sit around waiting while the British authorities tried to ascertain who was responsible for the shooting. To their minds the suspects were bound to be linked to the PLO in some shape or form, and the assassination attempt gave them the pretext they had been looking for. On the morning of June 6, 1982, Begin ordered the Israeli army to invade Lebanon. On June 10, Saddam declared a unilateral cease-fire with Iran, and ordered his troops to withdraw from the small pockets of Iranian territory that they still occupied. He proposed that both Iraq and Iran should make use of the cease-fire to divert their resources to helping the Palestinians defend themselves against the Israeli assault. Even though Saddam had managed to start a new Middle East war in his desperation to extract himself from the conflict with Iran, the ploy was a miserable failure. On July 14, Ayatollah Khomeini rejected Saddam's cease-fire offer and launched a new offensive against the Iraqis. From Khomeini's point of view, this was a war to the death.

The assassination attempt on Argov was not the only desperate measure Saddam was prepared to contemplate to end the war. Once it became clear that Iran was not going to be defeated easily, Saddam was keener than ever to employ his various nonconventional weapons. As usual, it was the nuclear research project that particularly interested him. Before the war started, Saddam had been promised that the reactor would be ready to produce weapons-grade material by July 1981. Although the French, responding to international pressure, were still dragging their feet on supplying Saddam with the enriched uranium necessary to power the Tammuz reactor cores, by July 1980 the first shipments had arrived at Al Tuwaitha, on the outskirts of Baghdad, where the nuclear research establishment was being built. Iraq was also engaged in a worldwide search for uranium. A hundred and twenty tons were acquired from Portugal in 1980, and a further two hundred tons from

Niger. Saddam clearly hoped that he would have use of an atomic bomb by either late 1981 or early 1982, and had his scientists succeeded in their mission, there is little doubt that he would have used it against Iran. When, later in the 1980s, Saddam renewed his efforts to acquire a nuclear capability, Britain's Secret Intelligence Service (SIS) issued an assessment that if the Iraqis were successful in producing a nuclear weapon, Saddam would most likely use it to bring the war with Iran to a speedy conclusion.[13]

Saddam's hopes of acquiring a nuclear arsenal at this juncture, however, were to be frustrated by the Israelis, who would have been high on Saddam's list of targets if the Iraqi scientists successfully completed development of an indigenous atomic bomb. Having seriously damaged the reactor cores in 1979, Israeli agents were blamed in June 1980 for the murder in a Paris hotel of Yahya al-Meshad, an Egyptian-born nuclear scientist who had been recruited to work on Iraq's nuclear program. Saddam was undeterred by these setbacks and insisted that development of the Tammuz reactors continue. "Whoever antagonises us must know that the nation he is antagonising today will be different in five years."[14] The next blow against Saddam's pet project came three months later, on September 30, shortly after Saddam had invaded Iran and the French had delivered the first consignment of enriched uranium, when the Iranians launched a surprise air raid against Al Tuwaitha. The attack failed, but on June 7, 1981, the Israelis completed what the Iranians had failed to do when the Israeli air force successfully bombed the plant, just one month before it was to become operational. The reactor was completely destroyed, although most of the enriched uranium, which had been stored in a deep underground canal, remained intact; this would enable Saddam to recommence his beloved nuclear weapons project at a later date.

Even after this disastrous setback, Saddam was not to be diverted from his determination of acquiring a weapons of mass destruction arsenal. Speaking during his annual address to mark the Baath revolution in July, Saddam declared: "We will not succumb to the Zionist aggression and we will not deviate from the war we have chosen."[15] He also took the opportunity to grant a rare television interview to Barbara Walters of the U.S. ABC News network, in which he claimed that Israel wanted "to maintain the Arabs in a state of underdevelopment to be able to dominate them and persecute them."

While the nuclear project had to be shelved, Saddam achieved considerably more success in his attempts to acquire chemical and biological weapons. Saddam's obsession was to acquire "strategic reach" weapons that could inflict a devastating blow on an enemy such as Iran or Israel. Many of the proposals for chemical weapons plants that had been hidden in Iraq's five-year plan by Adnan al-Hamdani had lain dormant. Following the Israeli bombing of the Tammuz reactors, Saddam resurrected these projects and ordered his scientists to redouble their efforts to develop chemical and biological weapons. This time they were greatly assisted in their endeavors by a variety of West German companies, which, for the next few years, worked shoulder to shoulder with Iraqi chemists, ballistic engineers, and nuclear scientists to develop one of the most diversified arsenals of unconventional weapons to be found anywhere in the world. U.S. Senator Jesse Helms, whose staff assistants spent months tracking them down, called these companies and their cohorts "Saddam's Foreign Legion."[16] And it was this "foreign legion" of German companies that was mainly responsible for building the Salman Pak military complex at Suwaira, thirty kilometers south of Baghdad, near the ancient site of Ctesiphon. Work was started on the plant in late 1981 and, despite Iraqi claims that it was a "university" project, when it was completed two years later it became Saddam's first nerve gas plant.[17] A German company was also responsible for building the other main Iraqi chemical weapons plant at Samarra. The official explanation was that the Samarra plant had been commissioned by a newly created Iraqi entity, the State Establishment for Pesticides Production (SEPP) to help develop the country's agricultural production. Even though they could see this claim was fictious, the Germans helped the Iraqis to build six separate chemical weapons manufacturing lines at Samarra called Ahmed, Ani, Mohammed, Iesa, Meda, and Ghasi. The first was completed in 1983; the last, sometime in 1986. These plants made everything from mustard gas and prussic acid to the nerve gas compounds Sarin and Tabun. With typical German efficiency, the plant was designed so that the poisons were funneled from the production "reactors" to an underground packing plant, where they were put into artillery shells, rockets, and other munitions. By the time work on the complex was completed, Iraq could boast one of the largest chemical weapons manufacturing plants in the world.[18] For good measure, a third chemical weapons plant was constructed in the Iraqi desert at Rutbah, near the Syrian border.

The Iraqis wasted no time boasting about their new capability, and in April 1983 the Iraqi High Command, of which Saddam was supreme commander, broadcast an explicit warning to the Iranians that Iraq was now armed with "modern weapons [which] will be used for the first time in war," and which had "not been used in previous attacks for humanitarian and ethical reasons." In a desperate attempt to ward off any further Iranian attacks, the warning went on to declare that "if you execute the orders of the Khomeini regime . . . your death will be certain because this time we will use a weapon that will destroy any moving creature on the fronts."[19]

The Germans were not the only Western country supporting Saddam in the war against the ayatollahs. The French were outraged by the Israeli raid on the Tammuz reactors, and immediately promised to rebuild it. The new French president, François Mitterrand, had surrounded himself with pro-Arab ministers who wanted to redress what they regarded as America's "lopsided" support for Israel. The first batch of the new Mirage F1 fighter-bombers that Saddam had purchased during his negotiations with Jacques Chirac had been delivered to Baghdad in February 1981. From then on, new Mirages continued to arrive in Baghdad at the rate of two a month. With most of the American-built Iranian air force grounded because of the U.S. arms embargo against Teheran, the new fighter-bombers were an important contribution to the Iraqi war effort. In February 1982, President Mitterrand concluded France's new $2.6 billion deal with Baghdad. Not to be left out, in September 1980, just days before Iraq invaded Iran, the Italians signed a $2.6 billion deal to provide Saddam with a new, almost purpose-built navy.

The new arms deals reflected Saddam's determination not to be reliant on one supplier, a philosophy that derived from the difficulties he had experienced with the Soviets when they were Iraq's main arms suppliers in the early 1970s. At the start of hostilities with Iran, the Soviets had again proved their unreliability as an ally of Baghdad when Moscow suspended all arms shipments. The official Russian position was that Moscow wanted to maintain its neutrality in the conflict, while privately Leonid Brezhnev wanted to punish Saddam for continuing his appalling treatment of Iraqi communists.[20] There was disquiet in Moscow about Saddam's attempts to effect a rapprochement with the West, a development that the Russians interpreted as a threat to their plans to extend their influence into the Gulf region. This might explain the claim (see above this chapter) that the Soviets had secretly provided the Iranians with Iraq's invasion plan. Abolhassan Bani-Sadr, the former Iranian president who oversaw the early years of the Iranian war effort, insisted that the Soviets arranged for Teheran to receive details of the invasion plan after they discovered that Saddam had opened a secret dialogue with Washington.[21]

Officially the United States and Britain maintained a policy of neutrality toward the combatants, but there were clear indications that both London and Washington were more favorably inclined toward Baghdad than Teheran. President Carter, in particular, was desperate to find an ally to help him extricate himself from the political situation caused by the American embassy hostage crisis in Teheran, which seriously threatened his prospects of his being elected for a second term in the autumn of 1980. Even though Washington still had Iraq on its list of countries that sponsored terrorism and had not enjoyed full diplomatic relations since the 1967 Israeli-Arab Six Day War, from mid-1980 onward there was a distinct shift in the Carter administration, which began to regard Saddam as a potential counterweight both against the ayatollahs and as an ally that might provide a bulwark against Soviet expansionism in the Gulf. According to President Bani-Sadr and the *New York Times,* Carter's desire to explore the possibility of a clandestine alliance with Saddam resulted in a top-secret meeting taking place in Amman, Jordan, during the first week of July 1980 between Zbigniew Brzezinski, Carter's national security adviser, and Saddam Hussein. According to the *Times,* the purpose of the meeting was to discuss ways that the United States and Iraq could coordinate their activities "to oppose Iran's reckless policies."[22] Brzezinski and his former aides have always denied that there was a face-to-face meeting, although Brzezinski did meet with King Hussein of Jordan, whose own survival instinct had already persuaded him to befriend his dictatorial namesake and neighbor. It is possible that a high-level Iraqi emissary was also present. As with Iraq's invasion of Kuwait ten years later, various former Carter administration officials, including Gary Sick, the former national security adviser, have claimed that the Americans led Saddam to assume that they had given Iraq a green light to invade Iran in the summer of 1980. Certainly from that moment on there was a distinct thaw in U.S. relations with Baghdad. While the U.S. Senate continued to block any attempt to export military equipment to Baghdad, in July Carter approved the sale of five Boeing airliners for Iraq's national airline, America's first significant commercial contract with Iraq since the Baathists came to power.

By the summer of 1982 the glory Saddam had hoped to acquire from the "second Qadisiya" was fast becoming a distant memory. The brutal reversal in Iraq's fortunes in a war that Saddam had predicted would last just two to three weeks was developing, as it neared the end of its second year, into a crisis for the Iraqi leader. With an estimated one hundred thousand Iraqi dead, thousands more injured, and the remnants of his invasion force rotting in Iranian prison camps, for the first time in his presidency Saddam's personal survival was starting seriously to be questioned.

The first indication that Saddam's popularity was on the wane emerged in April when an assassination attempt was made on the information minister, Latif Jasim. The gunmen were members of the Dawa, Iraq's militant Shiite group, although the assassination attempt itself was inspired more out of a desire to avenge Saddam's execution of Sadr, their leader, and his sister. Saddam responded in his customary fashion by rounding up hundreds of Shiites, many of whom were never to be seen again. A few months later a serious attempt was made by the Dawa to assassinate Saddam himself when he was visiting the village of Dujail in the Balad district of Iraq, about forty miles northeast of Baghdad. In the ambush, which lasted for more than two hours, the presidential party was pinned down and had to be rescued by the army. Several of Saddam's companions died in the attack and eight of the assassins were killed. The assassins named their operation *Um Al Hada,* after the sister of Ayatollah Sadr executed by Saddam. A few days later the inhabitants of Dujail were evicted from their homes and relocated to a new town while the village itself was destroyed by the army. According to one report, the village was attacked by helicopters dropping napalm. Bulldozers were then sent in and turned the village into agricultural land. The failed assassination attempt was to make a lasting impression on the way Saddam conducted his presidency. Until this attack Saddam had been in the habit of making impromptu appearances around the country as part of his ongoing campaign to present himself as a populist. From this point on he would make no more impromptu appearances.

From the start of the war Saddam had tried hard to insulate the Iraqi population from the reality of what was taking place at the front. The Iraqi population was fed on a constant, and somewhat repetitive, diet of pro-Saddam propaganda. From the moment they glanced at the morning paper, through their journey to work, to the family evening gathered in front of the television, the Iraqi people was inescapably exposed to the towering presence of the "Struggler President." They saw him posing with a rocket launcher on the front lines or paternally embracing young children; as a statesman meeting heads of state and as a military leader discussing war plans. Saddam was depicted as an efficient bureaucrat in a trendy suit and as an ordinary peasant, helping farmers with their harvest, scythe in hand. His portraits pervaded the country to such an extent that a popular joke put Iraq's population at 26 million: 13 million Iraqis and 13 million pictures of Saddam.[23]

In addition to maintaining a constant stream of propaganda in the state-owned media in praise of the country's armed forces and leader, Saddam used the oil wealth to ensure living standards were maintained at a high level. At the outbreak of hostilities Saddam was widely quoted as having said that Iraq had two years' supplies of all key commodities.[24] Instead of concentrating most of Iraq's resources on the military effort and, like Iran, stressing the virtue of sacrifice, the Iraqi president sought to prove to his people that he could wage war and maintain a business-as-usual atmosphere at the same time. Ambitious development plans that had commenced prior to the war went ahead, and public spending rose from $21 billion in 1980 to $29.5 billion in 1982. The lion's share of this expanded budget was spent on civilian imports to prevent commodity shortages. This guns-and-butter policy meant that most Iraqis were relatively immune from the ferocious war being waged on the battlefield. Instead the country was buzzing, much to the delight of foreign contractors. Construction projects of all sorts, begun prior to the war, continued apace with the result that Baghdad was being transformed at a feverish pace from a medieval into a modern city. Daily life in the capital was largely unaffected by the war. The blackouts imposed at the start of the fighting were soon lifted once it became clear that the dwindling American-built Iranian air force, starved of spare parts by the U.S. embargo, was unable to extend the war to the Iraqi hinterland. Most foodstuffs were readily available, and the black color of mourning was not too visible in the streets of Baghdad.

Apart from the protective shield Saddam had thrown around the civilian population, he took great care to look after those directly involved in the fighting or affected by the war. With the Iraqi authorities forced to admit that casualties were running at the rate of 1,200 a month, Saddam saw to it that all the participants were handsomely rewarded. The already high standard of living of the officer corps was further improved, and members of the armed forces were given priority for car and house purchases. Officers who had displayed any measure of heroism were presented with Rolex watches, which naturally had Saddam's face on the dial. Bereaved families, for their part, were compensated with a free car, a free plot of land, and an interest-free loan to build a house. To ensure the Baathists were clearly identified with the war effort, Saddam ordered all leading party officials to dispense with their tailor-made suits and wear olive green battle fatigues, which soon became one of the distinguishing features of televised meetings of the Baath.

Another example of Saddam's attempts to maintain a facade of normality was his insistence on keeping to his plan to host the Non-Aligned Nations Conference in Baghdad in the autumn of 1982. Saddam's interest in the Non-Aligned Movement, formed in the 1950s to represent the interests of developing countries that sought to be independent of the superpowers, dated back to 1978 when he had attended the quadrennial conference in Havana, Cuba. Despite his hatred of communism, Saddam is said to have befriended Fidel Castro and to have developed a taste for fine Havana cigars, which were henceforth exported to Baghdad on a regular basis. In his desire to prevent Iraq being subjected to either superpower's sphere of influence, it was natural for Saddam to turn his attentions toward the Non-Aligned Movement. In arranging for the movement's 1982 conference to be held in Baghdad, Saddam was hoping that he might prevail upon its membership to elect him as Castro's replacement when his term ended as head of the Non-Aligned Movement. Much of the frenetic construction work taking place in Baghdad in the early 1980s was the building of new hotels and conference centers for the planned conference. Millions, if not billions, of dollars were spent on various construction projects, and existing buildings and facilities underwent substantial renovation.

By mid-1982, however, as Iran began its determined drive into Iraq, the butter-and-guns policy, the main buttress of Iraqi national morale, could no longer be maintained. Iran's success in attacking and destroying many of Iraq's oil installations around Basra was one reason the country's financial reserves could no longer finance both the war and a prosperous domestic economy. Another was the decision by Baghdad's rival Baathist colleagues in Damascus to order the closure of the Iraqi pipeline to Banias on the Mediterranean, which passed through Syria. President Asad had been itching for an opportunity to avenge Saddam's purge and execution of pro-Syrian Baathists when he assumed the presidency in 1979, and for the duration of the Iran-Iraq War, Damascus proved to be one of Teheran's staunchest allies. With Iraqi foreign reserves plunging from $35 billion before the war to just $3 billion at the end of 1983, Saddam was forced to reduce radically all spending on nonessential goods. As a consequence civilian imports to Iraq dropped from a peak of $21.5 billion in 1982 to $12.2 billion in 1983, and $10–11 billion between 1984 and 1987. Saddam was even forced to cancel plans to hold the Non-Aligned Movement conference in Baghdad; the meeting was moved to New Delhi and in Saddam's absence India's Indira Gandhi assumed the leadership of the nonaligned world for the next four years.

The reversal in Iraq's war fortunes and the dramatic economic downturn combined for the first time to raise serious doubts about Saddam's leadership qualities. The setbacks the Iraqis suffered following the Iranian counteroffensives meant Saddam was being held directly responsible for the failures of the armed forces. He was also blamed for exercising poor political judgment in declaring war on Iran in the first place. His insistence on taking personal command of the military meant that he had no alternative other than to accept responsibility for the military setbacks. From the outset of hostilities Saddam had ordered that military command be subjected to Baath Party control. In the early weeks of the conflict Saddam had personally overseen operations from a bunker located beneath the Presidential Palace in Baghdad. Every order had to be referred back to Baghdad and Saddam insisted on being involved in every military decision, from a platoon-level action to the bombing of major targets. Even Adnan Khairallah, his cousin and brother-in-law who was the army chief of staff, had to defer to Field Marshal Saddam on the smallest of issues.

As the conflict developed, Saddam transformed the Revolutionary Command Council (RCC) into his personal headquarters, thus enabling him to maintain tight control over all war operations. The result was a lack of flexibility and initiative on the part of Iraq's field commanders, who were severely handicapped in their ability to respond quickly and effectively to whatever new tactics the Iranians might deploy. Saddam's insistence, for political reasons, that his military commanders keep Iraqi casualties to a minimum was but one example of how his amateurish interference hindered his commanders' effectiveness. Far from reducing casualties, Saddam's interventions, which were often diametrically opposed to the view of the professional soldiers, had devastating consequences. Unable to exploit their initial successes in southern Iran, the Iraqis were forced to commit their troops in worsening operational conditions as Iran strengthened its defenses, causing thousands of unnecessary Iraqi deaths. When he was in the wrong, Saddam's hold over the military was so complete that the most experienced battalion and brigade commanders were unwilling to make independent decisions for fear of upsetting their commander in chief. Instead they referred decisions back to division or corps headquarters, which in turn approached the highest command in Baghdad. It should also be remembered that the political commissars who had been appointed by the Baath to keep a watchful eye on the military high command were present throughout, sending back their reports to the RCC on the performance of individual officers.

Saddam was well aware that his popularity was skin-deep among the majority of the Iraqi population and, true to character, he took care that the necessary preemptive measures were in place to keep him in power. The nation's security apparatus now employed an estimated 208,000 people—twice the present size of the British army—which amounted to about 15 percent of all government employees.[25] The special presidential security service, Amn al-Khass, remained under the watchful, and vengeful, eye of Saddam's half brother, Barzan al-Tikriti. Despite the burdens of war, Saddam's executioners hardly missed a beat; in 1981 and 1982, it is estimated, more than 3,000 civilians were executed in addition to those executed for purely political crimes.

The atmosphere of mounting suspicion that permeated the inner sanctum of the Baathist government is reflected in the infamous incident of March 1982 when Saddam shot dead one of his own ministers during the weekly cabinet meeting. While the government later claimed that the minister had been shot for profiteering—a crime punishable by death—the real reason for Saddam's precipitate action was that Riyadh Ibrahim Hussein, the minister of health, had had the temerity to suggest that Saddam stand down in favor of former president Ahmad Hassan al-Bakr, to enable a cease-fire to be negotiated in the Iran-Iraq War. By this stage in the hostilities the war had become a titanic struggle between the overinflated egos of Saddam and Khomeini, and by removing Saddam from the front line, the Iraqis might have been in a better position to sue for peace. When the minister made the suggestion, Saddam showed no outward sign of irritation. He merely interrupted the cabinet meeting and asked the minister to escort him outside. "Let us go to the other room and discuss the matter further," said Saddam. The minister agreed and the two left the room. A moment later a shot was heard and Saddam returned alone to the cabinet as though nothing had happened.[26] When the Iraqi news agency reported the execution of the health minister, it stated that he had been punished for importing medicine that had killed innocent Iraqis, and that he was therefore a "traitor." When the dead man's wife asked for the return of her husband's body, it was delivered to her chopped into pieces. Soon after this incident Saddam sent a team of doctors working for his security forces to make sure that his ailing predecessor, former president Bakr, did not cause him any further problems in the future (see Chapter Seven).

Saddam's insistence on maintaining direct control of the military campaign meant that he personally had to deal with the first rumblings of discontent within the armed forces. The war had never been particularly popular from the outset, especially as Iraq's Sandhurst-educated officer corps were deeply skeptical about launching an offensive that lacked clearly defined goals. There had been intermittent reports of officers being executed for openly disagreeing with Saddam's war aims, and matters came to a head in the summer of 1982 when a group of officers attempted to articulate what they regarded as constructive criticism of how the war effort might be better directed. Saddam, still nurturing his inferiority complex about the military establishment, did not see it that way, and about three hundred high-ranking officers were executed, together with a small number of party officials who had supported the officers' point of view. Saddam showed no mercy to those officers he suspected of not doing their duty at the front. In one incident it was reported that Saddam personally executed an officer who had ordered a tactical retreat. The officer was brought before Saddam, who calmly drew his pistol and shot the man in the head.[27]

The Baathists had to contend with a rising number of deserters, although the security forces were easily able to deal with this particular problem. At first deserters who were unfortunate enough to be caught were returned to their homes, where they were executed. Later they were taken to the Abu Ghraib prison on the outskirts of Baghdad, which was quickly earning itself a reputation as Saddam's Lubianka. According to one prisoner who survived the horrors of the prison, which had replaced the Palace of the End as the Baathists' main interrogation center, "the section of the Abu Ghraib reserved for those under sentence of death is a hall surrounded by rooms measuring four metres by four metres into each of which fifteen to twenty prisoners are packed. They have to use their rooms as toilets and rubbish dumps. The sun never finds its way into these rooms. A very small proportion of these prisoners are common criminals but the majority are from the military, men who have opposed the Iran-Iraq war."[28] Other inmates described a department of the prison dealing with "special sentences," a category including all opposition members, but particularly those from the Dawa and the Communist Party. Many of these people were kept in basement dungeons, and allowed out for exercise only once a month.

In an attempt to dilute responsibility for Iraq's failure to achieve its war aims, in June Saddam undertook a series of measures designed to ensure that the ruling echelon of the Baath accepted its fair share of the blame and to remove those for whom he had no further use. Saddam started by convening meetings of the RCC, whose members were invited to make their own plea to the Iranians to accept a cease-fire. This was duly rejected by the Iranians, thereby showing that removing Saddam would not end the war. At the next meeting Saddam staged a minipurge of the RCC, and eight of the sixteen members were removed. The most symbolic change was the removal of General Saadoun Ghaydan, the last survivor from the officers who had brought the Baath to power in 1968. Another indication of Saddam's murderous mood during the summer of 1982 concerns an incident that is alleged to have occurred during a meeting of the National Assembly. As Saddam addressed the assembly he noticed a man in the audience passing a note to another man. Without thinking twice the president drew his pistol and killed both of them. Saddam assumed that they were plotting his assassination, and when the piece of paper was examined, the president was proved correct. Whether this story is true or apocryphal, it certainly enjoyed wide circulation in the coffee shops of Baghdad and reinforced the view that the Iraqi president was not a man to be trifled with.

The most serious challenge to Saddam's position came from within his own family the following year when he was forced to place his three half brothers—Barzan, Watban, and Sabawi—under house arrest. Precisely what caused this family fallout has never been adequately explained. It has been suggested that Barzan was involved in a coup attempt against his half brother, in which he was approached by a group of military officers and offered the presidency if he would support a putsch against Saddam. Another version blames the failure of Barzan, who was head of security, to detect a plot against Saddam, which was ironic given that the previous year Barzan had actually published a book entitled *Attempts to Assassinate Saddam Hussein* in which he provided details of seven alleged plots, some of which had taken place before Saddam became leader, and accusing such disparate forces as Syria, Israel, and the United States of being the masterminds behind the schemes.

A more likely explanation is that Saddam and his half brothers became embroiled in a family feud. It is probably no coincidence that these tensions developed soon after the death of Saddam's beloved mother in August 1983; she was fiercely protective of her sons by her second marriage. The rivalry between the al-Majids, Saddam's blood relatives through his natural father, and the al-Ibrahims, his relatives through his mother's second marriage, was to become one of the key causes of tension within his regime. During her life Subha Tulfah had promoted the interests of all her sons, and the fact that all three of Saddam's half brothers had occupied such prominent positions in the government was as much due to Subha's persuasive talents as Saddam's proclivity for filling key positions with fellow Tikritis and family. The most likely explanation for the fallout between Saddam and his half brothers in late 1983 was Saddam's choice of bridegroom for his eldest daughter, Raghda. For all the Baathist propaganda about the emancipation of women that had taken place under the Baath, in Saddam's family traditional, tribal customs still prevailed, and it was the duty of the father to choose a suitable son-in-law. In this case Saddam had opted for Hussein Kamel al-Majid, one of his cousins. An officer of limited talent, Hussein had managed to ingratiate himself with both Saddam and Sajida. He had accompanied Sajida on her shopping trips to New York and, thanks to his family connections, occupied several key positions in Saddam's security apparatus. Saddam's choice of Hussein, however, caused deep offense to Barzan, who had been hoping that his own son would become betrothed to Raghda. Barzan was so incensed by the news that Saddam had opted for Hussein Kamel that, in typical Tikriti fashion, he threatened to kill Hussein rather than let him deprive his own son of his chosen bride. Thus a country that was in the midst of a murderous war and that was in the process of developing an arsenal of chemical, biological, and nuclear weapons found itself suddenly paralyzed by a family squabble over tribal marriage arrangements.

That the dispute was more tribal than conspiratorial was revealed a few days after the three half brothers had been placed under house arrest. Saddam made a public declaration of support in favor of Barzan's loyalty, something he would not have done had there been a shred of proof that had implicated any of the three half brothers in a plot against Saddam. Had such evidence been forthcoming, they would have experienced the same fate as any other conspirator, and been dispatched by one of Saddam's firing squads. Once tempers had cooled, the recalcitrant Barzan was treated in the same way as previous high-ranking Baathists who, for one reason or another, had fallen out of favor with the Baath hierarchy. Barzan was sent into exile as an ambassador, in his case in the unlikely role of Iraq's official representative to UNESCO in Geneva. Three years later the two other half brothers were rehabilitated. Sabawi took over Barzan's previous position as head of Amn al-Khass and Watban was made head of State Internal Security. The first significant crisis in Saddam's relations with his family had been resolved without recourse to bloodshed. It was an example that would not always be followed in the troubled years that lay ahead.

NINE

The Victor

The war was taking its toll on Saddam. The military setbacks of 1982, together with the incipient signs of popular unrest, affected Saddam's outlook. Saddam had always been susceptible to the idea that Baghdad was awash with plots and conspiracies, but the pressures of a war that showed no sign of abating only served to exacerbate his profound sense of paranoia. The carefree days when he could entertain his people with surprise visits, as he had on many occasions during the early years of his presidency, were long gone. No person or institution—not even his own family—was to be trusted. An elaborate and extensive security cordon was thrown up to protect the president from the numerous assassins, both foreign and domestic, who he had convinced himself were out for his blood. Whenever and wherever he traveled, decoy convoys of armored limousines with blacked-out windows and surrounded by heavily armed security guards would make dummy runs, trying to lure the would-be assassins from their lairs. With his own experience of plotting and carrying out assassinations, Saddam knew a thing or two about the mind of an assassin, and it was second nature for him to try to beat the assassins at their own game.

Similarly, visiting dignitaries would be required to go through a lengthy vetting procedure before they would be allowed into Saddam's presence. No one, not even his closest aides, could safely predict where Saddam would be at any given time. On the rare occasions that Iranian fighter-bombers were able to reach Baghdad, Saddam was sure that the bombs were aimed directly at him. Consequently the president took to sleeping in various "safe houses" in the Baghdad suburbs, an old habit that he had practiced during his years as an underground organizer of the Baath in the 1960s and one he would repeat many times in the future when he felt his personal safety was at risk. Saddam's mounting paranoia had many bizarre manifestations. When wearing his favorite hunting clothes, his hat would be lined with Kevlar bulletproof material. From the late 1970s he had employed his own cooks, but now they were supplanted by his personal food tasters, who accompanied him on trips when he ventured outside Baghdad. Rather than consult Iraqi doctors, who might easily be recruited by his enemies, Saddam hired a number of foreign physicians to care for his ailments. Former officials have claimed that he increasingly relied on the use of doubles to represent him at official ceremonies; one of the doubles is said to have been shot dead in 1984 after being mistaken for the real Saddam. Even Saddam's eldest son, Uday, was reported to have his own double. General Wafic al-Samurrai, who for a period in the 1980s was one of Saddam's most trusted military officers and was on intimate terms with the president, has confirmed that he saw doubles standing in for Saddam at minor official functions on several occasions.

Saddam had already created his own intelligence service, the Amn al-Khass, and in 1984 he took his personal security to new extremes when he created his own army, the revitalized version of the Republican Guard that had been in existence since the 1960s. The Baath prided itself on having its own militia, the Popular Army, which at the start of the war numbered around 250,000. In the early years of the war the Popular Army, which was in reality little more than a collection of enthusiastic Baathist amateurs, had carried out civil defense duties; on no account did it ever run the risk of seeing genuine combat. In 1984 Saddam decided to replace the Baath army with his own army unit, which owed its allegiance solely to the president. Beginning with just two brigades, the Republican Guard rapidly developed into an army within an army. It was equipped with the best available military equipment: Soviet-built T72, T62, and T55 tanks, French-manufactured 155-millimeter guns, and advanced ground-to-air missiles. Members of the Guard, drawn, like Saddam, from peasant Sunni stock, were imposing physical specimens. They received special training and better salaries than the other soldiers, and were totally dependent on Saddam for their existence. If the Iranians ever came close to invading Baghdad, the Republican Guard, like their praetorian forebears, would be expected to defend their president to the death. An elaborate security structure was imposed on the regular armed forces to prevent them from carrying out assassination and coup attempts. Army units were not allowed within one hundred miles of Baghdad, and when they relocated they did so without ammunition. Political commissars and security agents reported directly to Saddam's office on the performance of individual officers, who were frequently moved from unit to unit to prevent them from becoming too close to their troops.

Saddam had been badly shaken by the Israeli air raid the previous year that had destroyed Iraq's nuclear weapons program, and to protect himself and the regime from future air attacks he launched a costly program to build a network of underground bunkers to shelter both himself and the country's strategic resources. Although Saddam claimed the plan was being commissioned in the interests of national security, there was more than a suggestion that Saddam's own "bunker mentality" lay behind his interest in the project. British companies submitted designs for enough underground bunkers to hide forty-eight thousand soldiers. One of Saddam's personal bunkers was built beneath a cinema in the basement of the Al-Sijood administrative complex, located close to the Presidential Palace. Small by Saddam's standards (thirty feet by fifteen feet), it nevertheless contained enough electronic equipment, computers, teleprinters, and fiber-optic communications links for Saddam to maintain contact with his troops throughout the country.

Another Saddam bunker was built close to the new Presidential Palace complex he had started to build. This bunker, which was built by a German firm, was buried about three hundred feet beneath the Tigris River. The walls contained six to eight feet of reinforced concrete and the structure rested on huge springs, two feet in diameter, on a cushion of hard, molded rubber. In the event of a Hiroshima-sized bomb being detonated just a quarter of a mile away from the bunker, "Saddam would only feel a jolt." The bunker contained two escape routes, including an earthquake-proof elevator. Both the entrances to this James Bond–like fantasy hideout were guarded by automatically controlled machine-gun nests.[1] Saddam ordered special security arrangements to be included in the construction of the VIP lounge at Saddam International Airport, which was then under construction. He ordered the French contractors to build an underground escape route and a separate access road. "If the airport came under attack," recalled one of the French engineers, "Saddam could escape through a 15-kilometre-long tunnel beneath the VIP lounge that led to a secret helicopter landing pad out in the desert."[2]

Members of Saddam's immediate family were reaching the age when they could assume positions of responsibility in the government. It has become the habit among secular Arab despots to groom their sons as their political heirs; Bashir Asad became president of Syria on the death of his father, and both President Mubarak of Egypt and Colonel Gadhafi of Libya gave their sons privileged government positions in the hope that they might prove worthy successors. Saddam was no different, and when Uday graduated in engineering from the University of Baghdad in 1984, he rewarded his eldest son by appointing him director of Iraq's Olympic Committee. Even the most committed sports enthusiast would be hard-pressed to recall the last occasion on which an Iraqi athlete qualified for an Olympic event, but the Olympic Committee was more of a showcase position that enabled the twenty-year-old Uday to learn the art of government. In fact most of Uday's responsibilities concerned youth development, a task for which he was singularly unsuited in view of the unruly, selfish, and thuggish demeanor he had displayed both in high school and the university. Uday had graduated with an average grade of 98.5 percent, an unlikely score given his known preference for nightclubs over classrooms. It has also been claimed that tutors who were not prepared to give him the highest grade possible were tortured and lost their jobs.[3]

With both sons reaching marriageable age, Saddam had an opportunity to further his family's dynastic ambitions. In late 1984 Saddam arranged for Uday to marry his cousin Saja, who was the daughter of Saddam's half brother Barzan. As Saddam himself had shown with his own marriage to his first cousin, it was not uncommon for Iraqi men to marry close relatives. Although the Baath Party had made a heroic effort to modernize Iraq's economic and social structure in the sixteen years it had been in power, the ties of family and tribe remained immutable, and arranged marriages remained the norm. Barzan was still living in exile in Geneva following the family feud that had broken out the previous year over Saddam's refusal to allow Barzan's son to marry Saddam's eldest daughter, Raghda. By allowing one of Barzan's daughters to marry his eldest son, Saddam clearly hoped to settle the feud and persuade Barzan to return home and provide him with some much-needed moral support during the dark days of the war.

The union between Uday and Saja duly took place, and everything appeared set for a formal reconciliation between Saddam and his half brother. But Saddam had failed to appreciate just how out of control his eldest son had become, even after entering adulthood. Neither son had exactly been subjected to much discipline during their childhood, and the coffee shops and bazaars of Baghdad were frequently regaled with tales of the latest indiscretions of both Uday and Qusay. Their favorite haunt was the rooftop discotheque of the Melia Mansour Hotel, and Qusay, who was rather more fastidious in his choice of companion, was said to import blondes from Scandinavia for his personal entertainment. Even though both sons aspired to a playboy lifestyle, the failure of Uday's marriage after less than three months was truly scandalous even by the low moral standards of the Hussein clan. The precise reason for the marital breakdown has never been adequately explained, although it has become generally accepted within Iraqi society that the principal cause of the split was Uday's impotence.[4] Despite Uday's love of fast cars and racy nightclubs, suggestions persisted that he rarely achieved sexual fulfillment, which was the underlying psychological cause of his violent temper. When the brokenhearted Saja returned to her father's home in Geneva, it was generally accepted that the marriage had not been consummated. She returned home covered with cuts and bruises, the result of a savage beating she had received as a parting gift from Uday. Frustrated by his own inadequacy, violent outbursts were to become one of Uday's defining characteristics. Barzan, meanwhile, was less inclined than ever to contemplate a reconciliation with his half brother.

Saddam enjoyed more success in arranging the marriage of his other son, Qusay, who was quieter in temperament and more studious than his elder brother. For once one of Saddam's children was allowed to marry outside the family, although not outside the Tikriti clan. Qusay took for his bride Sahar, the daughter of one of the few genuine heroes of the war with Iran, General Maher Abdul Rashid, the Iraqi officer who was credited with having saved Saddam from capture by the Iranians in 1982. Although Saddam and Rashid had their differences (see Chapter Eight), Rashid was a Tikriti, after all, and a marriage into one of the more respectable Iraqi military families would undoubtedly raise the Husseins' social standing, a factor that was as important for Saddam as it was for his wife, Sajida. Qusay's marriage in 1985 was as much a political affair as it was dynastic, and any romantic element seems to have been completely lacking. As soon as two children had been produced, the marriage was dissolved. The collapse of this marriage might also have had something to do with the fact that, by the end of the war, Saddam, who was preternaturally jealous of the success enjoyed by any of his military officers, had placed his son's father-in-law under house arrest. The final piece in Saddam's dynastic jigsaw was put in place the same year when his second eldest daughter, Rana, married another of Saddam's first cousins, Saddam Kamel al-Majid, who was the younger brother of her elder sister's husband, Hussein Kamel al-Majid. By strengthening the ruling family's ties to the al-Majids, the relatives of Saddam's natural father, Saddam increased the estrangement of the al-Ibrahims, his stepfather's family, for his three half brothers had all nurtured the aspiration that their own sons might become betrothed to one of the president's daughters.

Saddam's preoccupation with feathering his family's nest while the rest of the country was suffering the bitter privations of war did little to improve his popularity among Iraqis. Stories about the venality of the Hussein clan, and particularly their interest in acquiring property, became commonplace. In 1985, to accommodate the requirements of his growing family, Saddam was said to have sequestered an entire town along the banks of the Euphrates. The owners of the valuable land and houses were paid sums of money determined by Saddam's family rather than by market conditions. When Saddam came to hear that the evicted landowners were less than pleased with the compensation they had received, he exploded, "They were without jackets and shoes before me."[5] Any number of lurid myths began to circulate about Saddam's family. It was widely believed, though never confirmed, that a young man who had taken a fancy to Saddam's youngest daughter, Hala, his favorite and the only one of his five children who was unmarried, was buried up to his neck and stoned to death. And even though Saddam had passed draconian anticorruption laws to deter Iraqis from profiteering from foreign contracts, his ruling inner circle seemed to have no qualms about ostentatiously flaunting their wealth. Adnan Khairallah, Saddam's brother-in-law and defense minister, collected a huge fleet of expensive cars. He would import a dozen Mercedes at a time and had a chauffeur for each. Adnan's greed made a deep impression on his nephews, Uday and Qusay, who began collecting their own fleets of cars, although the younger members of the Hussein clan were more interested in sports cars. In Saddam's view, the wealth being accumulated by his family was nothing less than what they deserved. "We have grabbed the lines of the sun," he declared on one occasion, "and we will not go."[6] So far as Saddam was concerned, Iraq's vast oil wealth was the exclusive domain of his family.

The lavish expenditure of Saddam's ruling elite contrasted sharply with the sacrifices demanded from ordinary Iraqis to fund the war effort. In 1983, for example, when Iraqi oil exports were at their lowest, Saddam called on Iraqi civilians to donate their jewelry and savings to the nation, "to allow women or elderly people to take part in the battle for the homeland, each according to his or her ability." Taha Yassin Ramadan, the Iraqi deputy prime minister, put it more succinctly. "This is a referendum in favour of the party . . . in favour of the revolution and the leadership of Saddam Hussein." The response was immense, whether from peasant farmers donating their life savings or elegant Baghdad ladies carrying their Moroccan leather jewel cases to the collecting centers. The finance minister was so impressed by the amount collected that he claimed "the gold amassed will be an extra reserve to strengthen the Iraqi currency." In theory, all the money and valuables handed over were merely on loan for the duration of the war, and would be handed back when the war ended. In most cases, however, the Iraqis received nothing in return for their generosity.

By far Saddam's biggest achievement during the mid-1980s was to turn Iraq's disastrous performance in the war against Iran to his, and the nation's, advantage. Iraq's "voluntary withdrawal" from Iran in the summer of 1982, as the regime referred to the defeats it had suffered at the hands of the Iranians, had fooled no one, least of all the Iraqi public. The "second Qadisiya" was now more commonly known as "Saddam's war," and the wholesale failure of the Iraqi military to achieve any of the stated war aims was Saddam's personal responsibility. The setbacks, however, only made Saddam more determined than ever to reassert himself as the undisputed ruler of the Iraqi people and their destiny. The purges carried out on senior military officers during the disastrous summer of 1982, together with the reorganization of the RCC, had reaffirmed Saddam's position as the country's supreme leader. In late 1982 he convened a special meeting of the Baath Party's Regional Command at which he sought, and received, confirmation of his absolute control over the machinery of government. The final report of the Ninth Party Congress stated unequivocally that "Saddam Hussein is the symbol of freedom, independence, pride, integrity and hope for a better future for Iraq and the Arab nation." But with absolute power came absolute responsibility, and the responsibility for the perilous plight Iraq faced from the ayatollahs rested squarely on Saddam's shoulders.

From the summer of 1982 onward the main thrust of the Iranian counteroffensive was directed at Basra, Iraq's second largest city and the capital of the country's Shiite community. The Iranians' objective was to cut the main Baghdad-Basra highway and to take control of the Shiite heartlands. The

Iraqis, however, proved better at defending their positions than they had been at going on the offensive, and were able to repulse the Iranian attacks and inflict heavy losses. From this point onward the conflict was locked in stalemate, with neither side able to make a significant breakthrough. The Iraqi engineers were fully occupied constructing an elaborate network of defensive positions that were not so very different from those constructed in northern France during the First World War. Well dug in, with a plentiful supply of ammunition and two other major defensive lines to protect the Iraqi heartland in the event of an Iranian breakthrough, Saddam's approach was to grind the Iranians into submission. The Iranians persisted with the same tactic that had succeeded in driving the Iraqis out of Khorramshahr. The *basij*, the young suicidal Iranian volunteers who were prepared to walk through minefields to claim their place in heaven, persisted with their human-wave attacks against the Iraqi positions. But the Iraqis had learned their lesson during the humiliating retreat from Khorramshahr, and were easily able to fight off these kamikaze tactics. On the rare occasions that the Iranians succeeded in making a breakthrough, the Iraqis were able to regain the initiative by calling in their helicopter gunships and fighter aircraft.

Saddam displayed considerable political skill during this period in turning the Iranian counteroffensive to his advantage. Somehow the Iranian attempts to capture Iraqi territory enabled the Iraqi government to achieve something it had failed to do in the early years of the war—unite the nation. With their backs to the wall, fighting to defend their territory and to prevent an invasion by the Iranians, the people of Iraq were transformed. Not only did the army fight with greater tenacity, there was also a noticeable drop in the volume of dissent. As one Western diplomat who was based in Baghdad during this period recalled, the bottom line was that the Iraqis were more afraid of the Iranians than they were of Saddam. "The Iraqi people were well aware that Saddam was a dictator and treated people badly if they crossed him, but they were far more alarmed at the prospect of the Iranian revolution being exported to Iraq. They wanted Saddam to be strong and they wanted him to win."[7]

The Iranians' three-pronged attack on Basra in late summer 1982 set the pattern for the dozens of others that would follow. The Iranians gained ground—in this instance about four miles—but were eventually stopped and driven back, losing large numbers of men in the process. Well protected behind their fortifications, the Iraqis showed a new spirit, fighting with skill and determination as they defended their homeland rather than having to hold some nebulous, unnatural line inside Iran. Saddam was highly successful in publicizing the military's success in halting these Iranian onslaughts as a great victory. Rallies and celebrations were held in Baghdad and in towns and villages throughout the country. The speeches made by Saddam and the Baath leadership made a point of blaming Iran for the outbreak of hostilities in 1980. The demands made at the start of the war, such as the realignment of the border along the Shatt al-Arab and the resolution of Iraq's claim to Arab territories in Iran, were quietly dropped. All Saddam was looking for now was the restoration of the status quo ante of 1980.

Iraq's success in repelling the Iranian human-wave attacks, however, made little impression on the ayatollahs in Teheran. The Iranians' main objective remained the capture of Basra and the overthrow of Saddam Hussein. Their strategy was to besiege the city and destroy its garrison or force it to surrender, or to bypass it completely and drive into the west, effectively cutting Iraq in two. The Iranians reasoned that by seizing a sizable slice of territory in southern Iraq, the Shiite heartland, it would be possible to announce a provisional government to which the opponents of Saddam Hussein could rally. The fear that the Iranians would attempt to implement a similar strategy in the aftermath of Operation Desert Storm in 1991 was one of the reasons the victorious allies refused to support the Shiite revolt against Saddam.

The Iranians remained determined to take Basra even though they were unable to achieve a significant breakthrough. Different attacks were launched in different sectors, each one gaining a little ground and nibbling away at the Iraqi border areas. No matter how great the sacrifice, the ayatollahs would not give up on their objective. As a consequence the casualties on both sides were horrendous. By 1984 Iraq had suffered at least 65,000 killed, with at least three to five times as many wounded and between 50,000 to 60,000 combatants taken prisoner. By comparison the Iranians had lost up to 180,000 killed, with as many as 500,000 injured.[8] The casualty figures were far higher than anything Iraq had experienced since independence, and there was hardly a family in the country that had not suffered some loss. The manpower situation was so bad by the end of 1984 that the government had to revert to calling up seventeen-year-olds for service. Saddam tried to cushion the discontent caused by the appalling waste of life at the front by making generous payments and benefits available to bereaved families and widows. Even so, there was further public disquiet in Iraq about the level of casualties and from

1984 Saddam ordered a change in tactics that were designed to reduce the level of casualties at the front. The Iraqis relied even more on heavy artillery and air strikes to repel the frequent human-wave attacks being launched by the Iranians. And the Iraqis managed to harass the Iranians by launching raids deep inside Iranian territory, in the hope of demonstrating the incompetence of the authorities in Teheran in protecting their own people.

The only breakthrough of any significance made by the Iranians during the war of attrition, as this period in the conflict became known, came in early 1984 when the Iranians captured the Majnun Islands, two thin strips of territory, loaded with oil, that commanded the northern approach to Basra. The Iranian operation was brilliantly executed. Attacking at night, Iranian commandos in small fiberglass boats had made their way silently through the Howeiza marshes, taking the few Iraqis guarding the levees by surprise. By dawn the Iranians were fully in control of both islands, north and south, and well dug in. They constructed a pontoon bridge to bring up supplies and fresh troops. Within days they had increased the bridgehead to some 30,000 troops and had built a dirt causeway linking the Majnun Islands to the mainland in Iran. The Iraqis counterattacked time after time, trying to drive the Iranians into the swamps and back over the border. But the reed-filled marshes got the better of them. The heavy undergrowth fouled the propellers of Iraq's amphibious tanks, making them an easy target for the Iranian gunners. Saddam, furious that his troops were unable to dislodge the stubborn Iranians, decided that there was only one option available to him—to use the poison gas now being manufactured at his new chemical weapons plants that had come on-line at Salman Pak and Samarra.

Iraqi pilots dumped canisters from Soviet-, German-, and French-built helicopters. A small electric pump inside the drums triggered on impact, dispersing the mixture into a deadly cloud. In other attacks the helicopters sprayed the Iranians with a greasy yellow liquid that filled the area with the odor of garlic. The Iranians, who had no protective clothing, fell ill immediately. Within minutes they began vomiting a yellowish liquid, and their skin turned red. By the time the medics reached the battlefield, some of the troops were already dead, their faces horribly blackened by the gas. Others had amber-colored blisters all over their bodies and were having trouble breathing.[9]

The Iraqis, of course, strongly denied using chemical weapons, but in March 1984 a group of UN experts visited Iran to investigate the claims. The UN team concluded that Iraq had used mustard gas and the chemical nerve agent Tabun, which had first been developed by the Nazis and was now being manufactured at the Salman Pak military complex at Suwaira, which had been constructed with the help of a number of German companies. Although Tabun had been developed by the Nazis, Hitler himself had refrained from using it on the battlefield. Saddam, clearly, had no such qualms.

The use of chemical weapons against the Iranians rebounded on Saddam in more ways than one. To start with, the use of poison gas was counterproductive. Although the first use of the gas caught the Iranians by surprise, and inflicted significant casualties, the weather conditions were rarely right for its use, and when the wind changed direction, it could blow back onto the Iraqi troops. "The Iraqis hated using poison gas," according to a former Western military attaché who was based in Iraq at the time. "It was difficult to use and posed as much of a threat to their own forces as it did to the enemy."[10] The Iranians also proved adept at changing their tactics to deal with the new threat. When the Iraqis used poison gas the following year, the Iranian front-line troops had all been equipped with West German respirators and personal phials of Atropin, a fast-acting agent used to counter nerve gas. And confirmation by UN inspectors that Iraq was using chemical weapons against the Iranians resulted in most Western countries reassessing their policy of supporting Iraq.

Prior to the scandal surrounding Iraq's use of nerve gas on the battlefield, Saddam had deployed the same skill abroad as he had at home in turning the war to his advantage. At the start of the war the general view of those not directly involved in the conflict had been best articulated by Dr. Henry Kissinger, the former U.S. secretary of state, who had lamented the fact that both sides could not lose. Thanks to Saddam's remarkable propaganda skills, however, by 1984 most of the Western powers, together with the majority of Arab states, had swung behind the Iraqi war effort. It would be fair to say that at the start of the Iran-Iraq War few people outside the closed arena of international diplomacy had heard of Saddam, despite his obsession with propaganda and self-promotion. On the other hand by the early 1980s most people were well aware of the Iranian revolution, and the fanaticism of Khomeini's Revolutionary Guards. The American embassy siege in Teheran, and the disastrous U.S. military mission to rescue the hostages in late 1980, had destroyed Jimmy Carter's presidency. The attempts by the Iranians to export their revolution to the Gulf states and Lebanon, where the establishment of the Hizbollah militia, which was funded, equipped, and trained by Iran's

Revolutionary Guards, posed a direct threat to Western interests in the eastern Mediterranean, had turned Iran into a pariah state. Although the blame for provoking hostilities lay with Saddam, by early 1983 the Iraqis were able to claim, with ample justification, that the Iranians were wholly responsible for their continuation.

No matter how unappealing Saddam's totalitarian regime might have appeared to the outside world, Baghdad found itself attracting an eclectic mix of backers who saw the Iraqi cause as a crucial bulwark against the advancing tide of Islamic fanaticism as personified by the ayatollahs in Teheran. Saddam's first breakthrough was with the Soviets, traditionally one of Baghdad's largest military suppliers, which had responded to Iraq's invasion of Iran by declaring its neutrality and imposing an arms embargo. Relations between Moscow and Baghdad had become strained before the war because of the Soviets' increasing displeasure at Saddam's persecution of the Iraqi Communist Party. But Saddam's anticommunism was manageable when compared with the rabid anticommunist and anti-Soviet rhetoric emanating from Teheran, which culminated in 1983 with the ayatollahs executing the leaders of the Tudah Party, the Iranian Communist Party. The Soviets had resumed moderate levels of arms shipments to Baghdad in 1981, but by 1983 Moscow was prepared to sell the Iraqis top-of-range equipment, such as its SS-12 ballistic missiles, which, with a range of 800 kilometers (500 miles), were capable of hitting targets deep inside Iranian territory. The Soviets also dispatched twelve hundred military advisers to help with the Iraqi war effort.

Relations with Egypt, which had deteriorated after the Camp David peace agreement, were repaired after the assassination of President Anwar Sadat in 1981. Hosni Mubarak, the new Egyptian president, who was trying to contain his own Islamic firebrands, agreed to provide Iraq with spare parts for its Soviet weapons systems, as well as tanks and other equipment. The French, who had enjoyed a lucrative arms trade with Baghdad since the mid-1970s, negotiated a loan deal for the Iraqis to have five Super Étendard warplanes, equipped with heat-seeking missiles and guidance systems and which were to be used mainly for attacks on Gulf shipping.

From 1983 onward Iraq received considerable backing from the Gulf states that were keen to contain the menace posed by the Iranian revolution. Iraq's oil revenues had collapsed as a result of its inability to ship oil through the Gulf after Syria had closed its pipeline outlet to the Mediterranean. Iranian oil revenues, on the other hand, which were buoyed by the fact that

Iran's southern ports were relatively unscathed during the early stages of the war, had nearly trebled between 1981 and 1983.[11] With the war effort costing the Iraqis an estimated $1 billion a month, the donations made by the Gulf states were crucial to keeping the Iraqi economy afloat, even after Saddam had cut back his spending on consumer goods in 1982. If the Iranians succeeded in making a breakthrough of the Iraqi lines, the defenseless Gulf states were well aware that they were on the ayatollahs' agenda. Consequently Iraq received donations worth $25 billion toward its war effort, most of which was spent on rearming the armed forces.

The Western powers, with the notable exception of France, publicly professed a policy of studious neutrality in the war while privately backing the Iraqis. There was a general consensus that an Iranian victory would have disastrous consequences for the stability and security of the Gulf. Perhaps the most surprising diplomatic development during this period was the rapprochement between Baghdad and Washington. The U.S. State Department was starting to view the dramatic developments on the battlefield with alarm. The initial hope of the Carter administration that an Iraqi invasion might deter the Iranians from trying to export their revolution throughout the Middle East had come to nothing. Indeed, unless Saddam received help, there was a genuine expectation in Washington that Iran might win the war. As a first step toward resolving fifteen years of mutual hostility between Washington and Baghdad, the State Department in 1982 took Iraq off its list of countries suspected of supporting international terrorism. Countries on the list were subjected to "foreign policy controls," and by removing Iraq from the list the United States had more freedom of movement if it wanted to funnel aid to Baghdad. Later that year the shift in policy resulted in the Reagan administration authorizing the sale of sixty Hughes helicopters, a type of aircraft specifically designed for battlefield observation. Soon after the new helicopters arrived in Iraq in 1983 they were easily adapted to fire TOW antitank missiles, and were deployed in an offensive capacity against Iranian positions.

Washington's delicate diplomatic dance with Baghdad continued in the summer of 1983 with a visit to Washington by Ismat Kittani, the Iraqi undersecretary for foreign affairs. This was reciprocated the following December with a visit to Baghdad by Donald Rumsfeld, who was then a special Middle East envoy for President Ronald Reagan. Given Rumsfeld's position as one of the leading cheerleaders in favor of military action against Saddam in the aftermath of the September 11, 2001, terrorist attacks against the United

States, it is somewhat ironic that Rumsfeld played such a key role in helping to bring Iraq out of its diplomatic isolation in the 1980s. According to David Mack, a former U.S. diplomat who accompanied Rumsfeld on his Baghdad mission, the American desire to reopen formal channels with Iraq reflected the different U.S. geopolitical priorities that existed for the Middle East at that time. "We were looking to bring pressure to bear on Syria, and it seemed a good idea to patch up our differences with Baghdad." The Syrian regime, which enjoyed close ties with Moscow, was then backing the radical Lebanese Shiite Muslim groups such as Hizbollah, which destroyed the American embassy and U.S. marine compound in Beirut earlier in 1983. "Relations had been improving with Baghdad from the late 1970s onward, but it was a difficult and slow process. It was very difficult for us to read the signals coming out of Baghdad. But with the war going so badly for Saddam, and the Syrians causing us a lot of grief in Beirut, we thought it made sense to deal with Saddam. We wanted to build a Cairo-Amman-Baghdad axis that would drive President Asad crazy."[12]

The bombing of the American embassy and the U.S. marine compound in Beirut was in fact the key turning point in Washington's decision to build bridges with Baghdad. The embassy bombing, in April 1983, had taken place during a meeting of the CIA's station chiefs in the Middle East. In one stroke most of the CIA's best Middle East experts had been wiped out. Within weeks satellite intercepts of telephone conversations confirmed American suspicions—the terrorists responsible for the bombing had been guided by Teheran. The United States was now unofficially at war with Iran. The United States moved quickly, and the following month Secretary of State George Shultz met secretly with Tariq Aziz, the Iraqi foreign minister, during a trip to Paris. Shultz and Aziz both saw the logic of pooling resources in the fight against the ayatollahs, but the United States was still wary of normalizing relations so long as Saddam continued to harbor Abu Nidal, who only the previous year had masterminded the attempted assassination of Shlomo Argov, the Israeli ambassador to London (see Chapter Eight). In order for Washington to agree to normalize relations with Baghdad, Shultz insisted that Saddam must first get rid of Abu Nidal. The Iraqi leader duly obliged, but in the most bizarre way imaginable. Soon after the Shultz-Aziz meeting the government-owned Iraqi media solemnly announced that Abu Nidal had died of a heart attack. The report was confirmed by "sources" close to the Palestinian terrorist. A month later, just as the report was starting to acquire credence in the international intelligence community, Libya's Colonel Gadhafi announced that Abu Nidal was alive and living in Tripoli, thereby undermining Saddam's rather ingenious attempt to wash his hands of the Abu Nidal issue.

The U.S. rapprochement with Saddam gathered momentum in December 1983 when Rumsfeld flew to Baghdad. During the visit Rumsfeld met with Saddam and delivered a personal letter from President Reagan. The visit must have been a success for, after Rumsfeld returned to Washington, the United States began to exert pressure on its allies not to supply arms to Iran. In November 1984 warmer U.S.-Iraqi relations resulted in the full restoration of diplomatic relations and American companies were encouraged to participate in the construction of Iraq's new pipelines through Jordan and Saudi Arabia to provide Baghdad with new outlets for its oil sales. Saddam responded by sending Tariq Aziz, his foreign minister, to Washington, where he delivered a message from Saddam to President Reagan and other leading members of the administration. The United States may have quietly maintained a CIA office in Baghdad from as early as 1979;[13] certainly the CIA was active in Baghdad from 1984 onward. At this time, however, the United States was still holding back from directly arming the Iraqis and maintaining a policy of neutrality, with the exception of sixty Hughes helicopters that were sold in 1982 "for use in agriculture." David Mack insisted that Washington did not sell any arms to Iraq. "We never provided any military equipment to Iraq," he said. "The only U.S. equipment we ever sent to Baghdad was two pearl-handled revolvers which Saddam asked for especially to give someone as a present. But that was it. Nothing else."

The most important contribution the United States made to the Iraqi war effort was undoubtedly the high-grade intelligence of Iranian troop dispositions provided by the CIA spy satellites. Soon after the restoration of full diplomatic relations, the Americans sent a CIA liaison team to Baghdad to deliver satellite photos and other intelligence gleaned from U.S. AWACS surveillance aircraft based in neighboring Saudi Arabia. The intelligence liaison between Langley, Virginia, the CIA headquarters, and Baghdad was soon established on such a regular footing that Saddam designated three senior officers from the Estikhbarat, Iraq's military intelligence, to liaise directly with the Americans. The American assistance soon paid dividends. When in June 1984 Saudi Arabian fighters shot down an Iranian F-4 attempting to attack a target in Saudi territorial waters, Washington acknowledged that this skirmish had been directed from a "Saudi" AWACS plane manned by American personnel.

General Wafic al-Samurrai, who was one of the Iraqi officers liaising with the United States, recalled that the information was enormously helpful to the Iraqi war effort. When preparing for an attack, his officers would routinely request specific intelligence from the Americans. "I used to say, for example, 'Give us information on the Basra sector.'" Even though the Americans provided the information, Saddam remained deeply suspicious about the relationship, so much so that he put Samurrai under intensive surveillance by his Amn al-Khass security forces. Saddam personally advised his generals on how to go about seeking information from their CIA allies. When Saddam wanted information about the Basra sector, for example, he would tell Samurrai, "Ask them to give us information from the north of Iraq to the south, because if we tell them it's Basra, they will tell the Iranians." Samurrai would sometimes have his memos on his U.S. contacts, which Saddam was constantly demanding from him, returned with cautionary notes scribbled in the margins in Saddam's distinctive scrawl. "Be careful, Americans are conspirators."

Saddam's suspicions about the duplicity of the American intelligence infrastructure was borne out with the exposure of the infamous Iran-Contra scandal in 1986. One of the reasons why the revelation, in late 1986, that the United States had been secretly shipping antitank missiles to Iran since 1985 caused such embarrassment in Washington was that U.S. policy was directed toward supporting Iraq in the war with Iran. The Irangate scandal, as it became known, which was hatched by Lieutenant Colonel Oliver North of the National Security Council, was designed to buy the release of American hostages being held in Lebanon, but was abandoned when details of the deal were made public. Some of the TOW antitank weapons supplied by the United States actually found their way to the Iranian front, where they helped the Iranians achieve a strategic breakthrough on the Basra battlefield.

In the early 1980s Britain was still attempting to maintain a neutral posture. Sir John Moberly, who was Britain's ambassador to Iraq between 1982 and 1985, said that, unlike the United States, Britain did not believe that Iraq was in danger of being overrun by Iran. "The American view was that there was a real danger of Iraq being defeated by the Iranians and so they had to do everything they could to bolster the Iraqis. We, however, were slightly more skeptical about things." Because of Britain's intransigence over supplying Iraq with arms, Moberly only saw Saddam on rare occasions, but when he did he was impressed with what he saw. "He was a man who clearly had a strong personality who was very much in control of events. Everyone in Iraq knew where they stood. And they were well aware that if they stepped out of line that would be the end for them. Most Iraqis accepted that Iraq needed a strong leader to maintain law and order and hold the country together. Saddam fulfilled all these criteria." Moberly was, however, in constant contact with Tariq Aziz, Saddam's foreign minister, who was forever berating the British envoy about the Thatcher government's position. "Aziz was always complaining that he got a better reception from the Americans than he got from the British and that, as the former colonial power, we should have a better understanding of the Iraqi people. Aziz would say: 'You people should understand us, but instead we find in practice that we get a far better hearing from the U.S. than we do from the U.K.'"[14]

Indeed, for most of the war the British position on the Gulf was encapsulated by the now infamous guidelines on arms sales provided to the House of Commons by Geoffrey Howe, the foreign secretary, in 1985, when he stated that Britain refused to supply "lethal defense equipment" to either side as part of Britain's policy "of doing everything possible to see this tragic conflict brought to the earliest possible end." By late 1984 there was growing evidence that the Iraqis were using chemical weapons as a means of countering Iran's human-wave attacks, and a number of human rights organizations were starting to investigate the claims. The UN reports were particularly resonant in London, where confirmation of Iraq's use of chemical weapons, combined with Iraq's appalling human rights record, persuaded the Thatcher government to impose tough restrictions on British trade with Iraq. There were a number of deals to supply Baghdad with nonlethal equipment, such as radar electronics, which were approved by the British government. It was only toward the end of the war that the Thatcher government quietly adopted a more liberal interpretation of what constituted "nonlethal" equipment, and the decision to allow the Midlands company Matrix-Churchill to export to Baghdad equipment designed for making sophisticated armaments would result in the "Iraqgate" scandal.

With money and arms coming into Baghdad, the war moved into a new phase from 1984 onward. In an attempt to force the Iranians to the negotiating table Saddam sought to undermine the morale of the civilian population by destroying the Iranian economy. In February 1984 he began using the newly imported Soviet missiles to target Iranian cities, much as the German V2 "doodlebug" rockets had been fired at Britain during the closing stages of World War II. This provoked what became known as the first Battle of the Cities, for the Iranians soon responded in kind. The second Battle of the Cities took place in March and April 1985 and, from Saddam's point of view, began to pay dividends as the constant targeting of Teheran by Iraqi missiles provoked widespread demonstrations against the Iranian government.

Apart from trying to demoralize the Iranians, Saddam's other main goal from the mid-1980s onward was to internationalize the conflict in the hope that the West could be persuaded to end the war for him. On this basis in March 1984 he ordered his newly acquired French Super Étendard warplanes to launch long-range attacks on Iran's oil terminals and shipping in the Gulf. Initially the Iraqi attacks were concentrated on tankers bound for Iran's ports, especially the Kharj Island terminal. In the first months some seventy ships were hit by the Étendard's highly efficient Exocet missiles.

The war continued along similar lines until February 1986 when the Iranians made a surprising breakthrough on the battlefield and captured the Fao Peninsula south of Basra, which put Iraq's second largest city in serious jeopardy of falling to Teheran. Even though the Fao Peninsula itself was militarily irrelevant, the Iranian breakthrough nonetheless constituted a significant political setback for Saddam at a time when Iraq appeared to be making headway on the war front. Saddam compounded this setback by instructing his generals to retake Foa, even though by the time he gave the order it was too late. The Iranians were too well dug in to be dislodged. Obeying Saddam's orders, the Iraqi generals poured men and equipment into the peninsula, and suffered appalling casualties. Iraq's total manpower losses in early 1986 were put at between 8,000 and 10,000 dead and the Iraqi military was forced to organize special trains to carry its wounded; the corresponding casualty figure for Iran was 20,000 fatalities.[15]

The failure to recapture Fao prompted Saddam to make another strategic error. Desperate for a victory, he ordered the Iraqi army to launch an offensive on the central front to take the Iranian town of Mehran. Saddam's strategy was twofold: he wanted to demonstrate to the Iraqi people that their armed forces were still capable of taking offensive action; and he wanted to capture Iranian territory that could be used as a bargaining chip to recover Foa. Initially the Iraqis, who attacked in May with four divisions, succeeded in capturing the town, which was lightly guarded by five thousand Iranian troops who were quickly overwhelmed, suffering heavy casualties in the process. The victory certainly boosted the morale of the armed forces, and Saddam was quick to exploit its propaganda potential. But the victory was short-lived. The Iranians refused Saddam's offer to exchange Mehran for Fao, and at the end of June launched a counteroffensive, which caught the Iraqi occupiers by surprise. By early July, Mehran was back under Iranian control and the Iraqis had suffered further casualties.

The loss of Fao, and the heavy Iraqi losses suffered as a result of Saddam's demand that the Iraqi armed forces launch a series of futile attempts to recover the territory, was deeply wounding for him. The Mehran adventure was a further example of the problems caused by having civilians in charge of military operations. Saddam's insistence on personally directing the war effort had in no small measure contributed to the failure of Iraq's superior military firepower to react adequately to the initial Iranian attack. The loss of the Fao Peninsula prompted a reaction from the Iraqi president that bordered on the irrational. All Iraqis were urged to donate money and blood and to work longer hours. Some 100,000 men, women, and children were enlisted to cut reeds in the southern marshes to help facilitate Iraq's military operations in the area. In an attempt to offset Iran's overwhelming demographic superiority, Saddam personally launched a nationwide campaign to encourage procreation. "Our motto must be that each family produces five children and that families failing to produce at least four children deserve to be harshly reprimanded." He strongly advised female students to choose childbearing over studying. The heavy losses suffered during the Fao counterattacks saw the Iraqi authorities resorting to desperate measures such as forced blood donations, trying to mass recruit the staffs of some leading tourist hotels, and forcing empty taxis going north from Basra to carry corpses inside the vehicle or on the roof racks.

It was at this juncture in the conflict that Iraq's military commanders, frustrated at Saddam's constant interference in their conduct of the war, came close to staging a mutiny. An example of the military's growing disillusion with Saddam manifested itself in the winter of 1986, when he clashed with General Maher Abdul Rashid of the Seventh Corps. Rashid, a fellow Tikriti and the father-in-law of Saddam's second son, Qusay, was one of Iraq's genuinely successful officers. Rashid had a reputation for speaking his mind, and the huge loss of Iraqi life at Fao, which he thought could have been avoided, caused him to criticize publicly Saddam's tactics. In a candid interview published in the Kuwaiti press, Rashid stated unequivocally that the high number of Iraqi casualties incurred during the Fao battle had been unnecessary. Saddam was incensed, and ordered Rashid to Baghdad to explain himself. Well aware of what the order meant, Rashid's officers transmitted a warning to Saddam, implying that they would refuse to continue the war effort should anything untoward happen to their commander. On arrival at the Presidential Palace, Rashid was decorated by a beaming Saddam, who deferred his vengeance for later. After the war Rashid was forced to resign his commission and was put under house arrest.

It is significant that, unlike previous military coups in Iraq, the officers were not seeking political power in their confrontation with Saddam; they simply desired to be able to use their own professional judgment to prosecute the war against Iran. And for the moment they were successful. For the rest of the war the commanders were able to insist that they were running the war, not the politicians. Saddam was seen less and less at meetings of the Supreme Defense Council, the body overseeing the war effort, and though he continued to visit frontline positions, it was plain that his trips were to raise morale among the troops, and the fiction that Saddam was personally directing successful operations was quietly dropped.

Indications that Saddam was getting more and more irrational in his conduct were not confined to the military arena. In the mid-1980s it was reported that he had sacked Hamed al-Jubari, his foreign minister, after the workaholic Saddam had twice telephoned the minister's office and received no reply. Assuming that the minister was late for work, Saddam dismissed him the moment he arrived at the office. Saddam refused to rescind his decision even after the minister informed him that he had a perfectly legitimate reason for not being at his desk—he had been at Baghdad airport receiving an official delegation. Despite the venality of his own family, Saddam also initiated a big anticorruption drive against Iraqis accused of taking illicit commissions on government contracts. Since the 1970s corruption had been regarded as a serious offense by the Baathists, but during the boom years of the late 1970s and early 1980s a blind eye had generally been turned to the Iraqi entrepreneurs who were making small fortunes for themselves in commissions on large foreign contracts. The austerity of the mid-1980s saw Saddam revive much of the anticorruption legislation with the result that Abdul Wahab Mufti, the mayor of Baghdad, who had taken over from

Khairallah Tulfah, was hanged following allegations that he had received bribes from a British company supplying Baghdad with refuse trucks and fire engines.

The collapse in the oil revenues resulted in the Iraqis having to default on payments for their arms supplies. Until the start of the war with Iran, Baghdad had enjoyed a reputation as a prompt payer, which was one of the main reasons that Western governments had been so keen to do business with the Baathists. By the mid-1980s, however, money was scarce and Saddam was unable to meet the payments on the arms shipments he needed to sustain the war effort. The French and the Russians were the worst affected, though their constant complaints on the Baghdad diplomatic circuit that they could not get the Iraqis to settle their debts evoked little sympathy from their fellow diplomats. "I think we all took the view that, particularly with the French, that they got what they deserved," commented one former Western diplomat.[16]

Realizing that his position was getting increasingly desperate, Saddam made yet another attempt to sue for peace. But the ayatollahs remained insistent that one of their key conditions for halting hostilities was Saddam's removal from power. As Saddam's entire raison d'être was his own survival, the Iranians' demand was clearly out of the question. Saddam responded with a ferocious aerial assault against Iran's main population centers—Teheran, Isfahan, and Kermanshah—and renewed the assault on the ayatollahs' economic infrastructure.

In one of the most significant developments of the war, in August 1986 Iraqi aircraft mounted their first successful raid on the Iranian oil terminal of Sirri Island, just 150 miles north of the Strait of Hormuz at the mouth of the Gulf, thereby demonstrating to Teheran that none of Iran's strategic targets was beyond Iraq's operational reach. By extending the conflict to the lower reaches of the Gulf, Saddam was making another attempt to escalate the conflict in a manner that would invite international intervention. In particular he was hoping to provoke the Iranians into a reaction that would make the Gulf unsafe for shipping, thereby closing one of the world's most important oil arteries. At first the Iranians would not be drawn into Saddam's trap, and the Strait of Hormuz remained open. As Saddam maintained his assault on Iran's economic infrastructure, however, the Iranians came to the view that they had no alternative other than to respond in kind. In late 1986, the Iranians began intimidating the Kuwaitis, who were assisting Iraq with its oil exports, so much so that the Kuwaitis approached both superpowers with a request for protection. The Soviets were the first to offer their services, and the prospect of the Soviet navy assuming responsibility for policing the Gulf shipping lanes prompted the United States to intervene on Kuwait's behalf. By early 1987 both superpowers, and a number of Western countries such as Britain and France, had deployed some fifty warships in the Gulf. Saddam had gotten his way and managed to embroil the world's powers in a dispute they had been desperately hoping to avoid. Moreover Saddam in effect had the might of the world's navies protecting him from attacks by Iran while he remained able to attack Iranian targets with relative impunity. Even when an Iraqi Super Étendard mistakenly fired two Exocet missiles at the American frigate USS *Stark,* killing thirty-seven American servicemen, there was no letup in the international protection effort.

The international intervention to protect Iraqi oil supplies, together with the maintenance of Saddam's intensive bombardment of Iranian cities, gradually combined to sap Iranian morale and gave the regime in Teheran a growing sense of isolation. There was a sharp drop in the number of young Iranians volunteering for the front, particularly after the costly failure to capture Basra in late 1987. The constant Iraqi bombing had caused many Iranians to flee the main cities. The peace lobby in Teheran became more vocal as the pattern of the war changed from being a defensive campaign to repel the Iraqi invaders to an offensive assault to capture Iraqi territory and overthrow Saddam. Saddam correctly calculated that one big offensive was all that was required to force the Iranians to the negotiating table, and in February 1988 the Iraqis launched their most ferocious campaign of the entire war. During the next two months about 150 missiles and numerous air raids were launched against Iran's major population centers. In April the Iraqis launched their first ground offensive in nearly six years, and managed to recapture the Fao Peninsula. Apart from receiving the assistance of U.S. military intelligence, the Iraqis received direct military assistance from the United States, which sent teams of military advisers to assist the Iraqi top brass direct operations at the front. Emboldened by this success the Iraqis launched more offensives during the spring and succeeded in driving out the Iranians from all the Iraqi territory they had captured since 1982. In early July the Iraqi forces drove the remaining Iranian forces out of Kurdistan and even managed to capture a small strip of Iranian territory in the central part of the Iran-Iraq border, the first Iraqi incursion into Iran since the heady days at the start of the conflict in 1980.

Throughout this period the Iranians were incapable of providing an adequate response to the Iraqi assaults. The lack of volunteers for the front meant they were unable to consider launching a ground offensive and their air force was grounded through lack of spare parts. The only tactic available to them was to attack Iraqi shipping, but as Saddam had now inveigled an array of Western navies to protect all Gulf shipping, any Iranian move would run the risk of provoking a direct confrontation with the United States and its allies. Small detachments of Revolutionary Guards did manage to attack several ships by using small, high-speed boats and also succeeded in mining the main shipping lanes. These tactics made the Iranians appear the main threat to Western interests, and the high state of alert that was being maintained by the American forces against the possibility of an Iranian attack resulted, in early July, in the USS *Vincennes* accidentally shooting down an Iranian civilian airliner, with the loss of more than three hundred lives.[17]

A combination of all these factors enabled the peace camp in Teheran finally to persuade Ayatollah Khomeini that it was time to bring hostilities to a halt; the aging ayatollah reluctantly agreed that Saddam Hussein, his mortal enemy, would not be overthrown during his lifetime. On July 18, 1988, Iran accepted UN Security Council resolution 598 for a cease-fire in the Iran-Iraq War and a month later the guns along the common border fell silent. Khomeini claimed that agreeing to the cease-fire was like drinking from a poisoned chalice. Saddam simply declared himself the victor. A war that had cost an estimated one million fatalities, had wrecked the Iraqi economy, and had come close to destroying Saddam's presidency was now proclaimed a triumph for the Iraqi people. And in many respects the conclusion of the war did represent a significant achievement. In spite of the brutal totalitarianism that characterized his regime, Saddam had managed to persuade the outside world that a secular and progressive Iraq was infinitely preferable to the fanatical hordes of the Iranian revolution. He had managed to attract the financial and moral support of his Gulf neighbors and even had the world's superpowers competing against each other to ensure his success in the war with Iran. Domestically he had demonstrated that he was not afraid to engage in repression, even in time of war. He had made it abundantly clear that no sacrifice was too great to keep him in power.

The only blemish on his victory was Saddam's proclivity for using nonconventional weapons in conventional warfare. For most of the Iran-Iraq War, Saddam used chemical weapons sparingly against the Iranians, for fear of turning international opinion against Baghdad. Thus chemical weapons were used against the Iranians on isolated occasions, such as when Iraq was confronted by the massive human-wave attacks by suicidal volunteers, or to dislodge the Iranians from strategically sensitive targets, such as the Majnun Islands. Apart from the 1984 UN report on the use of mustard gas and Tabun nerve agent, the Iraqis were accused by UN inspectors of using chemical weapons in both 1986 and 1987. The inspectors concluded that "chemical weapons have been used once again by the Iraqi forces against the Iranian forces and resulted in many casualties." Even so, Saddam was relatively restrained in his use of nonconventional weapons, enabling him to secure the support of most Western powers, who turned a blind eye to the damning evidence produced by the UN inspection teams.

If Saddam was sparing in his use of chemical weapons against the Iranians, the same did not hold true when it came to dealing with his own people. Throughout the conflict the Kurds had been hoping to take advantage of the hostilities to pursue their own goal of total independence. At one point Saddam became so exasperated with them that he actually colluded with the Turks and the United States to allow a Turkish offensive against Kurdish territory. From 1983 the Iranians, aware of the vulnerability of Saddam's forces in the region, concentrated part of their effort on trying to make a breakthrough in Kurdistan. Saddam initially responded by repeating his offer to grant the Kurds limited autonomy. The Kurds spurned the offer, and Saddam reacted by launching a ferocious campaign to subjugate the area. The assault was led by General Ali Hassan al-Majid, Saddam's cousin, who was to become known as "Chemical Ali" for his preference for using nonconventional weapons. Al-Majid, who was Saddam's first cousin by his natural father, had been in charge of the Mukhabarat, the state security service, since Saddam's falling-out with Barzan al-Tikriti and the Ibrahim branch of the family. As the situation with the Kurds deteriorated, Saddam appointed al-Majid his viceroy to the north and ordered him to use any means necessary to resolve the Kurdish problem.

The campaign started with the execution of eight thousand Kurdish prisoners, who had been captured and held since 1983. The government also attempted to reinstitute its policy of uprooting the rebellious population and moving them to areas where they posed less of a threat to Baghdad. By the end of the war in 1988, it is estimated that more than half of the towns and villages in Kurdistan had been razed and their populations deported to the main towns, or else to concentration camps in the southwestern Iraqi desert. When the population tried to resist, Majid resorted to using a wide range of chemical weapons against the defenseless civilian population.

The first chemical attacks were reported in May 1987, when about twenty Kurdish villages were gassed in an attempt to deter the local population from collaborating with the advancing Iranian forces. The most infamous attack, however, took place in March 1988, when the prospect of an Iranian break-through in Kurdistan prompted Saddam to employ chemical weapons on an unprecedented scale against the Kurdish village of Halabja. As the thick cloud of gas spread by the Iraqi planes evaporated into the clear sky, Western television crews were rushed into the town by the Iranians and the world was shown the full extent of the massacre. Five thousand people—men, women, children, and babies—were killed that day, and nearly ten thousand were wounded. They had been gassed with a hydrogen cyanide compound that the Iraqis, with the help of their German advisers, had developed at their new Samarra chemical weapons plant.[18] The new death agent bore a striking similarity to the poison gas the Nazis had used to exterminate the Jews more than forty years before. The attack on Halabja provided Saddam with another dubious record in the unhappy history of chemical warfare. Having been the first war leader to authorize the use of nerve gas on the battlefield (during the battle at Majnun Islands), he could now lay claim to be the first national leader to use chemical weapons against his own people. Finally, the outside world was being forced to confront the reality that was Saddam Hussein's Iraq.

Despite the grueling demands of the war, Saddam still found time in his busy schedule to eliminate his enemies. Although the savage measures he had taken against the Shiites had effectively destroyed their ability to oppose his rule, Saddam was concerned about the activities of Ayatollah Sayyed Mahdi al-Hakim, a highly respected and influential Shiite cleric who lived in London with his wife and four children. Hakim had been living in exile in Britain since 1969 when he had been accused of being a spy by the Baathists and forced to flee. Seventeen members of his family, men and women, young and old, had been executed by Saddam's government. During the Iran-Iraq War, Hakim had become involved in attempts to rally Iraqi opposition groups to intensify their efforts to remove Saddam. His activities soon came to the attention of Saddam's ever-watchful security services. Toward the end of 1987, Hakim received an invitation to address a Muslim conference in Sudan. Accepting the invitation, he arrived there on January 17, 1988. As he was waiting in the lobby of the Hilton Hotel in Khartoum, three members of an Iraqi assassination squad walked over to where the learned man was sitting. One shot him at point-blank range while the others each fired two shots in the air. The three assassins then walked calmly out of the hotel and headed for a waiting car bearing diplomatic number plates, which then drove them to the Iraqi embassy in Khartoum. A few days later they flew back to Baghdad.

TEN

The Invader

Saddam had won the war and, for him, that was all that counted. The country was virtually bankrupt, its infrastructure lay in ruins, and the population was exhausted by the demands of the war effort. But Saddam was only interested in making sure the victory played to his advantage. The guns had hardly fallen silent at the front before Saddam's *arc de triomphe* appeared in the center of Baghdad. It consisted of two pairs of giant crossed swords, held by huge bronze fists embedded in concrete. Lest anyone be in any doubt about who was responsible for the triumph over Iran, the fists holding the sabers were modeled on those of the Iraqi president.[1] Throughout the war Saddam's propaganda machine had constantly sought to compare the exploits of the Iraqi president with heroic figures from antiquity. With the war over, Saddam sought to pay tribute to these illustrious ancestors by holding official burial ceremonies for the remains of the Babylonian kings and building new tombs on their graves. At the same time he ordered a massive reconstruction of the site of ancient Babylon. Whole sections of the ancient ruins were bulldozed to be replaced by yellow-bricked walls. Tens of thousands of bricks used in the construction bore a special inscription reminding future generations that the "Babylon of Nebuchadnezzar was rebuilt in the era of the leader President Saddam Hussein."

Despite Saddam's attempts at triumphalism, however, there were clear signs that eight years of relentless conflict had severely dented his confidence. Saddam's sense of paranoia was highly developed at the best of times, and the pressures the war had brought to bear on his leadership had made him even more suspicious. His public appearances became fewer, and he made good use of the network of bunkers and palaces that had been set up during the war to protect himself against any possible coup attempts. While Iraqis took to the streets of Baghdad in their hundreds of thousands in the immediate after-math of the cease-fire announcement to celebrate the war's end, Saddam was well aware that the euphoria would be short-lived, and that it would not be long before the people began to ask searching fundamental questions about their president's judgment, and in particular whether the eight years of sacri-fice that they had just endured was either necessary or worthwhile. Saddam suspected, correctly, that his political and military colleagues would soon be engaged in attempts to overthrow him. Foreign diplomats based in Baghdad at the conclusion of the Iran-Iraq War noted that Saddam had become more reclusive in his general demeanor. In their view he did not enjoy the fruits of victory, but locked himself away from the public view. As one former diplo-mat commented: "After the war there was very little triumphalism in evi-dence in Baghdad."[2]

During the latter stages of the conflict Saddam had formed the habit of moving from one of his presidential palaces to another every few days. Each palace looked much like the other, and was fully equipped with its own orchards and vegetable gardens, which provided a guaranteed food supply. The walls of all the palaces were specially reinforced to withstand a missile attack, and each of them had its own security units. It is not known pre-cisely how many of these palaces were built during the 1980s; one indica-tion of their preponderance is the fact that no fewer than fifteen of Saddam's palaces were known to exist within a thirty-one-mile radius of northern Kurdistan. A Western diplomat who traveled widely throughout Iraq during the late 1980s reported that virtually everywhere he visited he found large, high-walled fortresses under construction, even in the most remote areas of the country. All of them had a similar design, and when he asked local people what they were, he was informed that they were regional centers of government. The diplomat later learned that the fortresses were in fact Saddam's new palaces, places where he could seek protection from his enemies. Apart from providing a sanctuary for the president, the heav-ily fortified palaces provided a convenient hiding place for Iraq's military assets, particularly the nonconventional weapons. All the palaces were linked to one another by a number of different communications systems so that, if one system failed, there were at least two or three others that could keep the presidential party in touch with developments elsewhere in the country at any given time.

A meeting convened by Saddam of the director-generals of the country's key ministries in the late 1980s provides a chilling insight into his state of mind at this time. The officials were ordered to assemble at a certain point at 8 A.M. When they arrived they were put on a bus with blackened windows and then driven around Baghdad. They changed buses twice, and the exercise was repeated. The officials were then taken to a palace on the outskirts of the city, where they were searched and required to empty their pockets of all their belongings, which were placed in envelopes with their names written on them. Again they boarded the bus and were driven to another palace, where they were searched again and were ordered to wash their hands in disinfectant. They were then shown into a large hall and ordered to take a seat, where they waited for three hours. By now it was late afternoon, and none of the officials had been given anything to eat or allowed to go to the bathroom. "We were simply too afraid to ask," recalled one of the officials present. "We thought Saddam was going to declare a new war or something. All his bodyguards seemed so serious."

Finally, at about 6 P.M., Saddam entered the room, and the officials duly rose to their feet and started clapping. Saddam made a short, rambling speech about the state of the nation, and the need for government officials to carry out their duties efficiently. "He did not say anything interesting or anything that was new." After thirty minutes he left. The bemused officials were then invited to form a queue at the side of the platform. As they took their places they noticed that huge piles of Iraqi dinars were stacked on a table at one side of the stage. Each of the officials was invited onto the stage, and handed bundles of dinars, which were each worth thousands of dollars. Having collected their "present" from Saddam, they were taken into a garden at the side of the hall where an attempt had been made to lay out a sumptuous feast. The only problem was that little thought had been given to the presentation of the food, and the cakes and jellies were mixed up with legs of lamb and stuffed chicken, which had the effect of making the whole spread appear deeply unappetizing. The famished officials packed it away nonetheless, before being escorted from the palace, put on the bus, and returned to their original assembly point, having made various detours along the way. "As government officials all of us knew the country pretty well, but none of us had the faintest idea where we had been," said the official who attended the meeting. "The sole purpose of the exercise was intimidation; Saddam simply wanted to remind us who was the boss. He gave us the money and the banquet to show how we would be rewarded if we did as he asked."[3]

If anything, Saddam's personal security after the war increased, rather than diminished. So long as Iraq was at war Saddam calculated it was unlikely that there would be a popular movement to remove him, and by murdering his health minister at a cabinet meeting in 1982 he was confident that he had persuaded his close colleagues against trying to unseat him. After the war Saddam convinced himself that he was under threat, with the result that his security arrangements intensified. He maintained the nomadic existence he had undertaken during the war years. The fact that the palaces looked alike was very much to his advantage. If he gave a television interview, for example, it was impossible to work out his location from the backdrop. On the increasingly rare occasions that Saddam appeared in public, details of the event would appear in the Baghdad press only after it had taken place. If Saddam's enemies wanted to get rid of him, their first task was to find him.

Of all the problems with which Saddam had to contend at the end of the war the one that immediately caused him most difficulty was the conduct of his own family. During the war years Saddam had succeeded in containing the rivalries among various clans within his family that were forever jostling to increase their power and influence within the government's ruling Tikriti clique. Relations between the Ibrahims and the Majids had not quite reached the level of the Montagues and Capulets in Shakespeare's *Romeo and Juliet,* but Saddam had his work cut out repairing the rift with his three half brothers that had been caused by his choice of groom for his eldest daughter, Raghda (see Chapter Eight). Saddam had managed to effect a reconciliation with the Ibrahim wing of his family toward the end of the war, and his three half brothers—Barzan, Watban, and Sabawi—were rehabilitated and given high-ranking jobs in the regime. Sabawi took over Barzan's old job as head of the Mukhabarat and Watban was made head of State Internal Security, while Barzan remained in Geneva as ambassador to the United Nations.

Saddam's success in keeping his family under control, however, proved to be short-lived. The cause of the new rift that erupted in October 1988, just two months after the cease-fire with Iran had been negotiated, was Saddam's alleged infidelity to his wife Sajida. Rumors about Saddam's unfaithfulness to Iraq's first lady had become commonplace in Baghdad during the war. Saddam was known to have a penchant for blondes and, in an attempt to keep her husband from straying, at some time in the mid-1980s Sajida had changed the color of her own hair. Reports of Saddam's infidelities included the claim that he had an affair with the wife of an Armenian merchant living in Baghdad, while another girlfriend was supposedly the daughter of a former Iraqi ambassador. But the affair that was to provoke Saddam's biggest family crisis was his relationship with Samira Shahbandar, the wife of the director-general of Iraqi Airways.

Precisely when the affair began is not known, although it may have dated back to 1986, the period when Saddam was embroiled in a power struggle with his military chiefs and the first intimations of his mental instability began to manifest themselves. Samira filled all of Saddam's requirements for a potential mistress—she was tall, blonde, articulate, in her mid-thirties, and married. Numerous Iraqi exiles who were intimately involved in the regime at the time have claimed that from the mid-1980s onward Saddam's philandering was so well established that it followed a set pattern. "He particularly enjoyed having affairs with married women because it was his way of humiliating their husbands," commented an official who worked at the Presidential Palace for several years.[4] The woman would be taken against her will from her home while the husband was out and brought to a special house in the Mansour district of Baghdad, not far from the hunting club that had been Saddam's favorite socializing haunt in the early 1970s. Once Saddam had finished with his assignation, the woman would be returned to her home later that same night.

Most of Saddam's dalliances were arranged through one of his bodyguards, Kamel Hana Geogeo, who had worked for Saddam in one capacity or another for nearly twenty years. Geogeo was the son of Saddam's personal chef, and one of his duties was to act as the presidential food taster; Saddam reckoned that the cook would not deliberately poison his own son. It was through Geogeo that Saddam came to know Samira. Unlike his previous assignations, however, on this occasion Saddam struck up a serious relationship with Samira, who, unlike his wife, came from a well-respected Baghdad family. In the past Sajida, the mother of Saddam's five children, had been aware of her husband's philandering, but only intervened when one of Saddam's conquests looked as if she might pose a threat to the marriage. In those instances she would call on one of Saddam's half brothers, either Barzan or Sabawi, who ran the country's all-powerful security forces, to intervene. On one occasion, for example, Barzan had arrested one of Saddam's mistresses and sent her into exile in Turkey.

When Sajida learned that Saddam was becoming attached to Samira, she resolved to break up the relationship. With Barzan in Geneva, Sajida made the mistake of imploring her eldest son, Uday, to intervene. According to an account of the affair that was widely circulated in Baghdad at the time, Sajida was so consumed with jealousy that she almost had a nervous breakdown. She told Uday that unless he acted quickly, Saddam would marry Samira and their inheritance would be at risk. Uday reacted true to character. He learned that Geogeo had been invited to a party being hosted by one of Iraq's vice presidents on the "Island of Pigs," the island in the center of the Tigris not far from the Presidential Palace that was a favorite picnic spot for Baghdadis. The party was being thrown in honor of the wife of the Egyptian president, Hosni Mubarak, as part of Iraq's attempts to improve relations with the Arab world after the war with Iran. Uday arrived at the party with his bodyguards and went straight to Geogeo, whom he felled with a single blow from a heavy club. Uday then proceeded to beat the unconscious victim as he lay on the ground. Geogeo later died in the hospital.[5]

In the past Saddam had always turned a blind eye to his children's excesses. Neither of his sons had known much discipline during their child-hood. Since taking control of the Olympic Committee in 1984, Uday had done little to endear himself to the Iraqi people, even if, in his father's eyes at least, he was being groomed for the succession. His only contribution to the war effort had been to keep Baghdad's nightlife in business while most other young Iraqis of his age were engaged at the front. There were constant reports of him being involved in drunken brawls at nightclubs, and he was impli-cated in at least two other murders before killing his father's food taster. His first victim was an army colonel who had opposed Uday's attempts to seduce his teenage daughter, while the second was an army officer who had taken exception to him making passes at his wife in a Baghdad discotheque.[6] Perversely, Uday's previous murders had won approval at the Presidential Palace, where his father appeared to take pride in the fact that his son and heir had been "bloodied."

If Saddam had been willing to excuse Uday's past excesses, he was not pre-pared to have his son interfering with his own love life. The killing of Geogeo provoked a furious reaction from Saddam, who immediately denounced his son on television, and ordered that he should stand trial for murder. The Arab press was soon filled with lurid accounts of Saddam going to his son's house and beating him up and then, when his wife intervened on her son's side, beating her up, too.[7] Another account, provided by a man who acted as one of Uday's "doubles," claimed that Uday was so overcome with remorse that he swallowed a bottle of sleeping pills and was taken to the same hospital where Geogeo had been taken after Uday attacked him. Unlike Geogeo, Uday's life was saved by the medical staff. As they were pumping out his stomach, Saddam arrived in the emergency room, pushed the doctors aside, and hit him in the face, shouting: "Your blood will flow like my friend's."[8]

Given the considerable political strain Saddam was under following the disastrous war with Iran, the domestic scandal caused by Uday's murder of the presidential food taster did little to improve the president's popularity. Aware that he needed to take firm action if he was to stand any chance of salvaging the ruling family's reputation, Saddam ordered that both his wife and Uday disappear from public view. This was particularly embarrassing for Sajida, who had been hosting various state functions in Baghdad in honor of President Mubarak's wife Suzanne when the murder took place. When Mrs. Mubarak went to the Baghdad airport to catch her return flight home to Egypt on October 21, Iraq's first lady was curiously absent from the farewell ceremonies. The day after the killing Uday's name was dropped from the masthead of the local sports newspaper of which he was nominally editor in chief. A few days later he was stripped of his official positions as head of the Iraqi Olympic Committee and the Iraq Football Federation. A brief announcement stated simply that he had resigned "for personal reasons." Uday's resignation from the football association was particularly embarrassing as he had just been unanimously reelected by its members—all of whom belonged to the Baath Party—to serve another four-year term. He was also required to stand down from his newly acquired post as rector of the Saddam University for Science and Technology in Baghdad.

Initially Saddam tried to keep the scandal a family secret, but reports soon began to appear in the foreign press, and Saddam was obliged to go public. Uday was jailed and a special commission set up to investigate the killing, and Saddam declared that if the commission held Uday responsible, he would be put on trial for murder. The manner in which the court was set up and the background lobbying that took place to secure Uday's eventual release is highly revealing about the nature of the byzantine politics that lay at the heart of Saddam's regime. The judge appointed to conduct the investigation, Abdel Wahab Hussein al-Douri, was in fact a cousin of the vice-chairman of the Revolutionary Command Council, Izzat Ibrahim al-Douri. The commission was quickly assisted in its deliberations when Geogeo's father, who was, after all, employed as Saddam's personal cook, asked for the charges to be dropped. In addition he invoked the tribal custom of appealing to Saddam to spare the life of Uday. Saddam was subjected to intensive lobbying on Uday's behalf by Sajida and her brother, Adnan Khairallah, the Iraqi defense minister, and Saddam's first cousin. Sajida railed at Saddam, demanding to know why he should punish Uday for killing the food taster when he had done nothing about Uday's previous killings. "Why arrest him?" she reportedly asked her husband. "After all, it is not the first time he has killed. Nor is he the only one in his family who has killed."[9] The latter remark was clearly a dig at Saddam's own youthful transgressions.

The reluctance of the judicial commission to upset the president, combined with the intensive lobbying that was undertaken by Uday's relatives, resulted in the case being dropped. Saddam remained furious with Uday for having the gall to intrude upon his romantic liaisons, and his eldest son was sent into exile to Geneva to join his half uncle, Barzan al-Tikriti, who himself was still sulking over Saddam's refusal to allow his son to marry one of the president's daughters. Uday's banishment to a country like Switzerland, which prided itself on its civility, was no doubt intended to curb his wilder instincts. But Saddam's hopes that Geneva would become a finishing school for his errant son were short-lived. Reports of Uday's behavior in Baghdad had reached the attention of the Swiss authorities, and when Barzan and Uday applied for their diplomatic residence permits, they approved Barzan's while postponing a decision over Uday. A few weeks later the Swiss made a formal request to Uday to leave the country. Even while his application for diplomatic status was pending, he had managed to involve himself in an altercation with a Swiss policeman, in which he pulled a knife during a row at a restaurant in Geneva. Uday's departure was so abrupt that his plane crossed paths with that of his mother, who was unaware of his expulsion and was traveling to Switzerland to see him. He returned to Baghdad, where a reconciliation of sorts was effected with his father. Uday received a presidential pardon, was reelected unanimously as president of the Iraqi Olympic Committee, and was allowed to resume many of his former activities. Former Iraqi officials who went into exile after the Gulf War reported that Uday had developed into a carbon copy of his father. "He is rude and shows no respect. He is a bully and thug."[10]

If Saddam was prepared to come to terms with his son, the same cannot be said of his relations with his wife. It was because of Sajida's jealousy over

Saddam's mistress that Uday had been encouraged to murder Geogeo in the first place. As Iraq's first lady, Sajida herself was virtually immune from any form of retribution, especially as the press reports of Geogeo's murder had made it clear that it was Saddam, and not his wife, who was ultimately responsible for the scandal by having the affair in the first place. Unable to avenge himself directly on his wife, Saddam resolved to punish her by acting against her brother and his childhood friend, Adnan Khairallah.

By 1989 Saddam and Adnan, who had grown up together in Khairallah Tulfah's house in Tikrit, had been friends, companions, and colleagues for more than thirty years. Adnan had been a key ally in Saddam's rise to power. His appointment as defense minister in 1977 had been a watershed moment in Saddam's preparations to take over the presidency, as it meant Saddam no longer had to contend with any threat from the military establishment. Adnan had worked closely with Saddam during the Iran-Iraq War. Like his father, Khairallah Tulfah, he was not averse to exploiting his position for personal gain. Apart from acquiring a fortune in real estate deals with his father, Adnan had also skimmed off millions of dollars in commissions on the arms deals he had negotiated on behalf of the government. By 1989, when the rest of the country was still suffering the austerity of the war years, Adnan had acquired an estimated five hundred cars for his personal use.

Relations had already been strained between Saddam and Adnan before the row over Uday became public. As defense minister, Adnan had claimed some of the glory for the "victory" over Iran for himself, and was coming to see himself more and more as Saddam's heir apparent. Saddam was always deeply suspicious of colleagues who looked as though they might be in a position to challenge him. Unlike Saddam, Adnan had attended the prestigious Baghdad Military Academy as a young man, and had made a reputation for himself as a highly competent military officer. A long-standing member of the Baath, Adnan was courteous and was capable of presenting his ideas in a professional, military manner. Before becoming defense minister, he had served in Iraq's 10th Armored Brigade, the "Golden Brigade," and unlike most of the other members of the regime, he had not been involved in the atrocities and torture conducted by Saddam's security officials. Consequently he was popular with his fellow officers. During the war with Iran Adnan's superior military knowledge and capability became a source of constant friction with Saddam. If, for example, an Iraqi officer withdrew from an engagement with the enemy, Adnan was able to grasp the tactical explanation for the maneuver. Saddam, on the other hand, who had no military training, would interpret any retreat as cowardice, and demand that the officer responsible be executed. Relations between Saddam and Adnan had become so strained during the war that Adnan seriously considered resigning his position as defense minister, but was persuaded to stay by his father, Khairallah Tulfah, who, although elderly and infirm, continued to enjoy his status as the regime's unofficial "godfather" until his death in the 1990s.

After the war, as criticism of Saddam's leadership qualities mounted, articles began appearing in the Arab press suggesting the possibility that Adnan Khairallah might replace Saddam as president. The articles had a similar theme; Adnan was better trained, more professional, and more reasonable than Saddam and was better suited to running the country. Furthermore, Iraq was a nation in which successful military officers had previously taken control of the government. Saddam's intelligence officers kept him fully informed about the articles appearing in the foreign press, and also about the impact they were having on the ruling elite in Baghdad. His suspicions about Adnan were further heightened by reports that he had become rather too familiar with the CIA officials who had been based in Baghdad during the war, and had provided Iraq with crucial intelligence material.[11]

Adnan's decision to side publicly with his sister in the dispute over Saddam's mistress was the last straw. Saddam was aware that, true to the Arab tradition, Adnan would always stand by his blood relatives when it came to any dispute. And as defense minister Adnan was also responsible for Saddam's personal protection. In this respect Adnan's position was not helped in January 1989 when Saddam was forced to cancel the annual Iraq Army Day celebrations—the first held since the end of the war—after his ever-vigilant security agents uncovered a plot to kill him during the military procession. A group of dissident military officers, no doubt still seething at Saddam's bungling during the war effort, had planned to attack the reviewing stand during the official march past. There were even suggestions that rebellious pilots were to strafe and bomb the stand. Although the plot was uncovered in time, the fact that it had not been discovered earlier left the impression that Adnan was not paying sufficient attention to the fulfillment of his duties. Adnan did not have to wait long for Saddam to exact his revenge. Four months later he was killed in a helicopter crash. The official explanation was that Adnan, who was piloting the helicopter, was disoriented by a sandstorm, lost control, and crashed while returning from a tour of inspection in Kurdistan.

The true story of Adnan's death was provided a few years later by Hussein Kamel al-Majid, Saddam's first cousin and son-in-law. According to Hussein Kamel, Adnan had been to a family gathering near Mosul, in northern Iraq, with Saddam and Sajida. The meeting was an attempt by Saddam to heal the rift within the family that had been caused by the row over Uday. During the meeting, however, a dispute broke out between Saddam and Adnan, and Adnan decided to leave the gathering. At this point Saddam told Hussein Kamel "to take care of matters." Hussein Kamel admitted that he placed the explosives on Adnan's helicopter with a timer set to make them explode once the aircraft was airborne.[12]

Adnan's murder signaled the end of Saddam's relationship with his first wife. Shortly before Adnan had boarded the helicopter Sajida had had a premonition that it might not be safe for him to fly back to Baghdad, especially as it was getting dark. Saddam had attempted to reassure her, saying that Adnan must carry out his duty, and consoled her with the words "We must put our faith in God to protect us." After Adnan's murder Sajida was in no doubt who had been responsible for her brother's death, and she vowed never to speak to Saddam again. An official separation between Saddam and Sajida was later arranged whereby she acquired the official title "Lady of the Ladies," while Samira, who became Saddam's second wife soon afterward, took the title "First Lady."

Saddam's domestic difficulties no doubt had a bearing on the policies he pursued in the immediate aftermath of the war. For once Saddam appeared to be on the defensive, aware that his own position was susceptible to political challenges, both from within his own ruling elite and from the military. Between the end of the Iran war and 1990 several attempts were made on his life. The first took place in November 1988 and reportedly involved a plan to shoot down his plane on his return from a state visit to Egypt. The second was at the Iraq Army Day parade. This was particularly worrying for Saddam as it involved officers from the Republican Guard, his elite bodyguard unit. Dozens, if not hundreds, of officers were executed in the reprisals that followed. A third coup attempt was aborted in September 1989, at a time when the Iraqi leader was being hailed as the new Nebuchadnezzar at a national festival in the rebuilt Babylon. And in January 1990 Saddam narrowly escaped an assassination attempt by army officers while he was riding in his car through Baghdad.

Aware that his personal popularity was at a low ebb, Saddam embarked on an Iraqi form of perestroika, a program to liberalize some of the state institutions. One of his first steps was to hold new elections in April 1989 for the National Assembly, the body that came closest to providing a genuinely democratic platform for political expression. As in previous elections, however, all the candidates were carefully scrutinized by the security services. Non–Baath Party members were allowed to run as "independents," and a large number of these so-called independent candidates were elected, although the authorities were less keen to publicize the fact that any potential candidate who was regarded as being "dangerous to the state"—a status that enjoyed a broad definition—was not allowed to run. Apart from arranging the elections the regime indicated that it would in the future tolerate a degree of criticism of government ministers and policies, although it stressed that such criticism could only be directed at ministers, the technocrats responsible for running the country. The president, his relatives, and other members of the ruling circle were immune from adverse comment, which was just as well in view of the antics of some of Saddam's more headstrong relatives at that time.

A "Freedom Wall" was established at the University of Baghdad where students were encouraged to air their grievances. The state-controlled media began to carry a considerable number of articles detailing public complaints about everyday life, which enabled the minister of information and culture, Latif Nusseif al-Jasim, to claim, without any hint of irony, that "there is no censorship in Iraq. No person is asked about what he has written. The only limitations relate to issues of national security."[13] In order to demonstrate to the outside world the changes that were taking place in Iraq, a number of Western journalists were flown into the country to observe its flourishing "democratic process" firsthand. Saddam also initiated a charm offensive with the Arab press, and leading editors in Egypt who were invited to Baghdad reportedly received "spanking new red, white, blue and light brown Mercedes Benz 230 cars. . . . Lesser figures received Toyotas."[14]

Saddam's efforts at liberalizing the country's political institutions were accompanied by a systematic purge of the armed forces. By 1988 Iraq had developed the fourth largest army in the world. Saddam's inept handling of the war, and in particular his rash interventions during the Fao Peninsula crisis of late 1986, had resulted in the military high command imposing curbs on his political power (see Chapter Nine). In retrospect this would have been the ideal moment for the military to make their move against Saddam. But after more than a decade of close supervision by security agents and the Baath Party's highly effective network of commissars, the Iraqi military establishment had been virtually brainwashed against the notion of entertaining any political ambitions. Saddam had neither forgotten nor forgiven the humiliation he had suffered at the hands of his military commanders, even though the constraints they were able to impose on him had contributed to their success in eventually winning the war.

The discovery of various military plots to overthrow Saddam between 1988 and 1990 enabled him to reassert his authority over the military establishment. Apart from executing any officer suspected of being involved in the coup attempts, others were accounted for in mysterious accidents—more Iraqi military officers died in helicopter crashes in one year than had died during the eight years of war with Iran. Saddam was determined to break the bonds of comradeship that had formed during the war years which he believed, if left unchecked, could present a formidable challenge to his leadership. Thus his purge of the military was conducted with great brutality. For example, Lieutenant General Omar al-Hazzaa was sentenced to death after being overheard speaking ill of the Iraqi president. Saddam ordered that prior to his execution his tongue be cut out; for good measure, he also executed Hazzaa's son, Farouq. Hazzaa's homes were bulldozed, and his wife and children left on the street.

Even those officers who came from the same provincial background as Saddam, or were directly related by clan or marriage to the president's ruling circle, were not immune from prosecution. Saddam's treatment of General Maher Abdul al-Rashid was a case in point. Not only was Rashid a fellow Tikriti, but his daughter was married to Saddam's second eldest son, Qusay. But Rashid had become far too powerful for Saddam's liking, and he resolved to cut him down to size. First, Rashid's brother was killed in a mysterious accident. Then Rashid himself was forced to retire from his position and placed under virtual house arrest at his ranch outside Tikrit, a move that prevented him from maintaining contact with the substantial body of officers who were loyal to him. Although Saddam had other reasons for wanting his cousin and defense minister Adnan Khairallah out of the way, his death in the spring of 1989 in a helicopter crash fitted the pattern of purges that were being conducted in all areas of the armed forces.

For all the difficulties Saddam was experiencing with his relatives and in bringing the military to heel, by far the biggest challenge he faced was on the economic front. The war had wrecked the Iraqi economy. At its outset Iraq had been one of the most prosperous countries in the world; at the end it was one of the most bankrupt—apart from incurring $80 billion of debt, the cost of reconstruction was put at $230 billion. Iraq's oil revenues of $13 billion did not cover the cost of the nation's expenditure, and the regime needed an extra $10 billion per annum simply to balance the books.[15] As Saddam's regime relied heavily on patronage, the shortage of funds in a consumption-oriented economy like Iraq's created widespread resentment and led to charges of incompetence being leveled at the government. The extent of Iraq's indebtedness meant that Saddam was reliant on the goodwill of his creditors, a position that further weakened the president's image as an all-powerful leader.

In an attempt to revive the economy Saddam initiated a series of measures to accelerate the economic liberalization process that had begun during the war. Price controls were removed, entrepreneurial activity was encouraged, and a number of state factories were sold off to private individuals, as were some other minor state assets. The overall impression created by these changes was that Saddam was committed to dismantling Iraq's large public sector.[16] Licenses were granted for private industrial projects, which resulted in the private sector accounting for nearly a quarter of all imports. The regime went out of its way to attract lucrative investment from the oil-rich neighboring Gulf states. All these changes succeeded in achieving, however, was the creation of a small group of wealthy entrepreneurs, most of whom were closely connected to the ruling regime and who were able to exploit the opportunities presented by privatization.

In terms of improving Iraq's economic performance, therefore, Saddam's reforms made little impact. The high expectations aroused by the changes were matched only by high inflation, which forced Saddam to reintroduce price controls. In the spring of 1989 he sought to place the blame for the country's economic fortunes on his ministers, and two of them were sacked for incompetence. But with 50 percent of Iraq's oil income being spent on debt repayments, the economic situation deteriorated, rather than improved. Saddam was forced to implement a series of austerity measures, such as reductions in the number of government employees and the demobilization of thousands of troops from the armed forces, which only served to increase unemployment and did not help the growing sense of restlessness among the Iraqi people. Even so the postwar years were a period of grandiose ambition on the part of the Baathist regime. On one occasion Saddam announced that he was going to build a world-class subway system for Baghdad, a multibillion-dollar project, and then claimed he would construct a state-of-the-art national railway system around it. The only restriction on his undertaking these fantastic projects was a lack of funds. The country was, after all, broke.

According to Saad al-Bazzaz, the former editor of Baghdad's largest daily newspaper who was head of the ministry that oversaw all of Iraq's television and radio programming, the liberalization measures proposed by Saddam were mainly cosmetic. In 1989, for example, Saad found himself unexpectly summoned to see Saddam. Security officers drove him to a large villa on the outskirts of Baghdad. On arrival he was searched and then invited to sit on a sofa, where he waited for half an hour as people came and went from the president's office. When it was his turn, he was handed a pad and pencil, reminded to speak only if Saddam asked a direct question, and then ushered in. It was noon and Saddam was wearing a military uniform. Staying seated behind his desk, he did not approach Bazzaz or even offer to shake his hand. First, Saddam complained about an Egyptian comedy show that had been airing on one of the Iraqi television channels. "It is silly, and we should not show it to our people," he said. Bazzaz duly made a note. Then Saddam came to the issue that was causing him most concern.

Even in the new era of liberalization it was the practice of the state-owned broadcasters daily to air poems and songs that had been written in praise of Saddam. Most of the work was amateurish, written by Iraqis whose admiration of their president was significantly greater than their writing skills. Although the verses were still being broadcast, Bazzaz and his producers had cut down their number, and had become more rigorous in their selection. Saddam had noticed the change in policy and casually remarked, "I understand that you are not allowing some of the songs that carry my name to be broadcast." Bazzaz was suddenly gripped with terror, and replied, "Mr. President, we still broadcast the songs, but I have stopped some of them because they are so poorly written. They are rubbish." Saddam was unimpressed by the explanation. "Look, you are not a judge," he informed the terrified director of programs, who thought he was about to be taken away and shot. "How can you prevent people from expressing their feelings toward me?" All Bazzaz could do was to repeat "Yes, sir" and frantically write down everything the president said. Saddam continued with his tirade, giving new instructions about how the press and the arts were to be administered. Later that day Bazzaz was allowed to return to his office in Baghdad, where he immediately rescinded his earlier policy. That evening there was a full broadcast of poems and songs dedicated to Saddam.[17]

Another of Saddam's key priorities in the immediate aftermath of the war was to improve Iraq's international standing, especially with the Arab countries that had supported the Iraqi war effort. In February 1989 he helped to set up the Arab Cooperation Council (ACC), comprising Egypt, North Yemen, Jordan, and Iraq. Apart from encouraging economic cooperation, the ACC was conceived to present a unified bloc that would arrest Iran's expansionist aims, promote the Palestinian cause, and isolate Syria, Saddam's sworn enemy. The formation of the ACC was welcomed in the West, which noted a sea change in Baghdad's position, particularly with regard to the Palestinian issue. In this respect Saddam's prewar "rejectionist" rhetoric was scaled down to the extent that he was credited with helping sponsor the PLO's historic declaration of Israel's right to exist, which was made by Yasser Arafat in Geneva in December 1988.

The West, together with most moderate Arab regimes and the Soviet Union, had all backed Iraq toward the end of the war with Iran, and the perceived threat posed by the hard-line ayatollahs in Teheran meant that most of those countries wanted to continue their support for Iraq, if nothing else as a bulwark against the spread of Islamic fundamentalism throughout the Middle East. Although most Western powers were inclined to continue doing business with Baghdad, two issues impeded the full normalization of relations—Iraq's appalling human rights record and its continued development of weapons of mass destruction.

As in 1975, when Saddam's deal with the shah had enabled him to launch a devastating attack against the Kurds, so the 1988 cease-fire with Iran enabled him to resume hostilities against the Kurds. Within a couple of months of the end of the war about sixty-five Kurdish villages came under the same kind of chemical attack that had decimated Halabja the previous March as Saddam sought to impose a "final solution" on the troublesome issue of Kurdish independence. An estimated 5,000 people died in the chemical attacks, while another 100,000 fled in the direction of the Iranian and Turkish frontiers. By the autumn of 1989 the number of Kurdish refugees in Iran and Turkey had reached 250,000. The persecution of the Kurds provoked international outrage. In the United States the Senate Foreign

Relations Committee dispatched two staff members, Peter Galbraith and Christopher Van Hollen, to look at the situation in Kurdistan. When they reported back in October 1988 that Iraq was using chemical weapons as part of a policy to depopulate the region, the U.S. Congress responded by calling for sanctions. In France Danielle Mitterrand, the wife of the French president, took up the cause of the Kurds under the aegis of her Association France-Libertés and organized a Kurdish conference in Paris in October 1989. In Britain the foreign secretary, Sir Geoffrey Howe, issued a statement condemning Saddam's treatment of the Kurds.

Concern over Iraq's human rights abuses was mirrored by the mounting evidence that Saddam, despite the perilous state of the country's finances, was increasing the development of its military infrastructure in the aftermath of the war rather than concentrating his resources on peaceful reconstruction. In 1989 Iraq's military imports were running at $5 billion a year, accounting for nearly half of the oil revenues. At the end of the war a new organization was set up, the Military Industrialization Organization (MIO), to oversee development of an indigenous Iraqi arms industry. Hussein Kamel al-Majid, the man responsible for putting the bomb on Adnan Khairallah's helicopter, was placed in charge of the MIO and its vast budget. Saddam had learned from bitter experience that Iraq could not rely on its foreign arms suppliers in times of crisis, and so resolved to continue with his plan, first conceived in the mid-1970s, to make it self-sufficient in the manufacture of weapons, in particular weapons of mass destruction.

In this he seems to have been highly successful, for in October 1989 the Washington Institute for Near East Policy, a private research foundation, issued a report entitled "The Genie Unleashed," which cataloged Iraq's chemical and biological weapons production and suggested that the West might already have lost the battle to halt the proliferation of such weapons. The report stated: "Significantly, Iraq has continued and even expanded its efforts since the cessation of fighting with Iran in July 1988," and went on to say that international efforts to undermine the chemical weapons program by starving it of raw materials were increasingly irrelevant as Iraq was on the verge of becoming self-sufficient. "Baghdad's willingness to invest substantial resources in its chemical and biological weapons programs suggests that its leaders believe that these programs will continue to be of tremendous strategic importance." There were further indications that Iraq's biological weapons program was well advanced, and that the Salman Pak facility, twenty miles southeast of Baghdad, was producing botulin toxin. The other main biological plant at Samarra was said to be investigating the possible military applications of typhoid, cholera, anthrax, tularemia, and equine encephalitis.

Little attention was paid at this time to Saddam's nuclear program, mainly because most experts believed that Israel's attack against the Osirak plant in 1981 had destroyed Iraq's nuclear ambitions. But by the late 1980s American and British intelligence officials had reached the conclusion that Iraq was continuing to make good progress with its nuclear research program, with the result that by the early 1990s Baghdad would be in a position to build its own atomic bomb. Confirmation that Saddam was still determined to become the Arab world's first nuclear superpower emerged in 1989 when British and American investigators uncovered an Iraqi scheme to obtain a number of krytons—high-voltage switches that can be used for detonating nuclear weapons.

The progress on the program to make Iraq self-sufficient in the manufacture of weapons of mass destruction was matched by the Iraqis' success in developing their own delivery systems. During the war with Iran the Iraqis, with Egyptian help, had managed to develop an enhanced version of the Soviet-built Scud-B missile with a 180-mile range that was capable of hitting Iran. The Iraqis were also working on development of the Badr-2000, a 375-mile-range missile based on the Argentine Condor-2. And in December 1989, to demonstrate its technical prowess, Iraq announced that it had launched a three-stage rocket capable of putting a satellite into space and had tested two missiles with a range of 1,200 miles. By far the most intriguing military project the Iraqis undertook at this time was the development of a "supergun" that would supposedly be capable of launching nonconventional warheads for thousands of miles. The project was brought to an abrupt halt in March 1990 with the murder in Brussels of Dr. Gerald Bull, the Canadian ballistics expert responsible for designing the "supergun." Israel's Mossad intelligence service was widely blamed for the murder, although there was no shortage of other suspects. A few weeks later British customs officials confiscated eight large steel tubes that were destined for Baghdad, which were thought to form the barrel of the "supergun," and shortly afterward other parts of this ingenious project were located in Greece and Turkey.

Despite all the evidence that Iraq was guilty both of gross human rights violations and developing weapons of mass destruction, no serious attempt was made by the West to isolate Saddam at this juncture. While Western politicians made various statements condemning Iraq's behavior, Western businessmen were actively encouraged to trade with Baghdad. In Washington the Reagan administration continued to block any attempt by Congress to take action against Baghdad, while in Britain Trade Minister Tony Newton reponded to criticism of Saddam's treatment of the Kurds by doubling British export credits to Iraq from £175 million in 1988 to £340 million in 1989. And when, in April 1989, Saddam held a military trade fair in Baghdad, which was organized and hosted by his son-in-law Hussein Kamel, hundreds of Western companies sent representatives in the hope of picking up lucrative contracts.

Sir Harold Walker, who became Britain's ambassador to Baghdad in February 1991, recalled that his brief was to maintain Britain's relations on an even keel with Iraq so that British companies could "do good business." The West was still more concerned with Iran than Iraq, and there was a growing perception that Iraq could actually become a stabilizing factor in the Arab-Israeli conflict. "I'm afraid the whole human rights issue was brushed under the carpet. The main priority was trade," said Sir Harold.[18] Maintaining normal diplomatic contacts with the regime, however, was no easy matter. From the mid-1980s onward Saddam decided to stop greeting foreign ambassadors when they arrived on the grounds that he was too busy with the war. The practice continued after hostilities had ceased, and new ambassadors were required to present their credentials instead to Tariq Aziz, the foreign minister, at the Presidential Palace. Walker recalled that when he went to the palace in early 1991, long after the cease-fire with Iran had been implemented, he was taken aback at the level of security. He had to pass through several security checkpoints, and when he arrived at the final checkpoint, he found all the guards were wearing gas masks, as if they expected the palace itself to come under chemical weapons attack.

Saddam, however, remained deeply frustrated at the generally negative press he was receiving, particularly in the West. Western ambassadors, on the rare occasions they were called in to see him, were generally treated to a long list of complaints about media coverage of Iraq. The BBC's Arabic Service was a particular source of irritation, and successive British ambassadors received long lectures about what Saddam perceived to be the bias shown by the BBC to Baghdad.[19] Nor could he comprehend the international outcry that had greeted the evidence that Iraq was using chemical weapons against the Kurds. Saddam dismissed the criticism as a "Zionist" plot to discredit Iraq's "glorious victory" over Iran, and he launched a propaganda campaign that was designed to portray the relocation of the Kurds as a humanitarian act. Saddam's persecution complex was not helped by the overthrow, and brutal execution, of Romanian dictator Nicolae Ceausescu in December 1989. Like Saddam, Ceausescu was a despot whose rule depended on the ceaseless promotion of a personality cult and the efficiency of his security apparatus, the formidable East German–trained Securitate, to maintain himself in power. And like Saddam, Ceausescu had become increasingly removed from his people, retreating within the sanctuary of his opulent and heavily fortified palaces to protect himself from the reality of his impoverished and discontented people. Saddam was deeply shocked by Ceausescu's overthrow, and he ordered his security chiefs to study the videotapes of Ceausescu's demise to ensure that he did not suffer a similar fate.

Any hopes Saddam may have entertained of rehabilitating himself with the West, however, were irretrievably destroyed by his treatment of Farzad Bazoft, a British journalist who was arrested on espionage charges as he made his way to Baghdad airport in September 1989. Bazoft, who had been born in Iran and was working as a freelance journalist for the *Observer* newspaper in London, had been investigating a mysterious explosion that had occurred at a military plant at al-Hillah, south of Baghdad. The explosion had been so huge that it had been heard in Baghdad and, although Saddam ordered that news of the incident be kept secret, it soon emerged that the explosion had occurred at a missile production line. The blast killed scores of Egyptian technicians employed on the top-secret missile project, and Bazoft, hoping to secure a big scoop, traveled to al-Hillah dressed as an Indian doctor to investigate. Soon after his return he was arrested as he tried to leave the country and charged with espionage. In a subsequent televised confession clearly made under duress, Bazoft said he had been working as a spy for Israel. By making the confession he had hoped that he would be treated leniently. But this was not Saddam's way. Throughout his rule he had used the tactic of extracting false confessions to justify the purging of his opponents, as he had graphically demonstrated during the first days of his presidency in 1979 when he conducted a widespread purge of his colleagues in the Baath Party. On March 15, 1990, after a one-day trial at which the prosecution failed to produce any convincing evidence of his guilt, Bazoft was executed by firing squad.

Of all the acts of brutality that had been perpetrated under Saddam's auspices since the Baathists seized power in 1968, the summary execution of

Farzad Bazoft was the one that finally caught the attention of the West and drew its scrutiny to the barbaric nature of Saddam's regime. Whether it was because Bazoft's position as a journalist meant his case attracted more attention than Saddam's myriad other victims, or because his execution occurred at a time when international concern was already being expressed about Iraq's human rights abuses and development of weapons of mass destruction, Bazoft's judicial murder proved to be a watershed in the West's relations with Baghdad. The Western view of Iraq under Saddam Hussein in 1990 was succinctly summed up by Margaret Thatcher, the British prime minister: "Iraq was a country which had used chemical weapons—not just in war but against its own people. Saddam Hussein was not only an international brigand, he was also a loser who had done immense damage both to the Palestinian cause and to the Arabs and who over eight years had vainly thrown wave after wave of young Iraqis into the war against Iran."[20]

With the economy in ruins, his attempts to acquire weapons of mass destruction subjected to constant sabotage, and the frequent discovery of new coup attempts, Saddam was very much on the defensive in the spring of 1990. By executing Bazoft he had no doubt calculated, as he had done on so many occasions in the past, that he would send a defiant signal to potential enemies, both at home and abroad, that all those who plotted against him would pay the ultimate price. And it was in this advanced state of paranoia, when Saddam genuinely believed that there was an international conspiracy to destroy his regime, that he began to contemplate a dramatic new initiative that would both restore the country's finances and the people's faith in their leader.

During the first six months of 1990 Saddam had been increasing the diplomatic pressure on the Gulf states, in particular Kuwait and Saudi Arabia, to help alleviate Iraq's economic plight. Since the end of the war with Iran the Iraqis had been lobbying Gulf leaders to write off the $40 billion financial aid they had given to Baghdad. The low oil price of the late 1980s was also a serious concern for the Iraqis, as oil accounted for 95 percent of the government's revenue. In February 1990, at a summit meeting of the Arab Cooperation Council in Amman to mark the organization's first anniversary, Saddam virtually demanded that the Gulf states bail him out of his financial difficulties. Apart from an immediate moratorium on the wartime loans, he wanted fresh loans of $30 billion to pay for reconstruction work. "Let the Gulf states know," he declared, "that if they [do] not give this money to me, I [will] know how to get it."[21]

Tensions between Iraq and the Gulf states increased during the spring of 1990, particularly after Saddam became convinced that Israel, with American backing, was planning to attack his weapons of mass destruction facilities, similar to the Osirak attack of 1981. But the Gulf states took no notice of Saddam's threats and, to make matters worse, continued with their policy of exceeding their OPEC oil production quotas, which only served to deflate the international oil price at a time when Saddam could least afford it. At an Arab summit convened in Baghdad in May 1990, ostensibly to discuss the impact the recent influx of Soviet Jews to Israel would have on the region, Saddam launched a direct attack on the Gulf leaders, especially the Kuwaitis, who were deliberately exceeding their OPEC quotas. This policy, Saddam announced, was tantamout to a declaration of war on Iraq. But still the Gulf states refused to be intimidated. The emir of Kuwait was insistent that he would neither reduce oil production nor forgive his wartime loans to Iraq nor provide additional grants to Baghdad.

Although Saddam's anger was directed at all the oil-producing Gulf states, he was particularly irritated by the stance of the Kuwaitis, who, in his view, had a historic obligation to support Baghdad. Ever since Iraq's creation successive Iraqi regimes had complained that Kuwait, which had formed part of the administrative district of Basra during the Ottoman period, had been illegally separated from Iraq. Given the limited nature of Iraq's coastline on the Gulf, Kuwait's well-developed shoreline was looked upon with envy in Baghdad, particularly after the discovery and development of the region's oil fields. The arbitrary demarcation of the border between Iraq and Kuwait, which had been drawn up by Sir Percy Cox in the 1920s, was another source of complaint, as the Iraqis claimed it unfairly gave the Kuwaitis access to the lucrative Rumaila oil field.

Iraq had threatened action against Kuwait on several occasions in the past. In 1937 the Iraqi monarch King Ghazi had upset his British overlords by advocating its annexation. When Britain granted Kuwait independence in 1961, President Qassem had responded by insisting that it was an integral part of Iraq, and even announced the appointment of a new Iraqi ruler for the "province." And in the early 1970s a dispute between Iraq and Kuwait over the two Kuwaiti islands of Warbah and Bubiyan had resulted in them being occupied by the Iraqi armed forces. The islands dominate the estuary leading to the southern Iraqi port of Umm Qasr, and possession of them would have increased the size of Iraq's

Gulf shore and provided it with the opportunity to develop a much-needed deep-water port on the Gulf. The Iraqi troops were eventually persuaded to vacate the islands following the intervention of the Arab League and Saudi Arabia, but Iraq continued to press its claim to them.

In a final attempt to intimidate the Kuwaitis, in July, on the twenty-second anniversary of the Baath revolution, Saddam handed Kuwait a list of demands, which included the stabilization of the international oil price, a moratorium on Iraq's wartime loans, and the formation of an Arab plan similar to the Marshall Plan to assist with Iraq's reconstruction program. If the Kuwaitis failed to oblige, he warned, "we will have no choice but to resort to effective action to put things right and ensure the restitution of our rights."[22]

Dr. Ghazi Algosaibi, a Saudi Arabian diplomat who acted as a close adviser to King Fahd during the crisis of the summer of 1990, said that the Saudi monarch was deeply disturbed by Saddam's attitude toward the Kuwaitis and his other Gulf neighbors. "The king was worried about Saddam's state of mind. He was convinced that Saddam was about to do something catastrophic." According to Algosaibi, neither the Saudis nor the Kuwaitis had any realistic expectation that the war loans would be repaid, but both countries thought it would set a bad precedent if they were to announce publicly that they had written them off. However, with Saddam in a bellicose frame of mind and with the largest army in the Middle East at his disposal, the Saudis were prepared to make an exception, and urged the Kuwaitis to do the same. Throughout July King Fahd was in constant telephone contact with the Kuwaiti emir. Eventually he persuaded the emir to accept Saddam's conditions. The king phoned Saddam and told him, "I have incredible news for you. The emir has agreed to all your terms." But to King Fahd's surprise, rather than being relieved that the crisis had been resolved, Saddam gave the impression that he was not impressed with the Saudi initiative. "At that moment the king realized the Kuwait was doomed," said Algosaibi.[23]

In all probability Saddam had made the decision to invade Kuwait prior to the ultimatum he issued on July 18. On July 21 an estimated thirty thousand Iraqi troops began deploying near the Kuwait border. The only issue that prevented Iraq from launching a full-scale invasion of the emirate was Saddam's desire to win at least tacit consent for his adventure from Washington. With the collapse of the Soviet Union the previous year Saddam believed that the United States was the only power capable of obstructing his plans. Even after the Bazoft execution, Washington was still sending conflict-ing signals about its attitude toward Baghdad. While the Senate lobbied in favor of imposing sanctions against Iraq, President George Bush was still indicating an interest in cultivating bilateral relations with Baghdad. In June John Kelly, the U.S. assistant secretary of state for Near Eastern affairs, argued against a congressional attempt to impose sanctions on the grounds that such a move would be counterproductive to the U.S. national interest.

On July 25 Saddam summoned April Glaspie, the U.S. ambassador to Baghdad, for a one o'clock meeting at the Presidential Palace. Saddam wanted to test her reaction to his proposed adventure in Kuwait. Glaspie had already been involved in a diplomatic confrontation with Saddam over a Voice of America broadcast the previous February, which had drawn a direct comparison between Saddam's Iraq and Romania under Ceausescu, stating: "The success of dictatorial rule and tyranny requires the existence of a large secret police force, while the success of democracy requires abolishment of such a force." Glaspie had responded to Saddam's protests by offering an apology, and stressing that the United States had no intention of interfering in the "domestic concerns of the Iraqi people and government."

At the July meeting, Saddam made it clear that a conflict could result from his dispute with Kuwait. He accused the United States of supporting "Kuwait's economic war with Iraq" at a time when it should be grateful to Baghdad for having contained fundamentalist Iran. He further threatened the United States with terrorist retaliation should it continue with its hostile policy against Iraq. "If you use pressure, we will deploy pressure and force," said Saddam. "We cannot come all the way to you in the United States but individual Arabs may reach you."

According to a transcript of the conversation between Glaspie and Saddam, which was leaked by the Iraqis, and whose veracity has never been denied by the U.S. State Department, Ambassador Glaspie, rather than responding to Saddam's bellicosity, replied simply, "We have no opinion on Arab-Arab conflicts, like your border disagreement with Kuwait." She went on to compliment Saddam on his "extraordinary efforts" to rebuild Iraq after the war with Iran. And when Saddam reiterated his claim that the United States was supporting Kuwaiti attempts to undermine the Iraqi economy, she replied, "President Bush is an intelligent man. He is not going to declare an economic war against Iraq." Finally Glaspie said that she had been instructed "in the spirit of friendship" to ascertain Saddam's intentions with regard to

Kuwait, which, from the American point of view, was the main purpose of the meeting. Saddam repeated his contention that Kuwait was the aggressor, because it had deliberately driven down the oil price, thereby threatening the livelihoods of Iraqis, "harming even the milk our children drink and the pension of the widow who lost her husband during the war, the pensions of the orphans who lost their parents." He concluded the meeting by stating that, if an agreement was not reached with Kuwait, "then it will be natural that Iraq will not accept death."

Glaspie apparently came away from the meeting believing that Saddam was full of bluster, and was not intent on invading Kuwait. Five days later she flew back to Washington to consult with President Bush. Three days after that Iraq invaded Kuwait. When details of Glaspie's meeting with Saddam were published by the Iraqis in Baghdad, the forty-eight-year-old career diplomat, who had wide experience of the Arab world, was accused of, at best, naivete, or, at worst, having given Saddam a "green light" to invade Kuwait. It was an accusation she rigorously denied. In an interview published in the *New York Times* in late 1990, she said: "Obviously I didn't think, and nobody else did, that the Iraqis were going to take all of Kuwait. Every Kuwaiti and Saudi, every analyst in the Western world, was wrong too."

Sir Harold Walker, the British ambassador at the time, sympathized with Glaspie's position. In his view, none of the Western diplomatic missions took Saddam's posturing seriously. Furthermore, President Mubarak of Egypt had personally assured Washington and London that Saddam had no intention of invading Kuwait, and that the crisis would be resolved by Arab diplomacy. "For that reason," said Walker, "we all believed that Saddam was involved in a game of brinkmanship that would suddenly end with an agreement, and everybody would behave as though nothing had happened." When Glaspie announced she was taking a vacation, Walker followed suit without a moment's hesitation.[24]

Glaspie's comment, however, that she did not believe Saddam was "going to take all of Kuwait," was intriguing. Prior to the Iraqi invasion there had been a general expectation that if Saddam did take military action it would be confined to the Rumaila oil field and the disputed islands. Indeed, had he confined his activities to these areas, it is unlikely that the United Nations would have gone beyond the imposition of sanctions, or that the United States would have dispatched a single soldier to the region.

But this assessment gravely underestimated the basic pan-Arab principles of Baathist ideology, which looked forward to the complete eradication of the colonial boundaries imposed on the Middle East at the end of the First World War. Saddam's invasion of "all of Kuwait" was entirely consistent with Baathist ideology. It was also a policy that was, initially, immensely popular with the Iraqi people.

ELEVEN

The Loser

At 2 A.M. on August 2, 1990, 100,000 Iraqi troops, backed by 300 tanks, crushed the 16,000-strong Kuwaiti army and seized control of the principality. Unlike the invasion of Iran ten years previously, the Iraqis met with hardly any resistance. There was no resistance at the Kuwaiti border, and it was only when the Iraqi armed forces entered Kuwait City itself that they came across a few gallant Kuwaitis who tried to impede their progress, but they were easily overwhelmed by the Iraqis' superior firepower. The Kuwaiti air force took to the skies, but only to fly their fighters to safety in Saudi Arabia, and the Kuwaiti navy remained quietly at anchor.

The only setback for Saddam was that the Kuwaiti emir and all his ministers had managed to escape, thanks to a carefully orchestrated plan that had been arranged with the help of the CIA some months previously. An elite unit of the Republican Guard had been ordered to go straight to the Dasman Palace the moment they entered Kuwait and take the royal family prisoner. Had this happened, the emir would have been given the choice of cooperating with the invaders, and ordering a cessation of all resistance, in return for which his life would have been spared and he would have been appointed head of a quisling government directed from Baghdad. If as expected, the emir declined to cooperate, he was to be executed at the palace. The only member of the royal family who stayed behind was Sheikh Fahd, the emir's brother, who managed the Kuwaiti soccer team. He stood with a few guards at the top of the palace steps as the first Iraqis arrived, barring their way with his drawn pistol. One of the Iraqis casually shot him dead.

Within seven hours the invasion had been completed and Kuwait was firmly under the control of the Iraqis. The government had fled, together with an estimated 300,000 citizens, armed resistance was at an end, and the airport was closed. Saddam had the added bonus of capturing a British Airways plane that had inadvertently landed at Kuwait on a refueling stop just as the invasion began. The plane was on a scheduled flight from London to Delhi, and although Western intelligence knew that Iraq was in the process of invading Kuwait, no one thought to alert the airline. When the plane landed at Kuwait, the crew and passengers were taken prisoner, and the men moved to Baghdad to form part of the human shield that Saddam began to deploy to protect vital targets from attack.

Although Saddam was initially euphoric about the capture of Kuwait, his enjoyment proved to be short-lived. He had calculated that, while he might not expect any plaudits for his move, he would not meet much resistance. Indeed, U.S. satellite intelligence pictures taken shortly after the invasion clearly showed lines of Iraqi tanks deployed on Iraq's border with Saudi Arabia, and one of the great mysteries of the invasion of Kuwait was why Saddam halted his advance at the emirate, and did not advance farther south and take the oil fields of the United Arab Emirates. But as he had shown during the Iran war, Saddam was not tactically astute and his actions were always tempered with caution. He believed he had received a "green light" from April Glaspie to occupy Kuwait, and having done so, he decided to gauge the strength of international reaction to the invasion before considering his next move. For that reason the signals emanating from Baghdad in the immediate aftermath of the occupation were confusing.

Initially Saddam set up a "provisional revolutionary government," and he gave the impression that Iraq intended to withdraw from Kuwait once it had satisfied its strategic needs with the annexation of the Warbah and Bubiyan islands, together with some territories along the joint boundary, including the south Rumaila oil fields. It is, however, extremely unlikely that Saddam ever gave any serious thought to vacating Kuwait City; even if he had succeeded in setting up a government that was well-disposed to Baghdad, he would have been reluctant to do so. Arab apologists have suggested that Saddam would have withdrawn from Kuwait in time, but was forced into annexing the emirate by the uncompromising international response that greeted the invasion. Given his previous track record, however, it is unlikely that Saddam could ever have been persuaded to withdraw voluntarily.

Historically the Iraqis regarded Kuwait as their territory, the country's "nine-teenth" province, which had been denied to them by the perfidy of the British when they drew up Iraq's original boundaries in the 1920s. In Ottoman times Kuwait had been placed under the control of the provincial government in Basra, and it was almost an article of faith for the Iraqis that they should con-trol Kuwait.

Saddam's invasion of Kuwait will be remembered as one of the great mil-itary miscalculations of modern history. It was an unprovoked attack on an unprepared neighbor, and was widely condemned as such. The Iraqi action provoked international condemnation that was almost unprecedented in its ferocity. Within hours of the invasion President George Bush imposed an economic embargo against Iraq and ordered the aircraft carrier *Independence* to move from the Indian Ocean to the Persian Gulf. All Kuwaiti and Iraqi assets and property in American banks and companies were frozen, and the movement of goods and people to and from Iraq was suspended. Margaret Thatcher, the British prime minister, who was attending a conference at Aspen, Colorado, hosted by President Bush on the day the invasion occurred, drew an immediate parallel between Saddam's occupation of Kuwait and Adolf Hitler's occupation of the Sudetenland in the 1930s, and insisted that Britain's response be based on the policy that "aggressors must never be appeased."[1] The United States and the Soviet Union took the unusual step of issuing a joint declaration condemning the invasion. Iraq was also con-demned by the United Nations and the Arab League, the UN Security Council imposed a total economic and trade embargo on Iraq, and Iraq's oil export pipelines through Turkey and Saudi Arabia were promptly cut. Furthermore, Saudi Arabia, alarmed by the deployment of Iraqi armored units on its border, asked for U.S. military assistance. The United States, committing itself to the unconditional withdrawal of Iraq from Kuwait, began a military airlift that would ultimately result in the deployment of some 600,000 foreign troops in Saudi Arabia within the next six months. By any standard Saddam's invasion of Kuwait was a spectacular miscalculation.

The strength of the international response to the invasion undoubtedly took Saddam by surprise. Even though he appreciated that his occupation of Kuwait would attract criticism, he still believed that, one way or another, the invasion would ultimately be to his advantage. If he were forced to withdraw, he would surely be able to win some concession, such as the eradication of Iraq's foreign debt, recognition of Iraq's claim to the

Rumaila oil fields, or, alternatively, recognition of Iraq's claim to the disputed islands of Warbah and Bubiyan. At the very least he expected Iraq's enduring complaint about the inadequacy of its fifty-kilometer shoreline in the Gulf to be resolved. But when calculating the options available to him, Saddam had not reckoned on such an uncompromising response from the West.

One of the key factors that weighed heavily against Saddam was that, in 1990, the international community was still coming to terms with the new political realities of the post–cold war world. The collapse of the Iron Curtain in the autumn of 1989 had freed a number of East European countries who had been forcibly subjected to Moscow's communist dogma for more than forty years. As one tyranny ended in Europe, the leaders of the free world were unwilling to see another develop in the Middle East.

In an attempt to counter the mounting international criticism, Saddam claimed that Iraqi troops had entered Kuwait at the request of a revolutionary movement that was opposed to the ruling al-Sabah family, but this claim was soon discredited by his inability to find any Kuwaiti nationals willing to serve in a puppet government. Even so, the Iraqis pressed ahead with the establishment of a provisional cabinet on August 4, which three days later declared Kuwait a republic. On August 6, while Washington was considering how best to protect Saudi Arabia, Joseph Wilson, the American chargé d'affaires in Baghdad (who was acting ambassador in Glaspie's absence) had a meeting with Saddam at which he sought guarantees for the security of Saudi Arabia. Saddam was happy to provide them, telling Wilson to inform the Saudis, "We will not attack those who do not attack us, we will not harm those who do not harm us."

On August 7, President Bush announced in a televised address to the nation that the 82nd Airborne Division was being dispatched to Saudi Arabia. This was the start of Operation Desert Storm, the largest deployment of American troops overseas since the Vietnam War. In his address, Bush was uncompromising. He accused Saddam of an "outrageous and brutal act of aggression." And, consciously echoing the sentiments that had been expressed by Mrs. Thatcher, he indirectly compared Saddam with Hitler. "Appeasement does not work," he declared. "As was the case in the 1930s, we see in Saddam an aggressive dictator threatening his neighbors." The clear implication was that if the West did not act to evict Saddam from Kuwait, he would eventually take control of the Gulf, and with it more than 50 percent of the world's known oil reserves. Bush then went on to list the four guiding principles that would underpin his policy during the next six months: (1) the immediate and unconditional withdrawal of all Iraqi forces from Kuwait, (2) the restoration of the legitimate Kuwaiti government, (3) a reaffirmation of the U.S. commitment to stability in the Gulf, and (4) America's determination to protect the lives of its citizens. Saddam's response the following day was to proclaim the annexation of Kuwait, the first annexation of a sovereign state since the Second World War. On August 8 the Revolutionary Command Council rubber-stamped the return of the "branch, Kuwait, to the root, Iraq," and three weeks later, on August 28, Kuwait officially became the nineteenth province of Iraq. The announcement of "a comprehensive and eternal merger," as the Iraqis described it, turned out to be another grave tactical error on Saddam's part. Even his putative allies in the Security Council, Yemen and Cuba, now found it difficult to defend his actions.

Throughout the autumn of 1990, as he came to appreciate the ramifications of his Kuwait policy, Saddam embarked upon a number of desperate diplomatic initiatives whose sole defining characteristic was that they guaranteed his own survival. Having appointed his cousin Ali Hassan al-Majid, the man responsible for the gassing of the Kurds at Halabja in 1988, as the new governor of Kuwait, Saddam concentrated his energies on extricating himself from the Kuwait imbroglio while preserving his reputation, within the Arab world, at least, as the champion of Arab nationalism. From the outset Saddam acquired some surprising allies, such as King Hussein of Jordan, who insisted during his discussions with both London and Washington that the Kuwait crisis was an Arab problem that would best be resolved by the Arabs. Saddam also found himself supported by Yasser Arafat's PLO, a surprising development given that Saddam had previously devoted much energy to destroying Arafat's power base. Displaying his characteristic opportunism, Arafat calculated, wrongly as it would turn out, that Saddam's new position as the undisputed champion of Arab nationalism might strengthen his own position with regard to Israel.

Saddam certainly tried to link the Kuwait issue with the Arab-Israeli conflict. In the months preceding the invasion of Kuwait he had become convinced that Israel was planning an assault on Iraq's military infrastructure. Saddam's susceptibility to conspiracy theories had led him to conclude that the United States was encouraging Israel to attack him while at the same time encouraging the Kuwaitis to undermine the Iraqi economy. Saddam actually articulated this convoluted theory of American double-dealing to Joseph

Wilson, the U.S. chargé d'affaires, at their meeting in early August. In the following months much of the rhetoric emanating from Baghdad sought to link Iraq's occupation of Kuwait to the liberation of Jerusalem. By annexing Kuwait, so the argument went, Saddam had fulfilled "a dear Arab goal . . . to rectify what colonialism had imposed on our country."[2] This noble act, however, was opposed by the "imperialist" United States, which, backed by its ally Israel, wanted to maintain its dominance of the region by preventing the Arabs from asserting their true rights. On August 12, Saddam advanced his own peace initiative in which he suggested that Iraq would withdraw from Kuwait only after all the other occupied lands in the Middle East had been liberated. Israel should withdraw from Arab land it had occupied in Palestine, Syria, and Lebanon, while Syria would withdraw from Lebanon. Even though Saddam's peace proposal was dismissed by the West, his attempt to establish linkage between his predicament and the Palestinian issue met with some success. By September politicians in the United States, Britain, and France were all making statements in favor of convening a Middle East peace conference to resolve the Arab-Israeli issue, but only after Saddam had withdrawn from Kuwait.

Another tactic Saddam employed was to attempt to exploit differences of opinion between the members of the international coalition that was taking shape against him. Nearly twenty years previously, when he had masterminded the nationalization of Iraqi oil, Saddam had become expert at exploiting the rivalries of the great powers. In the 1970s he had successfully formed alliances with the Soviet Union and France to ensure the success of his oil nationalization program, and in the autumn of 1990 he pursued a similar diplomatic agenda in the hope of heading off an American-led campaign to drive him out of Kuwait. From the outset of the crisis the Soviet leader Mikhail Gorbachev invested a great deal of energy in attempting to find a nonmilitary solution. Yevgeny Primakov, Gorbachev's special envoy and a former KGB specialist on the Middle East, was an early convert to the concept of linkage between the Kuwait issue and resolving the Arab-Israeli conflict, and argued in favor of giving Saddam "some room for manoeuvre."[3] Saddam also offered the Soviets, whose economy was on the verge of collapse after seventy years of communist mismanagement, free oil supplies.

The French, who continued to value their "special relationship" with Baghdad, were similarly courted by Saddam. In September President François Mitterrand had embarrassed Washington by indicating, during his speech to the United Nations General Assembly, that he recognized the legitimacy of some of Iraq's territorial claims to Kuwait. In late November Saddam sought to capitalize on what he perceived as France's good intentions toward Iraq by releasing 327 French workers who had been held as "guests" since the invasion of Kuwait. The release of the French hostages was deliberately timed to coincide with a visit to Paris by James Baker, the U.S. secretary of state, to discuss the coalition's strategy on Iraq. Saddam's goodwill gesture inevitably aroused suspicions that the French had negotiated their own bilateral deal with Saddam, as they had during the oil nationalization negotiations. While the French vigorously denied the suggestion, the Iraqis leaked details of a secret meeting that had taken place between the two countries' respective foreign ministers in Tunis.[4] By releasing details of the deal, Saddam expected to exacerbate the tensions between the different members of the international coalition being formed to take action against Iraq. In fact it had the opposite effect, and the embarrassed French government felt it no longer had the moral authority to challenge the coalition's objectives.

By far the most egregious tactic employed by Saddam to counter the threat of military action by the West was the use of "human shields" to defend key installations. Saddam had convinced himself that, when it came to suffering casualties, the West had no stomach for a fight. He had intimated as much during his meeting with Ambassador Glaspie in July when, in a reference to the high number of casualties Iraq had sustained during the war with Iran, he stated, "Yours is a society which cannot accept ten thousand dead in one battle." Saddam had also taken note of the fact that a number of Western governments in the 1980s, including the United States, had been prepared to negotiate secret deals in their desperation to secure the release of their citizens who had been taken hostage in Lebanon.

In August Saddam passed an order to the effect that all foreign workers would be detained in Iraq until the threat of military action had passed. His tactic was designed to test the mettle of the governments forming the international coalition to liberate Kuwait. Saddam's "human shield" policy, as it became known, was designed to protect Iraq's most sensitive sites from attack. Saddam calculated that the West would be unlikely to bomb his key military and government facilities if they contained groups of foreign hostages. The tactic certainly had the effect of making him the center of world attention, although his intention of exploiting the publicity to defend his decision to invade Kuwait backfired in spectacular fashion. It soon became apparent that the fate of different groups of hostages depended solely on their government's attitude to Saddam. Thus the French, whose government was still keen to maintain the Franco-Iraqi axis that had served their business interests so well, were soon released en masse. The British, however, whose prime minister, Margaret Thatcher, was the most vocal opponent of appeasing Saddam, were moved from one Iraqi strategic location to another. The most sickening moment in this charade came when Saddam decided to pay a "goodwill visit" to a group of British hostages. Saddam reiterated his assertion that their presence in Iraq was necessary for the cause of peace, i.e., so long as they were there, the allies could not bomb them. At one point in the proceedings, which were televised live throughout the world, Saddam approached a seven-year-old British boy, Stuart Lockwood, patted his head, and asked him, in Arabic, "Did Stuart have his milk today?" The terrified expression on the boy's face articulated the feelings of all those unfortunates who were trapped in Saddam's Iraq.

Saddam's intimidation tactics may have succeeded over the years in terrifying the Iraqi population, but in the West they only succeeded in alienating whatever support he may still have enjoyed. Even so, the "human shield" policy was successful in attracting a wide spectrum of international luminaries to Baghdad, some of whom were even sympathetic, if not to Saddam himself, then to his predicament. The first visitor was Kurt Waldheim, the Austrian president, who attended a joint press conference with Saddam, and was rewarded with the release of the 140 Austrians held in Iraq and Kuwait. Waldheim was followed by the Reverend Jesse Jackson, who secured the release of American women and children, and men suffering health problems. Other visitors included the boxer Muhammad Ali and the former West German and British prime ministers, Willy Brandt and Sir Edward Heath, all of whom returned with a batch of hostages. Saddam's hostage policy, however, did not provide the change in Western opinion that he desired. The Bush and Thatcher governments, in particular, refused to be deflected from their determination to seek his unconditional withdrawal from Kuwait, and as the pressure grew at the UN Security Council to give the allies the mandate to evict Iraq by force, so Saddam became more desperate to appear conciliatory. He offered to release all the hostages over a three-month period if the threat of hostilities was lifted. On the eve of the key Security Council vote, he released 1,000 Soviet workers in a deliberate attempt to dissuade Moscow from supporting the resolution. But it was to no avail. On

November 29 the Security Council passed Resolution 678, which demanded Iraq's unconditional withdrawal from Kuwait by January 15, 1991, and authorized the use of military force if Iraq failed to comply.

Saddam's position was getting desperate, even though he continued to maintain a public posture of defiance. Rhetoric similar to that used to proclaim his greatness during the war with Iran was broadcast by the Iraqi media. "O Great Iraq, under the leadership of Saddam Hussein and his excellent management of the conflict, will remain proud and firm, challenging the gathering of evil-doers and tyrants."[5] The country, which had still not recovered from the ravages of the eight-year war with Iran, was again put on a war footing. A large-scale mobilization of reservists was announced and frantic efforts were made to turn Kuwait into an impenetrable fortress. A decree was passed making the hoarding of foodstuffs punishable by death.

In Kuwait, or Iraq's "nineteenth province," as it was now known, the new Iraqi provincial government, headed by Ali Hassan al-Majid, was working hard to eradicate any sign that Kuwait had ever existed as an independent nation. About 300,000 Kuwaitis, nearly one-third of the population, had fled the country, and those who remained were subjected to a systematic campaign of terrorism. The basements of the vacated palaces were turned into makeshift torture chambers by Saddam's intelligence agents. Ordinary workshop tools such as vises and electric saws were adapted as instruments of torture, as were electric wires. Street names were changed and residents had to acquire new identity documents and license plates. The time difference between Baghdad and Kuwait was abolished. A decree was implemented banning Kuwaitis from wearing beards, and some offenders were punished by having their beards plucked out with pliers."[6]

By far the most humiliating concession Saddam was forced to make as a consequence of the Kuwait crisis was the peace terms he offered Iran. Although a cease-fire had been in place since 1988, no final peace agreement had been signed between Iran and Iraq. With a massive international coalition being assembled to evict him from Kuwait, Saddam realized he could not afford to have his Iranian front exposed. Just two weeks after the invasion of Kuwait, when Saddam realized that he faced stiff international opposition, he made an approach to the Iranian president, Ali Akbar Hashemi Rafsanjani, offering him a final peace deal on the basis of the 1975 agreement he had negotiated with the shah. In the past Saddam had argued that the 1975 Algiers Agreement had unfairly denied Iraq control over the Shatt al-

Arab, and this had been his principal motivation for declaring war on Iran in 1980. But after waging one of the bloodiest wars of the twentieth century, Saddam, the nominal victor, was now prepared to concede all the key points. The Iran deal revealed once more that the only policy that really concerned Saddam was that which guaranteed his own survival.

This was certainly Saddam's main priority as he sought to prepare himself and the regime for the military challenge that almost inevitably lay ahead. Initially his policy on Kuwait had been to seek an advantageous withdrawal, i.e., on terms that benefited Baghdad, such as retaining the disputed islands and the Rumaila oil field, and with a pro-Iraq government established in Kuwait City. The international diplomatic momentum of the autumn of 1990, driven by Washington and London, made the prospect of such an outcome appear increasingly unlikely. As war seemed inevitable, Saddam changed his policy from one of advantageous withdrawal to one that might best be described as "survivable withdrawal."[7]

Saddam concentrated his energies on ensuring the survival of the regime, rather than the defense of the country. Ali Hassan al-Majid was brought back from Kuwait to help plan the defense of the Baathist homeland. Another trusted kinsman, Hussein Rashid al-Tikriti, was promoted from commander of the Presidential Palace and Republican Guard to chief of the general staff. The divisions of the Republican Guard were deployed in such a way as to ensure both that the heart of the regime in central and northern Iraq was secure and to block any attempted invasion of the country from the south. Saddam's half brothers—Barzan, Watban, and Sabawi—all occupied key positions in the country's intelligence services, guarding against the possibility of an internal revolt. With these forces in place Saddam was confident that he could survive any attack; if necessary he was even prepared to sacrifice his forces in Kuwait if it meant guaranteeing the safety of the heartland.

A last-ditch effort to resolve the conflict by diplomacy was undertaken by the United States at the end of November. Having secured UN approval for military action, President Bush offered to send James Baker, his secretary of state, to Baghdad and to receive Tariq Aziz in Washington. Although the United States insisted that it was seeking an unconditional Iraqi withdrawal from Kuwait, the unexpected initiative gave Saddam a face-saving formula. Saddam had been asking for direct negotiations with Washington since the start of the crisis and he was able to portray Bush's offer as a concession to Baghdad. In an attempt to capitalize on what he perceived as a softening of the American position, Saddam ordered the release of all the remaining foreign hostages held in Iraq and Kuwait. But he had been mistaken in interpreting Washington's offer of talks as a sign of weakness. At the very least he expected to be granted some concessions on Kuwait, such as a redrawing of the boundaries in Baghdad's favor, before he withdrew. If Saddam withdrew unconditionally from Kuwait, he would be humiliated in the eyes of his fellow Arabs. He reasoned that his standing, and his chances of survival, would both be greatly increased either if he confronted the international coalition, or won concessions for Iraq. As Washington categorically dismissed the latter option, armed conflict was inevitable. The dictator would not be dictated to.

The Allied attack, which began on January 16, 1991, subjected Iraq to one of the most intensive aerial bombardments known to the modern world. For six weeks Allied aircraft systematically bombed military, political, strategic, and economic targets in Iraq and Kuwait with impunity. Despite having the world's sixth largest air force and an extensive air defense system, Iraq was unable to contend with the awesome airpower launched by the Allies. The Iraqi air force did not try to challenge the Allied aircraft, and those planes that did take off did so in an attempt to escape to airfields in northern Iraq.

The coalition war plan envisaged a four-phased air, naval, and ground offensive operation that would be executed over the course of one month. The first phase of Operation Desert Storm, as the campaign was known, was aimed at softening up the Iraqi defenses in preparation for a ground offensive to liberate Kuwait. Having established total air supremacy, Allied bombers proceeded to attack a wide range of targets at will. The early bombing raids were directed at radar and communications bases, early warning stations and air defense batteries. These were followed by precision bombing attacks, using aircraft and cruise missiles, against strategic targets such as airfields, command and control centers, Iraqi troop concentrations in and around Kuwait, Iraqi oil refineries, and the long-range surface-to-surface missile batteries. In the first days of the bombardment Baghdad took the brunt of the Allied assault, and when Iraqis emerged from their shelters after the first night's bombardment they saw that the Presidential Palace, the headquarters of the Baath Party, and the Ministry of Defense building had all been largely demolished.

Within two hours of the commencement of the Allied offensive, Saddam made a defiant statement in which he informed the Iraqi people that "the mother of all battles" had begun, and he urged them to live up to their glorious reputation. A few hours later Iraqi television showed their president visiting a Baghdad street where he was greeted by an elderly woman who clasped his hand with great reverence. Saddam had taken great care to prepare the Iraqi people for war. Elaborate instructions had been issued regarding self-protection against chemical and nuclear attacks. Citizens were told to black out their homes and to store a medicine cabinet in every apartment. Individuals and institutions had been ordered to clear their shelters for immediate use, and to store oil products for an emergency. Even civil defense drills had been held, with a large-scale evacuation of Baghdad involving hundreds of thousands of people.[8]

Despite his public defiance, Saddam was under no illusions about the challenge that lay ahead. The conflict he now confronted was a very different proposition from that which he had faced during the war with Iran. Apart from the occasional air raid, and the missiles fired at Baghdad during the war of the cities, the majority of Iraq's civilian population had been protected from the conflict. There were shortages, it is true, and most families were affected by the appalling attrition rate at the front, but Saddam had generally succeeded in rallying the people behind him. The confrontation with the formidable international alliance that President Bush had assembled under the auspices of the United Nations mandate was an altogether different proposition. The Allies had the means and the will to take the battle to the heart of Iraq, and from the opening shots of the war, Baghdad was subjected to intensive bombardment. The longer the bombing continued, the greater the damage that would be inflicted on Iraq's infrastructure. One of the main reasons Saddam had, after all, invaded Kuwait was to distract attention from Iraq's woeful economic plight, itself the consequence of the eight-year war with Iran. Operation Desert Storm could only make Iraq's economic and military situation worse, and that would undoubtedly have repercussions for Saddam in the postwar world, assuming, that is, he survived the war. From the outset of the conflict, therefore, Saddam resolved to draw the Allies into a ground war as soon as possible. He still believed, as he had explained to Ambassador Glaspie the previous July, that the Western powers could not sustain a high level of casualties, and if he could tempt the Allies into committing their ground forces, he was confident that his forces would, at the very least, be able to inflict a substantial number of casualties on them. This in turn, or so he reasoned, would force the Allies to request an early cease-fire, and push them back to the negotiating table. As he remarked in another of the defiant speeches he made at the outset of the conflict, "Not a few drops of blood, but rivers of blood would be shed. And then Bush will have been deceiving America, American public opinion, the American people, the American constitutional institutions."[9]

An insight into Saddam's thinking at the outbreak of hostilities was provided by General Wafic al-Samurrai, who was Iraq's head of military intelligence during the Gulf War, and one of Saddam's most trusted military advisers.[10] According to al-Samurrai, shortly before the start of the Allied attack, Saddam had called a meeting of his generals at Basra at which he outlined his tactics. Saddam proposed capturing U.S. soldiers and tying them up around Iraqi tanks and using them as human shields. "The Americans will never fire on their own soldiers," he declared triumphantly. In the fighting that lay ahead, Saddam anticipated that thousands of enemy prisoners would be captured, and that the Iraqis would be able to use them for this purpose. In turn this would enable Saddam's forces to move unopposed into eastern Saudi Arabia, forcing the Allies to back down.

Al-Samurrai and the other generals were appalled by Saddam's naivete and inhumanity. To start with, it would be almost impossible for the Iraqis to capture Allied troops, whose bases in Saudi Arabia were well defended. And even if it could be done, the very idea of using soldiers as human shields was anathema to the professional military officers. To do so would be to breach all laws and international agreements, and it might so outrage the Allies as to provoke them into retaliating with nonconventional weapons. But even though Saddam's generals knew his scheme was irrational, dangerous, and impossible to implement, none of them said a word. They all nodded and dutifully took notes. To question Saddam's strategy would have meant to admit doubt, timidity, and cowardice. It might also mean demotion or death.

Even so, on the eve of the outbreak of hostilities, Samurrai, as chief of intelligence, regarded it as his duty to inform the country's commander in chief of the grave risk it faced from the coalition of more than thirty countries that were actively participating in Operation Desert Shield. Late in the afternoon of January 14, the general reported for a meeting in Saddam's office in the Presidential Palace. Dressed in a well-cut black suit, the president sat behind his desk as Samurrai delivered his grim assessment. It would be very hard for Iraq to defend itself against the assault that was coming, said Samurrai. No enemy soldiers had been captured, and it was unlikely that any would be. Iraq was ill equipped to defend itself against the number and variety of weapons ranged against it. The Iraqi positions were also difficult to defend because of Saddam's refusal to withdraw the bulk of his forces from Kuwait and move them back across the Iraqi border, where they might be more effective. According to Samurrai, the Iraqi forces were spread so thinly across the desert that there was little to stop the Americans advancing straight to Baghdad itself. The general then produced evidence to back his argument in the form of photographs and news reports. Iraq, he concluded, could expect nothing more than a swift defeat, and then it would have to face the possibility of Iran seeking to exploit its weakness by invading from the north.

When Samurrai had finished outlining this litany of disaster, Saddam responded by asking, "Are these your personal opinions or are they facts?" Samurrai replied that this was his educated analysis on the basis of the facts he had available to him. To which Saddam said, "I will now tell you my opinion. Iran will never interfere. Our forces will put up more of a fight than you think. They can dig bunkers and withstand America's aerial attacks. They will fight for a long time, and there will be many casualties on both sides. Only we are willing to accept casualties; the Americans are not. The American people are weak. They would not accept the losses of large numbers of their soldiers."[11] Saddam was repeating the same argument that he had presented to Ambassador Glaspie the previous July.

There is also the question of whether, had Saddam succeeded in luring the Allies into an early ground confrontation, he would have been tempted to use his considerable weapons of mass destruction arsenal to inflict heavy casualties.[12] Saddam had already won himself the distinction of being the first "field marshal" to use nerve agents on the battlefield. It was later established that at an early stage of the conflict he had deployed quantities of weapons-grade anthrax, botulinum toxin, and aflatoxin biological agents, together with their missile delivery systems, but it is generally accepted that they were not used.[13] The most likely explanation is that the United States warned Baghdad, through diplomatic channels, that it would retaliate with nuclear weapons if Iraq attempted to use weapons of mass destruction. Hussein Kamel al-Majid, Saddam's son-in-law and head of Iraq's weapons procurement program, who was later to defect to Jordan, admitted as much when interviewed by *Time* magazine in September 1995. When asked why Saddam had not used his nonconventional weapons, Hussein Kamel replied: "How can you use them while you are fighting the whole planet? Any mistake of using these non-conventional weapons would make the major powers use nuclear weapons, which would mean Iraq being exterminated."[14]

The one country, however, that had in the past indicated that it would resort to its nuclear deterrent if attacked with nonconventional weapons was Israel. Throughout the military buildup to Operation Desert Storm, Saddam's propaganda machine had accused the Israelis of masterminding the Allied assault on Iraq. In the speech Saddam made on the morning of the Allies' first air strikes, he had immediately implicated the Israelis. Referring to the aerial bombardment, Saddam proclaimed, "Satan's follower Bush committed his treacherous crime, he and the criminal Zionism." Later that same day the Iraqis accused Saudi Arabia, from which Operation Desert Storm had been launched, of allowing Israel to deploy sixty of its aircraft on the holy soil of the Prophet.[15]

In the circumstances it was hardly surprising that Saddam should launch missile attacks against Israel. His strategy was twofold. First, by attacking the Zionist state he hoped to rally the support of the Arab masses, who were always supportive of any Arab leader who confronted Israel. Second, by firing a series of Scud missiles at the Israeli coast, he anticipated an Israeli response, which in turn, he calculated, would force the Allies to launch their ground offensive earlier than they would have liked, as the Allies were desperate to prevent the conflict spreading to other areas of the Middle East. The leaders of all the Western powers involved in the international coalition were anxious for the conflict not to escalate into an Arab-Israeli conflagration. Thus when, in the early hours of January 18, three Iraqi ballistic missiles landed in Tel Aviv and a further two hit the northern port of Haifa, there were intensive diplomatic efforts to persuade the Israeli government from retaliating. This was not an easy option for the Israelis. For the first time since the establishment of their state, the country's main population centers had come under indiscriminate military attack by a regular Arab army. Even so, the Israeli leader Yitzhak Shamir was persuaded by Washington that the long-term advantages of restraint outweighed the immediate desire for revenge, and although Saddam continued to fire Scuds at Israel, the Israelis refused to be drawn into the conflict.

Having failed in his first attempt to draw the Allies into a ground offensive, Saddam tried a variety of other tactics. In late January he set fire to several oil installations in Kuwait and began pumping crude oil into the northern Gulf, creating the world's largest ever oil slick—an estimated 240 square miles. A number of captured Allied pilots appeared on Iraqi television. Most of them had been harshly treated and were made to read prepared scripts in which they were critical of the Allied war effort. But rather than provoking the Allies into launching a premature ground offensive, all these acts achieved was to rally Western public opinion behind the war effort. Saddam's acts of barbarism also prompted calls from some quarters for the war aims to be expanded beyond the liberation of Kuwait and to include the removal of the Iraqi leader from power. John Major, who had replaced Margaret Thatcher as Britain's prime minister shortly before hostilities commenced, hinted that Saddam could be tried for war crimes after the war if he continued to indulge in "inhuman and illegal" behavior.

Despite these setbacks Saddam appeared confident that he would eventually get his way. On January 20 he warned: "Our ground forces have not entered the battle so far. . . . When the battle becomes a comprehensive one with all types of weapons, the deaths on the allied side will be increased with God's help. When the deaths and the dead mount on them, the infidels will leave."[16] A few days later, in an interview with Peter Arnett, the Cable News Network correspondent, Saddam appeared relaxed and confident. Iraq, he said, had managed to maintain its "balance" by using only conventional weapons, and would undoubtedly "win the admiration of the world with its fighting prowess." When asked if he had any doubts that Iraq would win the war, he replied, "Not even one in a million." Saddam also raised the issue of nonconventional weapons, claiming that Iraq had the capability to fix chemical, biological, and nuclear weapons to its missiles. "I pray to God I will not be forced to use these weapons," he said, "but I will not hesitate to do so should the need arise."[17]

For all the public bravado, however, Saddam was becoming deeply frustrated by the course of the war. The intensity of the bombing campaign was taking its toll on the country. With Allied warplanes free to pick their targets at will, by the end of January Iraq's four primary nuclear research reactors had been wiped out, and the chemical and biological weapons facilities had been badly damaged. The country's strategic and economic infrastructure was being laid waste, with roads, bridges, power stations, and oil installations all coming under attack. Apart from being subjected to heavy bombardment, the armed forces were finding it increasingly difficult to operate as their command and control systems were put out of commission. Nor was the morale of the armed forces helped when an estimated 100 combat and transport planes of the Iraqi air force, including some of the country's most sophisticated aircraft, such as the Soviet MiG-29 and French Mirage F1, flew to Iran to seek sanctuary. Saddam tried to give the impression that the mass defection was a prearranged ploy to preserve some of his best military assets, an unlikely story in view of the fact that ten years later they were still in Iran. A more likely explanation was that the pilots wanted to escape after a failed air force coup, which had been prompted by Saddam's summary execution of his air force and air defense commanders for failing to repel the Allied attack.

Saddam's situation was becoming desperate, and in a final attempt to provoke the Allies to commence hostilities on the ground, in late January he launched a series of military assaults against the Allied positions. First a small Iraqi force comprising two infantry and one tank battalion crossed the Kuwaiti border and captured Khafji, a deserted Saudi Arabian town about twelve miles from the frontier. Despite its initial success, the force was quickly overwhelmed by the Allies' superior firepower, with the loss of dozens of men and hundreds of Iraqis taken prisoner. Even so, Saddam could claim a victory of sorts, as his troops had demonstrated that they had the ability to penetrate the enemy's lines. A few days later four Iraqi mechanized divisions with some 240 tanks and 60,000 soldiers were spotted massing near the Kuwaiti border town of Wafra. These units, which formed a ten-mile-long column, were subjected to ferocious air assaults, which exacted a heavy toll and forced Saddam to abandon what had clearly been intended as a second attack on the Allies. Much to Saddam's irritation, President Bush saw these maneuvers as indicating the Iraqi leader's desperation to engage the Allies on the ground before the air bombardment destroyed all his assets. The American president said the Allies would not be deterred from their war plan, and that the land offensive would be launched "if and when the time is right."

With the Allies failing to fall for his numerous ploys, Saddam had little going for him apart from his considerable talent for using his propaganda machine to portray every development as a triumph for the "hero president." Thus the Iraqi defeat at Khafji became a humiliation for the Allies. "Bush tried to avoid a meeting of men face to face, one on one, and substituted for such confrontation technology that fires from afar."[18] Western journalists were invited to Baghdad to inspect the damage caused by the air strikes, which inevitably had an effect on the collective conscience of Western public opinion, and sparked a series of protests around the Arab world. The antiwar movement became particularly vocal after thirteen American bombers destroyed an air raid shelter in Baghdad, killing three hundred civilians. The normally pro-Western King Hussein of Jordan even went so far as accusing the Allies of committing war crimes. And while the Allied bombing was undoubtedly effective in decimating Saddam's military capability, the daily bombardment had a dramatic impact on the everyday lives of Iraqi citizens. By early February there was no running water or electricity in Baghdad and the other main Iraqi cities. The government announced an indefinite ban on the sale of fuel, which effectively brought the country to a standstill. Saddam, of course, blamed the Allies for all these misfortunes, rather than his own disastrous miscalculation in invading Kuwait.

The growing unease about the course of the air war, and Saddam's desperation to extricate himself from certain defeat, resulted in the Soviet Union undertaking a diplomatic initiative to explore the possibility of arranging a cease-fire. Soviet leader Mikhail Gorbachev had been anxious to broker a cease-fire as soon as the fighting began, and by mid-February the Iraqis, who had scornfully dismissed previous mediation offers, indicated they were prepared to meet Gorbachev's special envoy, Yevgeny Primakov, who had spent much of his career developing Moscow's special relationship with Baghdad. Primakov arrived in Iraq and met Saddam on February 12 and was immediately given a tour of the bomb damage in Baghdad. The Russian envoy noted that Saddam had lost more than thirty pounds since they had last met in October 1990. Saddam appeared relaxed, even confident. To emphasize his sense of well-being, he did not meet Primakov in his bunker but rather in a guesthouse in central Baghdad, where the Russian was treated to a diatribe by Saddam, delivered in front of the leading members of the regime, against the Soviet position. Judging that the speech was directed more at Saddam's RCC colleagues than himself, Primakov asked Saddam for a private meeting. According to Primakov, he was struck by the practical nature of Saddam's outlook during their private conversation, which was different from the bravado of his public statements. "In the event of a withdrawal," Saddam asked, "would retreating Iraqis be shot in the back? Would the air strikes stop? Would sanctions be lifted? Was it at all possible to effect a change in the Kuwaiti regime [i.e., to establish a government in Kuwait that was better disposed toward Baghdad than the ruling al-Sabahs had been]?"[19]

Primakov came away from the meeting with the feeling that Saddam was seriously interested in a peaceful resolution of the conflict, and he returned to

Moscow to brief Gorbachev. Two days later the RCC in Baghdad issued a statement indicating Iraq's willingness to withdraw, a move that briefly caused much excitement among the Allies, who thought the horrors of a ground invasion might, after all, be avoided. It soon transpired, however, that Saddam had attached a number of conditions to withdrawal, such as the demand for Israel to withdraw from Palestine and the Arab lands it had occupied in Lebanon and Syria, the lifting of all UN sanctions against Iraq, and the cancellation of Iraq's $80 billion foreign debt. Just how Saddam believed he could get away with any of these conditions is something of a mystery, as Primakov had been quite explicit in telling him just how determined the Allies were to liberate Kuwait. At any rate, Saddam's proposal was dismissed as a "cruel hoax" by President Bush, who called upon the "Iraqi military and the Iraqi people to take matters into their own hands, to force Saddam Hussein the dictator to step aside."[20] Bush's explicit invitation to the Iraqi people to pursue the "Ceausescu option" did not go down well with Saddam. He responded by repeating his threat to employ chemical weapons.

By exploring the diplomatic options with the Soviets, Saddam had been hoping to exploit potential differences of opinion within the Security Council. Having successfully commandeered Soviet support for his own ends in the past, he clearly believed he had detected an opportunity to do so again. All he had succeeded in doing, however, was to embarrass Moscow at a time when the postcommunist Soviet Union was gently feeling its way in George Bush's self-proclaimed "new world order." It was one thing for Yevgeny Primakov to be harangued by Saddam in front of the other members of the Iraqi government; it was quite another to make Moscow look naive before the bar of international opinion. Primakov had made it clear to Saddam that the Americans meant business, and that Bush would accept nothing less than an unconditional withdrawal. For Saddam then to impose a whole raft of conditions just days after the Russians had indicated they had achieved a significant breakthrough in Baghdad meant that neither Saddam nor the Soviets was left with much credibility.

Even so, as the Allies began making the final preparations for a land invasion in earnest, Saddam made one last effort to avert disaster. On February 18, Tariq Aziz flew to Moscow and accepted the Soviet proposal to a full and unconditional withdrawal from Kuwait. Except that, yet again, the offer of withdrawal was not unconditional. The Iraqis stipulated that all UN resolutions against Iraq must be canceled and sanctions must be lifted before Iraq completed its withdrawal. There seemed no doubt that at this juncture Saddam was prepared to vacate Kuwait and that, in different circumstances, the Soviet proposal might have formed the basis of a diplomatic solution. Saddam was looking for a formula that would allow him to save face in the Arab world while also averting a catastrophic defeat. He was prepared to leave Kuwait, but he could not allow himself to submit to an American ultimatum. To do so, in his view, would be to sign his own death warrant. But by now Saddam had prevaricated so often since he first conceived his Kuwait adventure in the summer of 1990 that none of the Western leaders took him at his word. They wanted action, not promises, and unless Saddam began physically removing his troops from Kuwait, the Allies remained determined to do the job themselves.

With this in mind President Bush gave Saddam one last chance. "The coalition will give Saddam Hussein until noon Saturday [8 P.M. Iraqi time, February 23] to do what he must do—begin his immediate and unconditional withdrawal from Kuwait. We must hear publicly and authoritatively his acceptance of these terms."[21] The die was cast. While leaving Tariq Aziz to pursue what was left of the Soviet diplomatic initiative, Saddam set his mind to preparing for the inevitable. In anticipation of the land invasion, Saddam ordered his occupation forces in Kuwait to set fire to the Kuwaiti oil fields. Mass executions of Kuwaiti prisoners were also carried out.

Saddam did not have long to wait for the Allies to act. At 4 A.M. local time on Sunday, February 24, Bush announced that General Norman Schwarzkopf, the commander in chief of the Allied forces in Saudi Arabia, had been instructed "to use all forces available, including ground forces, to eject the Iraqi army from Kuwait." In fact the invasion turned out to be a complete rout of the Iraqi armed forces. Within less than forty-eight hours of fighting, the backbone of the Iraqi army had been broken. What Saddam had intended as a formidable line of defense in Kuwait, the so-called "Saddam line," was breached and collapsed within hours of the offensive's commencing. After six weeks of saturation bombing, the Iraqi troops were in no mood for a fight, and there were so many Iraqi soldiers trying to surrender that the Allied troops struggled to cope. By the end of the second day the Allies had taken 20,000 prisoners; an estimated 370 Iraqi tanks had been destroyed and seven Iraqi divisions—totaling some 100,000 men—were no longer able to fight.

Realizing that the future of his regime was now very much at stake, Saddam gave the order to his military commanders "to withdraw in an organized manner to the positions they held prior to August 1, 1990." But even though there were reports from military intelligence that some Iraqi units in Kuwait were turning and heading north back to Iraq, Bush refused to call a cease-fire until Saddam "personally and publicly" committed himself to a speedy withdrawal. Even at this stage in the conflict, when his army was being completely routed by the Allies' superior firepower, Saddam could not bring himself to make any public utterance that would in any way indicate that he had been mistaken to occupy Kuwait. From his point of view, it was better to let the Allies destroy his army than to undermine his reputation as the infallible "hero president." And as, on February 26, he announced that the Iraqi armed forces were to complete their withdrawal from Kuwait within the next twenty-four hours, Saddam used the occasion to urge the nation to applaud their heroism. "Applaud your victories, my dear citizens. You have faced 30 countries and the evil they have brought here. You have faced the whole world, great Iraqis. You have won. You are victorious. How sweet victory is."[22]

The fighting continued for another two days. While the Allies said they would not attack unarmed soldiers in retreat, they continued to attack Iraq's retreating armed combat units with devastating effect. By the end of February 26 the last Iraqi soldier had left Kuwait. The number of Iraqi prisoners of war now stood at 50,000, a further eight Iraqi divisions had been rendered ineffective, and total Iraqi casualties numbered an estimated 150,000. With the Iraqi armed forces in their death throes Saddam made various appeals to the United Nations to call a halt to the fighting in return for Iraq renouncing its annexation of Kuwait. But his approaches were accompanied by various demands, such as the immediate lifting of sanctions, which were still unacceptable to the coalition members.

The conflict was finally brought to a close on the morning of February 25 when President Bush, who felt he could no longer justify the continuation of Allied attacks against a defenseless Iraqi foe, announced that he was suspending offensive combat operations. Bush's decision was taken after Allied aircraft conducted a particularly devastating attack on a defenseless Iraqi convoy retreating from Kuwait at Mitla Ridge, a key intersection on the road to Basra. Believing that the convoy was an Iraqi unit attempting to link up with the Republican Guard, Allied commanders ordered American warplanes to attack it. The attack became what one American commander later described as a "turkey shoot," with American aircraft lining up in the skies above

Kuwait to attack the defenseless convoy.[23] Hundreds of vehicles were destroyed and many casualties inflicted. As the attack on Mitla Ridge also coincided with the arrival of Western television crews, who had accompanied the liberating Allied troops into Kuwait, the carnage was broadcast throughout the world.

The Mitla Ridge attack effectively ended the war. Even though General Schwarzkopf noted that the Allied forces could easily have overrun Iraq and captured Baghdad, there was mounting unease within the coalition partners about prosecuting the war beyond Kuwait. Public opinion in the West was uncomfortable about any unnecessary killing and there were fears that if the war ended on a sour note it might complicate the postwar political situation in the region. On that basis President Bush decided to end the war. "Kuwait is liberated," he said. "Iraq's army is defeated. Our military objectives are met. It was a victory for all the coalition nations, for the United Nations, for all mankind, and for the rule of law." The American announcement was received with enormous relief by Saddam, who responded by making a victory speech to the Iraqi people. "You have won, Iraqis," he declared. "Iraq is the one that is victorious. Iraq has succeeded in demolishing the aura of the United States, the empire of evil, terror and aggression."[24]

Whatever Saddam claimed, the Allies had achieved a devastating and comprehensive victory. In little more than 100 hours coalition forces had captured 73,700 square kilometers of territory, including 15 percent of Iraq. The Iraqi army had been cut to pieces; no more than seven of the original forty-three Iraqi divisions were capable of operations. The full extent of the Allied victory only became apparent to the Iraqis on March 3 when they attended the cease-fire meeting at Safwan air base. The Iraqi commanders listened in stunned silence as General Schwarzkopf explained that the Allies had taken 58,000 prisoners, and occupied large tracts of Iraqi territory. The Iraqis made only one request, namely to fly their helicopters, as most of the country's roads and bridges had been destroyed. Schwarzkopf agreed.

In the days shortly after the rout General Wafic al-Samurrai was once more summoned to meet his commander in chief, who had conveniently absented himself from the cease-fire negotiations. Saddam was now working at a secret office, having moved from one house to another in the Baghdad suburbs almost every night of the war to escape the attentions of the American smart bombs, which he believed, correctly, were trying to assassinate him. To his surprise, al-Samurrai found Saddam relaxed and strangely buoyed by all the excitement. "What is your evaluation, General?" Saddam asked. Samurrai replied bluntly: "I think this is the biggest defeat in military history. This is bigger than the defeat at Khorramshahr [the defeat in the Iran-Iraq War]."[25]

At first, Saddam did not reply. He was as well aware as anyone of the scale of the Iraqi defeat. He knew that his troops had been surrendering en masse; he knew about the slaughter at Mitla Ridge and the devastation that had been caused by the Allied bombing campaign. But even if Saddam agreed with the general's assessment, he was not going to say so. In the past, as at Khorramshahr, he had blamed the generals for the defeat, and had punished them accordingly, thereby giving the impression that he personally was not to blame for the military disasters. But on this occasion he knew that the defeat rested squarely with him and this was something that he could never admit. And so his reply to Samurrai was brief and to the point. "That's your opinion," said Saddam.

TWELVE

The Survivor

The greatest threat to Saddam's survival was not Operation Desert Storm, but the nationwide revolt that followed it. For once Saddam's rhetorical flourishes made little impact on a nation driven to the depths of despair by the catastrophe that had been inflicted on it by his ill-conceived adventure in Kuwait. For the first time in Iraq's modern history, the people rose in strength against their despotic leader. The first revolt occurred in Basra and within days the Shiite heartlands of southern Iraq, including the holy cities of Najaf and Karbala, had risen up against Baghdad. Many towns fell to the rebels, numerous armored vehicles were destroyed, and some Republican Guards units deserted. The fighting quickly spread to nearby Sunni cities and even reached Baghdad, where a number of fierce street clashes were reported.

Before long the rebellion had spread to the north, where the Kurds, encouraged by the Shiites' revolt, decided to capitalize on the collapse of the government's authority and assert their own national rights. The Kurdish revolt was launched in the belief that it had the support of the Bush administration, which had indicated its commitment to removing Saddam and protecting the Kurds.[1] Within a fortnight the Kurds had liberated 95 percent of Kurdistan and invited various factions of the Iraqi opposition to form a new government. Although the leaders of the Iraqi opposition declined, some three hundred delegates from twenty-three exiled opposition groups met in Beirut on March 10 in an unprecedented attempt to coordinate a joint strategy against Saddam.

The nationwide revolt against the Baath leadership in Baghdad caught the leaders of the Allied coalition by surprise. Throughout Operation Desert Storm several coalition leaders, including President Bush and British prime minister John Major, had called for Saddam's overthrow. In mid-February President Bush explicitly called on the Iraqi people "to force Saddam Hussein the dictator to step aside," while Mr. Major stated in parliament that Saddam "may yet become a target of his own people."[2] Indeed, soon after the cease-fire had been signed, President Bush was handed an intelligence assessment that predicted that Saddam would be out of office within a year. The only question mark hanging over Saddam's ability to survive was whether the formidable security apparatus he had created could withstand a widespread insurrection at a time when the country lay in ruins.

Although the Allies were keen to see Saddam deposed, the simultaneous revolts by the Shiites and the Kurds put them in a quandary. Although the coalition leaders had urged the Iraqis to overthrow Saddam, they were not prepared to commit Allied troops in support of the rebels. The war was fought on the basis that it was a military campaign to liberate Kuwait; removing Saddam was not part of the mandate. The argument against extending Operation Desert Storm to include the overthrow of Saddam's regime was articulated by the *New York Times,* which, for example, argued that if the war aims were broadened, they could result in higher Allied casualties and destabilize the region, particularly if Iraq's neighbors, such as Iran, were to exploit the weakness of the government in Baghdad for their own ends.[3] The Gulf monarchies, who had to contend with the constant threat posed by Iranian-backed Islamic militants, were unhappy at the prospect of Iran's influence being extended to the Shiite areas of southern Iraq.

The noninterventionist rationale was best summed up by Richard Cheney, the U.S. defense secretary, who, ten years later, would be a key player in a renewed American commitment to remove Saddam from office. "If we'd gone to Baghdad and got rid of Saddam Hussein—assuming we could have found him—we'd have had to put a lot of forces in and run him to ground some place. He would not have been easy to capture. Then you've got to put a new government in his place and then you're faced with the question of what kind of government are you going to establish in Iraq? Is it going to be a Kurdish government or a Shiite government or a Sunni government? How many forces are you going to have to leave there to keep it propped up, how many casualties are you going to take through the course of this operation?"[4]

Cheney would himself be searching for the answers to these key questions ten years later when he was elected vice president along with President George W. Bush, the son of the American president who had commanded Operation Desert Storm.

Although the Allies favored a change of regime in Baghdad, their preference was for a repeat of the conventional coup d'état that had historically brought about change in the Iraqi government, rather than a popular revolution. A popular uprising was full of hazards. No one knew what kind of regime would replace the Baathists and the State Department remained convinced that the Iranians would try to exploit whatever success the rebels achieved, whether it was the Shiites in southern Iraq or the Kurds in the north. The Allies, moreover, were more interested in tackling Iraq's substantial arsenal of nonconventional weapons, which they believed posed more of a long-term threat to the region than Saddam. Operation Desert Storm had been fought against the backdrop of the Iraqi regime's constant threats to use nonconventional weapons, some of which Saddam had already used against his own people.

With this in mind, the United States, Britain, and France on April 3, 1991, pushed through UN Security Council Resolution 687, the longest in the organization's history, which was known as the "mother of all resolutions." Apart from stipulating the inviolability of Iraq's boundary with Kuwait, which would be demarcated by an international commission, the resolution demanded that Iraq present the United Nations with full disclosure of all its chemical and biological weapons and facilities, its ballistic missile stocks, and production capabilities (over 150 kilometers range), and all nuclear materials. The Iraqis were then to cooperate fully with the destruction of their nonconventional weapons arsenal. In addition Baghdad was to facilitate the return of all Kuwaiti property and agree to compensation to those foreign nationals and companies that had suffered as a result of the occupation of Kuwait. All sanctions would remain in place for anything other than "medicines and health supplies." The sanctions were to be reviewed every sixty days, and Iraqi compliance with the UN resolutions, particularly with regard to the disarmament program, was central to any decision to reduce or lift sanctions. In the meantime Iraq would not be allowed to sell any oil.

With Iraq in ruins, and half the country in revolt and facing the most uncompromising sanctions against a regime ever devised by the UN Security Council, most Western leaders accepted the general assessment that Saddam would be gone within a year. The only drawback was that they were not prepared to assist with his demise. President Bush was content to utter platitudes such as "Saddam cannot survive . . . people are fed up with him. They see him for the brutal dictator he is."⁵ But supporting the insurrection being undertaken by the Shiites and the Kurds was another matter entirely. Marlin Fitzwater, the White House spokesman, was noncommittal, almost to the point of naivete, when asked about American intentions toward the rebels. "We don't intend to get involved in Iraq's internal affairs," he said. "We have these reports of fighting in Basra and other cities, but it is not clear to us what the purpose or the extent of the fighting is." Clearly Bush was not about to let his magnificent triumph in Kuwait become tarnished by allowing American troops to be ensnared in the maelstrom of Iraqi politics. He wanted U.S. troops home as soon as possible.

The manner in which Saddam managed to turn the perilous plight he faced in the spring of 1991 to his personal advantage was a textbook demonstration of the political cunning, and skill, that had enabled him to survive as the undisputed champion of Iraq for the better part of three decades. It showed that he remained a formidable foe when challenged on his own territory. Even though Saddam had badly misunderstood the West's attitude toward Iraq and the Baathist regime in the run-up to the invasion of Kuwait, he could detect that the West had no heart to take the fight to Iraq following the liberation of Kuwait. Saddam was quick to exploit the West's weariness with the Middle East and calculated that, if he gave the Allies no reason to intervene in Iraq's internal affairs, he could easily reestablish the government's writ. Thus in early March he allowed his foreign minister, Tariq Aziz, to write to the UN secretary-general informing him of Iraq's renunciation of its annexation of Kuwait, and agreeing to return Kuwait's plundered assets. Aziz finally accepted the terms of UN Resolution 687, although its implementation would soon be directly related to Baghdad's calculations on the readiness of the coalition, which was dissolving as quickly as it had been assembled, to resort to armed force to ensure compliance.

Having done enough to keep the UN off his back, Saddam made some important adjustments to the regime's structure to consolidate his own position and to guarantee absolute loyalty to his command in the struggle that lay ahead to suppress the Shiites and the Kurds. His deputy in the Revolutionary Command Council, Izzat Ibrahim, was made deputy commander in chief of the armed forces and sent to the south to supervise the suppression of the

Shiite uprising. Saddam's favorite son-in-law, Hussein Kamel al-Majid, was appointed minister of defense, and Taha Yassin Ramadan, Saddam's long-standing henchman, became deputy president. As a gesture to the Shiites Saddam gave up the office of prime minister, a significant concession, and appointed another of his longtime associates, Saadoun Hammadi, a prominent Shiite, to the position—although Hammadi was widely regarded a weak person with no power base. Finally Ali Hassan al-Majid was appointed minister of the interior. Given his atrocious record, both as the official responsible for gassing the Kurds at Halabja, and his recently vacated position as the brutal governor of Kuwait, Majid's appointment sent a clear signal to the rebels that Saddam was not intending to treat them with kid gloves. As he had done so many times in the past, Saddam had ensured that the fate of all the leading members of the regime was inextricably linked to his own.

Saddam made a concerted effort to raise the morale of his battered troops. An across-the-board pay raise was announced for the military and the security forces. Any officer whose loyalty was regarded as suspect was purged, and there were a number of executions. Saddam's network of military commissars had survived the war intact. A number of senior military commanders were replaced, including General Wafic al-Samurrai, the head of military intelligence, who was no doubt punished for having been so candid in expressing his opinions on the military implications of Operation Desert Storm.

The Republican Guard was unleashed against the rebellion in the south. Buoyed by their new command and pay structure, the battalions of the Guard that had survived the war were keen to redeem themselves from the disgrace that they had suffered at the hands of the Allies. They plunged into their new task with a brutality that was exceptional even by the harsh standards of the Baathist regime. In the holy cities of Najaf and Karbala thousands of clerics were arrested and hundreds were summarily executed. Any turbaned or bearded man who took to the street ran the risk of being arrested and shot. People were tied to tanks and used as human shields, while women and children were indiscriminately shot. The Baath Party commissioned a film to be made of Ali Hassan al-Majid, the newly appointed interior minister, conducting operations against the Shiites. On one occasion in the film Majid can be heard giving instructions to an Iraqi helicopter pilot on his way to attack a group of rebels holding a bridge: "Don't come back until you are able to tell me that you have burnt them; and if you haven't burnt them don't come back."[6] Later in the film, which was distributed to Baath Party activists after the revolt had been suppressed, Majid is joined by another senior Baathist, Mohammed Hamza al-Zubeidi, and the two men slap and kick some of the prisoners as they lie defenseless on the ground. "Let's execute one so the others will confess," says Zubeidi, who later was promoted to prime minister by Saddam as a reward for his distinguished service in southern Iraq. The film then shows a group of prisoners looking frightened and resigned. Majid chain-smokes while he carries out his interrogation of the prisoners. He points to one of them and remarks: "Don't execute this one. He will be useful to us." By the time Western correspondents were finally allowed to visit the area after the revolt had been fully suppressed, they reported that Karbala "looked as if it had been hit by an earthquake."[7]

In late March a major offensive was launched against the Kurds and within days the main cities of Kurdistan had fallen to government forces, and fearful Kurds began fleeing to the mountains in a desperate attempt to escape the advancing Iraqi army. Saddam's psychological hold over the Kurds was revealed when his forces, simply by dropping white flour on groups of refugees, instilled total panic, and the defenseless civilians thought they were being attacked with chemical weapons. In early April nearly one million Kurdish refugees were concentrated along the Iranian and Kurdish borders, and by the end of the month the number exceeded two million. In the mountainous regions of Kurdistan the refugees were reported to be starving to death at the rate of a thousand people a day.

The victorious Allies, who had only two months previously been toasting their triumph over Saddam, now had to deal with a humanitarian disaster for which they were mainly responsible. Backed by UN Security Council Resolution 688, which authorized humanitarian organizations to aid the Kurds and banned Iraqi aircraft from flying north of the 36th parallel, the embarrassed Allies launched Operation Provide Comfort, with transport aircraft and helicopters delivering tons of relief materials, including food, clothes, tents, and blankets. But the emergency international relief effort was hampered by appalling overcrowding in the refugee camps and by bad weather. The only solution to prevent the situation reaching catastrophic proportions was to find a way in which the refugees could return to their homes. In early April John Major proposed establishing "safe havens" for the Kurds, areas of Kurdistan where they would be protected from attack by Saddam's forces. Initially President Bush, whose overriding concern was to prevent American troops from becoming embroiled in Iraq's civil war, was lukewarm to the plan, but in mid-April he changed his mind and authorized the U.S. military to establish a number of secure sites in northern Iraq to facilitate the distribution of food aid. By the end of the month nearly 10,000 American, British, and French troops were deployed in northern Iraq supervising the relief effort for the Kurds.

From Saddam's point of view, his policies in the spring of 1991 were a great success. He had demonstrated that he was tactically astute; he had succeeded in putting down two major insurrections, and he had demonstrated to complacent Western leaders that he was still the undisputed leader of his country. It was in this confident frame of mind that Saddam set about dealing with the next challenge to his regime, the arrival in Iraq of teams of UN-sponsored weapons inspectors to dismantle his nonconventional weapons arsenal. In the immediate aftermath of Iraq's defeat, there was a clear consensus at the UN Security Council that the country should be prevented from launching similar acts of aggression in the future. Apart from passing a number of resolutions that required it to give formal recognition to the independent state of Kuwait and to pay massive war reparations, the UN ordered Saddam to open up all sites in Iraq for inspection by UN teams searching for evidence of its suspected programs of nuclear, chemical, and biological weapons development. Once discovered, these would be destroyed, as would any remaining long-range surface-to-surface missiles. The punitive sanctions would be lifted only when the Security Council was satisfied that Iraq no longer possessed these capabilities, had allowed monitoring teams to be installed, and complied with the stipulations contained in the UN resolutions.

When the first UNSCOM (United Nations Special Commission on Disarmament) team arrived to start work in May 1991, Saddam and his officials embarked upon a systematic campaign of obstruction and concealment so that, seven years later, when the UNSCOM teams finally departed, the UN was unable to ascertain the precise nature of Iraq's capacity for manufacturing and delivering chemical, biological, and nuclear weapons. The very notion of teams of foreign nationals conducting intrusive investigations into the most sensitive aspects of Iraq's military industrial complex was, of course, anathema to Saddam and the Baath's ruling clique. The Iraqis had grudgingly agreed to the inspections in the immediate aftermath of the war only because Saddam wanted to give the impression of cooperating with the UN so that he could have a free hand to subdue the revolts in Kurdistan and southern Iraq.

But even though on the surface the Iraqis had agreed to comply with the weapons inspectors, the reality was very different.

In late April an emergency committee was set up under Tariq Aziz to decide how best to defy the UN, with orders from Saddam to save as much of Iraq's weapons of mass destruction capability as possible.[8] Saddam was determined not to declare any aspect of his nuclear weapons program, code-named PC-3, which he had successfully concealed from inspectors working for the International Atomic Energy Agency (IAEA) for more than a decade. Saddam also ordered that no details of the biological weapons program should be revealed. The only nonconventional weapon that was to be disclosed was the chemical weapons program, as the UN already had evidence of its manufacture. Saddam authorized the disclosure of stocks of chemical agents and their delivery systems, but the extensive research and development facilities were to be hidden, as were stocks of Iraq's most advanced chemical weapons, VX, which were to be totally concealed from the inspection teams. The policy was clear; Saddam would go through the motions of disarmament, but would not disarm. Aziz's committee drew up a detailed list of what could and what could not be disclosed to the UN, and an emergency evacuation plan was drawn up to disperse all weapons-related material that was not to be handed over to the UN. The committee even went so far as to make preparations for dealing with the inspection teams, which included rearranging the layout of sensitive facilities to hide evidence of prohibited activity. Aziz ordered that elaborate exercises be conducted, complete with mock inspections, to train Iraqi officials in how to deal with the UN inspection teams. Finally on April 18, Iraq submitted its declaration to the UN outlining details of its nonconventional weapons programs.

Rolf Ekeus, the Swedish head of UNSCOM, was quick to spot the inconsistencies between the material contained in Aziz's declaration and the details of Iraq's nonconventional weapons infrastructure that had been compiled by American and British intelligence. Ekeus put Baghdad on notice that UNSCOM was conducting a comprehensive assessment of Iraq's weapons of mass destruction capabilities, and that on-site inspections would be conducted not only of Iraq's declared facilities, but of undeclared locations as well. Saddam was clearly unnerved by the uncompromising nature of Ekeus's response, and ordered that a new committee be formed, the Concealment Operations Committee, which was to be controlled by his second eldest son, Qusay.[9]

The appointment of Qusay to this key position did not go down well with Hussein Kamel al-Majid, Saddam's son-in-law, who, through his chairmanship of the Military Industrial Commission set up after the Iran-Iraq War to rearm Iraq, had spent billions of dollars enhancing Iraq's nonconventional weapons capability. Hussein Kamel was a cocky individual, whose arrogance and generally self-satisfied demeanor had alienated many key figures within the ruling elite. Furthermore he owed his rise to prominence to the patronage of Saddam's estranged wife Sajida, who had been alienated from Saddam since the death of her brother Adnan in a helicopter crash in 1989. In times of crisis Saddam turned to those he could trust, as he had demonstrated with the changes he had made in March to the Baath leadership and the military prior to launching the campaign to subdue the Kurds and the Shiites. With so much at stake, Saddam clearly felt more confident if he had his own flesh and blood in charge of protecting the precious nonconventional weapons arsenal than someone who was related to him only by marriage. Saddam's preference for Qusay over Hussein Kamel created much bitterness and would cause Saddam much heartache in the years to come.

Qusay's new committee met regularly at the Presidential Palace and discussed ways of ensuring sensitive material was hidden from the inspectors. At this juncture the Iraqis thought that the UN inspection program would last a few months, if not weeks. They expected to show the inspectors around the sites they had declared to the UN, most of which had been destroyed by Allied bombing during the war. The Iraqis based their expectations on their previous experience of dealing with the IAEA inspectors who had regularly inspected Iraq's nuclear research facilities without ever actually noticing that Iraq was developing nuclear weapons.

The UNSCOM inspectors proved to be far more conscientious in carrying out their duties. In June 1991 a team led by David Kay, the chief inspector, which was surveying Iraq's declared nuclear facilities, visited the Abu Ghraib military camp west of Baghdad. Although the Iraqis had admitted that part of the camp was used for nuclear research, another part of the camp had been commandeered by Qusay to conceal key equipment from Iraq's nuclear research program. In the course of inspecting the camp Kay discovered Iraqi soldiers attempting to move a number of huge electromagnetic isotope separators, known as Calutrons, which were being transported on heavy tractor trailers. When Kay tried to intervene, the Iraqi soldiers reacted by firing shots over his head. The Iraqis then drove the Calutrons away to another location in full view of the inspectors, who filmed the entire proceedings.

The Abu Ghraib incident set the tone for Iraq's relations with the weapons inspectors for the next six years. After this embarrassment, Qusay's concealment committee ordered that all the key components of Iraq's nuclear weapons program be concealed at a network of Saddam's palaces and villas around Tikrit, which were not mentioned in Iraq's declared list of sites. Any material that was not regarded as essential was blown up by the Iraqis, who then informed the UN that they had unilaterally destroyed their nonconventional weapons, in the belief that the weapons inspectors would not return. Having already caught Saddam out once, the UNSCOM inspectors were not convinced. Kay returned to Baghdad and in mid-September his team arrived unannounced at the Iraqi nuclear headquarters in Baghdad, scaled the fence, and burst into the building. To their amazement they discovered millions of pages of documents detailing all of Iraq's nuclear weapons programs. Although Qusay's concealment committee had ordered that all the nuclear hardware be secured, they had forgotten about the documentation. Embarrassed Iraqi officials rushed to the compound, and a four-day standoff ensued, in which Kay's inspectors were virtually held captive in the parking lot.[10] But the damage had been done, and the UNSCOM teams resolved to continue their inspections until they were convinced that Saddam had been completely disarmed.

The concealment committee reacted to this latest disaster by arranging to have the nuclear archive microfilmed and stored at the Ministry of Agriculture, which had previously played a prominent role in constructing Iraq's chemical and biological weapons programs. But the inspectors were not to be deceived, and in July 1992 they raided the Ministry of Agriculture building. Saddam's security forces responded by organizing groups of civilians to attack the UN inspectors as they tried to carry out their mission. That was the last time the weapons inspectors came close to making a thorough examination of the complete nuclear weapons archive, which soon afterward was removed to a secret presidential compound near Tikrit.

While Saddam concentrated his energies on finding ways to defy the UNSCOM inspectors, the Iraqi people were destitute and starving. The UN sanctions meant that Iraq was unable to sell its oil to earn foreign currency and was therefore severely limited in what it could import. Fertilizers, agricultural machinery, pesticides, and chemicals that might have a dual use, as well as parts for Iraq's ruined electricity and water purification systems, were all forbidden. As a consequence, disease and malnutrition were soon widespread, causing infant mortality rates to rise to levels not seen in Iraq for more than forty years. Food prices rose by 2000 percent within a year of the Kuwait invasion, and the devastation of the economy meant that previously affluent middle-class Baghdadis were reduced to penury.

The suffering of the Iraqi people, however, made little impression on the country's leader. In 1992 the UN responded to the mounting hardship suffered by ordinary Iraqis by offering the Iraqi government the opportunity to sell $1.6 billion worth of oil to pay for food and medicine. This was rejected by Saddam, who took exception to the UN's insistence that it control the funds, and that 30 percent of the profits would be deducted to pay for war reparations. For the next four years Saddam continued to block similar offers, preferring to let the Iraqi people suffer rather than allow any constraints to be imposed on the office of the presidency. It was not until 1996 that he finally agreed to accept the terms of UN Security Resolution 986, which allowed Iraq to sell $2 billion worth of oil every six months for the purchase of essential supplies.

Although the coalition Allies had been unwilling to back the Kurdish and Shiite rebellions, there was nevertheless a strong desire to see Saddam overthrown. In May 1991, when Saddam had successfully crushed the rebellions in the north and south and had reestablished himself at the strongman of Baghdad, President Bush signed a formal "finding" that authorized the CIA to mount a covert operation to "create the conditions for the removal of Saddam Hussein from power." Had the finding been signed a few months earlier, the CIA might have stood some chance of success. But by the time Bush finally came to the conclusion that Saddam must be removed from power, the Iraqi leader had been able successfully to strengthen his power base.

Frank Anderson, the recipient of the "finding" and head of the CIA's Near East Division at the Directorate of Operations, later commented: "We didn't have a single mechanism or combination of mechanisms with which I could create a plan to get rid of Saddam at that time."[11] Bush's finding seemed to echo an aphorism coined by Richard Helms, a former CIA director: "Covert action is frequently a substitute for a policy." Bush himself conceded that a key opportunity to overthrow Saddam in the immediate aftermath of Operation Desert Storm had probably been lost. Evidence had emerged that a group of senior Iraqi officers had planned a coup against Saddam shortly after the war, but were deterred from taking action because of the rebellions in the north and south.[12] Interviewed on American television in 1994, Bush commented: "I did have a strong feeling that the Iraqi military, having been led to such a crushing defeat by Saddam, would rise up and rid themselves of him. We were concerned that the uprisings would sidetrack the overthrow of Saddam by causing the Iraqi military to rally round him to prevent the breakup of the country. That may have been what actually happened."[13]

From the autumn of 1991 onward the American and British intelligence services explored various options for removing Saddam. The first priority was to find a person or group who would present an acceptable alternative to him. To this end the CIA made an approach to Saddam's half brother Barzan, who was still living in exile in Geneva,[14] an unlikely candidate in view of his previous activities as head of the Iraqi Mukhabarat and his personal involvement in the executions of fellow Baathists that took place after Saddam assumed the presidency in 1979 (see Chapter Seven). The next significant initiative was undertaken in June 1992 when, under CIA auspices, an estimated forty Iraqi opposition groups, including the Kurds, were brought together in Vienna to form a new organization called the Iraqi National Congress (INC), which committed itself to Saddam's overthrow. The publicly declared aim of the INC was to create a democratic Iraq with a government that would represent all races and creeds. The INC was little more than a propaganda vehicle, and most of its more realistic members were well aware that Saddam would not easily be dislodged. The INC was funded almost exclusively by the CIA, to the tune of $23 million in its first year alone.

The most serious threat to Saddam still lay with his own armed forces. In the summer of 1992 two mechanized Republican Guard brigades were linked to a plot to depose him. The plot—assuming it existed—was foiled by Saddam's ever-watchful security forces, and resulted in another round of executions and purges. Six officers were executed immediately, including two brigadier generals, and another four hundred were arrested.[15] The following year another plot was uncovered, whose purpose was to kill Saddam during the annual July celebrations marking the Baathist revolution. The Republican Guard was again suspected of involvement, and further executions took place. Concerned that even the elite units of the Republican Guard could not be trusted, Saddam formed a special unit, mainly drawn from Tikritis, called the Golden Division of the Republican Guard. Its members were paid higher salaries and accorded special privileges, and worked closely with the president's special security officers. Eventually the two groups merged to form the Organization of Special Security (OSS).

Saddam made some adjustments to the government, strengthening the position of his direct relatives in key positions. His half brother Watban replaced Ali Hassan al-Majid as minister of the interior, with Majid becoming defense minister. Another half brother, Sabawi, was made head of his private office and took control of the Mukhabarat. Uday, who was now twenty-eight and had effected a reconciliation with his father, was made head of national security and took control of the newspaper *Babel,* while continuing to run the Olympic Committee. Uday's younger brother, Qusay, twenty-five, was given the key role of heading the newly created OSS. Saddam also tried to keep his two sons-in-law, Hussein Kamel and Saddam Kamel, happy. Hussein Kamel, who was becoming increasingly irritated by Saddam's promotion of Qusay, continued to run the Military Industrialization Oorganization (MIO), Iraq's main weapons procurement agency, while Saddam Kamel, a less abrasive personality, headed an unspecified security department at the Presidential Palace.

In the absence of any effective plan to remove Saddam, the United States, Britain, and France sought to increase the diplomatic pressure on him by establishing a no-fly zone over southern Iraq below the 32nd parallel, which gave the Allies effective control over one-third of Iraq's airspace. The decision to impose the no-fly zone, similar to the one that was established to protect the Kurds in the north in 1991, was taken to protect the Marsh Arabs, the people who have inhabited the marshland around Basra for centuries, and who rebeled against Saddam in the summer of 1991. The revolt of the Marsh Arabs was unrelated to the rebellions of the Kurds and the Shiites, and was provoked by Saddam's decision to construct a new three-hundred-mile-long water channel—called Saddam's River—that adversely affected the marshes' natural drainage, thereby arbitrarily destroying a culture that had existed for centuries. Saddam responded with his customary savagery, and reports soon reached the West of chemical weapons again being used against a defenseless population. An underlying motive for the creation of the no-fly zone, however, was George Bush's desire, with the presidential election due in November, to impress the American electorate with his uncompromising stand against Saddam.

Bush's ploy failed, however, and in November 1992 Bill Clinton defeated him in the presidential contest. Saddam responded by appearing on the balcony of his palace and firing his gun in the air in celebration. While Saddam remained the undisputed leader of Iraq, his two key antagonists during the Kuwait crisis, Margaret Thatcher and George Bush, had been unceremoniously thrown out of office. Saddam believed the change of government in Washington would be to his advantage, and that the new president would be less interested in pursuing a personal vendetta against the Iraqi leader. In this, he was disappointed. Within hours of winning the election, Clinton warned Saddam not to flout any of the UN sanctions. He responded in early January 1993, just days before Clinton officially replaced Bush, by deploying antiaircraft missile batteries inside the no-fly zone, a clear act of provocation designed to test Washington's political will during the sensitive transition period. Again Saddam underestimated American resolve, and just six days before he handed over the presidency to Clinton, Bush responded by ordering more than 100 Allied aircraft to attack the Iraqi missile batteries.

Even after Bush stepped down as president, Saddam's tribal instincts would not allow him to drop the vendetta. In April 1993, when George Bush made an emotional return to Kuwait, the Kuwaiti authorities revealed that they had uncovered an Iraqi plot to kill him. The Kuwaitis found a car packed with enough explosive to devastate the center of Kuwait City; the bomb was primed to detonate as Bush was driving through the city's center. James Woolsey, Clinton's CIA director, sent a team of forensic experts to Kuwait to examine the bomb. They concluded that it bore the hallmarks of Iraq's Mukhabarat. Wafic al-Samurrai, the former head of military intelligence, who had much experience in carrying out such operations, said there was never any doubt that Saddam personally issued the order for the assassination attempt. "No one could do it without a direct order from Saddam Hussein himself." Five of the six suspects were Iraqis; they were subsequently convicted and hanged by the Kuwaitis. Two months after the failed assassination attempt Clinton retaliated by firing twenty-three Tomahawk guided missiles at the Mukhabarat headquarters in Baghdad. The United States might have changed its president, but it had not altered its policy toward Saddam Hussein.

While the Iraqi people were starving, destitute, and afflicted by outbreaks of typhoid and cholera, Saddam's ruling clique grew rich on the profits of oil smuggling. Within two years of the commencement of one of the most all-encompassing sanctions ever imposed by the UN, Saddam's security forces had set up a complex network of companies, middlemen, and smugglers that enabled him to sell large quantities of oil on the black market and use the proceeds to finance the regime. The favored smuggling routes were through Kurdistan and Turkey, and through Jordan, where King Hussein turned a blind eye to Iraq's illegal oil shipments through the Jordanian port of Aqaba. At the Habur checkpoint on the Iraqi-Turkish border, Iraqi trucks with specially adapted tanks capable of carrying substantial quantities of oil became a common feature of the everyday traffic. By 1992 it was estimated that 50,000 barrels of Iraqi oil were moving through this crossing point daily. The oil was then sold to Turkish middlemen for foreign currency, which was then passed back to Saddam's coffers at the Presidential Palace. Without any hint of irony, in the summer of 1992 Saddam ordered the execution of forty-two of Baghdad's leading merchants, who were accused of profiteering. Some of the merchants were tied to poles in public with signs declaring: "We are bloodsuckers." They were then taken to the Interior Ministry—which was controlled by Saddam's half brother Sabawi—and hanged.[16] The Iraqi public saw the executions as nothing more than a cynical attempt by Saddam to deflect the general discontent with the high living of his elite.

Sami Salih, who for many years was in charge of Saddam's oil smuggling operation, said he was recruited on the recommendation of Hussein Kamel, Saddam's son-in-law. Salih said he had previously worked with Hussein Kamel at the MIO on various secretive weapons procurement projects. Because of his expertise in running export-import companies, Salih was summoned to the Presidential Palace after the Gulf War for a meeting with Saddam and was asked to set up an international sanctions-busting network. "It would have been impossible for me to refuse," he said. "Had I declined they would not just have killed me; they would have murdered my wife, my children, my friends, my relatives—anyone remotely associated with me." Having accepted the assignment Salih set up a number of "front" companies through which Iraq sold its oil and bought arms. "The UN could do nothing to stop us," he said. Eventually Salih, like so many Iraqis who had contact with the West, was accused of spying and arrested.

The first he knew that he was in trouble was when a team of Iraqi intelligence officers arrived at his Baghdad office. "They told me, 'Saddam Hussein has personally ordered your detention and interrogation.' " He was blindfolded and driven to the Presidential Palace compound. He was taken to a place called the "property room," where he was stripped, given an old pair of blood-soaked pajamas, and thrown into a cell. At one point he managed to look beneath his blindfold. He saw that the walls of his cell were spattered with blood, and on them he found a number of inscriptions, which read "My name is so-and-so and I am to be executed on such-and-such a day." Salih was left in the cell for a week and fed a diet of bread and water.

Eventually the guards said they were taking him to the "operations room." He was led into the room blindfolded, and immediately heard the screams of other people being tortured. "They accused me of being a spy and demanded that I make a full confession," Salih recalled. "I was more than willing to comply, but I had no idea what I was supposed to confess to." The guards tied his feet together, hung him upside down, and whipped his body with lengths of cable and wire, until he was covered in blood. "I thought I was going to die then and there. But they were very expert in their trade. Just when I was losing consciousness they stopped and let me down." He was then given ten blank pieces of paper on which to write his "confession." As Salih lay on the ground recovering from his ordeal, he was able to look beneath his blindfold. All around him he saw other prisoners being tortured by teams of Saddam's tormentors. In one corner he saw a naked man being lowered slowly into a vat of boiling water. In another a victim was being tortured with electric shocks to his genitals. Yet another victim was strapped to a table in the center of the room, where the guards were extracting his toe- and fingernails. Unlike most of the other victims, Salih, by making use of the contacts he had developed when he was a key figure in the regime, managed to escape.[17]

Another key figure in the smuggling operation was Saddam's estranged half brother Barzan, who, from the comfort of his fortresslike villa overlooking Lake Geneva, combined his duties as Iraq's representative to the UN mission with working as Saddam's private financier. By 1993 it was estimated that Barzan, taking full advantage of the closed world of Swiss banking, controlled a complex web of undercover investments worth $20 billion.[18] Kroll Associates, the U.S.-based firm of financial investigators, reckoned that Saddam had personally siphoned off about $200 billion from Iraq's oil sales since 1981, and that he was able to exploit the secretive network of companies set up prior to the Kuwait crisis to circumvent the UN sanctions.

Despite the lucrative smuggling trade, however, little of the profits went to improving the lot of ordinary Iraqis. Indeed, much of the funds donated by the UN to assist the plight of ordinary Iraqi civilians went directly to Saddam and his ruling circle, and the main beneficiaries were the security forces and his family. Even the medical supplies shipped in by the UN were exploited by the regime, and ended up being sold on the black market in Jordan, the profits being channeled back to the Presidential Palace in Baghdad. The lion's share of the substantial income Saddam received from these various illicit activities was spent on arms. Secret arms deals were negotiated with such disparate countries as China, North Korea, Russia, several former East bloc satellites, and Serbia. By the mid-1990s it was estimated that Saddam had regained 80 percent of the military hardware destroyed during the Gulf War. The rest was spent on the increasingly opulent lifestyle of Saddam's immediate family and other leading members of the regime.

Uday was the most profligate and the most corrupt member of the ruling family, closely followed by his brother-in-law, the preening Hussein Kamel. Both men abused their power in the manner one would expect of a pair of mafiosi. Their homes were filled with valuable Persian rugs, gold fittings, and fixtures, much of which had been looted from Kuwait. Uday's garage was filled with Ferraris and other expensive models. Uday and Hussein Kamel were also heavily involved in an international smuggling operation, which was linked both to the Russian mafia and Latin American drugs smuggling rings.[19]

According to Abbas Janabi, who worked as Uday's private secretary for fifteen years before defecting to the West, by the mid-1990s Uday had become undoubtedly the wealthiest man in Iraq, and his private fortune was estimated at hundreds of millions of dollars, much of it secreted at locations throughout Iraq. Uday had no qualms about how he acquired his money. For example, he was personally involved in the resale of the humanitarian aid Iraq received from the UN on the black market. On one occasion he changed the labels on a consignment of Japanese milk, which had been donated to help Iraq's undernourished children, and sold it, keeping the profits for himself. Aid from Spain, which was donated to the Ministry of Health, met a similar fate. In the mid-1990s he expanded Iraq's oil-smuggling operations by forming an unlikely trading agreement with the Iranians. Uday personally controlled a fleet of barges based at the southern Iraqi port of Basra and paid an Iranian partner to protect the oil as it passed through Iranian waters. Another huge money market for Uday was cigarette smuggling, which he managed through a number of routes through Europe and Cyprus.

Despite his incredible wealth, Uday harbored a sadistic streak from which not even his closest colleagues and advisers were immune. On one occasion in 1991 Janabi inadvertently upset Uday by writing an article about the state of the Iraqi army. He was jailed and tortured. "Uday sent one of his body-guards to the prison and he used a pair of pliers to pull out one of my teeth. Then he wrapped it in a Kleenex and took it to Uday to show he had done the job." On another occasion Janabi saw Uday torture a man who had looked after his business interests in Jordan, beating him with a baseball bat on the soles of his feet, then suspending him from a revolving ceiling fan and flogging him with a cable. During the fifteen years he worked for Uday, Janabi was jailed on eleven separate occasions, including one spell in Uday's office at the headquarters of the Iraqi Olympic Committee.[20]

The Iraqi Olympic Committee's downtown headquarters had sufficient capacity to hold up to 520 detainees. The cells were located in the basement, and included sensory deprivation cells, which were sealed, painted red with red lightbulbs, and contained a tiny slot for the passage of food. Prisoners would be held for up to three months in these conditions. For many years Uday's prison complex at the Olympic Committee was kept secret from his father. Many of those held in Uday's cells had broken no law. They were mainly businessmen or the children of wealthy families who Uday thought were ripe for exploitation. Some of those held were simply ransomed by Uday—in 1995 the going rate was said to be $100,000. Others were imprisoned to force them to participate in a fraudulent scheme that Uday had devised. In one case an Iraqi businessman had arranged to import a shipment of steel for a construction project, and had deposited his payment with a bank in Baghdad to transfer to his foreign supplier. Uday arranged for the paperwork to disappear and had the man arrested. He then arranged to have the deposit transferred to his own account and the businessmen was brought in for interrogation at the Olympic Committee. He was given a stark choice: either make another payment for the steel, or die.[21]

While the regime flourished, the people suffered. By 1995 there was still no clean drinking water, the electricity system could only provide three to four hours of power a day. The per capita caloric intake was half what it was before the war. Crime was so widespread that in 1993 alone 36,000 cars were stolen. UNICEF claimed that in 1993 between 80,000 and 100,000 children died because of the sanctions. But the regime would do nothing to help. It suited Saddam to have the population weak and fearful. Limited medical aid was provided, but only to favored party members. Abbas Janabi claimed that during the period he spent working for Uday the regime could afford to buy anything it wanted, but preferred to spend the money on arms and expensive cars for the ruling elite. Saddam's only response to the growing desperation of ordinary Iraqis to feed themselves and their families in 1994 was to order that thieves should have their right hands cut off; frequent offenders were to have their left leg cut off from the knee and armed robbery would carry the death penalty. At the same time three high-ranking army officers were executed on Saddam's orders for questioning Uday's military capabilities.

The most essential aspect of the sanctions-busting operation was that it enabled Saddam to continue to defy the demands of the UNSCOM weapons inspectors. The pattern up to 1995 replicated that established when they first started work. Saddam's security forces would do everything in their power to impede the work of the inspectors, would make false claims about the true extent of the Iraqi weapons programs and devise new schemes for concealing the more sensitive material. Sami Salih, who spent five years based at the Presidential Palace running the sanctions-busting operations, said that Saddam never had any intention of complying with the requirements of the UN inspection teams. "There were missiles hidden all over Iraq. I saw them stored under swimming pools and on farms."[22] Despite all the provocations, the inspectors under the cool leadership of Rolf Ekeus continued with their painstaking task. They would present the Iraqis with incontrovertible evidence and force them to hand over the offending material. Ekeus struggled on with the mission despite Saddam's constant brinkmanship, one day threatening to reinvade Kuwait, the next threatening a new atrocity against the Kurds. Occasionally American and British warplanes would react to the provocation by bombing antiaircraft missile batteries in Iraq.

Although Saddam had the ability to cause the Allies immense irritation, the various schemes to remove him met with little success. This may have had something to do with the fact that from the autumn of 1993 onward the Clinton administration was deeply involved in efforts to resolve the Arab-Israeli conflict, which was enjoying one of its most constructive phases in years after the signing of the Oslo Accords. While Saddam was a nuisance, he was regarded in Washington as a containable nuisance, and any concerted effort to remove him might upset the delicate balance of the Arab-Israeli negotiations, particularly as many Palestinians were sympathetic to Iraq and would use any attack on Saddam as an opportunity to accuse the United States of anti-Arab bias.

Clinton was certainly less obsessed with the Saddam issue than Bush had been. Since April 1991, when President Bush signed his "finding" authorizing Saddam's overthrow, American policy had been based on a twin-track approach: to contain Saddam through a combination of sanctions and the no-fly zones while Western intelligence agencies worked within Iraq to bring him down. Initially the Clinton administration left the Bush approach essentially unchanged, and Clinton renewed Bush's "finding" authorizing Saddam's overthrow. Even so, Clinton was eager to avoid face-to-face confrontations with Saddam, and his advisers wanted to keep Saddam off the front pages. The phrase used by Anthony Lake, Clinton's national security adviser, to officials working on Iraq was: "Don't give us sweaty palms"—i.e., do not provoke any crises.[23] The CIA and Britain's MI6 were nevertheless still fully committed in their attempts to organize a coup. By late 1994 most of the intelligence activity was based in the Kurdish safe haven in northern Iraq. In September 1994 the CIA established its base at a heavily fortified villa at Salahdin while the Iraqi National Congress (INC) created a ministate for itself, complete with its own television station and newspaper. The INC had devised a plan to attack Mosul and Kirkuk, the two major cities in northern Iraq, which, if successful, would seriously weaken Saddam. The INC was greatly assisted in its planning by General Wafic al-Samurrai, Saddam's former head of military intelligence, who had defected in December 1994 after learning from his colleagues at the Presidential Palace that Saddam planned to kill him.

The INC and Samurrai were confident of success, although Washington was concerned that, if it supported the revolt, it could find itself embroiled in a messy war in Iraq, something successive U.S. administrations had been desperate to avoid since the end of Operation Desert Storm. On the eve of the INC's planned attack, Lake sent a message to the CIA team based at Salahdin ordering them to tell the INC that "the United States would not support this operation militarily or in any other way."[24] The INC, whose plans were already well advanced, went ahead with the attack and, even without American support, achieved a degree of success, capturing several hundred Iraqi prisoners. But without U.S. support, the INC, which was backed by Jalal Talibani's Patriotic Union of Kurdistan (PUK) Party, was unable to consolidate its gains, and the offensive petered out, leaving the Iraqi exiles deeply disillusioned about the sincerity of Washington's commitment to overthrowing Saddam.

The constant threat of plots, coups, and invasions, however, did little to ease Saddam's peace of mind. He was reported to be suffering from heart trouble and the resulting dizzy spells caused by a lack of blood reaching the brain. In the summer of 1995 yet another plot was uncovered, this one organized by Mohammed Madhloum, an air force commander who tried to launch an uprising against Saddam. The attempt failed and Madhloum and his accomplices were captured. Each of them was tortured by having all of their fingers cut off, one by one. Then they were shot.[25]

By this stage in his long career Saddam had developed a siege mentality. He had always taken his security to ludicrous extremes, but by the mid-1990s the aging tyrant had become almost dysfunctional in his obsession with it. Saddam spent most of his time at the Presidential Palace, which by the 1990s had become a massive, sprawling complex of about one thousand acres; on one side the Tigris provided a natural boundary, while the rest was protected by an electrified perimeter fence, with guard towers every fifty yards. The main road access was across a bridge, which had been rebuilt after being bombed in the war. Ordinary Iraqis were not allowed anywhere near the compound, and risked a jail sentence if they approached it without permission. Once past the main checkpoints, visitors were sent to one of several gates that were specially designated for different groups: the military, politicians, businessmen, or personal friends and acquaintances of Saddam's family. The gates and the fortress itself were guarded by a confusing number of different security forces, who were there as much to keep a watchful eye on one another as to protect Saddam and his entourage. The most basic security functions were performed by trusted members of the Republican Guard; more sophisticated measures, such as electronic surveillance, by the Special Republican Guard. Overall control of the complex was in the hands of the Republican Palace Guard, while the safety of Saddam and his family was entrusted to the Organization of Special Security (OSS) headed by Qusay.

The OSS guards were the elite corps. Most of them were recruited from Saddam's tribe in Tikrit, and they were afforded better privileges than most of the cabinet ministers to guarantee their loyalty. They were distinguished from the other guards by their olive green uniforms, a white lanyard, and special-issue guns. They lived with their families inside the presidential compound in comfortable villas. They had their own sports and health club, hospital, and schools for their children. They dined at their own restaurant complex, where their meals were served by waiters. Every six months they received a new car, usually a Mercedes. Most of them earned twice the wage of an Iraqi cabinet minister and, when off duty, they were generally allowed to do as they pleased, so long as they obeyed the command of their master, Saddam Hussein. As one former official at the Presidential Palace commented: "They fear only God, and their God is Saddam Hussein. They were so powerful that even ministers called them 'sir' when they entered the Presidential Palace. No one took any liberties with them."[26]

By now Saddam had established one of the most extensive security structures in modern history. Although he rarely appeared in public, by the mid-1990s he had some eight "doubles" who could impersonate him at public functions; sometimes they appeared at different events at the same time, causing difficulties for the state-owned media, which had to prepare daily reports on Saddam's itinerary. Visitors were still subjected to the routine where they were driven around Baghdad for hours in cars with blackened windows when invited to attend one of Saddam's guesthouses. Being such an expert himself in poisoning his opponents, Saddam not surprisingly took great care to ensure that he did not become a victim. Before meeting any member of his government, Saddam would insist that they first wash their hands, a precaution against the possibility that they might have poison on their fingers that could rub off in a handshake. In the interests of security no indignity was spared Saddam's guests. All of them had their photographs and fingerprints taken, and the OSS had the right to strip-search cabinet members prior to any meeting with Saddam. Even Tariq Aziz, one of Saddam's most trusted lieutenants, was not immune from such degradation. On rare occasions guests were subjected to an intrusive medical examination to check that they had not concealed any poison or explosives in intimate areas of their bodies. Even these elaborate precautions could not prevent the occasional security lapse. In 1996 Saddam narrowly escaped an assassination attempt when a young waitress at the Presidential Palace, who was supposed to serve him poisoned food, was overcome with fear and confessed. Saddam immediately had her taken outside the dining hall and shot. All her accomplices were tortured and executed.[27]

When off duty the guards terrorized the local population, and rumors circulated of their womanizing and dissolute behavior. One guard commander was seen one evening at a nightclub trying to attract the attention of an old girlfriend. When she rejected his advances, he pulled out a gun and shot her five times in the chest. They were also said to procure women for Saddam, who, despite his second marriage to Samira Shahbandar, still had a predilection for young, blonde women. For example Saddam might be attracted to a woman he had seen on television. He would order his bodyguards to bring her to him. When he had finished with her, the bodyguards would be told to pay her handsomely. But if for some reason the woman had not pleased him, she would be taken out and shot.[28]

Despite all the security, Saddam relied on a number of psychics to warn him of any impending misfortune. No doubt he had inherited his superstitious nature from his mother, who had used her collection of seashells to sell prophesies to the peasants of Al-Ouja. Saddam made particular use of an elderly blind woman psychic, to whom he paid particular attention in times of crisis. She once predicted that he would be the victim of an assassination attempt—not in itself a controversial prediction given the frequency with which he was attacked—and thereafter Saddam trusted her judgment.

Those who visited the palace regularly, such as Sami Salih, said there was always an air of tension about the place as no one—not even most of the OSS guards—knew whether or not Saddam was present. Most of the time he worked in a small building in a sealed corner of the presidential complex, and very few officials ever ventured into his inner sanctum. Visiting dignitaries were always received in the old Presidential Palace, and only Saddam's most trusted confidants were allowed into his private office. Access to Saddam was strictly controlled by Abdul Hamoud, his private secretary, who occupied a separate building in front of his private quarters. Whichever office Saddam used to receive his visitors was equipped with cameras and recorders. The meetings took the form of a royal audience, and guests were supposed to talk only after he had spoken, and then to keep their answers concise. Although Saddam had his sleeping quarters within the palace compound, he rarely slept there. In Baghdad alone there were at least five other palaces that accommodated his retinue, and he would move from one to the other regularly to escape detection. On those occasions when Saddam left the Presidential Palace, a number of decoy motorcades—never fewer than five—would sweep over the main bridge and into Baghdad. Saddam would not be in any of them, but would most likely have left by another exit, or through one of the secret underground tunnels that were connected to the presidential bunker.

The only area in which Saddam's elaborate security arrangements lacked effectiveness was in controlling the activities of his family. By the mid-1990s Uday's activities, in particular, were a cause of much friction. He had turned the Olympic Committee into his personal fiefdom, and by controlling much of the country's media output, he had unlimited access to one of the regime's key components, the propaganda machine. Uday's utter disregard for the state's institutions created friction with Watban, his uncle and Saddam's half brother, who controlled the Interior Ministry, and Hussein Kamel, who saw his own position as Saddam's potential successor being eroded both by Uday's acquisition of wealth and power, and to a lesser extent by Qusay's emergence as a more sober influence on the government. Matters came to a head in true Tikriti fashion in the spring of 1995 when Uday forced Watban's resignation by running a series of disparaging articles about him in his newspaper, *Babel.* A few days later Uday, in a drunken rage, attacked his uncle, shooting him in the leg and killing three of his companions while they were attending a private party in Baghdad. Watban, who feared for his life, claimed the shooting had been an accident, even though his injuries required him to have his leg amputated. Hussein Kamel and his younger brother, Saddam Kamel, believing that they were next on Uday's list, fled into exile in Jordan, taking their wives, Saddam's daughters Raghda and Rana.

The defection of Saddam's two sons-in-law in August 1995 was potentially the most damaging blow he had suffered since seizing power in 1979. For the first time two members of the Tikriti ruling circle had escaped Saddam's authority and were threatening to betray the regime's innermost secrets. Hussein Kamel, as head of Iraq's weapons procurement program, was particularly well equipped to provide Western intelligence with a treasure trove of detail about Saddam's weapons of mass destruction program. Hussein Kamel was fully debriefed by both the CIA and Britain's M16, and then by Rolf Ekeus, the head of UNSCOM. He provided a detailed account of Iraq's weapons program, including hitherto hidden chemical weapons plants and front companies helping with Iraq's weapons procurement and Saddam's VX nerve agent program. His most startling revelation was that Saddam had been within three months of testing an atomic bomb at the start of Operation Desert Storm in January 1991.

Hussein Kamel fully expected to be granted asylum in either the United States or Britain, from where he would base his campaign to overthrow Saddam. To this end he granted an exclusive interview to *Time* in which he said his defection was motivated by "the interests of the country." He was deeply critical of Saddam's regime. The country had spent nearly fifteen years at war and had accumulated debts that it would take "generations and generations" to pay. He also tried to distance himself from the brutality of the regime. "There are too many executions in our society, too many arrests," he complained. "Whatever the age of the critic—whether 80 or 15—many people are executed."[29]

Saddam was so enraged by the defections that for a time he was not able to eat and refused to talk to any of his close associates. Eventually, when he had calmed down, he called in Uday, whom he believed bore primary responsibility for the defections, and stripped him of all his positions. Saddam's security forces raided the headquarters of the Olympic Committee and freed all those being held in Uday's private jail. Saddam was forced to update his submissions to UNSCOM, including new data on biological weapons, such as anthrax and botulism, VX nerve gas, and new information on Iraq's attempts to acquire nuclear weapons. UNSCOM was readmitted to Iraq and Ekeus resumed the inspections, this time equipped with incontrovertible evidence of Iraq's nonconventional weapons infrastructure.

Saddam moved quickly to demonstrate that he was still the strongman of Baghdad, despite the shooting of his half brother Watban and the defection of his two sons-in-law. He announced that a referendum would be held on October 15, in which eight million Iraqis would vote on the question: "Do you agree that Saddam Hussein should be president of Iraq?" Even though he dyed his hair and suffered back problems, Saddam was still presented to the Iraqi people as a heroic, virile leader. His cousin and defense minister, Ali Hassan al-Majid, was the campaign's chief cheerleader. "Oh lofty mountain! Oh glory of God!" Majid said in an official broadcast. "By God we have always found you in the most difficult conditions as a roaring lion and courageous horseman, one of the few true men."[30] Saddam won the plebiscite with 99.96 percent of the vote. Majid performed another important service for Saddam by issuing a public denouncement of his cousins for defecting to Jordan. "This small family within Iraq denounces this cowardly act," said the statement, which was read live on Iraqi television. "His [Saddam Kamel's] family has unanimously decided to permit with impunity the spilling of blood."[31]

If Hussein Kamel had expected a hero's welcome in the West for his defection, he was sorely disappointed. Western intelligence officers were prepared to debrief him and his brother, but had no desire to perpetuate the relationship. In their view he was an arrogant, vainglorious individual who was too closely associated with Saddam's regime to be considered as a viable alternative. However much they wanted to see the back of Saddam, they did not want him to replaced by one his clones.[32] By the end of the year Hussein Kamel, Saddam Kamel, Saddam's daughters, and their retinue were confined to one of King Hussein's guesthouses in Amman, and all their overtures to be given a sanctuary in the West were met with a resounding silence.

Sensing an opportunity to avenge himself on his errant sons-in-law, Saddam established contact with them in Jordan through his security agents. He personally phoned the sons-in-law at their Amman hideout, offering them a presidential pardon if only they would return. Apart from the embarrassment their revelations on the arms program had caused, Saddam's honor as the family patriarch had been compromised by, as it appeared to Arab eyes, the abduction of his two daughters. Saddam gave Uday the opportunity to redeem himself by persuading the two families to return to Baghdad, tempting them with the offer of a presidential pardon. Disillusioned by the reception they had received, and arrogantly believing that they had taught Saddam a lesson, in February 1996 Hussein Kamel and Saddam Kamel agreed to return home with their families. For once Saddam Kamel protested against the decision of his overbearing brother, saying, "You donkey. You want us to go back to our deaths." Hussein Kamel responded by pulling out his pistol and replying, "You will come back."

The party set off on the journey to Baghdad on the morning of February 20. As soon as they crossed the border at Trebeil, they were met by Uday and his guards. No attempt was made to arrest the Kamel brothers, but Uday took his sisters Raghda and Rana and their children into his motorcade. On their arrival in Baghdad, the two men were summoned to the Presidential Palace. The two brothers were forced to sign papers sanctioning their immediate divorce from their wives. Saddam personally tore off their badges of rank from their uniforms—Hussein Kamel was a lieutenant general, while his brother was a lieutenant colonel. He then sent them to stay at their father's villa at Assadiyah, on the outskirts of Baghdad, to await their fate. Later that evening Saddam summoned relatives and associates of the disgraced men to the Presidential Palace. Sami Salih, who was still head of Iraq's oil-smuggling operation, was one of those present. He recalled that Saddam was "drunk, red-eyed, and wild. He was waving his gun around and screaming abuse." Saddam said that the brothers had shamed everyone in Iraq, particularly their family. He told them, "You must remove this shame. You must get hold of them and cleanse this stain. Get rid of them." Saddam then staggered out of the room and the "guests" were taken into the presidential compound, where they boarded three Toyota buses. Salih and his companions genuinely believed that they were going to be executed because of their association with the disgraced men.

Instead they were driven through the suburbs of predawn Baghdad. After about half an hour they came to a halt. One of the guards entered the bus and told everyone to stay quiet, on pain of death. Salih, who had worked with Hussein Kamel for many years, recognized the location; the buses had been parked a short distance from Hussein Kamel's family villa. The house was surrounded by Iraqi Special Forces, which were heavily armed. Salih could see the distinctive markings of Uday's silver Mercedes in a side street. The silence was eventually broken when a bulletproof Mercedes pulled up in front of the villa. A soldier, using a loudspeaker, called to those inside the house, "You must surrender, you are surrounded. You are not in danger." The occupants of the house responded by firing at the car, which sped away. The special forces, which were commanded by Ali Hassan al-Majid, the disgraced brothers' cousin, opened fire. The ensuing battle went on for about thirteen hours, and the entire proceedings were filmed by a presidential cameraman, while Uday and Qusay watched the proceedings from the safety of their bulletproof Mercedes. Although the Kamel brothers put up a brave fight, they eventually ran out of ammunition and were killed, together with their father, their sister, and her son. When the fighting was over, Majid went over to the body of Hussein Kamel, put his foot on the neck, and fired one last shot into the head. The bodies were then loaded onto a garbage truck and driven away.

Finally one of the special forces commanders walked over to the buses, where the terrified occupants had been trapped throughout the day's events. "We hope you enjoyed the show," the commander said. "I want this to be a lesson to all of you who knew these people. Iraq is not a country for traitors. No one betrays the Iraqi people and lives."[33] The buses were driven back to Baghdad while Saddam's cameraman returned to the Presidential Palace to deliver his videotape of the day's events. The widowed Raghda and Rana vowed never to speak to their father again, and went with their children to live with Saddam's estranged wife Sajida. A final postscript was added to this unhappy saga in February 2000 when the mother of Hussein Kamel and Saddam Kamel, the only surviving member of the family, was stabbed to death and her body cut into pieces in her home in Baghdad.

* * *

The skill with which Saddam countered the threat to his leadership posed by the defections of his sons-in-law left him in a stronger position than he had been in for many years. By persuading the al-Majid clan to do his dirty work for him, Saddam had demonstrated his supremacy over his fellow Tikriti tribesmen. By publicly humiliating Uday, who was stripped from his official positions and forced to make amends for provoking the defections in the first place, Saddam had reasserted his authority over his quarrelsome family. In the summer of 1996 he was able to consolidate his success at home by inflicting two humiliating defeats on the continuing attempts by Western intelligence to overthrow him.

Since the collapse of the INC's offensive to capture Mosul and Kirkuk in the spring of 1995, the CIA and MI6 had continued to explore ways of staging a coup in Baghdad. The American effort to overthrow Saddam had been stepped up following the appointment of John M. Deutch as director of the CIA in March 1995. After reviewing the record of the CIA's Iraqi operation to date, Deutch's new management team concluded that it should be made tighter and more focused on the single objective of overthrowing the Iraqi leader. Deutch was also under pressure from the White House to deliver a result before the 1996 U.S. presidential election.[34]

The failure of the 1995 offensive in Kurdistan had strained relations between the INC and the CIA, to the extent that Ahmed Chalabi had been banned by the White House from visiting CIA headquarters at Langley, Virginia. On the recommendation of British intelligence, the CIA was now dealing with a rival operation to the INC, the London-based Iraqi National Accord (INA) headed by Dr. Ayad Allawi, a former Baathist who had defected from Iraq after falling out with Saddam in the 1970s. Unlike the INC, which mainly conducted its operations outside Iraq, the INA had a network of high-placed contacts inside Iraq, mainly in the military and the senior echelons of the Baath. The INA was confident it could arrange a coup inside Iraq, which appealed to both the American and British governments.

One part of the INA's plan was for the three sons of Mohammed Abdullah al-Shahwani, a retired general with the Iraqi Special Forces and a helicopter pilot, who were based in Baghdad, to help orchestrate a military coup against Saddam. Unlike the INC's invasion plan of 1995, this scheme attracted the enthusiastic support of both the CIA and MI6. In early January 1996, a conference of high-level intelligence officials, which was attended by officers from both MI6 and the CIA, Saudi Arabia, Kuwait, and Jordan, was held in the Saudi capital, Riyadh, at which it was agreed to support fully the INA plan to overthrow Saddam. Scott Ritter, the UNSCOM chief inspector, claimed that backing for the INA plan was driven by MI6, which wanted a "quick, simple coup."[35] Apart from money and equipment, the INA was given a state-of-the-art satellite communications system, complete with high-technology encryption features to frustrate eavesdroppers.

Unfortunately for the INA, one of Shahwani's operatives was captured in Baghdad by Saddam's ever-vigilant security forces, together with the top-secret communications system. The Iraqis were careful to give no hint of their breakthrough, and simply monitored the INA as it finalized its plan for over-throwing Saddam. On June 26 Saddam's security forces finally pounced. One hundred and twenty Iraqi officers were arrested in the first sweep, including some of the ringleaders and Shahwani's three sons. The plotters were all from elite units such as the Special Republican Guards, the Republican Guard emergency forces, and the army. A number of officers arrested were from a highly secret special communications unit called B32, which worked directly with Saddam and was responsible for his secure communications with mili-tary units around the country. Senior officers in the Mukhabarat and other security services were picked up. Even two cooks at the Presidential Palace were arrested and confessed to a plot to poison Saddam, which had been part of the INA's fallback position if the military coup failed. In all about eight hundred suspects were detained, and the majority were tortured and exe-cuted. Flush with their success, the Iraqi intelligence chiefs could not pass up the opportunity of crowing over their victory to their CIA counterparts, who were anxiously awaiting news of the coup attempt in Jordan. On the morn-ing of the arrests, the captured communications system transmitted a mes-sage from the Mukhabarat in Baghdad to the CIA. "We have arrested all your people," the message said. "You might as well go home."[36]

The INA plot to overthrow Saddam was undoubtedly the most extensive ever attempted, and penetrated to the very heart of the regime. With so many supporters in key positions, the INA may have stood some chance of success had the Iraqis not captured the key communications system. All the credit for exposing the coup went to Qusay, the head of the Organization of Special Security. Saddam rewarded Qusay for his diligence by appointing him head of a new committee consisting of the heads of the Mukhabarat, special secu-rity, and military intelligence. While Uday languished in disgrace, his younger brother's star was very much in the ascendant.

In August Saddam inflicted another humiliating blow against the CIA when his forces reoccupied the Kurdish enclave that had been used the previous year by the INC for its assault on Kirkuk and Mosul. Tensions between the rival Kurdish factions of Talibani's PUK and Massoud Barzani's Kurdish Democratic Party (KDP) had been intensifying since Talibani supported the INC offensive. In the summer of 1996 fresh fighting erupted between the two groups. At first Talibani's forces got the upper hand, and Barzani appealed to Saddam for help. Saddam responded by dispatching the Republican Guard and Special Republican Guard units, which mounted a surprise attack on the PUK positions and routed Talibani's forces. It was a triumphant return to Kurdistan for Saddam, and a complete disaster for the CIA and the Iraqi opposition, which had been closely allied with the PUK. The Iraqi troops captured scores of INC followers who were operating under direct CIA control and thousands of documents that revealed the combined plans of both sides. Saddam ordered the execution of all the Iraqi CIA operatives, and the rest of the INC survivors were jailed. The INC infrastructure in Kurdistan was completely destroyed, and the United States had to make hurried arrangements to evacuate more than six thousand Iraqis and Kurds who were involved with the INC operation. Despite the PUK's call for military assistance to fight Saddam's forces, President Clinton would only authorize another series of cruise missile attacks against Baghdad, which made no impact on the operational capability of Saddam's forces in Kurdistan. William Perry, the U.S. defense secretary, summed up the government's position when he said: "My judgment is that we should not be involved in the civil war in the north."[37]

Saddam's success in exposing the INA's coup attempt and destroying the INC in Kurdistan effectively signaled the end of efforts by the Clinton administration and its allies to overthrow Saddam for the remainder of the 1990s. His rout of the INC in Kurdistan had been particularly embarrassing, and in the run-up to the 1996 presidential election contest the main priority of the Clinton camp was to ensure that the campaign did not attract any adverse publicity from its failed policy to overthrow Saddam. The sixty-five hundred Iraqi and Kurdish INC survivors and their families were evacuated to the remote island of Guam in the northern Pacific, where they were sequestered until the presidential election was safely out of the way. They were then given U.S. citizenship. The disasters of 1996 had taught Clinton a painful lesson in the limitations of Washington's ability to confront Saddam, and for the remainder of his presidency little interest was displayed in hatching plots to overthrow him. Although lines of communication were maintained with Iraqi opposition groups, they were kept to a bare minimum. "After 1996 it reached the point where we exchanged Christmas cards, but little else," commented one INA official.[38]

As 1996 drew to a close, Saddam had good reason to celebrate. Having eliminated his treacherous sons-in-law, he had successfully tested the limits of U.S. strength and resolve, and had found them both lacking. His regime had found a way of circumventing the effects of the UN sanctions and the only cloud on his horizon was the continued antics of his eldest son, Uday. One evening in December 1996, as he returned from feeding his pet dogs, Uday was badly injured in an assassination attempt in central Baghdad. The gunmen fired eight bullets into him at point-blank range before making good their escape, leaving him for dead. Saddam rushed to the hospital to see his injured son, as did Uday's mother, Sajida. It was the first time Uday's parents had been in the same room since the death of Adnan Khairallah in 1989. Although Uday was badly injured, the Cuban doctors who treated him informed Saddam that his son would live. There was no shortage of suspects, and in the next few days some 2,000 people were questioned, including Uday's uncle Watban, who was still recovering from the injuries he sustained when Uday shot him. The assassination was later attributed to a group calling itself al-Nahdah, or "the awakening," a group of middle-class Iraqi professionals that had been set up in 1991 to overthrow Saddam. A few days after the shooting Saddam summoned his family for an emergency summit around Uday's bed. Qusay, Saddam's two half brothers, Watban and Sabawi, and Ali Hassan al-Majid were all present as he delivered a scathing denunciation of their general conduct. All those present were given a dressing-down for either being incompetent or corrupt. Saddam saved his severest admonishment for Uday. "Your behavior, Uday, is bad," he lectured his stricken son. "There could be no worse behavior than yours. We want to know what kind of a person you are. Are you a politician, a trader, a people's leader, or a playboy? You must know that you have done nothing for this homeland or this people."[39]

The spring of 1997 saw Saddam concentrating his energies on the two issues that remained from the Gulf War, the UN sanctions and the UNSCOM weapons inspections. When the sanctions were originally imposed in 1991, the Iraqis were led to believe that they would be lifted once they had satisfied all the requirements of the UN weapons inspectors.

But by early 1997, with the second Clinton administration established in office, it became clear that Washington no longer regarded the sanctions as being related to the weapons inspections. In March 1997 Madeleine Albright, the new secretary of state, told an audience at Washington's Georgetown University, "We do not agree with the nations who argue that if Iraq complies with its obligations concerning weapons of mass destruction, sanctions should be lifted." Saddam duly noted this significant shift in policy. It was clear to him that he had nothing to gain from further cooperation with the UN inspectors. He was well aware that there was a limit to how far Washington was prepared to go militarily to enforce compliance with UNSCOM. In 1997 the threat of military force from Washington was declining. If the worst that the United States could throw at Saddam was a handful of cruise missiles, then he calculated that his interests would be better served by protecting his coveted nonconventional weapons arsenal from the prying eyes of the UNSCOM inspectors.

UNSCOM's main concern at this juncture was to track the remaining elements of the Iraqi biological and VX nerve gas programs, and any missile systems used to deliver them that Saddam might still be concealing. Another task delegated to UNSCOM was to investigate claims that Iraq had conducted biological weapons experiments between 1994 and 1995 on prisoners held at Abu Ghraib prison on the outskirts of Baghdad, and that there were human burial sites outside the Salman Pak facility.[40] Equipped with the new information supplied by Hussein Kamel and his fellow defectors, the UNSCOM inspectors became more confrontational as they went about their work, especially after the studious Rolf Ekeus was replaced as head of UNSCOM in 1997 by the more abrasive Austrialian diplomat Richard Butler. The increased pressure from UNSCOM, however, was matched by a more defiant attitude from Saddam. On one occasion during an UNSCOM inspection an Iraqi official grabbed the controls of an UNSCOM helicopter, almost causing it to crash, in an attempt to prevent the inspectors from photographing a sensitive sight. The Iraqis blacked out the cameras that were supposed to monitor sensitive sites, and moved restricted equipment without notifying UNSCOM. Saddam declared some of the more sensitive sites to be presidential or sovereign areas that were immune from the inspection process. In June, addressing a rare meeting of the RCC, Saddam issued a statement that summed up Iraq's new approach to the activities of the weapons inspectors. "Iraq has complied with and implemented all relevant resolutions. . . .

There is absolutely nothing else. We demand with unequivocal clarity that the Security Council fulfills its commitments toward Iraq. . . . The practical expression of this is to respect Iraq's sovereignty and to fully and totally lift the blockdade imposed on Iraq."[41]

Saddam's obstruction of the inspectors' activities intensified, with the Iraqis arguing, with some justification, that UNSCOM had been infiltrated by the CIA and other Western intelligence agencies.[42] In October Tariq Aziz announced that no more Americans would be allowed into Iraq to work on the inspection teams, and a few days later the remaining Americans were expelled. The Clinton administration responded by threatening to bomb Iraq, and on this occasion Saddam decided to back down, although not before his brinkmanship had demonstrated that, with the notable exception of Britain, the United States had little international support for a resumption of military action against Baghdad. Boris Yeltsin, the Russian president, even claimed that joint military action by the United States and Britain against Iraq would start World War III. Saddam, meanwhile, invited the foreign press to Baghdad to report on the devastating effects on Iraq caused by seven years of UN sanctions. The ensuing reports of hospitals without medicines, schools without books, and mothers without food duly appeared in the Western media and had a profound impact on public opinion. There was correspondingly less coverage either about how the regime was earning billions of dollars from its sanctions-busting activities, or about how UN food and medical aid was being sold on the black market by Uday's illegal smuggling network.

A final effort was made to defuse the mounting UNSCOM crisis through diplomacy when Kofi Annan, the UN secretary-general, visited Baghdad for talks with Saddam in February 1998. The key issues at stake were Butler's demand that the inspectors be allowed to visit so-called "presidential sites," where it was known that much of the proscribed equipment was concealed. Saddam had resisted this demand, which he claimed insulted the honor of the presidency. The Iraqis, on the other hand, wanted to know at what point the UN intended to lift sanctions. Annan arrived in Baghdad on February 20 and had a face-to-face meeting with Saddam a few days later. Like all visitors, Annan had no idea where he was going as he climbed into the government car to be taken to the meeting. He was driven to a new palace that Saddam had built in Baghdad since the Gulf War, where he found Saddam looking relaxed and confident and wearing a double-breasted blue suit, matching tie, and highly polished black leather boots. Annan began by flattering him.

"You're a builder, you built modern Iraq. It was destroyed, you've rebuilt it. Do you want to destroy it again?" Saddam listened attentively to what Annan had to say, and at one point produced a yellow notepad to take notes on Annan's points. After three hours of discussions the two men began working on a formula to resolve the crisis. Saddam objected to the word "inspections" in relation to the presidential sites, and wanted it replaced with "visits." Annan said Saddam's preference was too vague. Saddam replied, "Ok, they can enter," and on that basis Annan drafted the phrase "initial and subsequent entries for the performance of the tasks mandated." Saddam agreed to the amended text, in return for which he understood that Annan had made a commitment to lift sanctions if Iraq complied with a new round of inspections. As he said good-bye to Annan, Saddam said, "I want to thank you for coming to Baghdad personally. You must feel free to come here. You can even come for a holiday, if it won't embarrass you."[43]

Although the Annan mission was successful in defusing the immediate crisis, in the long term it signaled the end for UNSCOM. Annan's intervention confirmed that UNSCOM was no longer the sole interlocutor with Iraq on weapons issues, as Saddam knew he could now appeal above Richard Butler's head. Butler's authority had been usurped by Annan and the bickering members of the Security Council, a fact that Saddam was quick to exploit.

Following Annan's mission, the United States tried to back away from its confrontation with Saddam because the Clinton administration realized that, apart from bombing Baghdad, there was little it could do to enforce the UN resolutions. And rather than have the impotency of the West's position with regard to Iraq exposed, Washington put pressure on the UN to be less confrontational in its approach to the inspections. Butler in turn ordered Scott Ritter, the chief inspector of the UN team in Baghdad, to call a halt to the inspections, eventually causing Ritter to resign in protest, complaining of interference in his work from officials in London and Washington. Before departing, Ritter revealed that Saddam would have as many as three nuclear weapons ready for use as soon as he had laid his hands on the necessary fissile material (uranium 235 or plutonium). Ritter also severely damaged UNSCOM's credibility by revealing that he had worked closely with Israeli intelligence for much of his seven-year tenure with the supposedly independent UN inspection teams.

In August Saddam provoked yet another clash with Washington by demanding a speedy conclusion to the UNSCOM mission and threatening grave retaliation if sanctions were not lifted. In October the Republican-dominated U.S. Congress, which was becoming increasingly restless about President Clinton's disinclination to confront Saddam, voted the Iraqi Liberation Act into law on October 1, in which it pledged $97 million to Iraqi opposition groups working to overthrow Saddam. Saddam followed this in November by suspending all cooperation with UNSCOM's monitoring program. The inspectors were withdrawn, the United States and Britain prepared to bomb Iraq, and at the last moment Saddam allowed the inspectors back. Butler continued with the inspections, but the Iraqis were sufficiently obstructive for him to report back that Saddam was not fulfilling his UN commitments. By now Annan had concluded that both the Clinton administration and Saddam were intent on fomenting the long-awaited bombing attack. The timing especially suited Clinton, who was desperately seeking a diversion to draw attention away from the impeachment proceedings against him that had commenced in Washington.

On December 17 American and British warplanes launched Operation Desert Fox. Augmented by cruise missiles, the Allies conducted 400 bombing missions against targets that the weapons inspectors had been prevented from visiting. The bombing made little impact on Saddam. Ninety-seven targets overall were attacked, of which only nine were reported by the Pentagon to have been fully destroyed; of eleven chemical and biological weapons facilities targeted, none was destroyed. Saddam, as he had no doubt predicted, emerged from the seventy-hour bombing campaign unscathed, and declared that Iraq had emerged victorious from the confrontation. "God rewarded you and delighted your hearts with the crown of victory," Saddam said in a televised address that was broadcast throughout the Arab world. President Clinton also claimed victory with a more downbeat assessment: "I am confident we have achieved our mission."

The reality was that the bombing constituted a political victory for Saddam. Desert Fox ended UNSCOM's operations, and Iraqi officials insisted that there would be no more cooperation with UN weapons inspectors. Furthermore, unlike the international consensus that had presided over Kuwait, Clinton's decision to launch Desert Fox provoked international condemnation from France, Russia, China, and much of the Arab world. The UN Security Council was hopelessly divided on the future of UNSCOM and the issue of Saddam. Furthermore, the only policy left to the United States and Britain, the only countries that were still fully committed to forcing

Saddam's regime to observe its international obligations, was the maintenance of UN sanctions. Even this policy was now under fire. Although the
sanctions had been amended in 1996 to allow an "oil for food" deal, relief
agencies continued to publish harrowing reports on the plight of Iraq's undernourished children.

A UNICEF survey in March 1998, a year after the oil-for-food arrangements had taken effect, showed that a quarter of Iraqi children were chroni-
cally malnourished, and almost one in ten was acutely malnourished. Even
though Saddam's policies were mainly to blame for this appalling state of
affairs, public opinion in the West held that the UN sanctions were responsible. The difficulties of the American and British governments were compounded at the end of 1998 when Denis Halliday, the Irish Quaker who had
been appointed by the UN to supervise the oil-for-food program, resigned,
denouncing a policy that he claimed caused "four thousand to five thousand
children to die unnecessarily every month due to the impact of sanctions."

While Western public opinion began to turn against the continued
implementation of sanctions, the crucial issue of Saddam's weapons of mass
destruction arsenal lay unresolved. When the UNSCOM inspections ended
in 1998 Saddam had still not accounted for 20 tons of complex growth
media, essential for the production of biological weapons such as anthrax,
together with 200 tons of precursor chemicals for the production of VX nerve
gas. The UN still did not know the full extent of Iraq's capability to produce
long-range missiles. The strong suspicion remained that Saddam had a number of undisclosed Scud-type missiles that could be fitted with anthrax or VX
warheads.[44] In addition the Iraqis, at the very least, retained the ability to conduct active research and development of nuclear weapons and an effective
delivery system.[45] Scott Ritter, the former UNSCOM inspector, believed that
Iraq had the capacity to make several bombs, which could be moved from one
secret storage facility to another in specially modified vehicles.[46] Saddam had
already demonstrated his readiness to use weapons of mass destruction
against innocent civilians. The challenge that faced the West was how to prevent him from using them in the future.

The Idol

On April 28, 2002, the main road leading to Tikrit was jammed with lines of ramshackle buses and black-windowed Mercedes. Crowds of military personnel with thick mustaches, sheikhs in flowing robes, and farmers in shabby pants were congregating at an expansive parade ground in the center of the city for the official sixty-fifth birthday celebrations of Saddam Hussein, the Anointed One, the Glorious Leader, direct descendant of the Prophet, president of Iraq, chairman of the Revolutionary Command Council, field marshal of its armies, doctor of its laws, and great uncle to all its peoples.

The parade ground had been built for occasions such as this, when the people were given a rare opportunity to express their devotion to their president. It contained a reviewing stand, where specially selected guests were provided with high-backed chairs. As the crowds waited patiently for the guest of honor to arrive, groups of schoolgirls, including some who were dressed as suicide bombers, performed a series of dances that were dedicated to Saddam's "pulse of life." This was followed by a long procession of some ten thousand local soldiers and security officials. As each group passed the reviewing stand, they chanted, "Happy year to you, President Saddam Hussein, who brought victory to us." Eventually a convoy of sleek, bullet-proof Mercedes swept into the parade ground and stopped in front of the reviewing stand. A hush fell over the crowd as the security guards helped the long-awaited guest of honor out of the car.

The only problem was that the man emerging from the back of the presidential limousine was not Saddam Hussein, but his cousin General Ali

Hassan al-Majid, the man known throughout Iraq as "chemical Ali." After twenty-three years as the undisputed ruler of Iraq, by 2002 Saddam rarely showed himself in public, not even for special occasions such as his birthday. Fearful that one of his many enemies might take the opportunity to stage an assassination attempt, Saddam preferred to confine himself to the safety of the numerous presidential bunkers he had constructed throughout the country. Most of his appearances took place on television, where he would broadcast his message to the people from a secret location. Saddam's well-wishers in Tikrit were disappointed by his absence, but the crowd nevertheless continued with their birthday celebrations. As Majid raised his right arm with the palm open in imitation of Saddam's salute, the crowd chanted their slogans as if they were addressing Saddam himself. "We sacrifice our souls, our blood for you, Saddam."

Saddam's birthday celebrations lasted a full week. In deference to the suffering of the Palestinians, who were then being subjected to Israel's Operation Defensive Wall strategy to root out suicide bombers from the West Bank, Saddam asked the dancing girls who were to have entertained his thirty-five hundred guests at a special banquet in Baghdad to stay at home. "In Palestine they are demolishing villages and killing people," one of Saddam's officials explained. "This is not a time for dancing."[1] Saddam did, however, allow himself the luxury of having one of his plays performed at Baghdad's elegant new theater. *Zabibah and the King* was a play based on one of two novels written by Saddam since the Gulf War. The play related the story of a lonely monarch who falls in love with a virtuous commoner. Unfortunately for the monarch, the object of his desire is raped on January 17—the same day that the U.S.-led coalition launched Operation Desert Storm—and is killed by a jealous husband. The king resolves to avenge the woman's honor, but dies in the struggle. Although Saddam himself was not present for the gala opening, the play was well received by the audience, who had no difficulty in identifying the allegorical qualities of the plot. Zabibah represented the Iraqi people, who came to realize that their king, Saddam, was acting in their best interests and, if necessary, was prepared to sacrifice his life for them.

In the three and a half years since the UNSCOM inspectors had left Baghdad and President Clinton had launched his largely ineffectual air strikes in Operation Desert Fox, Iraq had undergone something of a transformation. With most of the Arab world openly boycotting the UN sanctions, trade was flourishing. There were regular flights to Baghdad's Saddam International Airport from Jordan, Syria, and Lebanon, where visitors were met with gaudy, bloodred "Down with America" slogans. All the capital's buildings, bridges, and roads that were damaged in the 1991 war had been rebuilt. The legitimate foreign currency earnings generated by the UN's oil-for-food program, combined with the enormous profits from Saddam's illicit oil-smuggling activities, meant that for the first time in more than twenty years signs of prosperity had returned to the streets of Baghdad. In the upscale al-Mansour district of Baghdad, the shops were filled with the latest designer fashions; in the poorer districts the markets were filled with plentiful supplies of food and cheap electrical goods imported from China.

For most of the 1990s, as Iraq wrestled with the UN over disarmament issues, Saddam had ruthlessly exploited the suffering of his people to persuade Western public opinion to abandon the UN's uncompromising sanctions. Now that he was no longer troubled either by the intrusive attentions of the weapons inspectors or by the worst effects of the sanctions, Saddam had decided to ease the economic constraints, mainly to prevent the long-suffering people from rebelling against him. Medicines were widely available, the electricity supply had been restored to normal, and ordinary Iraqis were starting to recover from the appalling privations that they had endured for most of the 1990s.

Apart from improving the welfare of the people, Saddam still had sufficient funds to indulge his obsession with grandiose schemes. In addition to the construction of more palaces, Saddam devoted enormous resources to building several giant mosques. One of the biggest, and the most expensive, was the Umm Al-Maarik, or "mother of all battles," mosque in central Baghdad, which had been completed in time for Saddam's birthday celebrations in 2001, the tenth anniversary of the Gulf War. The minarets were designed to resemble Scud missiles sitting on launchpads. Each of the four minarets—representing the Scud missiles Saddam fired at Israel during the Gulf War—was 43 meters high to mark the 43 days that Operation Desert Storm lasted. One of the mosque's more remarkable artifacts was a copy of the Koran that had been written in Saddam's own blood. All 605 pages were displayed for posterity in glass cases. The custodian of the mosque revealed that Saddam had donated 24 liters of blood over three years. The blood was then mixed with ink and preservatives, producing a red-and-brown color with a tinge of blue. A pool located at the foot of one of the minarets contained a 24-foot mosaic blob, which was supposed to be Saddam's thumbprint, and inside the thumbprint was a magnified version of Saddam's signature.[2]

Saddam's obsession with massive contruction projects, be they palaces, mosques, or nuclear weapons, was a product of his childhood in Tikrit, where, as a young boy, his family could not even afford to buy him a pair of shoes. It fitted in with Saddam's self-image as a giant of Arabian history. Like Saladin, the conqueror of the Crusaders, who also, according to legend, came from Tikrit, Saddam believed his destiny was to be remembered and revered as the leader who restored Iraq and the Arab world to their rightful glory. Accordingly Saddam's latest palace featured columns topped with his own head bearing Saladin's helmet.[3]

As Saddam grew older, he came to believe, as had Hitler, in providence. Just as Hitler had refused to accept the advice of his generals that the Third Reich was doomed, so Saddam refused to countenance the concept of defeat, even after he had suffered the catastrophic losses that had been inflicted on Iraq during Operation Desert Storm. By the time he reached his sixties Saddam had become more detached from reality than ever. No doubt the constant motion of moving from one palace to another, of never being able to tell anyone in advance, not even his own family, where he might be, had taken its own psychological toll. On those rare occasions when he had time to reflect on the course his life had taken, he would have been haunted, like Macbeth confronting Banquo's ghost, by the bloody images of his murdered friends, such as Abdul Karim al-Shaikhly and Adnan Khairallah. Then there was the havoc his success had wreaked on his once happy family—an estranged wife and two daughters, two murdered sons-in-law, and one psychotic elder son, not to mention the pathological tendencies of his other relatives, such as Ali Hassan al-Majid, and his half brothers, Barzan, Watban, and Sabawi.

Whichever palace or bunker Saddam slept in, he only needed a few hours' sleep a night. Often he would rise at 3 A.M. and go for a swim. In a desert country like Iraq water is a symbol of wealth and power, and all Saddam's palaces were filled with fountains, pools, and waterfalls. Saddam suffered from a slipped disc, and his doctors had prescribed swimming, together with walking, to help ease the condition. All Saddam's pools were scrupulously maintained, both to keep the right temperature and to ensure that the water had not been poisoned. Given that so many of the regime's enemies had suffered thallium poisoning, it was perhaps not surprising that Saddam had a deep-rooted fear of being poisoned. Consequently the security arrangements surrounding his food had reached almost surreal proportions. Twice a week fresh food was flown in to Baghdad, mainly lobster, shrimp, fish, lean meat, and dairy products. Before being taken to the presidential kitchens, the shipments were sent to a team of nuclear scientists, who x-rayed them and tested them for radiation and poison.[4] Saddam had about twenty palaces that were fully staffed and where three meals were prepared for him every day, even when he was absent.

Despite his age, Saddam remained a vain man, and his daily exercise regime was designed as much to keep him looking trim and fit as to help his bad back. Saddam wanted to look his best and had reverted to wearing smart, tailor-made suits rather than the olive green Baath Party uniform that he had worn throughout most of the 1990s. Saddam changed his sartorial attire after Kofi Annan, the UN secretary-general, suggested that a smart suit would vastly improve his image as a statesman. Saddam continued to dye his hair black, and he refused to wear his reading glasses in public. When he delivered a speech, his aides would print it out in huge letters, with just a few lines on each page. Because his back injury forced him to walk with a slight limp, he avoided being seen or filmed walking more than a few steps. Saddam continued to work long hours, as he had done since the early days of the Baath revolution in 1968. The only difference in his routine was that he had gotten into the habit of stealing short naps during the day. He would abruptly leave a meeting, shut himself off in a side room, and return refreshed a half hour later. For relaxation he liked to read, mainly books on Arab and military history, or watch television. He enjoyed monitoring cable news channels such as CNN, Al-Jazeera, and the BBC, and was also partial to watching movie thrillers that involved intrigue, assassination, and conspiracy. *The Day of the Jackal* was a particular favorite.

Despite his attempts to maintain contact with the outside world, Saddam had become more isolated than at any point in his career. This was reflected in his behavior at meetings with his officials. Whereas in the past Saddam had always run official meetings efficiently, properly briefing himself by reading the papers prepared for him in advance, they had become rambling, disorganized affairs. The meetings would go on for hours, without any proper resolution being reached. When they ended, Saddam would tell his officials, "Please give my regards to the people because I don't think I will be able to meet them for a while. I am rather busy these days."[5] In early 2002 Saddam noticed one of his ministers look at his watch during a cabinet meeting. When the meeting had finished he asked the minister to stay behind, and then asked him if he was in a hurry. When the minister replied in the negative, Saddam berated him for insulting him in this way. He then ordered the minister to be locked in the room for two days. The terrified minister sat locked in the cabinet room, expecting to be taken out at any moment and shot. When he was finally let out, Saddam merely sacked him.

If Saddam had become more subdued, he was certainly not benign. Freed from the constraints that had been imposed by UNSCOM, he renewed his efforts to rebuild Iraq's weapons of mass destruction arsenal. Hardly had the dust settled from the Operation Desert Fox bombing raids than it emerged that Saddam had signed a secret weapons deal with Moscow to rebuild his air defense system. A few months later, as the West prepared to take action to prevent the Serbian leader Slobodan Milosevic from ethnically cleansing Kosovo's Albanian population, Saddam signed a secret alliance with Belgrade to help the Serbian dictator survive Allied air strikes. In March a group of Serb chemical and biological weapons experts flew to Baghdad, where they were given a guided tour of Saddam's nonconventional weapons facilities.[6] Apart from assisting with each other's air defense requirements, Western intelligence suspected that the two countries were cooperating on nonconventional weapons production. Concern that Saddam and Milosevic were collaborating on the development of nuclear weapons intensified in the summer of 2000 when it was revealed that Milosevic had sufficient stocks of weapons-grade uranium to make several crude bombs. This was precisely the material Saddam required to complete work on the Arab world's first atomic bomb.[7]

Saddam ordered his security forces to renew their efforts to disrupt the activities of Iraqi exile groups. The Iraq Liberation Bill, which had been passed by the U.S. Congress in October 1998, had provided funds to enable Iraqi opposition groups to draw up new strategies for overthrowing Saddam's regime. Attempts to persuade the rival groups to work together had achieved little. Nevertheless Saddam's security agents did their best to disrupt the activities of the Iraqi opposition, and in August it was revealed that Saddam had hatched a plot in London to force a former Iraqi army general to assassinate Ayad Allawi, head of the Iraqi National Accord, which had masterminded the failed coup attempt of 1996. Saddam's security forces pressured Mohammed Ali Ghani, a former Republican Guard commander who had defected following the failed 1991 Shiite uprising, by arresting his twenty-year-old daughter, who was still living in Baghdad. Iraqi security agents threatened to torture Ghani's daughter unless he killed Allawi. Ghani tried to extricate himself from his predicament by attempting suicide. He survived the attempt, but the ordeal persuaded him against involving himself in the Iraqi opposition movement.[8]

Saddam's attempts to consolidate his position in Baghdad were constantly undermined by the waywardness of his eldest son, Uday. By the late 1990s Uday was reported to be fully recovered from the injuries he suffered during the 1996 assassination attempt, although in reality he was confined to a wheelchair most of the time. For official photographs and television appearances, he would appear standing, even though immediately afterward he would return to his wheelchair. He was so frustrated by the slow pace of his recovery that one evening, when drunk at a Baghdad nightclub, he demanded that his bodyguards "bring me the head of my surgeon." The unfortunate doctor was warned of Uday's ire, and fled into exile in Saudi Arabia.[9] Rumors continued to circulate about Uday's sexuality, with the oft-repeated allegation that he was impotent. Abbas Janabi, who worked as his private secretary for fifteen years before defecting to Britain, said Uday regained his sexual appetite and often seduced as many as four women in a single day. Sometimes his conquests would be young girls aged twelve or younger.[10] Uday's impetuous behavior was reflected in his treatment of Iraq's national soccer team. If the players lost an important game or played badly, they were taken to the cells at Uday's Olympic Committee headquarters and beaten.[11]

Another of Uday's former associates, Abu Zeinab al-Qurairy, a former brigadier general in the Mukhabarat who defected in early 2001, had personal experience of Uday's brutality. During an anticorruption purge initiated by Saddam in 2000, Qurairy had rather naively sent a secret report to Saddam detailing how Uday was defrauding his father's government in a multimillion-dollar scam. Although Saddam had given his officials his personal assurance that any information he received would be treated in the strictest confidence, the next time Qurairy saw Uday he knew all the details of the secret report. Uday "produced an electric cattle prod from nowhere, and he jabbed me with it between my legs. I lost consciousness. When I woke up, I was in a red cell in the Olympic Committee prison."[12]

Uday remained in charge of the highly lucrative oil-smuggling operation, and opened new routes through Syria. In August 1999 Saddam was deeply

embarrassed by his son's venality when a cargo of baby milk and medical supplies that were meant for Iraqi children was discovered being smuggled out of
the country in one of Uday's lucrative business deals. Saddam also had to contend with Uday's mounting jealousy of his younger brother, Qusay, who,
because he was more conscientious and responsible, was increasingly assuming the role of heir apparent. Uday had already caused one rift in the family
by prompting Barzan al-Tikriti, his uncle and Saddam's half brother, to defect
to Switzerland in late 1998. Barzan's defection was provoked by Uday's
attempts to take control of the billions of dollars of assets that Barzan controlled through a number of secret Swiss banks accounts. Saddam later
effected a reconciliation with Barzan, but Uday responded by turning his
attention on his younger brother. Matters came to a head in late 1999 when
Uday was held responsible for the execution of Saddam's intelligence chief
and cousin, Rafa al-Tikriti. Tikriti was a close ally of Saddam's half brother
Watban, and had been waging a campaign against Uday since he provoked
the defection of Saddam's two sons-in-law in 1995. Uday responded by fram-
ing him for leaking details of Iraq's secret arms deals with Moscow, and Tikriti
was executed for treason.[13]

   With Iraq effectively closed to the outside world, most of the details relating to the activities of Saddam's ruling family came from the increasing number of defectors who were making their way to the West, a process that was
accelerated in the aftermath of the September 11 terrorist attacks in New
York and Washington. One of the more revealing accounts of Saddam's clandestine attempts to rebuild his nonconventional weapons infrastructure was
provided by Adnan Ihsan Saeed al-Haideri, a civil engineer who escaped from
Iraq in the summer of 1991. In his debriefing by CIA and FBI agents,
Haideri said he had worked on the renovation of secret facilities for biological, chemical, and nuclear weapons in underground wells, private villas, and
even the Saddam Hussein Hospital in Baghdad.[14]

   Haideri's allegations confirmed the suspicions of arms control experts at
the UN who had been attempting to monitor Saddam's activities since
UNSCOM's demise. In December 1999 the UN had established a new body
to replace UNSCOM, the United Nations Monitoring, Verification, and
Inspection Commission (UNMOVIC), which, unlike its predecessors,
reported directly to the UN secretary-general. Because of the stalemate over
the future of UN sanctions, Iraq had resisted attempts by UNMOVIC to
conduct inspections in Iraq. The UN could only make an informed guess

about Iraq's nonconventional weapons capability on the basis of the work conducted by UNSCOM's inspectors and reports provided by defectors. These suggested that Saddam's development of nuclear weapons had been reestablished. Charles Duelfer, UNSCOM's former second-ranking official, said Iraq's known nuclear scientists had moved back to the country's five nuclear research sites.[15] Saddam had the equipment to construct a nuclear device—triggers, weapons housings, etc.—and all he lacked was weapons-grade uranium. In June Iraq was accused of smuggling components for constructing uranium-enrichment systems on aid flights after it sent relief to Syria to help villagers affected by the collapse of a dam north of Damascus.[16] Most estimates conducted by Western nuclear and intelligence experts concluded in the summer of 2002 that Saddam, left to his own devices, would be able to produce an atomic bomb within five years.

The level of Saddam's chemical and biological weapons development was even more difficult to assess. During the UNSCOM inspections Iraq had never accounted for all the 100,000 chemical weapons that it had produced during the Iran-Iraq War, and there were fears that thousands of them, filled either with VX nerve agent or mustard gas, had been hidden. George Tenet, the CIA director, told Congress in February: "Baghdad is expanding its civilian chemical industry in ways that could be diverted quickly to chemical weapons production."

Certainly, from Washington's point of view, Saddam's obsession with his nonconventional weapons arsenal became, in the radically altered post–September 11 political landscape, the principal casus belli for renewing hostilities against Iraq. As President George W. Bush had made clear in his State of the Union Address in January 2002, the "war on terror" that had been declared in the wake of the September 11 attacks had been extended to include those countries, such as Iraq, that continued to support and harbor terrorists and to develop weapons of mass destruction. Even if the evidence on all these counts was inconclusive, Bush was not prepared to make the same mistake his father had and let Saddam off the hook. In Britain Tony Blair came to much the same conclusion, despite the strong reservations expressed by leading members of his own Labour Party and most other European Union political figures. Indeed by the spring Bush's determination to target Saddam was such that he took the exceptional step of personally authorizing the CIA to conduct a covert operation to overthrow him, using lethal force if necessary. Bush had effectively given the CIA the green light to assassinate Saddam.

Bush's determination to remove Saddam provoked a characteristically defiant response from the Iraqi tyrant. Immediately after news leaked of Bush's decision to authorize Saddam's assassination, the Iraqi president summoned an emergency meeting of key regime members, which was held on the bottom floor of one of his heavily fortified bunkers at the Presidential Palace complex in Baghdad. Saddam started the proceedings by making a long, rambling speech, denouncing Bush and declaring that the American position had "left Iraq no room to be tolerant on this issue." Other ministers were invited to give their views. Ali Hassan al-Majid spoke first. He opened his remarks by declaring that the Americans were "silly and arrogant people." He then suggested that Iraq "take the fight to their own homes in America." Taha Yassin Ramadan, Saddam's long-serving vice president, a Baath activist from the 1960s who had helped him set up the People's Militia, responded in a similar vein, claiming that "the heroes of Iraq can become human bombs in the thousands, willing to blow up America in particular."

Saddam nodded his approval to both speakers, and then invited Qusay to address the gathering. "We know, and the brothers here all know," said Qusay, "that we have—with God's aid—every capability and ability. With a simple sign from you, we can make America's people sleepless and frightened to go out in the streets. . . . I only ask you, sir, to give me a small sign. I swear upon your head, sir, that if I do not turn their night into day and their day into a living hell, I will ask you to chop off my head before my brothers present." Qusay continued, "If bin Laden truly did carry out the September attacks as they claim then, as God is my witness, we will prove to them what happened in September is a picnic compared to the wrath of Saddam Hussein. They do not know Iraq, Iraq's leader, the men of Iraq, the children of Iraq."[17]

On July 17, 2002, the thirty-fourth anniversary of the Baath revolution, Saddam made his own feelings public about the new threat he faced from Washington during his annual speech to the Iraqi people. Speaking in his distinctive peasant accent in ungrammatical Arabic, Saddam declared, "July has returned to say to all the oppressors and powerful and evil people in the world: You will not be able to defeat me this time, not ever, even if you gathered to your side and rallied all the devils too."

In a somewhat transparent attempt to persuade Western public opinion not to support renewed hostilities against Iraq, in August Saddam invited the left-wing British Labour M.P. George Galloway to visit him in one of his presidential bunkers in Baghdad. Galloway wrote excitedly about how he was driven around Baghdad in cars with blacked-out windows to different destinations before he was finally shown into an elevator that descended at high speed to Saddam's cavernous, underground bunker.[18] Galloway was taken so far underground that it made his ears pop. At the meeting Saddam gave a demonstration of the carrot-and-stick approach that had become the hallmark of his presidency. On the one hand, he suggested to Galloway that he was ready to allow British officials—including Prime Minister Tony Blair—to inspect Iraq's alleged weapons sites; on the other, he threatened to inflict heavy casualties on any foreign force that invaded the country. "If they come, we are ready," he declared. "We will fight them on the streets, from the rooftops, from house to house. We will never surrender."[19]

For all the bravado, Saddam was preparing himself and his country for the many new crises that he would undoubtedly face in the future. But no matter how serious the challenge, how deadly the threat posed by the enemy, "the one who confronts" would respond in the same way that he had dealt with all the other tumults he had encountered during his many years in power. Survival would always be Saddam's number one priority.

NOTES

PROLOGUE: THE OUTLAW

1 Author's interview, May 2002.
2 Private source.
3 Private source.
4 *Wall Street Journal*, June 14, 2002.
5 Laurie Mylroie, *Study of Revenge* (Washington, D.C.: The AEI Press, 2001).
6 *Wall Street Journal*, June 14, 2002.
7 Iraqi television, December 14, 2001.
8 Private source.
9 Quoted in *Newsweek*, November 26, 2001.
10 *Daily Telegraph* (London), March 4, 2002.
11 Quoted in *Wall Street Journal*, June 17, 2002.

ONE: THE ORPHAN

1 There are two authorized biographies, or rather hagiographies, of Saddam's life: Amir Iskander, *Munadilan, wa Mufakiran, wa Insanan* (Paris: Hachette, 1981), and Fuad Matar, *Saddam Hussein: The Man, the Cause and His Future* (London: Third World Centre, 1981). There is also a thinly disguised autobiographical work of his early life: Abdel Amir Mu'ala, *The Long Days*, n.p., n.d.
2 Author's interview, April 2002.
3 Hamid al-Bayati, *The Bloody History of Saddam Al Tikriti*, p. 23
4 Geoff Simons, *From Sumer to Saddam* (London: Macmillan, 1994), p. 271.
5 *Vanity Fair*, August 1991.
6 Matar, p. 22.
7 Saddam Hussein, *Al-Dimuqratiyya Masdar Quwwa li al-Fard wa al-Mujtama*, p. 20.
8 Author's interview, February 2002.
9 Efraim Karsh and Inari Rautsi, *Saddam Hussein, A Political Biography* (London: Brassey's, 1991), p. 10.
10 Iskander, p. 11.
11 *Vanity Fair*, August 1991.
12 John Bulloch and Harvey Morris, *Saddam's War* (London: Faber and Faber, 1991), p. 31.

13 Karsh and Rautsi, p. 9.

14 Andrew Cockburn and Patrick Cockburn, *Out of the Ashes* (New York: HarperCollins, 1999), p. 62.

15 H. V. F. Winstone, *Gertrude Bell* (London: Jonathan Cape, 1978), p. 222.

16 David Fromkin, *A Peace to End All Peace* (New York: Andre Deutsch, 1989), p. 508.

17 Author's interview, April 2002.

18 Matar, p. 31.

19 Cockburn and Cockburn, p. 71.

20 Said Aburish, *Saddam Hussein: The Politics of Revenge* (London: Bloomsbury, 2000), p. 20.

21 Iskander, p. 29.

22 Matar, p. 292.

23 Quoted in Samir al-Khalil, *Republic of Fear* (Berkeley: University of California Press, 1989), p. 17.

24 Author's interview, November 2001.

25 Hani Fkaiki, *Dens of Defeat: My Experience in the Iraqi Baath Party* (London: Riad el Rayyes Books, 1993), p. 142.

26 Matar, p. 31.

27 Witness statement of Falih al-Nisiri al-Tikriti, proceedings of the People's Court, published by the Ministry of Defense, 1959, p. 410.

28 Cockburn and Cockburn, p. 71.

TWO: THE ASSASSIN

1 Matar, p. 31.

2 Ibid.

3 The full account of Saddam's involvement in the assassination attempt, and his subsequent escape, is provided in ibid. pp. 32–44.

4 Author's interview, April 2002.

5 Quoted in Adel Darwish and Gregory Alexander, *Unholy Babylon* (London: Victor Gollancz, 1991), p. 197.

6 *Independent* (London), March 31, 1998.

7 Dr. Hamid al-Bayati, *The Bloody History of Saddam al-Tikriti* (London, 1969), p. 25.

8 *Independent* (London), March 31, 1998.

9 Edith Penrose and E. F. Penrose, *Iraq: International Relations and Development* (London: Ernest Benn, 1978), pp. 362–363.

10 "I first met Comrade Saddam after the Ramadan Revolution of 1963." Michel Afleq quoted in Matar, p. 211.

11 Edward Mortimer, "The Thief of Baghdad," *New York Times Review of Books,* September 27, 1990, p. 8.

12 Iskander, p. 75.

13 Quoted in Cockburn and Cockburn, p. 73.

14 Author's interview, June 2002.

15 *New York Times,* October 24, 1990.

16 Al-Bayati, p. 63.

17 Simons, p. 274.

18 Three of Saddam's closest friends in Cairo have since perished—Abdul Karim al-Shaikhly (assassinated 1980), Medhat Ibrahim Juma'a (murdered 1986), and Naim

al-Azami (killed early 1980s). His only known surviving contemporary, Farouk al-Nuaimi, lives in Baghdad.

19 Quoted in Aburish, p. 54.

20 Matar, p. 44; Iskandar, p. 79.

21 Bulloch and Morris, p. 54.

22 Marion Farouk-Sluglett and Peter Sluglett, *Iraq since 1958* (London: Kegan Paul International, 1987), p. 283.

23 Samir al-Khalil, *Republic of Fear* (Berkeley: University of California Press, 1989), p. 59.

24 Quoted in Cockburn and Cockburn, p. 74.

25 Author's interview, May 2002.

26 Dr. Ali Karim Said, *From the Dialogue of Ideas to the Dialogue of Blood* (Beirut: Dar al-Kunuz al-Adabiyyah, 1999).

27 Al-Khalil, p. 6.

28 Hanna Batatu, *The Old Social Classes and Revolutionary Movements of Iraq* (Princeton, N.J.: Princeton University Press, 1978), p. 985.

29 Saddam quoted in Matar, p. 44.

30 Aburish, p. 61.

31 Judith Miller and Laurie Mylroie, *Saddam Hussein and the Crisis in the Gulf* (New York: Random House, 1990), p. 31.

32 Author's interview, March 2002.

33 Author's interview, November 2001.

34 Author's interview, October 2001.

35 Symons, p. 275.

36 Iskander, p. 97.

37 Author's interview, November 2001.

38 Matar, p. 45.

39 Author's interview, January 2002.

40 See Fkaiki, p. 325. Fkaiki claims Saddam frequently met President Arif and Bakr to inform them of various Baathist plots to overthrow them. This might explain why Saddam received benign treatment in prison.

41 Matar, p. 46; Iskander, pp. 80–81.

THREE: THE REVOLUTIONARY

1 Author's interview, April 2002.

2 Ibid.

3 *Le Monde,* October 9, 1968.

4 Quoted in Iskander, p. 110.

5 Matar, p. 46.

6 Iskander, p. 116.

7 Quoted in Matar, p. 47.

8 Author's interview, November 2000.

9 Matar, p. 47.

10 Aburish, p. 79.

11 Author's interview, January 2002.

12 Private source.

13 Private source.

14 Author's interview, January 2002.

15 Author's interview, November 2001.
16 Ibid.
17 Ibid.
18 Sluglett and Sluglett, p. 110.
19 Author's interview, February 2002.
20 Author's interview, November 2001.
21 Ibid.
22 Ibid.
23 Quoted in Batatu, p. 1100.

FOUR: THE AVENGER

1 Quoted in al-Khalil, p. 52.
2 Baghdad Domestic Service, March 20, 1971.
3 Quoted in Al-Khalil, p. 50.
4 Ibid., p. 51.
5 For a detailed analysis of Iraq's security structure, see Al-Khalil, Chapter One.
6 Author's interview, May 2002.
7 Batatu, p. 1099.
8 Quoted in al-Khalil, p. 231.
9 Majid Khadduri, *Socialist Iraq* (Washington, D.C.: The Middle East Institute, 1978), p. 54.
10 Karsh and Rautsi, p. 44.
11 Al-Khalil, p. 54.
12 Quoted in Karsh and Rautsi, p. 75.
13 J. Bulloch, *The Making of War: The Middle East from 1967 to 1973* (London: Longman, 1974), p. 131.
14 Bulloch and Morris, p. 31.
15 Ibid. p. 71.
16 Al-Khalil, pp. 292–296.
17 *Atlantic Monthly,* May 2002.
18 Author's interview, May 2002.
19 Ibid.
20 Private source.
21 Quoted in *Guardian,* July 4, 1973.
22 Iskander, p. 81.
23 Author's interview, February 2002.
24 Aburish, p. 97.
25 Author's interview, May 2002.
26 Ibid.
27 Khadduri, p. 65.
28 Kazzar also ordered the arrest of eleven other prominent Baathists, most of them friends or relatives of the president, whom he felt might conspire against him during the uprising. Ibid. p. 65.

FIVE: THE NATION BUILDER

1 Author's interview, April 2002.
2 Author's interview, May 2002.
3 Ibid.

4 Saddam Hussein, *Notre Combat et La Politique Internationale,* collected writings of Saddam Hussein (Lausanne: n.p., 1977), p. 57.

5 Quoted in Matar, p. 233.

6 Author's interview, May 2002.

7 *New York Times,* February 22, 1972.

8 *Le Monde,* June 20, 1972.

9 *Sunday Telegraph* (London), April 1, 1973.

10 Baghdad Domestic Service, October 17, 1971.

11 Phebe Marr, *The Modern History of Iraq* (Boulder, Colo.: Westview Press, 1985), p. 242.

12 Saddam Hussein, *Propos sur les Problèmes Actuels,* text of April 8, 1974, press conference, collected writings, pp. 98–99.

13 Author's interview, May 2002.

14 Matar, pp. 228–229.

15 Saddam Hussein, *Current Events in Iraq* (London: Longman, 1977), p. 38.

16 Quoted in Karsh and Rautsi, p. 81.

17 *Economist,* October 18, 1975.

18 Quoted in Matar, pp. 231–232.

19 Ibid.

20 *Economist,* June 24–30, 1978.

21 Edward Mortimer, "The Thief of Baghdad," *New York Review of Books,* September 27, 1990.

22 Karsh and Rautsi, p. 186.

23 Ibid., p. 88.

24 Efraim Karsh, *The Iran-Iraq War: A Military Analysis,* Adelphi Papers, No. 220 (London: International Institute for Strategic Studies, n.d.) pp. 10–11.

25 Marr, p. 229.

SIX: THE TERRORIST

1 *Der Spiegel,* August 6, 1990.

2 Kenneth R. Timmerman, *The Death Lobby: How the West Armed Iraq* (Boston: Houghton Mifflin, 1991), p. 20.

3 Ibid., p. 35.

4 Private source.

5 *Washington Post,* May 25, 1988.

6 Timmerman, pp. 49–50.

7 Matar, p. 217.

8 Aburish, p. 140.

9 Ibid., p. 139.

10 Timmerman, p. 31.

11 Quoted in ibid., p. 32.

12 Khidhir Hamza, *Saddam's Bombmaker* (New York: Scribner, 2000), p. 77.

13 Timmerman, pp. 59–60.

14 Quoted in ibid., p. 92.

15 Ibid., p. 116.

16 A. Baram, "Qawmiyya and Wataniyya in Baathi Iraq: The Search for a New Balance," *Middle East Studies,* Vol. 9, No. 2 (April 1983), pp. 188–200.

17 A detailed list of Abu Nidal's terror activities is provided in Patrick Seale, *Abu Nidal: A Gun for Hire* (New York: Random House, 1992), pp. 235–242.

18 *Vanity Fair,* May 2002.
19 Author's interview, April 2002.
20 *Newsweek,* July 17, 1978.
21 Author's interview, May 2002.
22 Author's interview, November 1998.
23 British Foreign Office spokesperson, speaking at the time of the expulsion.
24 Author's interview, May 2002.
25 Quoted in *U.S. News and World Report,* May 16, 1977.
26 Quoted in Seale, p. 112.
27 *New York Times,* April 12, 1975.
28 *Newsweek,* July 17, 1978.
29 Author's interview, March 2002.
30 Ibid.
31 Matar, p. 51.

SEVEN: MR. PRESIDENT

1 BBC Summary of World Broadcasts, July 18, 1979 (ME/6170/A/2).
2 *New York Times,* December 4, 1974.
3 *Newsweek,* May 9, 1977.
4 Author's interview, May 2002.
5 *Alif Ba* magazine (Baghdad), February 16, 1979.
6 BBC Summary of World Broadcasts, June 21, 1979 (ME/6147/A/3).
7 Patrick Seale, *Asad: The Struggle for the Middle East* (London: I. B. Tauris, 1988), p. 355.
8 Miller and Mylroie, p. 43.
9 Private source.
10 Matar, p. 54.
11 Author's interview, March 2002.
12 Excerpts from the film were shown on BBC *Panorama,* February 11, 1991.
13 Karsh and Rautsi, p. 115.
14 Miller and Mylroie, p. 45.
15 The five RCC members alleged to be involved in the plot were Muhie Abdul Hussein Mashhadi, Mohammed Ayesh, Adnan Hussein al-Hamdani, Mohammed Mahjub Mahdi, and Ghanem Abdul Jalil Saudi.
16 Author's interview, November 2001.
17 Private source.
18 Ibid.
19 Hamza, p. 114.
20 Baghdad Domestic Service, August 8, 1979.
21 Iraqi News Agency, August 8, 1979.
22 Author's interview, November 2001.
23 *Al-Thawra* (Baghdad), May 3, 1980.
24 Al-Khalil, p. 37.
25 Amnesty International, "Iraq, Evidence of Torture," April 29, 1981, p. 6.
26 Amnesty International, "Torture in Iraq 1982–84," pp. 10–11.
27 Quoted by Deborah Cobbett, "Women in Iraq," in *Saddam's Iraq: Revolution or Reaction?* (London: Zed Books and CARDRI [Committee Against Repression and for Domestic Rights in Iraq], 1989), p. 123.

28 *Human Rights in Iraq* (New York: Middle East Watch, 1990), pp. 23–24.

29 *New Scientist,* April 2, 1981.

30 Ali Hassan, "Profile—Modhaffar al-Nawab," in *Index on Censorship,* March 1981.

31 *As Safir,* December 5, 1985.

32 Iskander, p. 400.

33 Author's interview, May 2002.

34 Hassan Allawi, *The Borrowed State,* n.p., n.d., p. 90.

35 Mikhael Ramadan, *In the Shadow of Saddam* (New Zealand: GreeNZone, 1999), p. 12.

EIGHT: THE WARLORD

1 Iraq's Ministry of Foreign Affairs, *Iraqi-Iranian Conflict: Documentary Dossier* (Baghdad: January 1981), pp. 208–214.

2 Miller and Mylroie, p. 109.

3 Quoted in Efraim Karsh, *The Iran-Iraq War 1980–1988* (London: Osprey, 2002), p. 27.

4 John Bulloch and Harvey Morris, *The Gulf War* (London: Methuen, 1989), p. 47.

5 Quoted in Miller and Mylroie, p. 113.

6 Quoted in Karsh, p. 62.

7 Ibid., p. 114.

8 BBC Summary of World Broadcasts, June 22, 1982.

9 Dilip Hiro, *The Longest War* (London: Palladin, 1990), p. 35.

10 Ibid., p. 34.

11 Quoted in *Washington Post,* April 18, 1980.

12 Miller and Mylroie, p. 115.

13 Adel Darwish and Gregory Alexander, *Unholy Babylon* (London: Victor Gollancz, 1991), p. 129.

14 Baghdad Domestic Service, July 22, 1980.

15 Ibid., July 17, 1981.

16 Timmerman, p. 105.

17 Ibid., p. 106.

18 Ibid., p. 112.

19 BBC Summary of World Broadcasts, April 14, 1983.

20 Author's interview, May 2002.

21 Bulloch and Morris, pp. 47–48.

22 Ibid.

23 Karsh, p. 67.

24 M. S. el-Azhary, ed. *The Iran-Iraq War* (London: Croom Helm, 1984), p. 54.

25 Sahib Hakim, *Human Rights in Iraq* (London: Middle East Watch, 1992), p. 125.

26 *Wall Street Journal,* August 27, 1990.

27 Al-Khalil, p. 28.

28 Bulloch and Morris, p. 71.

NINE: THE VICTOR

1 Timmerman, pp. 116–117.

2 Ibid., p. 118.

3 Aburish, p. 236.

4 Author's interview, September 1995.

5 Author's interview, April 2002.
6 Wafic al-Samurrai, *The Destruction of the Eastern Gate* (Kuwait, 1997), p. 153.
7 Author's interview, February 2002.
8 These figures are taken from Anthony Cordesman, "The Iran-Iraq War in 1984: An Escalating Threat to the Gulf and the West," *Armed Forces Journal International,* March 1984, p. 24.
9 *Sunday Times* (London), March 11, 1984.
10 Author's interview, November 2001.
11 Marr, p. 297.
12 Author's interview, February 2002.
13 Aburish, p. 187.
14 Author's interview, May 2002.
15 Anthony H. Cordesman, *The Iran-Iraq War and Western Security, 1984–87* (London: Jane's Publishing, 1987), p. 99.
16 Author's interview, January 2002.
17 This incident is generally regarded, and especially by this author, as the main reason for the bomb attack against Pan Am flight 103 over the Scottish town of Lockerbie in December 1988, in which 270 people died.
18 Timmerman, p. 293.

TEN: THE INVADER

1 *Independent* (London), August 30, 1989.
2 Author's interview, May 2002.
3 Author's interview, June 2002.
4 Author's interview, September 1998.
5 *Sunday Times* (London), March 26, 1989.
6 Karsh and Rautsi, p. 184.
7 Simon Henderson, *Instant Empire: Saddam Hussein's Ambition for Iraq* (San Francisco: Mercury House, 1991), p. 82.
8 Cockburn and Cockburn, p. 155.
9 *Sunday Times* (London), March 26, 1989.
10 Author's interview, February 1999.
11 Private source.
12 Author's interview, June 2002.
13 *Guardian* (London), April 1, 1989.
14 *Wall Street Journal,* February 15, 1991.
15 Karsh and Rautsi, p. 202.
16 Charles Tripp, *A History of Iraq* (Cambridge, U.K.: Cambridge University Press, 2000), p. 251.
17 *Atlantic Monthly,* May 2002.
18 Author's interview, July 2002.
19 Author's interviews, Spring 2002.
20 Margaret Thatcher, *The Downing Street Years* (London: HarperCollins, 1993), p. 824.
21 *Observer* (London), October 21, 1990.
22 Baghdad Domestic Service, July 18, 1990.
23 Author's interview, February 2002.
24 Author's interview, July 2002.

ELEVEN: THE LOSER

1 Thatcher, p. 817.
2 Baghdad Domestic Service, August 8, 1990.
3 Thatcher, p. 827.
4 Dilip Hiro, *Desert Shield to Desert Storm* (London: HarperCollins, 1992), p. 222.
5 *Al-Thawra*, December 2, 1990.
6 *Economist* (London), December 22, 1990.
7 Tripp, p. 254.
8 *Iraqi National Accord*, December 14, 20, 21, 1990.
9 *Iraqi National Accord*, January 18, 1991.
10 Author's interview, August 2002.
11 *Atlantic Monthly*, May 2002.
12 As an accredited war correspondent with the British Armed Forces during Operation Desert Storm, the author can testify that Allied forces were on a constant state of alert for an Iraqi chemical weapons attack.
13 In 1998 UN weapons investigators confirmed that substantial quantities of weapons-grade anthrax were deployed in Kuwait and southern Iraq during the Gulf War. See *Sunday Telegraph* (London), February 15, 1998.
14 *Time*, September 18, 1995.
15 Baghdad Domestic Service, January 18, 1991.
16 Ibid., January 20, 1991.
17 CNN, January 28, 1991.
18 Baghdad Domestic Service, January 31, 1991.
19 Lawrence Freedman and Efraim Karsh, *The Gulf Conflict 1990–91* (London: Faber and Faber, 1993), p. 377.
20 *Times* (London), February 16, 1991.
21 Ibid., February 23, 1991.
22 Baghdad Domestic Service, February 26, 1991.
23 *Independent* (London), February 6, 1991.
24 Ibid., February 28, 1991.
25 *Atlantic Monthly*, May 2002.

TWELVE: THE SURVIVOR

1 Freedman and Karsh, p. 411.
2 *Hansard* (House of Commons), January 15, 1991.
3 *New York Times*, January 26, 1991.
4 BBC Radio 4, "The Desert War—A Kind of Victory," February 16, 1992.
5 *International Herald Tribune*, March 28, 1991.
6 Cockburn and Cockburn, p. 27.
7 *Sunday Times* (London), March 10, 1991.
8 Private source.
9 Private source.
10 Scott Ritter, *Endgame: Solving the Iraq Problem—Once and for All* (New York: Simon and Schuster, 1999), p. 111.
11 ABC News, *Peter Jennings Reporting* (New York), June 26, 1997.
12 Cockburn and Cockburn, p. 38.

13 Quoted in Michael R. Gordon and Bernard E. Trainor, *The Generals' War* (New York: Back Bay Books, 1995), p. 517.

14 Aburish, p. 319.

15 *Observer* (London), July 12, 1992.

16 *Times* (London), September 4, 1992.

17 Author's interview, September 1998. The name Sami Salih is a pseudonym.

18 *Daily Telegraph* (London), August 23, 1993.

19 Aburish, p. 326.

20 Author's interview, August 1999.

21 Author's interview, May 2002.

22 Private source.

23 *New Yorker,* April 5, 1999.

24 Cockburn and Cockburn, p. 189.

25 Author's interview, February 2002.

26 Ibid.

27 Ibid.

28 Ibid.

29 Quoted in *Time,* September 18, 1995.

30 BBC Survey of World Broadcasts, August 14, 1995.

31 Iraq television, August 12, 1995.

32 Private source.

33 Author's interview, September 1998.

34 Cockburn and Cockburn, p. 220.

35 *Times* (London), March 18, 1999.

36 Ibid., p. 229.

37 *International Herald Tribune,* September 9, 1996.

38 Author's interview, May 2002.

39 *Al-Wasat,* March 12, 1997.

40 Tim Trevan, *Saddam's Secrets: The Hunt for Saddam's Hidden Weapons* (London: HarperCollins, 1999), p. 365.

41 Iraq television, June 22, 1997.

42 A detailed examination of CIA penetration of UNSCOM is contained in "Saddam's Best Friend," by Seymour M. Hersh, in the *New Yorker,* April 5, 1999.

43 William Shawcross, *Deliver Us from Evil* (London: Bloomsbury, 2000), p. 243.

44 Trevan, p. 374.

45 Ritter, p. 223.

46 Ibid., p. 224.

EPILOGUE: THE IDOL

1 *Sunday Telegraph* (London), April 28, 2002.

2 *Guardian* (London), May 17, 2002.

3 *Time,* May 13, 2002.

4 *Atlantic Monthly,* May 2002.

5 Private source.

6 *Sunday Telegraph* (London), March 29, 1999.

7 *Scotland on Sunday,* April 2, 2000.

8 Author's interview, August 1999.

9 Private source.

10 Author's interview, October 1999.

11 *Sunday Times* (London), August 15, 1999.

12 Quoted in *Vanity Fair,* February 2000.

13 Private source.

14 *New York Times,* December 20, 2001.

15 *Time,* May 13, 2002.

16 *Times (London),* June 17, 2002.

17 *Al-Watan,* June 28, 2002.

18 *Mail on Sunday* (London), August 11, 2002.

19 Ibid.

SELECT BIBLIOGRAPHY

Aburish, Said. *Saddam Hussein: The Politics of Revenge.* London: Bloomsbury, 2000.

Algosaibi, Ghazi A. *The Gulf Crisis.* London: Kegan Paul International, 1991.

Axelgard, Frederick W. *A New Iraq? The Gulf War and Implications for U.S. Policy.* New York: Praeger, 1988.

Baram, Amazia. "Saddam Hussein, A Political Profile." *The Jerusalem Quarterly,* No. 17, 1980.

Batatu, Hanna. *The Old Social Classes and Revolutionary Movements of Iraq.* Princeton, N.J.: Princeton University Press, 1978.

Bengio, Ofra. *Saddam's World.* Oxford: Oxford University Press, 1998.

Bulloch, J. *The Making of War: The Middle East from 1967 to 1973.* London: Longman, 1974.

Bulloch, John, and Harvey Morris. *The Gulf War.* London: Methuen, 1989.

————. *Saddam's War.* London: Faber and Faber, 1991.

Butler, Richard. *The Greatest Threat.* New York: Public Affairs, 2000.

CARDRI (Committee Against Repression and for Democratic Rights in Iraq). *Saddam's Iraq: Revolution or Reaction?* London: Zed Books, 1989.

Chubin, Shahram, and Charles Tripp. *Iran and Iraq at War.* London: I. B. Tauris, 1988.

Cockburn, Andrew, and Patrick Cockburn. *Out of the Ashes.* New York: HarperCollins, 1999.

Cordesman, Anthony H. *The Iran-Iraq War and Western Security, 1984–87.* London: Jane's Publishing, 1987.

Dann, Uriel. *Iraq under Qassem: A Political History, 1958–63.* New York: Praeger, 1969.

Darwish, Adel, and Gregory Alexander. *Unholy Babylon.* London: Victor Gollancz, 1991.

Dobson, Christopher, and Ronald Payne. *War Without End.* London: Harrap, 1986.

Fkaiki, Hani. *Dens of Defeat: My Experience in the Iraqi Baath Party.* London: Riad el Rayyes Books, 1993.

Freedman, Lawrence, and Efraim Karsh. *The Gulf Conflict 1990–91.* London: Faber and Faber, 1993.

Friedman, Alan. *Spider's Web: Bush, Thatcher and the Decade of Deceit,* London: Faber and Faber, 1993.

Fromkin, David. *A Peace to End All Peace.* New York: Andre Deutsch, 1989.

Gordon. Michael R., and Bernard E. Trainor. *The Generals' War.* New York: Back Bay Books, 1995.

Hakim, Sahib. *Human Rights in Iraq.* London: Middle East Watch, 1992.

Hamza, Khidhir. *Saddam's Bombmaker.* New York: Scribner, 2000.

Harris Robert, and Jeremy Paxman. *A Higher Form of Killing.* London: Arrow Books, 2002.

Helms, Christine Moss. *Iraq: Eastern Flank of the Arab World.* Washington D.C.: Brookings Institution, 1988.

Henderson, Simon. *Instant Empire, Saddam Hussein's Ambition for Iraq.* San Francisco: Mercury House, 1991.

Hiro, Dilip. *The Longest War.* London: Palladin, 1990.

———. *Desert Shield to Desert Storm.* London: HarperCollins, 1992.

Hussein, Saddam. *Current Events in Iraq.* London: Longman, 1977.

The Iran-Iraq War, ed. M. S. el Azhary. London: Croom Helm, 1984.

Iskander, Amir. *Munadilan, wa Mufakiran, wa Insanan.* Paris: Hachette, 1981.

Karsh, Efraim. *The Iran-Iraq War 1980–1988.* London: Osprey, 2002.

———, and Inari Rautsi, *Saddam Hussein, A Political Biography.* London: Brassey's, 1991.

Khadduri, Majid. *Socialist Iraq.* Washington, D.C.: The Middle East Institute, 1978.

Khalil, Samir al-. *Republic of Fear.* Berkeley: University of California Press, 1989.

Longrigg, Stephen H. *Four Centuries of Modern Iraq.* Oxford: Oxford University Press, 1925.

Marr, Phebe. *The Modern History of Iraq.* Boulder, Colo.: Westview Press, 1985.

Matar, Fuad. *Saddam Hussein: The Man, the Cause and His Future.* London: Third World Centre, 1981.

Merari, Ariel, and Shlomo Elad. *The International Dimension of Palestinian Terrorism.* Boulder, Colo: Westview, 1986.

Middle East Watch. *Human Rights in Iraq.* New York, 1990.

Miller, Judith, Stephen Englelberg, and William Broad. *Germs: The Ultimate Weapon.* New York: Simon and Schuster, 2001.

Miller, Judith, and Laurie Mylroie. *Saddam Hussein and the Crisis in the Gulf.* New York: Random House, 1990.

Mylroie, Laurie. *Study of Revenge.* Washington, D.C.: The AEI Press, 2001.

O'Balance, Edgar. *The Gulf War.* London: Brassey's, 1988.

Penrose, Edith, and E. F. Penrose. *Iraq: International Relations and Development.* London: Ernest Benn, 1978.

Ramadan, Mikhael. *In the Shadow of Saddam.* New Zealand: GreeNZone, 1999.

Ritter, Scott. *Endgame: Solving the Iraq Problem—Once and for All.* New York: Simon and Schuster, 1999.

Samurrai, Wafic al-. *The Destruction of the Eastern Gate.* Kuwait, 1997.

Seale, Patrick. *Asad: The Struggle for the Middle East.* London: I. B. Tauris, 1988.

———. *Abu Nidal, A Gun for Hire.* New York: Random House, 1992.

Shawcross, William. *Deliver Us From Evil.* London: Bloomsbury, 2000.

Simons, Geoff. *From Sumer to Saddam.* London: Macmillan, 1994.

Sluglett, Marion Farouk-, and Peter Sluglett. *Iraq since 1958.* London: Kegan Paul International, 1987.

Smith, Colin. *Carlos: Potrait of a Terrorist.* London: Andre Deutsch, 1976.

Thatcher, Margaret. *The Downing Street Years.* London: HarperCollins, 1993.

Timmerman, Kenneth R. *The Death Lobby: How the West Armed Iraq.* Boston: Houghton Mifflin, 1991.

Trevan, Tim. *Saddam's Secrets: The Hunt for Saddam's Hidden Weapons.* London: HarperCollins, 1999.

Tripp, Charles. *A History of Iraq.* Cambridge, U.K.: Cambridge University Press, 2000.

Winstone, H. V. I. *Gertrude Bell.* London: Jonathan Cape, 1978.

INDEX

350 INDEX